D1431994

AMERICA'S CULTURAL REVOLUTION

AMERICA'S CULTURAL REVOLUTION

How the Radical Left
Conquered Everything

CHRISTOPHER F. RUFO

BROADSIDE BOOKS

HarperCollins books may be purchased for educational, business, or sales promotional use. For information, please email the Special Markets Department at SPsales@harpercollins.com.

Broadside Books™ and the Broadside logo are trademarks of HarperCollins Publishers.

FIRST EDITION

Library of Congress Cataloging-in-Publication Data
Names: Rufo, Christopher F., 1984– author.
Title: America's cultural revolution: how the radical left conquered everything / Christopher F. Rufo.
Description: First edition. | New York: Broadside, 2023. | Includes bibliographical references and index.
Identifiers: LCCN 2023002238 (print) | LCCN 2023002239 (ebook) | ISBN 9780063227538 (hardcover) | ISBN 9780063227545 (ebook)
Subjects: LCSH: United States—Social conditions—21st century. | Right and left (Political science)—United States. | Political culture—United States. | Education—Social aspects—United States. | Race relations—United States.
Classification: LCC HN59.2 .R836 2023 (print) | LCC HN59.2 (ebook) | DDC 306.0973—dc23/eng/20230502
LC record available at https://lccn.loc.gov/2023002238
LC ebook record available at https://lccn.loc.gov/2023002239

24 25 26 27 28 LBC 8 7 6 5 4

For Suphatra

CONTENTS

PART III: EDUCATION

PART IV: POWER

I have seen the hideous face of revolution.

My first encounter was in Seattle, Washington, where I began my career as a political journalist. When I started reporting on the city's homelessness crisis, Seattle's left-wing activists engaged in a relentless pressure campaign against my family, targeting our reputations, attempting to get my wife fired, publishing threats with our home address, and putting up menacing posters around my oldest son's elementary school.

Their objective was simple: silence, marginalize, and suppress—all, somehow, in the name of tolerance and an open society. At the time, I thought of myself as a moderate. But that experience opened my eyes to the real nature of left-wing politics. It radicalized me.

A few years later, when my reporting shifted to critical race theory, I discovered the same dynamic at a national scale: American institutions were playing the same cynical game, marshalling the forces of guilt, shame, and scapegoating in order to enforce a left-wing political orthodoxy. Government agencies were teaching that "all white people" are racist. Public schools were separating children into "oppressor" and "oppressed." Fortune 100 corporations were pushing the idea that the United States was a "white supremacy system."

Just as it had been in Seattle, most Americans—liberal, moderate, and conservative—could see the falsehood and danger in these ideas, but they were too afraid to speak out. They were not "oppressors" or "white supremacists"; they were normal people raising their families and trying to do right by their neighbors. And they needed a voice.

During this period, as I was doing my reporting, I also discovered a way to fight back. In the summer of 2020, I went on the television program *Tucker Carlson Tonight*, laid out my reporting on critical race theory in the federal government, and directly asked President Donald Trump to take action. "The president and the White House, it's within their authority and power to immediately issue an executive order abolishing critical race theory trainings from the federal government," I said. "I call on the president to immediately issue this executive order and stamp out this destructive, divisive, pseudoscientific ideology at its root."

I made the ask at precisely the right moment. At 7 a.m. the following day, I received a telephone call from the president's chief of staff, Mark Meadows, who told me the president had watched the segment and instructed him to take immediate action. Three weeks later, the president issued an executive order abolishing critical race theory in the federal government, nationalizing the issue, and sending American politics into a period of contentious and consequential debate.

I have been at the center of that debate since the beginning. As a journalist, I broke the stories exposing critical race theory in America's institutions and, as an activist, I led the successful campaign to ban critical race theory from the public school systems in twenty-two states. I was lionized in the conservative press, which hailed my work as writer and policy leader. Even my enemies were forced to acknowledge my influence, with the *New York Times* calling me the "architect of the right-wing crusade against critical race theory" and Vox calling me "the most important intellectual entrepreneur on the political right today."

This book is an effort to understand the ideology that drives the politics of the modern Left, from the streets of Seattle to the highest levels of American government. Over the past two years, as I fought against left-wing ideologies in the political arena, I was also studying my adversaries through deeper research. I read hundreds of books, papers, studies, and newspaper articles that revealed the historical development of the modern Left and its ideological foundations. Over time, I began to see the bigger picture: the campaign to embed critical race theory in American life was only one facet of the radical Left's "long march through the institutions," which had begun fifty years ago.

America's Cultural Revolution tells the full story. I outline the progression of the left-wing ideology from the student radical movement of the 1960s to the so-called anti-racism movement, which set fire to the country in 2020. As an activist, I often have to communicate in small bursts of simplified rhetoric. As an author, I'm able to be expansive, tracing the patterns of history, exploring the intricacies of ideology, and plumbing the depths of the personalities that have shaped the way we think, feel, and act.

The lesson of this book is a serious one. There is a rot spreading through American life. The country's foundations are starting to shake loose. A new nihilism is beginning to surround the common citizen in all of the institutions that matter: his government, his workplace, his church, his children's school, even his home. He knows we have been given a gift—the American Republic—but there is no guarantee that it will last. He can feel it in his bones.

My hope in writing this book is to substantiate these intuitions and to reveal the inner history of America's cultural revolution. It is a genealogy of darkness: an attempt to establish the human lineage of the new nihilism that threatens to overwhelm the country. But it is also a work of determined optimism: if we are to save this country from disintegration, we must first see the crisis clearly and confidently. We cannot look away.

America's Cultural Revolution

I n 1975, the Soviet dissident Aleksandr Solzhenitsyn spoke to a coalition of labor leaders in New York City and denounced the American radical Angela Davis, who had become a symbol of international communism and violent revolution against the West.

During this period, the Soviet government had churned out propaganda celebrating Davis as a world-historical figure and instructed millions of schoolchildren to send her cards and paper flowers. "In our country, literally for one whole year, we heard of nothing at all except Angela Davis," Solzhenitsyn said.

But this campaign was based on a lie. The Soviets had created a global slave state, with a network of gulags, dungeons, and prison camps extending from Vladivostok to Havana; Solzhenitsyn himself had spent eight years enduring imprisonment, torture, and forced labor.

Davis, however, followed the propaganda line. During a publicity tour of the Soviet Union in 1972, she praised her hosts for their treatment of minorities and denounced the United States for its oppression of "political prisoners." But during an unscripted encounter, Solzhenitsyn said, a group of Czech dissidents approached Davis with a plea: "Comrade Davis, you were in prison. You know how unpleasant it is to sit in prison, especially when you consider yourself innocent. You have such great authority now. Could you help our Czech prisoners? Could you stand up for those people in Czechoslovakia who are being persecuted by the state?"

Davis responded with ice: "They deserve what they get. Let them remain in prison."

For Solzhenitsyn, this moment revealed everything. Davis embodied the spirit of left-wing revolution: sacrificing the human being in service of ideology. Her commitment to the great abstractions—liberation, freedom, humanity—was a ruse. "That is the face of Communism," he said. "That is the heart of Communism for you."[1]

The Soviet Union eventually collapsed and many Americans considered the question of left-wing revolution settled. It had proven disastrous everywhere it had been tried—Asia, Africa, Latin America. The world had learned its lesson, they believed, and moved beyond the promises of Marx, Lenin, and Mao.

But they were wrong. Although the left-wing cultural revolution had self-destructed in the Third World, over time it found a new home: in America.

This new revolution patiently built itself in the shadows and then, after the death of George Floyd in the spring of 2020, exploded onto the American scene. All of a sudden, the old Angela Davis narrative appeared everywhere: America was an irredeemably racist nation; whites constituted a permanent oppressor class; the country could be saved only through the performance of elaborate guilt rituals and the wholesale overturning of its founding principles. All of the formative institutions—universities, schools, corporations, government agencies—repeated the revolution's vocabulary like a mantra: "systemic racism," "white privilege," "diversity, equity, and inclusion." Meanwhile, in the streets, mobs of left-wing rioters expressed the ideology in physical form, toppling statues of Washington, Jefferson, and Lincoln and burning entire city blocks to the ground.

The question of left-wing revolution was suddenly reopened. How did this happen? Where did these ideas come from? Who was responsible for the chaos?

In order to answer these questions and understand the dizzying cultural changes that have swept across the United States—the capture of America's institutions, the Black Lives Matter street revolution, the spread of racialist ideology in public education, and the rise of the "diversity, equity, and inclusion" bureaucracy—one must return to their origins.

The story of America's cultural revolution begins in 1968, as America endured a long season of student uprisings, urban riots, and revolutionary violence that has provided the template for everything that followed. During this period, left-wing intellectuals developed a new theory of revolution in the West and their most dedicated disciples printed pamphlets, detonated homemade bombs, and dreamed of overthrowing the state.

The ambition of this book is to reveal the inner history of America's cultural revolution, tracing the arc of its development from its origin point to the present day. The book is divided into four parts: revolution, race, education, and power. Each part begins with a biographical portrait of the four prophets of the revolution: Herbert Marcuse, Angela Davis, Paulo Freire, and Derrick Bell. These figures established the disciplines of critical theory, critical praxis, critical pedagogy, and critical race theory, which, in the subsequent half century, multiplied into a hundred subdisciplines and devoured the university, the street, the school, and the bureaucracy. Together they represent the intellectual genesis of the revolution. Their ideas, concepts, language, and tactics shaped and now suffuse the politics of the present.

Herbert Marcuse was the preeminent philosopher of the so-called New Left, which sought to mobilize the white intelligentsia and the black ghetto into a new proletariat. Angela Davis was one of Marcuse's graduate students and, after pledging to violently overthrow the state, became the face of racial revolt in the West. Paulo Freire was a Brazilian Marxist whose work on turning schools into instruments of revolution became the gospel of left-wing education in America. Derrick Bell was a Harvard law professor who set the foundation for critical race theory and recruited a cadre of students who would capture elite institutions with their new racialist ideology.

During the 1970s, the most violent elements of the New Left coalition—the Weather Underground, the Black Panther Party, and Black Liberation Army—fell apart, but the spirit of their revolution carried on in a subtler but equally dangerous form. As Solzhenitsyn revealed the bankruptcy of the communist movements in the West, the most sophisticated activists and intellectuals of the New Left initiated a new strategy, the "long march through the institutions," which brought their movement out of the streets and into the universities, schools, newsrooms, and bureaucracies. They developed intricate theories along the lines of culture, race, and identity, and silently rooted them into the entire range of America's knowledge-making institutions.

Over the subsequent decades, the cultural revolution that began in 1968 transformed, almost invisibly, into a structural revolution that changed everything. The critical theories, first developed by Marcuse, Davis, Freire, and Bell, were not designed to operate as mere abstractions. They were designed as political weapons and oriented toward the acquisition of power.

As the disciples of the New Left gained purchase over the great bureaucracies, they advanced the revolution through a process of relentless negation: it gnawed, chewed, smashed, and disintegrated the entire system of values that came before it. And their strategy was ingenious: the capture of America's institutions was so gradual and bureaucratic, it largely escaped the notice of the American public, until it burst into consciousness following the death of George Floyd.

Today, America's cultural revolution has reached the endgame. The descendants of the New Left have completed their long march through the institutions and installed their ideas into school curricula, popular media, government policy, and corporate human resources programs. Their core set of principles, first formulated in the radical pamphlets of the Weather Underground and the Black Liberation Army, has been sanitized and adapted into the official ideology of America's elite institutions, from the Ivy Leagues to the boardrooms of Walmart, Disney, Verizon, American Express, and Bank of America.

The critical theories of 1968 have turned into a substitute morality: racism is elevated into the highest principle; society is divided into a crude moral binary of "racist" and "anti-racist"; and a new bureaucratic logic is required to adjudicate guilt and redistribute wealth, power, and privilege. To enforce this new orthodoxy, left-wing activists have established departments of "diversity, equity, and inclusion" across an entire stratum of the public and private bureaucracies. Allies are rewarded with status, position, and employment. Dissenters are shamed, marginalized, and sent into moral exile.

America's cultural revolution has culminated in the emergence of a new ideological regime that is inspired by the critical theories and administered through the capture of the bureaucracy. Although the official political structures have not changed—there is still a president, a legislature, and a judiciary—the entire intellectual substructure has shifted. The institutions imposed a revolution from above, effectuating a wholesale moral reversal and implementing a new layer of "diversity, equity, and inclusion" across the entire society.

Nobody voted for this change; it simply materialized from within.

The ultimate goal is still revolutionary: the activists of the radical Left want to replace individual rights with group-identity-based rights, enact a scheme of race-based wealth redistribution, and suppress speech, based on a new racial and political calculus. They want a "total rupture" with the existing order.

Fortunately, despite its successful blitz through the institutions, the revolution has its limits. The political Left might have succeeded in unmasking and delegitimizing the old order—the critical theories have supplanted the mythology of the American Founding, and the substitute morality of "diversity, equity, and inclusion" has become the new operating system of the elite institutions—but the revolution cannot escape the fundamental contradictions that have plagued it since its beginning.

The intellectual movement that began in 1968 was able to initiate the process of disintegrating the old values, but it could not build a new set of values to replace them. Instead, the New Left's call to commit "class suicide" and renounce "white-skin privilege" unleashed a torrent of narcissism, guilt, and self-destruction. The terror campaigns of the Weather Underground and Black Liberation Army alienated the public and led to a swift reaction. The student radicals eventually abandoned their armed revolution and transformed themselves into patronage-seeking academics, activists, and bureaucrats.

The same dynamic holds today. The descendants of the New Left have captured the elite institutions but have not been able to reorder the deeper structures of society. The war of negation has failed to deliver the world beyond. It has, instead, yielded a world of failure, exhaustion, resentment, and despair. The universities have lost the ancient telos of knowledge, replacing it with an inferior set of values oriented toward personal identities and pathologies. The resurgence of politically motivated street violence with the Black Lives Matter movement—itself a crude reincarnation of the Black Panther Party—has wreaked havoc on American cities. The public schools have absorbed the principles of revolution but have failed to teach the rudimentary skills of reading and mathematics. Critical race theory bears all the flaws of traditional Marxism, then amplifies them with a narrative of racial pessimism that crushes the very possibility of progress.

Over the span of fifty years, the cultural revolution has slowly lowered its mask and revealed its hideous face—nihilism. The anxiety that has spread through every corner of American life is wholly justified: the common citizen can sense that a new ideological regime has been established in the institutions that provide the structure for his social, political, and spiritual life. He understands intuitively that appeals to a new system of governance based on "diversity, equity, and inclusion" are a pretense for establishing a political order that is hostile to his values, even if he does not yet possess the vocabulary to pierce through the shell of euphemism and describe its essence.

The aspiration of this book is to open his eyes. It is to reveal the nature of the critical theories, to establish the facts about the new ideological regime, and to prepare the grounds for revolting against it. This book will raise the questions that exist beneath the surface of the cultural revolution. Does the public want an equality society or a revenge society? Will it work to transcend racialism or to entrench it? Must it tolerate destruction in the name of progress?

Although it may seem that America's cultural revolution has entered a period of dominance, the space between its ambitions and its outcomes has left open the possibility of reversal. The simple fact is that society under the critical theories does not work. The revolution is not a path to liberation; it is an iron cage.

This is, in short, a work of counter-revolution. The basic premise is that the enemies of the cultural revolution must begin by seeing the critical theories and the "long march through the institutions" with clear eyes. They must help the common citizen understand what is happening around him and mobilize the vast reservoir of public sentiment against the ideologies, laws, and institutions that seek to make the cultural revolution a permanent feature of American life. The task for the counter-revolutionary is not simply to halt the movement of his adversaries but to resurrect the system of values, symbols, myths, and principles that constituted the essence of the old regime, to reestablish the continuity between past, present, and future, and to make the eternal principles of freedom and equality meaningful again to the common citizen.

This counter-revolution is already forming and staking out the territory for the fight ahead. The question now is which vision of America will prevail and which vision will return into the void.

PART I

Revolution

CHAPTER 1

Herbert Marcuse

Father of the Revolution

I n the summer of 1967, an elderly philosopher named Herbert Marcuse took the stage at the Dialectics of Liberation conference in London and calmly called for total revolution against the West.[1]

Speaking in a thick, Weimar-era German accent, Marcuse excoriated "the syndrome of late capitalism" and "the subjugation of man to the apparatus." The audience, which included pedigreed Marxist intellectuals, counterculture artists such as Allen Ginsberg, and black militants such as Stokely Carmichael and Angela Davis, sat in hushed silence.[2] They had gathered at the conference in order to "create a genuine revolutionary consciousness" and devise strategies for "physical and cultural 'guerrilla warfare'"—and the old man, who wore a formal suit and peppered his conversation with references to the great philosophers of the past, seemed to hold the key to unlocking it.[3]

Marcuse's lecture, titled "Liberation from the Affluent Society," praised the hippies and the counterculture for initiating a "sexual, moral and political rebellion"[4] and argued that the Marxist revolution must begin with a "new sensibility" and "the emergence of a new type of man, with a vital, biological drive for liberation, and with a consciousness capable of breaking through the material as well as ideological veil of the affluent society."[5] At the end of his speech, audience members circulated joints around the auditorium.[6] Marcuse took a puff and called for the negation of the existing society and the realization of utopia: "the abolition of labor," "the termination of the struggle for existence," "the total reconstruction of our cities," "the elimination [of] ugliness," "the transition from capitalism to socialism."[7]

His message reverberated around the world. Within months, the carefully mannered and meticulous scholar of Kant, Hegel, and Marx would become a beacon for left-wing radicals everywhere. Students in Rome, Paris, Frankfurt, and Berlin carried banners with the slogan "Marx, Mao, Marcuse!" emblazoned in enormous block letters.[8] The militants of the Weather Underground, the Black Panther Party, and the Baader-Meinhof Gang read dog-eared copies of Marcuse's books as they plotted robberies, bombings, assassinations, and urban guerrilla warfare against the state. Although Marcuse shunned the title of "father" of the revolution that was roiling the West—the radicals "did not need a father figure, or grandfather figure, to lead them to protest," he chided—his ideas became the guiding light for the youth revolts and the so-called New Left.[9]

In a sequence of three popular books—*One-Dimensional Man*, *A Critique of Pure Tolerance*, and *An Essay on Liberation*—Marcuse had sketched out the rationale and the methods for revolution in the West. He argued that modern capitalist society had created the perfect means of repression, anesthetizing the working class with material comforts, manufactured desires, and welfare programs, which stabilized the system and allowed for the creation of external scapegoats.

The only solution, he believed, was the Great Refusal: the complete disintegration of the existing society, beginning with a revolt in the universities and the ghettos, then dissolving "the system's hypocritical morality and 'values'" through the relentless application of his "critical theory of society,"[10] a philosophy described by Marcuse scholar Douglas Kellner as "Western Marxism," "neo-Marxism," or "critical Marxism."[11]

Meanwhile, as Marcuse's call for revolution was being heralded by the young radicals, his rise to prominence sparked a furious backlash. In San Diego, members of the American Legion hung an effigy of "Marxist Marcuse" on the flagpole in front of City Hall, demanding that the University of California, San Diego, terminate his employment.[12] California governor Ronald Reagan denounced the professor for his "communist" ideology that contributed toward the "climate of violence" on university campuses.[13] Vice President Spiro Agnew demanded that UCSD fire Marcuse for "poisoning a lot of young minds."[14] Pope Paul VI, delivering a homily at St. Peter's Basilica, criticized Marcuse's revolutionary theory for opening the way to "license cloaked as liberty" and spreading "animal, barbarous and subhuman degradations."[15]

The professor's domestic enemies sent him threats in the mail, cut his phone lines, and fired gunshots at his home.[16] "You are a very dirty Communist dog," read one letter. "We give you seventy-two hours to [leave the] United States. Seventy-two hours more, Marcuse, and we kill you."[17]

Today, America is living inside Marcuse's revolution. During the fever pitch of the late 1960s, Marcuse posited four key strategies for the radical Left: the revolt of the affluent white intelligentsia, the radicalization of the black "ghetto population," the capture of public institutions, and the cultural repression of the opposition.[18]

All of these objectives have been realized to some degree—and have begun the "transvaluation of all prevailing values" that Marcuse had envisioned.[19] Marcuse's "critical theory," which he wryly called "the power of negative thinking,"[20] has steadily devoured America's institutions, becoming the dominant mode of thought for the new elite. The young radicals who were ready to wage war against the state simply brought their revolution inside, bringing the critical theories to power by a long march through the universities, media, corporations, and central government.

This revolution is still hurtling forward. The modern Left is aggressively pursuing Marcuse's prophecy that, once society had been liberated from capitalist repression, their "rebellion would then [take] root in the very nature, the 'biology' of the individual" and unleash a pure freedom beyond necessity, exploitation, and violence.[21] They believe that Marcuse's negative dialectic, developed over a century of theory and practice, might finally dissolve the oppressive foundations of the West and lead to a "rupture of history, the radical break, the leap into the realm of freedom," even if it means the subversion of democracy and the cataclysm of political violence.[22]

Marcuse was willing to pursue his vision into the apocalypse—the chaos was the cost of change; the violence was the catalyst of progress. Along this path, thousands of young and alienated radicals were willing to follow.

*   *   *

Carl and Gertrud Marcuse of Berlin welcomed their first child, Herbert, into the world in the summer of 1898. Carl, a successful businessman, and Gertrud, the daughter of a prosperous industrialist, had established a life of bourgeois comfort that their son would spend his entire adulthood railing against.

During Marcuse's childhood, the family lived in a luxurious ten-room apartment in Berlin, then a suburban mansion with "five reception rooms, an elegant English fireplace, and accommodation for a household staff of two housemaids, a cook, a pair of laundry maids, and the driver of the family Packard."[23] Carl and Gertrud sent Herbert to the elite Mommsen Gymnasium, favored by the imperial ruling class,[24] and the Kaiserin-Augusta Gymnasium, which had been attended by the famed sociologist Max Weber.[25]

The family was Jewish, but not devout. Marcuse would later explain that his childhood was typical for an affluent, assimilated German family and that his religious heritage never caused a sense of alienation during his childhood.[26] Marcuse was a sensitive student who suffered from poor eyesight and completed his primary education without any thought to politics.

That changed with the outbreak of the First World War. Following his graduation from the gymnasium, Marcuse was swept into the military draft. Administrators exempted Marcuse from combat on account of his eyesight and assigned him to work the horse stables in Berlin. During this period, the capital city was awash in unrest: Marcuse witnessed protests, riots, strikes, profiteering, and political upheaval. The country was fighting a war abroad and a war within, as Kaiser Wilhelm II sought to suppress an internal democratic revolt.[27]

By 1917, Marcuse had joined the left-wing Social Democratic Party (SPD) and flirted with Rosa Luxemburg's radical Spartacus faction, which sought to overthrow global capitalism and advance the international Marxist revolution. The following year, Germany was on the verge of collapse: the Allied Powers had routed the German army, the kaiser had abdicated, and revolution had broken out from Kiel to Hamburg to Berlin. Citizens organized "workers' and soldiers' councils," modeled on the Russian soviets, to assume authority and provide security for the new political factions.

Marcuse, following the radical line, supported the revolution for social democracy and, in order to prevent counter-revolutionaries from reestablishing imperial rule, joined the left-wing "civilian security force" in Berlin.[28]

During the November Revolution, which would establish the ill-fated Weimar Republic, the twenty-year-old Marcuse found himself armed with a rifle, standing guard in Alexanderplatz, under orders to shoot any counter-revolutionary snipers on the spot. This moment—one can imagine the young intellectual dressed in a military overcoat, smoking cigarettes, dazzled by the great orators of the revolution—would contain all of the themes that occupied Marcuse until the end of his life: revolution and counter-revolution, utopia and dystopia, hope and betrayal.

Marcuse was elected to one of the soldiers' councils but quickly noticed that the councils were electing all of the old officers from the previous regime—a bad omen. Meanwhile, the Social Democratic Party coalition, now tasked with administering the new Weimar state, splintered. Rosa Luxemburg and her Spartacus faction cast their lot with a newly created Communist Party of Germany, and their most fervent members rallied for a putsch in order to bury capitalism once and for all. The SDP leadership, hoping to stabilize the country and consolidate power, unleashed nationalist paramilitaries on Berlin, who arrested, tortured, and executed Luxemburg, then dumped her body in a canal. The other Spartacus leaders met a similar fate.[29]

Marcuse, disgusted down to his core, resigned from the SDP and abandoned practical politics altogether. The revolution, he believed, had been betrayed and absorbed by the "reactionary, destructive, and repressive forces" of the German bourgeoisie.[30] "I remember standing with a rifle in Berlin on the Alexander Platz and during all that time I began to be more and more interested in Marx," Marcuse recalled sixty years later. "When the German revolution was gradually—or not so gradually—defeated, suppressed, and their leaders assassinated, I withdrew and devoted myself practically entirely to study at the university."[31]

The subsequent decades of Marcuse's life followed the same pattern of revolution and disenchantment. Marcuse earned his doctorate in literature from the University of Freiburg in 1922, worked briefly as a partner in an antiquarian bookstore in Berlin, then returned to Freiburg to study under the philosopher Martin Heidegger—who would later become a member of the Nazi Party—and eventually completed a second thesis, "Hegel's Ontology and the Theory of Historicity," which qualified him for a career in academia.[32] But as Adolf Hitler rose to power in 1932, Marcuse fled Germany alongside other Jewish academics and joined the Institute for Social Research, an association of prominent Marxist theoreticians who had escaped the Nazis, first to Switzerland, then to France, then to the United States.[33]

The group, led by scholars Max Horkheimer, Theodor Adorno, Leo

Löwenthal, and Friedrich Pollock, would pioneer the "critical theory of society," which synthesized a vast range of concepts from philosophy, psychoanalysis, and political theory in an attempt to explain the failure of traditional Marxism and to create a new, more sophisticated dialectic that could finally inspire the "radical act" of transforming the world. Their theory would contain three essential parts: radical criticism of the existing society, a method for the "alteration of society as a whole," and a "utopian spirit" that could guide humanity beyond necessity.[34]

The institute's scholars were careful to shroud their language in academic code—self-consciously replacing words such as "Marxism" and "communism" with "dialectical materialism" and "the materialist theory of society"[35]—but the implications were clear: the true object of the new Marxism was not the pursuit of truth, but the pursuit of revolution.

Marcuse eventually fled abroad, arriving in the United States on Independence Day, 1934. "When I saw the Statue of Liberty, I really felt like a human being," he recalled.[36] For the better part of the next two decades, Marcuse would work for the institute, then for the US Office of War Information and Office of Strategic Services, where he conducted research to help fight Nazism. Following the war, he moved into academia, securing positions at Columbia, Harvard, Brandeis, and, finally, the University of California, San Diego.

But Marcuse's faith in the postwar world quickly went sour, too. Internationally, Marcuse watched the Soviet Union descend into tyranny and the United States initiate hot and cold wars around the globe. Domestically, he watched capitalism expand into mindless consumerism, conformity, and excess, while the poor were mollified with the false promises of the Great Society welfare programs.

The United States, Marcuse concluded, was little more than a "Welfare State and Warfare State": a twin engine of repression, no longer capable of realizing any higher principle. "If I compare the country as it was, let's say, in 1934, when I came, and as it is now, I doubt sometimes that this is the same country," he said. "At that time, this country effectively fought inflation and unemployment, and prepared the war against fascism. You cannot say today that this country is opposed to fascism, if it helps to sustain and establish fascist governments in quite a few countries of the world."[37]

Marcuse elaborated on this theme in a probing and pessimistic 1964 book, *One-Dimensional Man*. His main line of argument was that modern liberal societies had transcended their original purpose, perverted the methods of technological rationality, and become repressive. "A comfortable, smooth, reasonable, democratic unfreedom prevails in advanced industrial civilization," he wrote.[38] The capitalist economies had created mass prosperity, but rather than liberate man, they had created a new structure of manipulation and control. Rationality had devolved into irrationality. Freedom had turned into slavery. Progress had produced barbarism.

For Marcuse, modern liberalism had reduced man's existence to a single dimension and hidden the social, economic, and political contradictions of the previous age, which had animated classical Marxism. In the new flattened society, he wrote, "domination—in the guise of affluence and liberty—extends to all spheres of private and public existence, integrates all authentic opposition, absorbs all alternatives. Technological rationality reveals its political character as it becomes the great vehicle of better domination, creating a truly totalitarian universe in which society and nature, mind and body are kept in a state of permanent mobilization for the defense of this universe."[39]

The consequence of this transformation was twofold. First, the working class had been stripped of its revolutionary potential. Second, the political system had become a "pseudo-democracy" with no authentic opposition.[40] For Marcuse, this was cause to despair. The theory of classical Marxism had been predicated on the revolutionary conflict between the proletariat and the bourgeoisie. But after the rise of the one-dimensional society, these conditions had been subsumed: capitalism had seduced the working class with its "supreme promise" of "an ever-more-comfortable life for an ever-growing number of people." The outcome was a new form of alienation. The proletarians had been reduced to "preconditioned receptacles" for production, advertisement, and domination.[41] They had become "sublimated slaves," unable to comprehend their own wishes and desires.[42]

The political outlook, Marcuse concluded, was grim. "The reality of the laboring classes in advanced industrial society makes the Marxian 'proletariat' a mythological concept; the reality of present-day socialism makes the Marxian idea a dream."[43] Modern man was condemned to "the hell of the Affluent Society" through a soft, diffused totalitarianism.[44] He was deprived of his own imagination and found his "soul in [his] automobile, hi-fi set, split-level home, kitchen equipment."[45] America had become a society characterized by "repressive tolerance," promising freedom of conscience, speech, and assembly, while, in practice, depriving men of the mechanisms for making those rights meaningful. These essential elements of political life—word, action, opposition—are allowed to exist as symbols, but deprived of any real power.

The implications of Marcuse's theory were ominous. He painted Western society as a series of inversions: democracy was "pseudo-democracy"; liberty was "repressive tolerance"; freedom was "sublimated slavery." The public, corroded by false consciousness and subjected to rational management, could no longer be trusted. "As long as this condition prevails, it makes sense to say that the general will is always wrong," Marcuse wrote in *An Essay on Liberation*.[46] The only solution, therefore, was to break through the illusion and enact a revolution against the system as a whole. "If democracy means self-government of free people, with justice for all, then the realization of democracy would presuppose abolition of the existing pseudo-democracy," Marcuse wrote. "In the dynamic of corporate capitalism, the fight for democracy thus tends to assume anti-democratic forms, and to the extent to which the democratic decisions are made in 'parliaments' on all levels, the opposition will tend to become extra-parliamentary."[47]

If not democracy, what should replace it? Here, appealing to Plato and Rousseau, Marcuse gently introduced his ideal political form: the "educational dictatorship"—or rule by elites who can distinguish false from true consciousness and freedom from slavery. "[Society] must first enable its slaves to learn and see and think before they know what is going on and what they themselves can do to change it. And, to the degree to which the slaves have been preconditioned to exist as slaves and be content in that role, their liberation necessarily appears to come from without and from above," Marcuse wrote. "They must be 'forced to be free,' to 'see objects as they are, and sometimes as they ought to appear,' they must be shown the 'good road' they are in search of."[48]

Following the orthodoxy of Marx and Lenin, Marcuse believed there must be a temporary dictatorship in order to move society from slavery to freedom. But, breaking from his predecessors, Marcuse offered an ironic twist: instead of the "dictatorship of the proletariat," which represented the will of the working class, Marcuse proposed a "dictatorship of the intellectuals"—which, presumably, represented the will of men like him.[49]

At the time, however, Marcuse was pessimistic about the prospects for revolution. Despite the passage of the Civil Rights Act and the Great Society programs in the mid-1960s, Marcuse believed that the progressive political project was doomed by its own limitations.[50] The one-dimensional society had swallowed up the very possibility of meaningful progress.

The only hope, Marcuse believed, was to unleash the destructive power of the slums and to hasten the collapse of the entire system. In the final passage of *One-Dimensional Man*, he appealed to "the substratum of the outcasts and outsiders," which, he believed, could constitute the physical, if not intellectual, forces of last-ditch resistance. "They exist outside the democratic process; their life is the most immediate and the most real need for ending intolerable conditions and institutions. Thus, their opposition is revolutionary even if their consciousness is not," Marcuse wrote. "It is nothing but a chance. The critical theory of society possesses no concepts which could bridge the gap between the present and its future; holding no promise and showing no success, it remains negative. Thus it wants to remain loyal to those who, without hope, have given and give their life to the Great Refusal."[51]

This, for Marcuse, was all that remained: the Great Refusal; the symbolic revolt; the negative charge of the dialectic.

But he had spoken too soon. Almost immediately after the publication of *One-Dimensional Man*, a new cultural revolution would sweep through the nations of the West, overturning a series of economic, political, sexual, religious, and artistic orthodoxies—and making Marcuse's lament about the permanence of the Establishment seem naïve. By the end of the decade, Marcuse's Great Refusal would end up setting the contours of the new "counterculture." College-educated bohemians would begin to "turn on, tune in, and drop out" of mainstream society. The war in Vietnam would start to alienate young people with sympathies for the Left. And the "outcasts and outsiders" of the American ghettos would riot, loot, smash, and steal in more than one hundred cities.[52]

The dialectic—against all expectations—had turned.

*   *   *

As the unrest spread through the United States, Professor Marcuse retreated to his little office at UCSD, settled himself at the typewriter, lit a cigar, and furiously updated his theory of the revolution. Between 1967 and

1969, Marcuse entered the most fertile period of his career, publishing a new edition of *A Critique of Pure Tolerance*,[53] a collection called *Negations: Essays in Critical Theory*,[54] and the seminal book *An Essay on Liberation*. During the same period, he also traveled across the world, delivered dozens of public lectures, and sat for lengthy press interviews, leaving behind a detailed record of his thought as it changed over time.[55]

This body of work would soon become the blueprint for the "New Left," a loose coalition of student protestors, race activists, radical feminists, and counterculture figures in the United States and Europe. Marcuse, then turning seventy, would become their father, their guru, their guide. As the New Left rose to prominence, Marcuse abandoned his earlier pessimism and laid out an ambitious intellectual program for the new radicals. In a speech at the Free University of Berlin in 1967, Marcuse outlined the basic philosophical orientation of the movement: "The New Left is, with some exceptions, neo-Marxist rather than Marxist in the orthodox sense; it is strongly influenced by what is called Maoism, and by the revolutionary movements in the Third World."[56]

The new movement was not the "'classical' revolutionary force" of the proletariat. It was, instead, the coalition of opposites that Marcuse had imagined in *One-Dimensional Man*: the intellectuals and the slum-dwellers, the privileged and the dispossessed. "It is an opposition against the majority of the population, including the working class," Marcuse said. "It is an opposition against the system's ubiquitous pressure, which by means of its repressive and destructive productivity degrades everything, in an increasingly inhuman way, to the status of a commodity whose purchase and sale provide the sustenance and content of life; against the system's hypocritical morality and 'values'; and against the terror employed outside the metropolis."[57]

This movement, Marcuse believed, was beginning to develop into a real political opposition: anti-war, anti-capitalist, anti-imperialist, anti-democratic. The new radicals were building a base of support on the Ivy League campuses and in the West Coast ghettos, beginning the process of "awakening the consciousness of the need for socialism, and that we must struggle for its realization if we are not to be barbarized and destroyed." The goal, Marcuse explained to the university students in West Berlin, might still be "socialism and the expropriation of private property in the means of production and collective control," but, he cautioned, in order to arrive at this stage, they must adopt a strategy of masking their intentions. "We must proceed from one step to the next."[58]

Marcuse told the students that they could not call for the immediate seizure and redistribution of wealth, but they could create the conditions for it to happen in the future.

Marcuse became their hero. His book *One-Dimensional Man* sold one hundred thousand copies and was translated into sixteen languages. In Rome, students swore their allegiance to "Marx, Mao, and Marcuse." In Paris, students occupied university buildings and embarked on a spiritual quest they called "la journée marcusienne."[59] In New York, white bourgeois radicals and black militants flocked to hear Marcuse speak about the revolution at the Fillmore East auditorium.[60] The *New York Times*, *Saturday Evening Post*, *BusinessWeek*, *Fortune*, *Time*, and *Playboy* all published features on Marcuse and his role as the "Father of the New Left."[61]

Over the following two years, Marcuse would crystallize his program for the New Left in *A Critique of Pure Tolerance* and *An Essay on Liberation*, which he dedicated to the "young militants." Together these texts outlined Marcuse's new theory of the revolution. Technological progress, he argued, had finally made communism possible. The new proletariat could use race, rather than class, to prepare the grounds for revolution. The radical minority could legitimately use violence and suppression in pursuit of the "total rupture." Marcuse had moved beyond classical Marxism and brought a coherent theory of neo-Marxism into being—the goal of making "the transition from capitalism to socialism" was the same, but the context, protagonist, and strategy had all changed with the progression of history.[62]

In the opening pages of *An Essay on Liberation*, Marcuse explains that the evolution of material conditions under advanced capitalism had finally created the material base necessary to meet the needs of all citizens. "Marx and Engels refrained from developing concrete concepts of the possible forms of freedom in a socialist society; today, such restraint no longer seems justified," he wrote.[63] The advanced nations of the West—and the newly industrialized nations of the East—simply needed to shift the control of the means of production and the distribution of goods in order to achieve the long-lost Marxian dream. "Utopian possibilities are inherent in the technical and technological forces of advanced capitalism and socialism,"

Marcuse said. "The rational utilization of these forces on a global scale would terminate poverty and scarcity within a very foreseeable future."[64]

This process of liberation could occur in two steps. First, through creating a system of "collective ownership" over economic production. Second, through a "qualitative change" in human nature "in accordance with the new sensitivity and the new consciousness," which would extinguish the spirit of exploitation once and for all.[65]

Next, Marcuse addresses the question of who will initiate this revolution. Under classical Marxism, the industrial working class—the soot-covered and alienated men who labored in the factories, shipyards, and warehouses— was the great Subject of the revolution. But, as Marcuse had concluded, the old proletariat had lost its revolutionary potential and assumed a "stabilizing, conservative function" within the capitalist system. And so Marcuse shifted his hopes to the emerging proletariat of the New Left—the coalition between the "young middle-class intelligentsia" and the "black militants"—which had the potential to become a new locus of resistance.[66]

He squared this apparent contradiction by arguing that new conditions of advanced capitalism necessitated a new revolutionary Subject, and that the New Left coalition served an analogous function to the Marxist political parties that were able to destabilize the ruling order and radicalize the masses in the past.[67] "The apparently impregnable economic fortress of corporate capitalism shows signs of mounting strain," Marcuse wrote. "The ghetto populations may well become the first mass basis of revolt. . . . The student opposition is spreading in the old socialist as well as capitalist countries."[68]

The emergence of this new proletariat also suggested a new axis for revolution: racial conflict, Marcuse believed, could provide a viable substitute—and eventual catalyst—for class conflict. "The fact is that, at present in the United States, the black population appears as the 'most natural' force of rebellion," he said. "Confined to small areas of living and dying, it can be more easily organized and directed. Moreover, located in the core cities of the country, the ghettos form natural geographical centers from which the struggle can be mounted against targets of vital economic and political importance."[69]

Marcuse had watched as the black urban centers had erupted in rioting, looting, arson, and bloodshed during the tumultuous years of the mid-to late 1960s. Although not a conscious revolutionary force, the ghettos provided an instinctual, physical resistance to the forces of law and order. They were a living refutation of the capitalist system, which, even after the passage of the Civil Rights Act, Voting Rights Act, and Great Society programs, had failed to absorb the minority populations into its mythology.

"The vital need for change is the very life of the ghetto population," Marcuse explained.[70] He saw the black militant movement, in particular, as a viable means of breaking the Establishment's stranglehold on language and culture. These groups, which were coalescing under the banner of Black Power, had developed a "subversive universe of discourse" that threatened to subvert the smooth, packaged language of corporate America. They had, for example, desublimated the Platonic word "soul" and loaded it with "black, violent, orgiastic" connotations; they had coined the slogan "black is beautiful" and imbued it with the feeling of "darkness, tabooed magic, the uncanny."[71]

Marcuse was careful to explain that this new coalition was not yet capable of revolution against the American regime. "The situation is in no sense revolutionary, it is not even pre-revolutionary," he told the French newspaper *Le Monde* in the summer of 1969. "But I am not a defeatist, ever." He hoped that the white radicals and black militants could soften the grounds for revolution at home and move beyond the confines of the university and the ghetto by uniting with the Third World revolutionaries who were leading the struggle for socialism abroad.

For Marcuse, the primary strategic necessity in the West was to relentlessly apply the negative dialectic, subvert the one-dimensional society, and destabilize the social order. As he explained in *An Essay on Liberation*, "the development of a radical political consciousness among the masses is conceivable only if and when the economic stability and the social cohesion of the system begin to weaken."[72] The white radicals and black militants, he believed, represented a "powerful force for disintegration" that might spur a crisis and, subsequently, develop into a real revolutionary class.[73] "Radical change in consciousness is the beginning, the first step in changing social existence: emergence of the new Subject," Marcuse wrote. "Historically, it is again the period of enlightenment prior to material change—a period of education, but education which turns into praxis: demonstration, confrontation, rebellion."[74]

The precondition for revolution, in other words, was the complete disintegration of the existing culture, economy, and society.

By 1969, Marcuse believed that these conditions were beginning to appear. That year, he republished *A Critique of Pure Tolerance*, which featured his provocative essay "Repressive Tolerance" and a new postscript relating his ideas to the political turmoil of the moment.

Building on the argument of *One-Dimensional Man*, Marcuse argued that the liberal-democratic notion of tolerance was an illusion. The "society of total administration" promoted the appearance of freedom and the simulation of dissent, but in practice it repressed and absorbed any real opposition into the system.[75] Thus, the major power centers—corporations, media, the state—had created a "perverted" form of tolerance that served "the protection and preservation of a repressive society."[76] Meanwhile, political radicals, lacking the requisite economic and democratic power to influence society, are "left free to deliberate and discuss, to speak and to assemble—and will be left harmless and helpless in the face of the overwhelming majority, which militates against qualitative social change."[77]

The solution to this state of "repressive tolerance," Marcuse believed, was to destroy and replace it with a new regime of "liberating tolerance," which would reverse the directionality of power and suppress all "institutions, policies, [and] opinions" that did not move the nation toward liberation and, eventually, revolution. As Marcuse put it: "Liberating tolerance, then, would mean intolerance against movements from the Right, and toleration of movements from the Left. As to the scope of this tolerance and intolerance: . . . it would extend to the stage of actions as well as of discussion and propaganda, of deed as well as of word."

For Marcuse, the practice of "liberating tolerance" would justify censorship, repression, and, when necessary, violence.[78] "Surely," he wrote, "no government can be expected to foster its own subversion, but in a democracy such a right is vested in the people. This means that the ways should not be blocked on which a subversive majority could develop, and if they are blocked by organized repression and indoctrination, their reopening may require apparently undemocratic means."[79]

Those means would include the censorship of ideas, the suppression of the political opposition, and the "suspension of the right of free speech and free assembly" for the enemies of the revolution, who constituted, in

Marcuse's words, a "clear and present danger." The new regime would apply strict censorship to all universities, corporations, media outlets, educational institutions, political parties, and the state itself. The radicals would enforce a policy of "intolerance even toward thought, opinion, and word" in order to inoculate the public against reactionary politics at the deepest substratum of consciousness.[80]

This program represented a radical departure from the basic principles of the Constitution, but Marcuse, intoxicated by the fervor in the streets, went a step further.

In the pages of "Repressive Tolerance," Marcuse patiently builds a step-by-step argument to justify left-wing political violence. First, he sets the premise: the modern capitalist democracies have produced the superficial appearance of peace, but in truth, they have simply masked and legitimized their own war of repression against the people. "Even in the advanced centers of civilization, violence actually prevails: it is practiced by the police, in the prisons and mental institutions, in the fight against racial minorities."[81] Next, he argues that, if the system of law and order is, in fact, a system of suppression, democracy becomes pseudo-democracy; morality becomes immorality; legitimacy becomes illegitimacy. Moreover, under such conditions, the minority—the student radical with his Molotov cocktail, the black liberation soldier with his semiautomatic rifle—has the right to engage in physical resistance.

Marcuse makes this explicit. "I believe that there is a 'natural right' of resistance for oppressed and overpowered minorities to use extralegal means if the legal ones have proved to be inadequate," he says. "If they use violence, they do not start a new chain of violence but try to break an established one. Since they will be punished, they know the risk, and when they are willing to take it, no third person . . . has the right to preach them abstention."[82]

In other words, in the revolutionary moment, the oppressed can exercise their right to overthrow their oppressors; they can justify their own violence as necessary for turning the wheel of history forward. "In terms of historical function there is a difference between revolutionary and reactionary violence," Marcuse concludes. "In terms of ethics, both forms of violence are inhuman and evil—but since when is history made in accordance with ethical standards? To start applying them at the point where the oppressed rebel against the oppressors, the have-nots against the haves is serving the cause of actual violence by weakening the protest against it."[83]

Marcuse's new theory of revolution was an instant success. The young radicals of the New Left, seeking intellectual justification for their revolt against the Establishment, immediately adopted Marcuse's vision as their own and celebrated the old man as their prophet. Meanwhile, the historical process was accelerating on all fronts. Police were tossing tear-gas canisters into throngs of student protestors in Europe. National Guard troops were firing live ammunition at rioters in the United States.[84] Mao Zedong was implementing the Cultural Revolution in China. Marxist-Leninist guerrillas from Cambodia to Mozambique had begun their long march toward liberation.

The world seemed poised for the "total rupture"—and Marcuse, abandoning any pretense of scholarly caution or detachment, gave permission for the "new barbarians" of the West to unleash havoc in the streets and in the halls of power. This was his chance, the moment that had escaped him in the crowds of Alexanderplatz in 1918 and on the ship passing by the Statue of Liberty in 1934. The revolution was finally within his reach. Man could escape the nightmare of necessity, liberate his instincts from repression, and create "the forms of a human universe without exploitation and toil."[85] At long last, the vast literature of the revolution, from Hegel to Marx to Lenin, could be realized on earth.

All that was needed was the gun.

CHAPTER 2

The New Left

"We Will Burn and Loot and Destroy"

The revolution was building momentum as the 1960s reached its end point. Marcuse continued to travel around the world, following the wave of student protests and giving interviews to the press in Frankfurt, Berlin, Paris, London, Rome, Turin, Milan, Bari, Oslo, Amsterdam, and Korčula.[1] He found himself at the center of the left-wing radical movements on both sides of the Atlantic and developed close connections with the most militant factions of the New Left.

In San Diego, Marcuse rallied with students to establish a Marxist-Leninist college at UCSD and, along with his graduate student Angela Davis, was among the first to break down the door and enter the registrar's office during a student occupation.[2] He was a regular guest at the Red House, a left-wing commune that was under FBI surveillance,[3] and gave the eulogy for a campus radical who had died by self-immolation in protest of the Vietnam War.[4] Davis would become a famed communist revolutionary and, after providing the firearms used in a murder-kidnapping plot, a fugitive from the law. As one San Diego resident told reporters, every time political violence erupted, "Marcuse, somewhere, is in the background."[5]

In December 1968, Marcuse presided over the twentieth-anniversary celebration for the Maoist newspaper the *Guardian* in New York City. His cohost was Bernardine Dohrn, who praised Marcuse as "the ideological leader of the New Left" and would later establish the Weather Underground terrorist organization. The other featured speaker was H. Rap Brown, a black militant who promised to wage a "continental liberation struggle" and was arrested a few years later, after going into hiding and engaging in a shoot-out with police.[6] During his speech, Marcuse signaled his support for the New Left's "political guerrilla force," which comprised "small groups, concentrated on the level of local activities" and might fore-shadow "what may in all likelihood be the basic organization of libertarian socialism, namely councils of manual and intellectual workers, *soviets*, if one can still use the term."[7]

These were not idle metaphors. Although Marcuse and his followers would later claim that the professor's use of the term "guerrilla force" was figurative,[8] the context is inescapable. Brown was already on the record promoting an armed "Negro revolution"[9] and agitating for "guerilla war-fare in all the cities."[10] Dohrn had already declared herself a "revolutionary communist"[11] and, months after her appearance with Marcuse, would sign the Weathermen's declaration of war against the United States,[12] inaugurat-ing a long string of bombings, prison breaks, and terror campaigns. An-other one of Marcuse's former students, Naomi Jaffe, would join Dohrn as a signatory and go into hiding after the FBI placed her on a wanted list.[13]

The young radicals were restless and soon pushed Marcuse to go further. In Rome, they heckled him onstage. In West Germany, they accused him of working for the CIA. Marcuse had touched the limits of academic inquiry, crafting an erudite philosophical justification for the revolution—but the students were growing impatient with the scholar's intricate abstractions and wanted liberation now, by whatever means necessary.[14]

The journalist Michael Horowitz, who had once studied under Marcuse at Brandeis University, captured the prevailing mood in a feature story for *Playboy*, detailing the professor's visit to the State University of New York at Old Westbury. Horowitz crafts a picture in contrasts: Marcuse, formally dressed in a vest, suit jacket, and French cuffs; and the student radicals, arriving in a dented Volkswagen, hoping to see "if Marcuse is radiating revolutionary vibrations."

The attendees represented the constellation of activist groups of the New Left: Students for a Democratic Society activists, the East Village Dig-gers performance troupe, campus Marxists and ethnic studies proponents, an academic sociologist, a gaggle of teenage libertines, and the radical press, carrying along old tape recorders and newsreels. During Marcuse's lecture, the young radicals shouted at him and bristled with hostility. They dismissed the value of a university education for black youth, arguing that "the white man's economic courses" could teach them nothing. "If he's seen rats, junkies, and the General Motors Building, he knows all he has to know!" they insisted.

Marcuse fired back with scorn: "I detect here what I have found on many campuses I have visited: a growing anti-intellectual attitude among the students. There is no contradiction between intelligence and revolution. Why are you afraid of being intelligent?"[15]

However, despite Marcuse's insistence that the young people in the audience represented a betrayal of his ideas, they also represented the natural consequence of his philosophy. They embodied the Great Refusal, the liberation of aesthetic form, the unleashing of the instincts. They followed Marcuse's call to participate in "the refusal to grow up, to mature, to perform efficiently and 'normally' in and for a society which compels the vast majority of the population to 'earn' their living in stupid, inhuman, and unnecessary jobs."[16] They were the "counter-culture," the inevitable carriers of the negative dialectic.

Horowitz, keenly aware of this contradiction, concludes the profile with a note of pity: "Poor Marcuse. Even in his popularity, he is out of step with the youth he seeks to guide. The campus left wants to burn libraries and he continues to defend reading, 'riting and 'rithmetic—albeit Marxist reading, 'riting and 'rithmetic. The kids thrill to phrases like 'undermine the foundations of the system' and 'the liberation of instinctual needs,' while the professor would have them temper such excitement with the reading of *Das Kapital* in the original German."[17]

As the campus movements grew more volatile, there was a sense that things might get out of hand. Even Marcuse's former colleagues at the Institute for Social Research warned the philosopher that he was becoming too radical, too zealous, too irrational. In a long exchange of letters, the critical theorist Theodor Adorno, having returned to Germany after the war and taken a position at Frankfurt University, warned his old friend Marcuse that he had lost sight of their shared commitment to rational inquiry.

When Marcuse requested to speak to Adorno's students in Frankfurt, Adorno refused, telling Marcuse that he would inflame the campus radicals, who were on the verge of succumbing to a kind of "left fascism" that resembled "something of that thoughtless violence" from the prewar era.[18] "To put it bluntly," Adorno wrote, "I think that you are deluding yourself in being unable to go on without participating in the student stunts."[19]

Throughout 1969, student protestors interrupted Adorno's lectures, topless women heckled him at the lectern, and a small group of radicals occupied the offices of the Institute for Social Research, prompting the professor to call the police. Believing that Adorno had betrayed them by summoning the authorities, the students passed out leaflets declaring that "Adorno as an institution is dead" and scrawled a message on his blackboard: "If Adorno is left in peace, capitalism will never cease."[20]

Marcuse, breaking painfully with Adorno in a return letter, sided with the radicals. "To put it brutally," he wrote, "if the alternative is the police or left-wing students, then I am with the students."[21] Adorno, beleaguered by the mob and suffering an "extreme depression,"[22] retreated to a chalet at the foot of the Matterhorn in Switzerland, where he died of a sudden heart attack.

Adorno did not live to see the New Left's full descent in violence, but his warnings were prescient. As the year turned from 1969 to 1970, the New Left embraced armed revolution as its new political strategy. During that critical juncture, Marxist-Leninist radicals formally established the Weather Underground Organization, the Black Liberation Army, and the Baader-Meinhof Gang, known formally as the Red Army Faction, all of which were committed to overthrowing the governments of the West. Marcuse was connected with them all. He had taught, mentored, and appeared publicly with leaders of the Weather Underground;[23] he had engaged in a high-profile struggle against the University of California Board of Regents alongside the spiritual leader of the Black Liberation Army;[24] and he had directly influenced the student radicals in West Germany who founded the Red Army Faction terror organization.[25]

The FBI was so concerned by these connections that Director J. Edgar Hoover personally elevated Marcuse to "Security Matter –C" status, classifying the professor as a "revolutionary," "anarchist," "grandfather of the New Left," and "threat to national security."[26] Agents recruited informants and monitored Marcuse closely, detailing his financial support for the Black Panther Party, meetings with Communist Party officials, and connections with the Marxist intellectual Angela Davis, black revolutionary H. Rap Brown, and German student leader Rudi Dutschke.[27]

Soon the young radicals would put Marcuse's theory of revolutionary violence into action. They had studied the books, written the manifestos, and prepared their weapons; they were simply waiting for the moment to strike.

*   *   *

On the evening of June 9, 1970, a bomb composed of fifteen sticks of dynamite ripped through the walls of the New York City Police Department headquarters in Manhattan.[28] The bomb blew out the second-floor windows and injured seven people inside the building with glass, construction material, and blast debris.

The next morning, the Associated Press received a handwritten letter from the Weathermen taking responsibility for the bombing. "The pigs in this country are our enemies," the letter said. "They build the Bank of America, kids burn it down. They outlaw grass, we build a culture of life and music. The time is now. Political power grows out of a gun, a molotov, a riot, a commune . . . and from the soul of the people."[29]

The Weathermen were members of the Weather Underground Organization, a group of white, college-educated radicals who were fed up with the institutional Left and saw armed revolution as the only viable path forward. The Weathermen were deeply influenced by Marcuse. The spiritual leader of the organization, Bernardine Dohrn, thought of Marcuse as a guiding light for the movement, and her close collaborator, Naomi Jaffe, "started to develop an identification as a radical" while studying under Marcuse as an undergraduate.[30] The literature that they produced, which justified their revolution and attracted recruits, was suffused with Marcuse's concepts and themes.

The nucleus of the group had formed in Students for a Democratic Society, a left-wing student movement that had mobilized on the issues of civil rights, free speech, and the Vietnam War. But as the 1960s drew to a close, the most radical elements of the SDS wanted to push further. Bernardine Dohrn, Bill Ayers, Mark Rudd, and others wanted to align with the black militants in America and the liberation armies in the Third World in order to achieve revolution on a global scale. "The goal is the destruction of US imperialism and the achievement of a classless world: world communism," they wrote in their 1969 manifesto, *You Don't Need a Weatherman to Know Which Way the Wind Blows*, referencing the famous lyric from Bob Dylan's "Subterranean Homesick Blues." "We want to smash cops, and build a new life."[31]

That fall, the Weathermen had established revolutionary collectives in more than a dozen cities and set up a centralized headquarters, which they called the Weather Bureau.[32] "A revolution is a war," they wrote. "This will require a cadre organization, effective secrecy, self-reliance among the cadres, and an integrated relationship with the active mass-based Movement. . . . Because war is political, political tasks—the international communist revolution—must guide it. Therefore the centralized organization of revolutionaries must be a political organization as well as military, what is generally called a 'Marxist-Leninist' party."[33]

Self-consciously modeling themselves on Che Guevara, Mao Zedong, and Mao's Red Guards, the Weathermen directed street protests, occupations, vandalism, and sabotage campaigns across the country, culminating in the "Days of Rage" protest in Chicago, in which several hundred Weathermen smashed windows and fought against a full contingent of police officers. The Chicago police put down the mob with fists, clubs, guns, and tear gas. They shot three demonstrators and arrested nearly three hundred more.[34]

The Weathermen were defeated, suppressed, and humiliated, but they had their first taste of blood—and they wanted more.

In the final days of 1969, the Weathermen gathered their most loyal soldiers in a crumbling dance hall in a Flint, Michigan, ghetto to convene a "war council." The event turned into a multiday bacchanalia. The young attendees endured long drug binges, participated in orgies, and entertained political hallucinations. The speeches, which slurred together in long sequences, captured the revolutionary ethos: "It must be a really wonderful feeling to kill a pig or blow up a building"; "we will burn and loot and destroy"; "we are the incubation of your mother's nightmare." Bernardine Dohrn, the most charismatic Weather Underground leader, celebrated the serial killer Charles Manson, the cult leader who had recently butchered the pregnant actress Sharon Tate and four of her friends. "Dig it!" Dohrn exclaimed to the menagerie in Flint. "First, they killed those pigs, then they ate dinner in the same room with them. They even shoved a fork into the victim's stomach! Wild!"[35]

The Weathermen followed Marcuse's theory, outlined in his book *Eros and Civilization*, that sexual and political liberation were intertwined. They deliberately broke up monogamous relationships and asked members to submit their sexuality to the collective in order to surpass bourgeois norms and "commit suicide as a class."[36] In Flint, the Weathermen confronted one another in all-night, Mao-inspired criticism/self-criticism sessions, confronting their racial privilege, their sexual inhibitions, and their commitment to the revolution.[37] They engaged in macabre thought experiments and contemplated the question of whether it was "the duty of every good revolutionary to kill all newborn white babies," who would otherwise "grow up to be part of an oppressive racial establishment."[38]

Violence was the highest theme of the war council discussions. Dohrn suggested that terrorism and political assassination were legitimate means of revolution and the organizers hung up a massive twenty-foot banner with the names of their enemies, such as Chicago mayor Richard J. Daley, illustrated onto pictures of bullets.[39]

According to an FBI informant who infiltrated the group, the Weather Bureau leadership was already making plans for what they would do after violently overthrowing and seizing control of the state. They would establish reeducation centers in the Southwest to rehabilitate the capitalists and guard against the counter-revolution. "Well, what is going to happen to those people that we can't re-educate, that are die-hard capitalists?" the informant asked. "And the reply was that they would have to be eliminated. And when I pursued this further, they estimated that they would have to eliminate 25 million people in these re-education centers. And when I say 'eliminate,' I mean 'kill' 25 million people."[40] The young radicals were utterly disillusioned with Western society and ready to enact Marcuse's dictum that "counter-violence" was necessary in "the struggle for changes beyond the system."[41]

The war council concluded on New Year's Day 1970 with a declaration of war. The Weathermen had made the decision to go underground and to commit themselves to revolution in their time. "Armed struggle," they said, "starts when someone starts it."[42]

That spring, Dohrn released a tape recording of the Weathermen's Communiqué #1, announcing the revolutionary intentions of the New Left. "Black people have been fighting almost alone for years. We've known that our job is to lead white kids into armed revolution," Dohrn said. "Within the next fourteen days we will attack a symbol or institution of Amerikan injustice. This is the way we celebrate the example of Eldridge Cleaver and

H. Rap Brown and all black revolutionaries who first inspired us by their fight behind enemy lines for the liberation of their people." The strategy of peace had failed. The new strategy of war would succeed. "Now we are adapting the classic guerrilla strategy of the Viet Cong and the urban guerrilla strategy of the [Uruguayan leftist] Tupamaros to our own situation here in the most technically advanced country in the world," said Dohrn, echoing Marcuse's language on the technological society. "Protests and marches don't do it. Revolutionary violence is the only way."[43]

Two weeks later, they set off the bomb at the NYPD headquarters, inaugurating a five-year campaign of bombings, robberies, escapes, and communiqués. Operating in small revolutionary cells, the Weathermen would claim responsibility for a string of symbolic bombings, including detonations at the US Capitol, the Pentagon, military bases, courthouses, police stations, government buildings, financial institutions, and a state attorney general's office.[44] The Weathermen, who considered themselves "white revolutionaries inside the oppressor nation," believed that their work against the United States represented "the unique contribution [they could] make to the world revolution."[45]

The scale of left-wing political violence during this period was enormous. The Weathermen, black nationalist organizations, and other left-wing groups perpetrated a stunning number of property bombings, police assassinations, bank robberies, prison breaks, and violent assaults. During a fifteen-month stretch between 1969 and 1970 alone, police recorded 4,330 bombings that resulted in forty-three deaths.[46] The militants, drawing on Che Guevara's *foco* theory of revolution, which held that focused action could inspire a broader movement, believed they were on the cusp of sparking a national revolt.

Marcuse, too, had succumbed to the romance of the Marxist-Leninist guerrillas and the armed revolution against the state. In *An Essay on Liberation*, he had expressed admiration for the revolutionaries in Vietnam, Cuba, and China, who he thought represented "the possibility of constructing socialism on a truly popular base."[47] Like his young disciples in the Weathermen, he praised Fidel Castro and Che Guevara as the living embodiment of "'freedom,' 'socialism,' and 'liberation'"[48] and told a French newspaper that "every Marxist who is not a communist of strict obedience is a Maoist."[49] When another reporter asked him if he agreed with the student slogan "Marx as the prophet, Marcuse as his interpreter, and Mao as the sword," Marcuse replied modestly: "I think they do me much too much honor."[50]

The New Left's wave of violence, however, did not advance the revolution. It alienated the public and precipitated a forceful response from the government.

In the summer of 1970, President Richard Nixon mobilized the intelligence services against the Weathermen and other radical organizations, which, he believed, were "determined to destroy" the country.[51] The United States Congress launched an investigation into the organization[52] and the FBI placed Bernardine Dohrn on its list of the Ten Most Wanted fugitives.[53] By 1972, law enforcement agencies had captured or killed dozens of left-wing militants and sent the remaining holdouts into deep hiding. Finally, Nixon—the architect of the counter-revolution—sealed his victory against the revolutionaries with a forty-nine-state landslide against liberal candidate George McGovern, promising a return to law and order.

For the remaining members of the Weathermen, the initial euphoria of revolution was overtaken by despair. Life underground turned painful, lonely, and monotonous. The all-night orgies resulted in hangovers, jealousies, gonorrhea, and lice.[54] The bombings lost their sheen and slipped to the back pages of the *New York Times*.

Eventually the movement shriveled down to a dozen hard-core followers, who managed to secure a bourgeois, if clandestine, existence with the help of left-wing lawyers and financial supporters—a pink houseboat in Sausalito, California, a cozy bungalow on Hermosa Beach, an apartment in San Francisco.[55]

By 1974, as Marcuse was openly conceding the defeat of the New Left, the Weathermen, too, realized that they were at the end of the line. The revolutionary coalition had fallen apart. The relationship between the white radicals and the black militants—Marcuse's new proletariat—had ended in recriminations. The black liberation organizations turned against their white counterparts, arguing that "the White Left" was a "bankrupt" political movement that "subsumes its hunger for White bourgeois legitimacy behind marxist rhetoric and intellectual lip masturbation."[56]

At the same time, the Weathermen's plan to radicalize the white working class had failed. When the Weatherman Mark Rudd tried to recruit a group of down-class white teenagers loitering outside a restaurant, they sent him to the hospital with a vicious beat-down.[57] As Marcuse had feared, the laboring classes, which Marx had considered the ultimate engine of revolution, had become "antirevolutionary," absorbed into bourgeois mythology and decisively opposed to large-scale social change.[58] The blue-collar worker, despite the best efforts of the young radicals, was still a one-dimensional man, sated with a paycheck, a television, and a wife and children at home.

Marcuse was shell-shocked. The forces of Thermidor, which had once devoured Robespierre, had smothered the spirit of revolution yet again. The reactionaries had won.

*　　*　　*

Marcuse's twilight years were a long, contemplative gloom. His revolution, which he had chased since the bracing days of his youth, was over.

From 1972 until his death in 1979, Marcuse retreated to his single-level suburban home in La Jolla to publish his final political manuscript, *Counterrevolution and Revolt*, and to contemplate the failures of the New Left. He still maintained a small office at UCSD, but following the conflict with Governor Reagan and the Board of Regents, the university had let his contract expire, putting Marcuse into early retirement and ending his career as a teacher.

Marcuse was unsparing in his diagnosis of what went wrong. In 1975, he told students in Irvine, California, that the counterculture was a spent force. It had become anti-intellectual, decadent, and authoritarian. "The countercultures created by the New Left destroyed themselves when they forfeited their political impetus in favor of withdrawal into a kind of private liberation—drug culture, the turn to guru-cults, and other pseudo-religious sects," he said.[59] "The strong libertarian, anti-authoritarian movements that originally defined the New Left have vanished in the meantime or yielded to a new 'group-authoritarianism.'"[60]

The student radicals of 1968, in other words, had taken one of two roads: they had either dropped out of society, rendering them politically inert, or joined the militant groups, rendering them vulnerable to infiltration, disruption, and despair. The young rebels had convinced themselves that the revolution was imminent, but, as Marcuse had tried to warn them, the United States had never met the Marxist preconditions for revolution. The students, playing the role of the avant-garde, failed to recruit the working classes. The ghettos, despite the objective conditions of poverty and oppression, failed to develop a political consciousness.[61]

Still, despite these setbacks, Marcuse refused to accept defeat. "I do believe that a democratic Communism is a real historical possibility. Worse still, I believe that only in a fully developed Communist society is a general democracy possible," he argued in a 1972 debate, insisting that the only path to liberation was a "socialist regime, with collective ownership of the means of production and collective control of central planning."[62] For Marcuse, the end was the same—traditional Marxism—but, he conceded, the means must change.

The revolution, he told his young followers, would not be achieved through LSD or guerrilla warfare. They had failed at the ballot box and failed in the streets, but there was still one thin glimmer of hope: returning to the origins of the critical theories—the universities—and rebuilding the revolution from the ground up.

CHAPTER 3

The Long March Through
the Institutions

During the chaos of the Chinese Civil War, the communist revolutionary Mao Zedong found himself besieged. The Nationalists had routed and encircled his army. His men were panicked, bloodied, and undersupplied. In October 1934, after deliberations, the Communists, who then chose Mao as their leader, initiated one of the most desperate and audacious maneuvers in military history: a five-thousand-mile strategic retreat that would become known as the "Long March of the Red Army."

Over the course of the yearlong retreat, Mao's ranks were devastated. His men died of starvation, cold, disease, and violence, and defeat seemed imminent. But after securing his defenses in the mountain stronghold of Yan'an and patiently rebuilding his forces, Mao launched a counterattack against the Nationalists, chased his enemies into the sea, and declared the Communist Party the sole and legitimate ruler of the People's Republic of China—a stunning reversal of fortune.

Marcuse believed the New Left was in a similar position. The FBI had hunted down and dismantled the revolutionary organizations. Nixon had won decisively in the court of public opinion. And the counterculture had succumbed to hedonism, guru worship, and despair. But Marcuse, like Mao, was relentless. He believed the left-wing radicals could engage in a strategic retreat to the universities and, rebuilding their forces, turn defeat into victory.

During the early 1970s, as the radical movement was disintegrating, Marcuse turned to the young activists in his political orbit, especially the German student leader Rudi Dutschke, who had helped spread the campus revolts across Europe and, after the failure of the terror campaigns, had proposed a new strategy of the "long march through the established institutions"—a direct allusion to Mao's military campaign.

In 1971, as the prospects of the revolution continued to narrow, Marcuse put his hopes in Dutschke's new concept, which meant entering the established institutions and changing them from within. "Let me tell you this," he wrote to Dutschke, "that I regard your notion of the 'long march through the institutions' as the only effective way, now more than ever."[1] Both men thought that the terror campaigns were a dead end and that participation in the democratic process was futile. They believed that the New Left needed to return to its origins: abandoning the radical path and, instead, rebuilding its power in the universities and turning the students into "potential *cadres*" who, over time, could move their "revolution in values" from university to society—and, for the time being, spread their influence outside the confines of electoral politics.[2]

Marcuse outlined his theory in his final political book, *Counterrevolution and Revolt*. The long march did not have the allure of the total rupture, but it provided a way to keep the revolution alive and to shift the focus from the war of cataclysm to the war of values. He encouraged the student radicals to put down their arms and burrow themselves in the universities, schools, media, and social services, capturing the means of knowledge production in order to subvert them—or, in Marcuse's words, "working against the established institutions while working in them." He believed that the Left's primary objective was to gain control of the "great chains of information and indoctrination,"[3] through which it could begin the "vast task of political education, dispelling the false and mutilated consciousness of the people so that they themselves experience their condition, and its abolition, as vital need, and apprehend the ways and means of their liberation."[4]

Marcuse encouraged the young radicals to create a series of "counter-institutions" that could serve as a new apparatus for social change. He thought that the New Left, using the university as its starting point, should regroup around "the organization of radical caucuses, counter-meetings, counter-associations, in short, the development of what have been called counter-institutions such as radio, television, press, workshops, anything and everything that promises to break the information monopoly of the establishment."[5] Through these new bases of support, Marcuse believed, the young radicals could launch their "cultural revolution" and usher in "a transformation of values which strikes at the entirety of the established culture, material as well as intellectual."[6] Race politics, women's liberation, radical environmentalism, the Great Refusal—all could be harnessed for the process of disintegration.

Marcuse implored the students to do this work slowly, patiently, and methodically. It would take time, but they would eventually be able to take the theoretical knowledge they developed in the universities and spread it by "contagion" through society,[7] undermining traditional culture and shattering the existing hierarchy of values. "The outcome depends, to a great extent, on the ability of the young generation not to drop out and not to accommodate," he wrote, "but to learn how to regroup after defeat, how to develop, with the new sensibility a new rationality, to sustain the long process of education—the indispensable prerequisite for the transition to large-scale political action."

They might not see the transvaluation of values in the near term, but their slow and steady work to dissolve the foundations of the West could create the possibility of utopia beyond their own lifetimes. "For the next revolution will be the concern of generations, and 'the final crisis of capitalism' may take all but a century."[8]

*   *   *

The radicals heeded Marcuse's advice. After graduation, many of the left-wing students cleaned up, put on solid-colored ties, and went to work in the institutions. Their united front had been defeated, but the dialectic carried on.

Even the Weathermen, who had retreated to a network of safe houses and hiding places, devised a plan to reestablish their credibility with the activist Left and resurface in a leadership role. In 1974, the remaining members of the group, led by Bernardine Dohrn, Bill Ayers, and Jeff Jones, published a new manifesto called *Prairie Fire*—an allusion to the Mao Zedong aphorism "a single spark can start a prairie fire"—and distributed it to radical organizations, coffeehouses, and college-town bookstores.

Gone was the language of the counterculture. They no longer spoke in the blunt language of "kill a pig or blow up a building."[9] Instead, they spoke in a high-minded intellectual tone and railed against the great "isms": capitalism, racism, sexism, imperialism, colonialism. They tacitly acknowledged their mistake in believing their bombing campaign would bring about the revolution and proposed a new theory of revolution, which would open a new "dialectic among those in the mass and clandestine movements"[10] and use the "weapon of theory" to awaken the masses and build the political consciousness required for revolution.[11]

The general line of *Prairie Fire*, which was radical at the time, now reads as something quite familiar: the United States was founded on racism, sexism, slavery, and genocide; the ruling class then set about with "the institutionalizing of white supremacy,"[12] which was "maintained and perpetuated over the generations by the schools, the unemployment cycle, the drug trade, immigration laws, birth control, the army, the prisons";[13] and, as a result, the current system was full of rot, enriching the elites while oppressing racial minorities and appeasing poor whites with "white-skin privilege."[14]

The solution, for the Weathermen, was to rebuild Marcuse's two-part proletariat and engage in an inside-outside game of marching through the institutions while exerting pressure through targeted violence. Dohrn, Ayers, and Jones put special emphasis on radicalizing the education system. They understood that public schools, which facilitated the transmission of values, could be co-opted by white, college-educated activists. They called on "radical teachers" to form an "anti-racist white movement"[15] and enter working-class and minority schools in order to "radicalize other teachers, organize the parents, teach and encourage [the] students."[16] Meanwhile, the Weathermen suggested, the black radicals emerging from the prisons could "[stir] the imagination and [raise] the vision of victory"[17] through riots, disruptions, sabotage, and prison revolts.

"Revolutionary action generates revolutionary consciousness," they said. "Growing consciousness develops revolutionary action."[18]

The Weathermen printed forty thousand copies of *Prairie Fire* and surreptitiously organized a national conference that was to augur their rightful return as the vanguard of the activist Left.[19] They assembled the entire spectrum of radicals on the University of Illinois campus in Chicago and planned for a unity summit. But the conference, despite the high-minded rhetoric about "cultural identity," "anti-racism," and "white privilege," turned into a farce. The black radicals feuded with the white radicals. The women denounced the men. The vegetarians revolted against the cafeteria chicken. Accusations of racism ricocheted across the floor.

Later that year, the Weathermen splintered for the last time. Dohrn, subjecting herself to punishing criticism/self-criticism sessions, finally broke. "I am making this tape to acknowledge, repudiate, and denounce the counterrevolutionary politics and direction of the Weather Underground Organization," she said in a rambling audiotape confession. "We followed the classic path of white so-called revolutionaries who sold out the revolution." She was guilty of "naked white supremacy, white superiority, and chauvinist arrogance"—and, with this final admission, the Weather Underground was done.[20]

After Dohrn's confession, the Weathermen made their final pivot: they would slowly come out of hiding and reenter the bourgeois world. They were tired of living as fugitives, wanted to start families, and desired the simple comforts of a middle-class life. Beginning in 1977, the Weathermen gradually negotiated their surrender and came out of the shadows. To their surprise, only one Weatherman, Cathy Wilkerson, served any prison time—just eleven months—for the string of bombings. Ayers had charges against him dropped. Dohrn, Rudd, and others escaped with sentences of probation for various misdemeanors.[21]

Although the Weathermen's final gambit with *Prairie Fire* and the Chicago conference was a failure, it established a deeper precedent. The way forward was not through the messy politics of revolutionary action, but through the manipulation of symbols and ideas. The language of *Prairie Fire* was not enough to revive the New Left, but over time it would become the entire vocabulary of American intellectual life: "institutionalized racism," "white supremacy," "white privilege," "male supremacy," "institutional sexism," "cultural identity," "anti-racism," "anti-sexist men," "monopoly capitalism," "corporate greed," "neocolonialism," "Black liberation." The rhythm of accusation and confession of the unity summit was not enough to reconstitute Marcuse's new proletariat, but it would establish the basic rituals for left-wing institutions: emotional manipulation, confessions of privilege, elaborate displays of guilt, and moral submission to the new hierarchy.

Beginning in the late 1970s, the entire constellation of New Left radicals, from the graduate students of Herbert Marcuse to the urban guerrillas of the Weather Underground, shed the trappings of the counterculture and returned to the place where their activism had once begun: the university campus. They followed Marcuse's counsel to move beyond the "pubertarian rebellion"[22] of the radical movements and turn to the education system as their primary "counter-institution." As the student radical turned

Brown University professor Paul Buhle explained in his book *Marxism in the United States*: "To the question: 'Where did all the sixties radicals go?,' the most accurate answer would be: neither to religious cults nor yuppiedom, but to the classroom."[23]

This transition was nearly invisible. The public considered the radical movement as good as dead. In 1981, the *New York Times* summarized the entire Weather Underground affair as a "classic tragedy" and portrayed the Weathermen as entitled, narcissistic, delusional, and irrelevant—out of step with the country, including the liberal establishment of the era. In the end, the *Times* concluded, the Weathermen had transformed themselves from "idealistic students" into "a chilling perversion of every purpose they had ever had: the children of the rich killing the less privileged in the name of revolution. It was clear that their rage had become psychosis, their struggle was with self-hatred, and the only revolution they would fight was the one taking place in their own minds."[24]

Despite these public dismissals, however, the New Left was silently making inroads in academia. Over the years, Marcuse's students and followers gained professorships at dozens of prestigious universities, including Harvard; Yale; Georgetown; Duke; University of California, Berkeley; University of Pennsylvania; University of California, Santa Barbara; University of California, Los Angeles; University of New Mexico; University of Texas; Bard College; Rutgers; University of San Francisco; and Loyola University Chicago.[25]

The Weathermen, in spite of their participation in political terror campaigns, found a welcome home in the academy, too. Dohrn, who had promised to "lead white kids into armed revolution,"[26] became a professor at Northwestern. Ayers, who had laid bombs at the Pentagon and the US Capitol, became a professor at the University of Illinois. Even Kathy Boudin, who served a long prison sentence for her involvement in an armored car robbery that left one Brinks guard and two police officers dead, became a professor at Columbia. In total, approximately half of the most active Weathermen managed to secure positions in the education field, from prestigious appointments at Duke, Fordham, and Columbia to more modest sinecures in the public school systems of Chicago, New York, and San Francisco, where the old revolutionary cells had been most prominent.[27]

The rise of the New Left in academia is symbolic of a larger shift in

American education. While the public was lulled to sleep by the resolution of the Cold War, the radicals in the West patiently executed their long march through the institutions, never abandoning their faith in the old dialectic. Over time, the radicals shifted the university as a whole, securing positions of influence, legitimizing their ideas in sympathetic journals, purging reactionaries from the faculty, and recruiting cohorts of graduate students who would transform the spirit of the revolutionary communiqués into a dense academic mass.

In retrospect, their ascension was inevitable. The radicals had learned bare-knuckled politics in student protests, guerrilla factions, and underground bomb factories. It was only a matter of time before they asserted dominance over faculty meetings and academic conferences. They were able to use their old tactics of manipulation—accusations of racism, evocations of guilt and privilege, rituals of criticism/self-criticism—to push out more conservative scholars and delegitimize traditional conceptions of knowledge. Their revolution might have failed in society, but it worked all too well in academia.

As critic Bruce Bawer has documented in *The Victims' Revolution*, this new hybrid ideology, which combined the critical theory of society with the identity politics of the New Left, had a corrosive effect on department after department. "Once, the humanities had been concerned with the true, the good, and the beautiful; now they were preoccupied with an evil triumvirate of isms—colonialism, imperialism, capitalism—and with a three-headed monster of victimhood: class, race, and gender oppression," Bawer lamented. "Once, the purpose of the humanities had been to introduce students to the glories of Western civilization, thought, and art—to enhance students' respect, even reverence, for the cultural heritage of the West; now the humanities sought to unmask the West as a perpetrator of injustice around the globe."[28]

The result is a curious contradiction. Over the course of the 1980s and '90s, the country's political center moved to the right—Presidents Ronald Reagan, George H. W. Bush, and Bill Clinton presided over the end of global communism and the triumph of democratic capitalism—while academia continued to move to the left, undeterred by the ideological failures of "Marx, Mao, and Marcuse" and the long trail of death and destruction in Communist China, Africa, Latin America, and the Soviet Union.

Today, Marcuse and Dutschke's long march through the universities has reached its conclusion. The American university is now a "counter-institution" driven by the ideology of the New Left and the critical theories. The empirical evidence is overwhelming. According to survey data, 24 percent of college professors in the social sciences self-identify as "radical," 21 percent as "activist," and 18 percent as "Marxist"; in the humanities, the numbers are 19 percent, 26 percent, and 5 percent, respectively.[29] In another study of faculty partisan affiliation at forty leading universities, one researcher found even greater dominance, with the ratio of liberal to conservative faculty reaching 8:1 in political science, 17:1 in history, 44:1 in sociology, 48:1 in English, and 108:0 in race and gender studies.[30]

The consequence, scholars argue, is an "academic caste system": the departments at the most prestigious universities administer hiring, funding, and placement of new professors on a majoritarian and consensus basis, which serves to further concentrate and reinforce ideological power. "Once the apex of the disciplinary pyramid becomes predominately left-leaning, it will sweep left-leaners into positions throughout the pyramid," they write. As a result, the ratio between liberals and conservatives in the social sciences and humanities increased from 3.5:1 in 1970 to 10:1 in 2016—and promises to become even more concentrated in the future as the "one-party" system replaces older professors with younger ideological allies.[31]

Like their hero Mao Zedong, whose Long March began as a strategic retreat, Marcuse, Dutschke, Dohrn, and the student radicals turned the defeat of the New Left into an eventual coup. Marcuse's "critical theory of society" spawned an enormous brood of new academic disciplines, which matured into hundreds of new departments, programs, and subfields: Critical Studies, Critical Identity Studies, Critical Race Studies, Critical Ethnic Studies, Critical Whiteness Studies, Black and Africana Studies, Women's Studies, Feminist Studies, Gender Studies, and Race, Class, and Gender Studies.

The old radicalism has shed the need for its prefixes—"counter-sociology" has become sociology; "counter-psychology" has become psychology; "counter-education" has become education—and the new disciplines have cannibalized every traditional field in the humanities and social sciences.

The political culture of these programs is textbook critical theory and New Left activism. When Marcuse articulated the concept of "liberating tolerance," he made the unapologetic argument for "intolerance against movements from the Right"[32] and the direct suppression of conservative intellectuals.[33] This is now the prevalent mood on campus, with conservative faculty, already vastly outnumbered, reporting hostility, fear, exclusion, and intimidation.[34] When the Weathermen subjected themselves to "criticism/self-criticism" as they sought to resurface, they confessed to their complicity in "white supremacy," "white privilege," and "male privilege,"[35] which had "betrayed [their] revolutionary principles."[36] This method of reconditioning is now second nature in the universities, where students participate in reeducation programs for "deconstructing whiteness"[37] and twelve-step programs on "recovery from white conditioning."[38]

The language, too, has been devoured by the critical ideologies. The vocabulary of subversion in *Prairie Fire*, dismissed at the time as fringe and marginal, has become the lingua franca of academia. A search of the scholarly journals yields 105,000 results for "white supremacy," 61,000 for "white privilege," 52,000 for "neocolonialism," 35,000 for "monopoly capitalism," 34,000 for "male privilege," 29,000 for "male supremacy," and 28,000 for "institutionalized racism."[39] There are now thousands of academics producing derivative scholarship that establishes dominance not through quality, but through volume. They promote their ideas in a circular fashion, agreeing with and promoting one another while insulating themselves from the very possibility of criticism.

The purpose of flooding the discourse with these concepts is not merely to shape public consciousness, but to precondition the population for left-wing political conclusions. Marcuse called this process "linguistic therapy," which he described as "the effort to free words (and thereby concepts) from the all but total distortion of their meanings by the Establishment" and to initiate "the transfer of moral standards (and of their validation) from the Establishment to the revolt against it."[40]

The process works like this: The public consciousness is primed with new language—for example, "male supremacy" or "institutionalized racism"—and then subconsciously filters all subsequent experience through these conceptual frames, whether or not they correspond with reality. The conclusion is loaded into the very language of the premise. Once the web is spun, it catches everything.

The result has been a sea change in the left-liberal consensus. During the 1970s, the *New York Times* mocked Marcuse as "an elder who isn't an adult"[41] and the Weathermen as spoiled children spreading "Big Lies about America."[42] When Bernardine Dohrn introduced Marcuse as "the man that the *New York Times* calls the ideological leader of the New Left" at the *Guardian* newspaper anniversary, the professor replied, "I'm not responsible for what the *New York Times* calls me," drawing jeers and whistles from the crowd.[43]

Fifty years later, Marcuse and his disciples have had their revenge. The modern Left now thinks almost exclusively in the terms of the New Left. The fringe ideas of *An Essay on Liberation* and *You Don't Need a Weatherman to Know Which Way the Wind Blows* are now dominant not only in academia, but in mass media. The *New York Times* has adopted the language of the New Left as its house style; the commentators of MSNBC engage in an endless reenactment of New Left activism.[44] The critical theories proved to be irresistible: through persuasion or through force, they were able to attract followers, undermine certainties, suppress enemies, and establish a foothold in the knowledge-forming institutions.

Taken together—as idea, language, position—the new disciplines of the critical theories have disemboweled the old institutions and captured the "linguistic universe of the Establishment."[45] But for the activists and intellectuals who followed Marcuse's vision, domination of the universities and the country's political vocabulary was not enough. They did not want to merely seize the goods; they wanted to seize the machine that produced them. This would mean moving beyond the classroom and the op-ed page. It would mean taking authority over the institutions as a whole and learning how to replace the Establishment in deed as well as word.

It would, in short, require power.

*   *   *

The training ground for the New Left's capture of institutional power was the university. They had achieved dominance over the discipline, but, as Marcuse had patiently explained, critical theory was a totalizing ideology. The cultural revolution would begin with a change in consciousness but must end with control over the means of production, which, in the advanced technological society, meant the production of knowledge and sensibility.

In order to initiate this shift, the New Left–inspired academics and activists worked to extend their power to the administration, which held the ultimate authority over the direction, hiring, training, and financing of the university. The process was simple. They took the basic building blocks of their academic program—a composite of critical theory, ethnic studies, racial quotas, civil rights compliance, and consciousness training—and formalized them in the bureaucracy. Over time, this regime of "liberating tolerance" came to be known as "diversity, equity, and inclusion," or DEI. Even the choice of language was brilliant. From the beginning, it had the attributes of a moral bulldozer: to oppose "diversity" was bigotry; to oppose "inclusion" was racism; to oppose "equity" was domination.

The critical theorists had spent a generation teaching that the university establishment was vicious, oppressive, and one-dimensional. Then, as administrators, they promised to change it.

One of the key figures in this transition from critical theory to "diversity, equity, and inclusion" was Herbert Marcuse's former teaching assistant and third wife, Erica Sherover-Marcuse, who was forty years his junior. Sherover-Marcuse was a deep student of Karl Marx—she wrote her doctoral thesis on Marx's early philosophical works—and believed that the revolution would occur through the cultivation of "emancipatory consciousness."[46] Beginning in the 1970s, Sherover-Marcuse became a pioneer in leading "consciousness-raising"[47] and "multicultural awareness" groups throughout California.[48]

In an interview with her then husband, Herbert, Sherover-Marcuse explained that these training programs could transform people's subconscious attitudes and, over time, advance the cause of political liberation. "It seems to me that the difficulties the left had in the sixties and also in the thirties are precisely because there wasn't in the Marxist tradition a theory of the development of subjectivity . . . it didn't deal with how do you transform people's consciousness? How do we actually transform our own consciousness?" she said. "I'm talking about a practice which would think about how people actually do get rid of unaware racism, unaware sexism, and unintentional classism."[49]

Sherover-Marcuse designed a series of training programs that became the prototype for university DEI programs nationwide. In the 1980s, Sherover-Marcuse led workshops on "institutionalized racism," "internalized oppression," and "being an effective ally," and invented the now-famous "privilege walk" exercise, in which participants sort themselves into an oppression hierarchy, then atone for their racial, sexual, and economic privilege.[50] The basic premise of Sherover-Marcuse's program was that racism is ubiquitous in every aspect of society and, consequently, that whites must eliminate the racist ideologies that have shaped their lives in order to prepare themselves for building the new society.

"The achievement of human liberation on a global scale will require far-reaching changes at the institutional level and at the level of group and individual interactions," Sherover-Marcuse said. "These changes will involve transforming oppressive behavioral patterns and 'unlearning' oppressive attitudes and assumptions."[51]

These programs were an immediate success. Sherover-Marcuse traveled throughout the world hosting these workshops and developing a new model for "diversity training" in universities, nonprofits, and corporations.[52] In little more than a decade, she had developed the entire theoretical and linguistic framework for the DEI industry writ large. She had redefined the word "racism" to mean "a whole series of attitudes, assumptions, feelings and beliefs about people of color and their cultures which are a mixture of misinformation, fear and ignorance." She had argued that "all white people have undergone some variety of systematic conditioning or 'training' to take on the 'oppressor role' in relation to people of color" and that "reverse racism" was impossible, because whites can never be the victims of the "systemic and institutionalized mistreatment experienced by people of color." She also had popularized a number of slogans that have come to define DEI: "be a 100% ally"; "everyone's oppression needs to be opposed unconditionally"; "do not expect 'gratitude' from people in the target group";[53] "colorblindness will not end racism."[54]

This move from critical theory to "diversity, equity, and inclusion" was a stroke of genius. With one hand, the critical theorists invented subtle new oppressions; with the other, they administered the cure. Marcuse had once lamented the "language of total administration" that moved in "synonyms and tautologies" and made itself "immune against contradiction."[55] A few decades later, his disciples were wielding that technique in their favor. By combining the academic program of the critical theories with the bureaucratic program of diversity training, left-wing activists discovered the formula for expanding their power over the university as a whole. They designed their programs to appear neutral while, in reality, they exist to promote left-wing orthodoxy, suppress dissent through the punishment of supposed "bias" crimes, and harness the university to a campaign of social activism. They are, in short, political offices that carefully manage the cultural life of the universities and force all knowledge and scholarship through the filter of ideology.

These newly created DEI initiatives have led to an explosion in college administration. Between 1987 and 2012, colleges and universities added more than 500,000 administrators[56] and, by 2015, the total number of administrators was rapidly approaching 1 million[57]—vastly outstripping the growth of both students and professors. The driving force behind the recent hiring binge, according to the *Economist*, is "diversity," with colleges boosting spending to "promote the hiring of ethnic minorities and women, launch campaigns to promote dialogue, and write strategic plans on increasing equity and inclusion on campus."[58]

Despite their outward appearance as neutral stewards of the university, this new cadre of campus administrators is even more left-leaning than the faculty. According to a recent survey, liberal administrators outnumber conservative administrators by a 12:1 ratio, with 71 percent of administrators identifying as "liberal" or "very liberal," compared to 6 percent who identify as "conservative" or "very conservative."[59]

These administrators serve as empire builders and enforcers of left-wing orthodoxy. At most public universities, the diversity bureaucracy has cemented itself as a dominant power center. The University of California, Berkeley's Equity & Inclusion Division has 400 employees and an annual budget of $25 million.[60] The University of Michigan's DEI programs have 163 employees[61] and an annual budget exceeding $14 million.[62] The University of Virginia's diversity programs have 94 diversity program employees and a multimillion-dollar budget.[63] From this new position, administrators can control the ideology of the university from all angles—vertically, from within the bureaucratic hierarchy, and horizontally, within the departments. They can lead decisions about hiring, funding, and tenure, which invisibly shape the limits of inquiry and concentrate power. Thus, from the earliest stages, the institution is able to screen out the ideologically incompatible without publicly deviating from a commitment to "academic freedom."

The state-affiliated University of Pittsburgh provides a good illustration of this process of bureaucratic conquest. In recent years, administrators at Pitt have created an elaborate web of programs, norms, incentives, and sub-institutions to consolidate power around diversity ideology. The university now boasts an Office for Equity, Diversity, and Inclusion, Racial Equity Consciousness Institute, Center for Race & Social Problems, Black Action Society, Black Experience Events, Black Lives in Focus, Black Senate, PittEd Justice Collective, Annual Social Justice Symposium, and a steady feeding of "diversity" forums, "white co-conspirators groups," "white privilege" seminars, "racialized capitalism" lectures, "anti-racism" modules, "diversity and inclusion" certificates, and "racial equity consciousness" trainings.[64]

In 2020, Pitt administrators announced that the university would expand the diversity bureaucracy even further, implementing racial quotas for admissions, establishing racially segregated "affinity" spaces for minorities, providing "anti-racism" training for all university employees,[65] and requiring all first-year students to attend a mandatory course on "anti-black racism," which presents critical theory and the ideology of "anti-racism" as catechesis, rather than contested debate.[66]

Hiring and promotion, too, are designed to create political filters and reinforce diversity ideology. Pitt's Department of Political Science, for example, recently posted a job listing for an assistant professor of "Structural Racism, Oppression, and Black Political Experiences" as part of the School of Arts and Sciences' "cluster in Race, Representation, and Anti-Black and Systemic Racism."[67] The listing, which encourages "applications from scholars working on problems of racial oppression and racialized inequalities and hierarchies," serves to pre-filter dissenting scholars. Existing faculty, too, must submit to a regular examination of their loyalties: candidates for leadership positions in academic departments must submit "diversity statements" that acknowledge "the challenges of navigating power and privilege," confess "one's own role in the systematic way in which people are oppressed," and commit to incorporating diversity ideology into their "teaching materials and methods."[68] At the end of the academic production line, output conforms to the input: tenured faculty bolt together an interchangeable mass of papers and books on "tacit racism,"[69] "social justice mathematics,"[70] "queer enchantment," and "confronting settler colonialism in higher education,"[71] adding new weight, without new insight, to the diversity corpus.

Some faculty have spoken out against the corrosive effects of these programs. At Pitt, professor of pharmaceutical sciences Michael Vanyukov, who was born and raised in the Soviet Union, denounced Pitt's diversity programming as "neo-Marxian agitprop" that is "no different than [what] Soviet propaganda taught about the West and capitalism."[72] At the University of California, Davis, mathematics professor Abigail Thompson issued a statement comparing mandatory diversity statements to the anticommunist loyalty oaths of the 1950s.[73] At the University of Michigan, economist Mark Perry has raised the alarm about the diversity bureaucracy's relentless expansion, which begins in the central administration, then "starts to decentralize down to all of the different schools and colleges and programs" until "even the library at the University of Michigan has a diversity officer."

The intention, Perry says, is to create an "intellectual echo chamber" that institutionalizes a "Marxist political ideology" through a pretextual focus on "race," "equity," and "diversity." The outcome is a commissar-style bureaucracy. Diversity officers monitor academic departments, diversity statements enforce loyalties, and, in Perry's words, the resultant "culture of fear" prevents most faculty from expressing opposition.[74]

Such protests, however, have proven ineffectual. Through department politics, faculty deck-stacking, and bureaucratic capture, administrators of the great public universities have managed to elevate the critical theories and quietly suppress most internal opposition. The University of California, which Marcuse had once criticized as a "pillar of the establishment,"[75] has now transformed into a system of one-party progressive rule.[76] The diversity bureaucracy is the ruler of university life and, among faculty, liberals often outnumber conservatives by 20:1.[77] Moreover, this new status quo is now so deeply woven into public expectations that it functions one-dimensionally, transmitting and maintaining the ideology of the critical theories without significant opposition.

When a conservative professor is suppressed for expressing a controversial opinion or suspended for refusing to reduce grading standards for black students, it hardly makes a blip.[78] There are no protests in the university plaza; no administrator's office is occupied. Administrators feel no pressure to reply beyond releasing a generic public relations statement affirming their commitment to "the marketplace of ideas,"[79] concealing the real nature of the political reality under the same "pseudo-neutrality" that had incensed Marcuse during his time.[80]

Observing the universities as a whole, the conclusion is inescapable: the critical theory of society has achieved its intellectual revolution. Metaphysics, tradition, religion, literature, history—all have been critiqued, categorized, disassembled, and displaced by the new ideology of liberation. The critical theorists and their allies in the bureaucracy have turned the university into what Marcuse called the "initial revolutionary institution," which, Marcuse believed, could serve as a template for "collective ownership" and finally make possible "the creation of a reality in accordance with the new sensitivity and the new consciousness."[81]

Marcuse's dream of "liberating tolerance" has been achieved. The universities have enacted the "the systematic withdrawal of tolerance toward regressive and repressive opinions" and "rigid restrictions on teachings and practices in the educational institutions."[82] The DEI departments, using the techniques of Erica Sherover-Marcuse, probe, test, and police students and staff for "oppressive attitudes" and the subliminal crimes of "unconscious bias," "internalized racism," and "microinequities."[83]

The practice of "liberating tolerance" has frozen the universities in an endless loop of 1968. Professors and students imagine themselves heroes of the counterculture, "decolonizing" and "disrupting" enemy ideologies, but their work has become mimicry, not genuine creativity. The New Left's language of subversion, which was authentically transgressive at its point of origin, has created its own "conformist and corrupted universe of political language."[84] It has hardened into the new "armor of the Establishment," defending the left-wing orthodoxy of the new elite[85] while exempting itself from the "radical criticism" of its own concepts, language, and power.[86]

The result is a total reversal. In 1967, Marcuse told the young revolutionaries at the Dialectic of Liberation conference: "We must confront indoctrination in servitude with indoctrination in freedom." He argued that the long march through the universities was just the beginning. "Education today is more than discussion, more than teaching and learning and writing," he said. "Unless and until it goes beyond the classroom, until and unless it goes beyond the college, the school, the university, it will remain powerless."[87] The revolution demanded that it extend itself through society as a whole and establish sovereignty over every institution of the past. "We must meet this society on its own ground," he said. "Total mobilization."[88]

The capture of the universities, more than anything, represents a model for the future. The critical theorists and DEI administrators believed they could manufacture the new set of values in the academic departments and perpetuate them through the bureaucracy. They understood that critical theory could no longer remain a pure negation. After its conquest over the disciplines and then over the administration of the university, it inherited, for the first time, the responsibility of governing. Once their critical theory turned into the governing principle of the university—sanitized as "diversity, equity, and inclusion" and concretized in the sprawling bureaucracy—it was only a matter of time before it sought to extend itself beyond the campus gates.

As Rudi Dutschke once explained, the revolution had begun in the universities out of necessity but would require the activists to reshape every domain of human life. "Our historically correct limitation of our action to the university should not be made into a fetish," he said. "A revolutionary dialectic of the correct transitions must regard the 'long march through the institutions' as a practical and critical action in all social spheres. It must set as its goal the subversive-critical deepening of the contradictions, a process which has been made possible in all institutions that participate in the organization of day-to-day life."[89]

The revolution, in other words, would not succeed until it captured everything.

CHAPTER 4

The New Ideological Regime

The long march through the institutions has wrought a strange kind of revolution. The images of the old revolts—soot-covered laborers burning down prisons and sacking ministry buildings—do not apply. The critical theory revolution, by contrast, was almost invisible. The long march through the institutions was so gradual, so bureaucratic, it went nearly unnoticed.

But today, after it has come to a conclusion, the dynamics of this new ideological order have become clear. It is revolution from above, rather than from below. It is revolution in the abstract, rather than the concrete. It is a revolution of information, rather than production—and it is a revolution no less significant than the great revolutions of the past.

In the 1960s, Marcuse had sketched out the beginning stages of this process, arguing that bourgeois capitalism and state communism were both destined to fail. Like Marx, he was convinced that "capitalism produces its own gravediggers,"[1] but, additionally, he had lost faith in Stalinist communism, having written a bitter book denouncing the Soviet Union's descent into tyranny.[2]

Marcuse proposed a third way, encouraging his predominantly white, college-educated followers to learn the methods of managing the large enterprises and to gradually install the critical theories as their governing ideology. Although Marcuse lamented that the working class had become "antirevolutionary," it was also rapidly becoming obsolete: the "means of production" in the advanced technological society were increasingly abstract, rather than concrete, affairs, and the most urgent task was to constitute a new elite, rather than a new proletariat.

This revolution has now run its course. Marcuse established the ideology with his critical theory of society. His disciples developed the model for elite capture in the universities. And the next generation of left-wing activists expanded it everywhere.

The result of this process is the creation of a new ideological regime—composed of a unity between the university, the media, the state, the corporation—that has coalesced around the critical theories, transmitted them through the public bureaucracy, and enforced the new orthodoxy through the top-down management of private life. This regime is decentralized and diffused. It functions through the maintenance of myths, beliefs, and incentives, rather than central leadership or direction.

The universities served as the initial hub, but the language of the critical theories was quickly translated into the language of the state and the corporation. The practices of the New Left were professionalized as "social science" and "diversity, equity, and inclusion."

When the New Left was in the minority, Marcuse preached "extra-parliamentary" political mobilization and criticized the Establishment for using manipulative language. Today the roles are reversed. After the left-wing ideologues began to dominate the institutions and consolidate power in the bureaucracy, they created their own one-dimensional linguistic universe, seeking to put their authority beyond political opposition. Thus the political concept of "liberation" becomes the mathematical concept of "equity." The ideological concept of "white privilege" becomes the scientific concept of "implicit bias." The moral concept of "racism" becomes the statistical concept of "racial disparity." They framed their revolution in terms of the social sciences because, they believed, it would legitimize elite management of society—and freeze out the "antirevolutionary" working classes, which had, since Marcuse's time, opposed their rule.

The new regime is a synthesis of Marcuse's critical theory, which he supported, and one-dimensional society, which he opposed. The university, the media, the state, and the corporation have all submitted to this strange hybrid and, together, now function as the "vital center" that mediates the relationship between the institutions and the public.[3] The new elites participate in this governing system through osmosis, absorbing the concepts and vocabulary created by the critical theories, then transmitting them through the management of the institutions.

The story of the long march through the universities was largely complete a generation ago—but that was only the beginning.

*   *   *

Marcuse believed that the university could serve as the "initial revolutionary institution"[4] but was not, in and of itself, powerful enough to transform the broader society. The intellectuals could produce knowledge but, left alone, could not break through the one-dimensional universe of the Establishment. "Under the rule of monopolistic media—themselves the mere instruments of economic and political power—a mentality is created for which right and wrong, true and false are predefined wherever they affect the vital interests of the society," he said. "The meaning of words is rigidly stabilized. Rational persuasion, persuasion to the opposite is all but precluded."[5]

The solution, then, was to extend the "long march through the institutions" to the media and to build a counter-narrative apparatus with the power to subvert the Establishment narrative and replace it with the narrative of the critical theories. He implored the students to learn "how to use the mass media, how to organize production," as part of a "concerted effort to build up counterinstitutions" and develop mastery over "the great chains of information and indoctrination."[6]

Over time, they did. The radicals waged a generational war for the prestige media and the critical theories became the house style of establishment opinion.

The triumph of this "long march through the media" can be represented in miniature through the conquest of the *New York Times*, which has long been the top prize in American media. Fifty years ago, the *Times* ridiculed Marcuse. One reviewer trashed *An Essay on Liberation* as a "rehash of discredited fantasies" that "reeked of totalitarianism."[7] Another published a snide criticism of *Counterrevolution and Revolt*, portraying the philosopher as a ridiculous, if slightly dangerous, figure who gave false legitimacy to violence and revolution.[8] When Marcuse died in 1979, the paper published an obituary dismissing the professor as a transitory historical artifact, noting that "as the social unrest of the 1960's dissipated, Dr. Marcuse faded from view just as suddenly as he had become a visible, if reluctant, folk hero."[9]

But the Establishment voices at the *Times* underestimated Marcuse, whose ideas would outlast and eventually supplant the moderate position at the paper of record. Like one of the Weathermen's time-controlled bombs, Marcuse's philosophy would eventually explode—and consume the newsroom.

This conquest came late but progressed quickly. According to a veteran *New York Times* reporter, who requested anonymity out of fear of reprisals, the paper's ideological shift began in the aftermath of the Great Recession, as executives laid off many veteran writers and began hiring hundreds of younger reporters who had been steeped in the critical theories at elite universities. These new employees waged a "generational battle" against existing leadership at the paper and the writers' union, eschewing traditional labor concerns in favor of agitating for the implementation of diversity programs and left-wing ideological priorities. "I think what's happening in the larger body of the *Times* very much mirrors what was happening in the union," said the reporter, "and now we're deeply immersed in DEI battles and battles over race [and] gender."

It was, in the words of another writer, a "revolution."[10]

Following their takeover of the union, the faction of younger, ideologically driven employees—not just writers, but designers, coders, marketers, and other creatives—set a new tone for the newsroom and shifted the paper dramatically leftward. As the social scientist Zach Goldberg has meticulously documented, the vocabulary of the critical theories rapidly conquered the paper's linguistic universe. Between 2011 and 2019, the frequency of the word "racist(s)" and "racism" increased by 700 percent and 1,000 percent; between 2013 and 2019 the frequency of the phrase "white privilege" increased 1,200 percent and the frequency of the phrase "systemic racism" increased by 1,000 percent. This new sensibility quickly captured the op-ed page, as well as the hard news sections and the offices of management, human resources, and diversity programming.[11]

Meanwhile, the spirit of Marcuse's "liberating tolerance," in which accusations of racism and sexism are wielded to silence dissent, has become the dominant internal culture. According to the veteran *Times* reporter, there is a pervasive fear among many older managers and editors, who "feel which way the wind's blowing" and disappear during moments of controversy, hoping to maintain their reputation and avoid public condemnation. "There was a strain of left-liberal thinking on free speech that owes very much to Marcuse, and that's probably true in our newsroom as well," said the senior reporter, noting that the old stalwarts of free expression, such as the American Civil Liberties Union, have also succumbed to the logic of Marcuse's philosophy. "It could be a real disaster," the writer said. "You can't just keep calling everything racist and think that that's going to hold forever."[12]

The capture of the *New York Times* was a pivotal turn in the long march through the institutions. The New Left–inspired activists had already achieved hegemony over the academic journals, but these publications reached a limited, insular audience of professors and administrators. The *Times*, by contrast, penetrates the consciousness of 100 million readers, plus immense secondary audiences on television, radio, and social media.[13] If the university provided the theory of the revolution, the paper provided the mechanism for transmission, turning the fringe ideas formulated in *An Essay on Liberation* and at the Flint War Council into the new liberal consensus. As the *Times* changed, the other primary channels of left-leaning media followed suit: the *Washington Post*, NPR, MSNBC[14]—even the wire services[15]—all converged on the framing and language of the New Left.

After securing power, the activists in the new "counter-media" deployed the model of political change that had been developed in the universities: flooding the discourse with heavily loaded political concepts in order to shape the popular consciousness and precondition the public for left-wing political conclusions. This process could be called "linguistic overload," in which a key set of ideological phrases is repeated at mass scale and embedded into the public mind through the force of repetition. As Marcuse had counseled the young activists, "the sociological and political vocabulary must be radically reshaped: it must be stripped of its false neutrality; it must be methodically and provocatively 'moralized' in terms of the Refusal."[16]

When this is accomplished, the activists believed, the masses will interpret their experience through the language of revolution—say, "systemic racism" or "police brutality"—and arrive at the predetermined conclusions almost automatically.

*   *   *

The next conquest in the long march through the institutions was the state.

Already, by the time Marcuse had emigrated to the United States, the New Deal had established the federal government as the great shaper of American life. It employed more than 1 million citizens and scattered an army of managers, bureaucrats, and technical workers throughout the country.[17] With President Lyndon Johnson's Great Society, the federal government redoubled its efforts and pushed the bureaucracy even deeper into social, political, and family life.

The situation today has, if anything, intensified: public agencies employ approximately 24 million Americans,[18] spend more than $1 trillion per year on means-tested welfare programs,[19] and subsidize approximately half of all households through entitlements and transfer payments.[20] Moreover, the modern state has a much more sophisticated technology of control: through advances in the social sciences and specialization of the managerial professions, the state not only seeks to build suspension bridges and administer Social Security, as it did following the New Deal, but to quantify and manipulate the most intimate expressions of human behavior, down to the relationship between parent and child.

Thus, for activists who want to influence society in a profound way, the state is the ultimate mechanism, both through its direct political power and its subtler capacities for social engineering. By the 1970s, the ambitious and highly educated activists of the New Left came to see the state, especially the vast administrative bureaus that operated outside of meaningful legislative control, as the highest prize. They realized, as Marcuse had suggested, that the most effective way to circumvent the democratic process was to administer the institutions of knowledge production and to ensure that the discourse was guided by the spirit of liberation—that is, according to the critical ideologies.

The state, it turned out, was an easy capture. The revolutionaries were able to easily translate the strategies, tactics, and policies of the universities to the state bureaucracy. There was barely any resistance at all.

The activist-bureaucrats had a simple list of objectives: capture the culture of the federal agencies; enforce political orthodoxy with critical theory–based DEI programs; turn the federal government into a patronage machine for left-wing activism.

The first step has already been accomplished. The political culture of the federal agencies is almost indistinguishable from that of the universities. Using political donations as a proxy for political culture, the federal departments are overwhelmingly left-wing. In the 2020 presidential election cycle, employees at the Department of Justice sent 83 percent of all contributions to Democrats. At the Department of Housing and Urban

Development, the number was 84 percent. At the Department of Health and Human Services, 88 percent; and at the Department of Education, a full 93 percent.[21] Overall, according to analysis by Bloomberg, nondefense federal employees sent 84 percent of all presidential donations to Democratic nominee Joseph Biden—within striking distance of the rate in universities, 93 percent.[22]

This culture is further reinforced through the creation of permanent "diversity, equity, and inclusion" programs that turn the narrative of the critical theories into orthodoxy and use the methods first developed by Erica Sherover-Marcuse to enforce codes of speech and behavior. These programs are now pervasive. The administration of President Joseph Biden has mandated "diversity, equity, and inclusion" in every department of the federal government[23] and the largest agencies have phalanxes of "diversity officers" who administer the bureaucracy in accordance with left-wing ideology.[24]

The programming at Sandia National Laboratories, which designs America's nuclear weapons arsenal, is representative of the general orientation of "diversity and inclusion" in the federal government. In 2019, executives at Sandia sent a group of white male employees to a three-day reeducation program in order to expose their "white privilege" and deconstruct their "white male culture." The mandatory training, which was called the "White Men's Caucus on Eliminating Racism, Sexism, and Homophobia in Organizations," utilized the techniques of the New Left–style "consciousness-raising" groups to humiliate, degrade, and disintegrate the participants, so they could be reoriented toward "anti-racism."[25]

To begin the sessions, the trainers explained that their intention was to expose the "roots of white male culture," which consists of "rugged individualism," "a can-do attitude," "hard work," and "striving towards success"—which might be superficially appealing but are, in fact, rooted in "racism, sexism, and homophobia" and "devastating" to women and minorities. This culture, according to the program materials, imposes a "white male standard" on others and leads to "lowered quality of life at work and home, reduced life expectancy, unproductive relationships, and high stress."

In order to break down this culture, the trainers for Sandia demanded that the white male employees make a list of associations about "white men" and read a series of statements about their "white privilege," "male privilege," and "heterosexual privilege." The trainers wrote down the answers to the first question, which included "white supremacists," "KKK," "Aryan Nation," "MAGA hat," "privileged," and "mass killing," then asked the men to accept their complicity in the white male system and repeat a series of confessions: "white people are more wealthy"; "white privilege is viewing police officers as there to protect you"; "white privilege is being first in line."

As the reeducation program concluded, the trainers asked the men to write letters "directed to white women, people of color, and other groups regarding the meaning of this Caucus experience." The men were exhausted and apologetic, pledging to atone for their whiteness and to become "a better ally" to the cause. "The caucus allowed me to see the [privilege], although not previously realized, that I have as a white male in society and at Sandia," wrote one. "I'm sorry for the times I have not stood up for you to create a safe place. I'm sorry for the time I've spent not thinking about you," wrote another. Their submission was complete.

Finally, as a broader structural matter, the new federal "diversity and inclusion" apparatus also functions as a patronage machine for left-wing activism.

All of the major grantmakers in education, humanities, and sciences—the Department of Education, the National Endowment for the Arts, the National Endowment for the Humanities, and the National Science Foundation—have become permanent benefactors of the critical theories, no matter which political party holds the presidency and the legislature. For decades, these entities have showered hundreds of millions of dollars on universities, artists, researchers, writers, and cultural figures who echo the euphemisms of the revolution, as if they constituted a secret password for support. The institutes function as their own fiefdoms: career bureaucrats outmaneuver political appointees and, through long-built patronage networks and a "one-party" selection process similar to those in the universities, funnel enormous gifts to outside activists, who are not subject to federal oversight and transparency requirements.

The list of approved arts and humanities grants during the Obama and Trump presidencies—the latter of which was ostensibly opposed to the critical ideologies—illustrates the absolute nature of this patronage system.

During this period, the Department of Education funded hundreds of left-wing programs, including an endless repetition of programs and studies that repeated the basic mantras of DEI: "educational equity," "using data to achieve equity," "equity through action," "building school capacity to address equity at scale," "equity-driven research-practice partnerships," "efficacy, efficiency, and equity," "systemic change to improve equity," "equity-focused educators," "opening pathways to institutionalize equity," "creating an equity-minded campus," "building equity through sustainable change."[26]

Meanwhile, the NEA and the NEH pursued the same political line, funding, for example, a speaking series on "race, reconciliation, and transformation," a national black writers' conference on "reconstructing the master narrative," an artist-in-residency program for "racial equity," a leadership certificate program in "diversity, equity, and inclusion," an art exhibit on "race, gender, and globalization," an overseas research program that "aims to dismantle hierarchies of race and civilization," and a biography exploring "the Black Power movement," a "dance theater trilogy on race, culture, and identity," and a stage play for "a manifesto on race in America through the eyes of a black girl recovering from self-hate."[27]

Even the National Science Foundation, which one might assume to be insulated from the critical theories, has succumbed. Through Democratic and Republican administrations, the institute has subsidized left-wing political work, including a multimillion-dollar initiative for dismantling "the institutional and intersectional barriers to equity" in universities, a million-dollar partnership to "accelerate diversity, equity, and inclusion systemic change," a plan for "creating faculty change agents" who implement policies related to "unconscious bias," a program to explore "the use of technology in building more socially conscious systems to mitigate institutional racism," a dissertation on "the lure of whiteness and the politics of 'otherness,'" a postdoctoral fellowship on "racial/ethnic subjectivity and grassroots community organizing," a conference to advance "diversity, equity, and inclusion" in the astronomical sciences, and dozens of other programs on "diversity," "equity," and "inclusion."[28]

Together, these programs direct hundreds of millions of dollars toward left-wing activism and have become the dominant culture of the agencies. The federal bureaucracy, which was designed to be neutral, or at least accountable to the executive, is now a creature of its own prerogatives. The bureaucrats claim to pursue knowledge, but, in truth, pursue power, all under the justification of technical expertise. The state becomes the primary vehicle of revolution. It no longer seeks to serve the public but, following the dictates of critical theory, seeks to subvert itself.

It is a revolt of the state against the people—and, to that end, it is rapidly gaining power.

*   *   *

The final conquest in the long march through the institutions is the extension of the critical theories into America's largest corporations.

At first, this seems like an insuperable contradiction: the critical theorists were vicious critics of capitalism and wanted nothing more than to abolish it. Yet their ideas have made inroads into the centers of capitalist power. Today, every one of the Fortune 100 corporations has submitted to the ideology of the critical theories, filtered through the language of "diversity, equity, and inclusion." They have established new bureaucracies, created new programs, and organized new training regimens for their employees on "whiteness," "systemic racism," "racial capitalism," and "prison abolition."[29]

How is this possible? Because the corporation is no longer the domain of the conservative establishment.

In fact, the cultural orientation of the most profitable companies matches, or even exceeds, the liberalism of academia, government, and education. According to employee political donations, Google and Facebook are more liberal than the University of California, Berkeley, and the University of Michigan; the consulting firms Deloitte, Accenture, KPMG, PwC, and Ernst & Young are more liberal than the departments of the federal government; and the employees of Disney, Nike, Starbucks, and Capital One are more progressive than the teachers and administrators of the public schools.[30]

Part of this is due to a change in cohort and, as with the *New York Times*, a generational "revolution." For the graduates of the prestige universities who then enter the corporate world, the critical theories serve as a proxy for a sophisticated, progressive worldview and an aesthetic connection to the 1960s counterculture, which is still perceived as high-status. They see Marcuse's "new sensibility" and the managerial-class career ladder as methods of personal liberation from suburban upbringings and Middle American values. For many of them, the culture captures the mind and the politics follows.

Meanwhile, for executives, adopting the principles of the critical theories, watered down as "diversity, equity, and inclusion," functions as an insurance policy against left-wing activism campaigns and costly, often frivolous discrimination lawsuits under Title VII of the Civil Rights Act. By circulating materials and requiring training programs on "racial equity" and "systemic racism," corporations can signal their liberal bona fides and create a preemptive defense for any "hostile work environment" or "race and gender discrimination" claims.

In addition, under the aegis of "diversity and inclusion" initiatives, executives can direct financial contributions to left-wing activist organizations, which serve as protection payments against protests, boycotts, and public relations campaigns. The major corporations have made a simple calculation: they have achieved all of their desires from the political right on economics—tax cuts, free trade, deregulation—and so they are looking to appease their potential enemies from the political left on culture. It is a classic inside-outside game. Corporate lobbyists quietly secure favorable legislation through congressional Republicans, while corporate executives publicly announce their contributions to "racial equity" and pledge allegiance to "social justice."

This dynamic was crisply illustrated following the death of George Floyd, which inspired months of rioting, looting, and violence in American cities. As looters sacked retail stores and burned commercial districts to the ground, the CEOs of the great companies announced themselves not on the side of "law and order," as they had in the 1960s, but on the side of the protestors and rioters. The largest fifty companies in America immediately pledged $50 billion toward "racial equity,"[31] with the CEOs of companies such as Cisco, Pepsi, and Nike publicly repeating the street slogan "Black Lives Matter,"[32] JPMorgan Chase chief executive Jamie Dimon kneeling in simulated protest of the national anthem,[33] and McDonald's declaring the social-justice martyr George Floyd "one of us."[34]

These businesses understand there is always a tax: in the past, they might have paid the mob or the union to achieve peace; today they pay the equity consulting firm and the racial activist organization. The latter is perhaps more sophisticated—after all, it was created by elite intellectuals rather than working-class toughs—but the arrangement is the same. The outside pressure group, backed up by the threat of violence, extracts payments from the dominant economic player, which calculates them as a cost of doing business.

The problem, however, is that the critical theories can never be satisfied. Petty corruption eventually congeals into bureaucracy: one-time cash payments to activists become long-term contracts with diversity consultants; the discovery of subliminal bias in the workplace leads to an endless inquisition; temporary initiatives harden into full-time departments. Once corporate managers have accepted the premise of the critical theories, they can never rid themselves of the consequences.

The content of corporate "diversity, equity, and inclusion" programs is nearly identical to those of the universities and the federal agencies. In recent years, these programs have become enormously popular at Fortune 100 companies, such as American Express, Bank of America, Lockheed Martin, Raytheon, Disney, Verizon, AT&T, Google, and Facebook.[35] Some of these firms now force white male executives to repeat a series of self-criticisms and renounce their "white privilege," "male privilege," and "heterosexual privilege";[36] others encourage employees to "identify [their] privilege," "defund the police," "participate in reparations," and "decolonize [their bookshelves]."[37]

But this style of program is not limited to the high-tech corporations in the coastal cities. Walmart, for example, is hardly the stereotype of the left-wing corporation—the company is based in deep-red Bentonville, Arkansas, and has traditionally supported conservative causes—and yet its executives have bought into the critical theories hook, line, and sinker.

In 2021, chief executive Doug McMillon announced the creation of the Walmart.org Center for Racial Equity and pledged $100 million to "address the drivers of systemic racism" and "[shift] power, privilege, and access" in American society.[38] According to whistleblower documents, the company has also instituted a mandatory training program for executives that denounces the United States as a racist society and teaches lower-income, white store employees that they are guilty of "white privilege" and "internalized racial superiority."

The training manual, designed in partnership with a Greensboro, North

Carolina–based consulting company called the Racial Equity Institute, reads like the text of *Prairie Fire* transliterated into the language of the corporation. The program begins by explaining that the United States is a "white supremacy system" designed by white Europeans "for the purpose of assigning and maintaining white skin access to power and privilege." Walmart frames American history as a long sequence of oppressions, from the "construction of a 'white race'" by colonists in 1680 to President Barack Obama's stimulus legislation in 2009, "another race neutral act that has disproportionately benefited white people."

Following Erica Sherover-Marcuse's "emancipatory consciousness" model, the program maintains that limitations in white consciousness uphold social oppressions. Therefore, according to Walmart, the objective is to create a psychological diagnosis of "whiteness," which can then be treated through "white anti-racist development." Whites, the manual explains, are inherently guilty of "white supremacy thinking," which is based on the belief that "one's comfort, wealth, privilege and success has been earned by merits and hard work," rather than through the benefits of systemic racism. As a result, white Americans have been subjected to "racist conditioning" that indoctrinates them into "white supremacy," which includes the racist values of "individualism," "objectivity," "paternalism," "defensiveness," "power hoarding," "right to comfort," and "worship of the written word."

Racial minorities, on the other hand, are constantly suffering under the yoke of "constructed racist oppression" and "internalized racial inferiority." Their internal psychology is considered shattered and broken, dominated by internal messages such as "we believe there is something wrong with being a person of color," "we have lowered self-esteem," "we have lowered expectations," "we have very limited choices," and "we have a sense of limited possibility." Minorities, Walmart claims, thus begin to believe the "myths promoted by the racist system" and have feelings of "self-hate," "anger," "rage," and "ethnocentrism," and are forced to "forget," "lie," and "stop feeling" in order to secure basic survival.

The company's proposed solution, again following the model of the old "consciousness groups," is to encourage whites to participate in "white anti-racist development," a psychological conditioning program that reorients white consciousness toward "anti-racism" and cedes power to minorities inside and outside the corporation. To this end, white employees must accept their "guilt and shame" and the idea that "white is not right," acknowledge their complicity in racism, and, finally, begin taking responsibility and moving toward "collective action," whereby "white can do right." The goal is for whites to climb the "ladder of empowerment for white people" and re-create themselves with a new "anti-racist identity."[39]

On the surface, there is a glaring contradiction in such corporate DEI programs: the corporation is oriented toward the profit motive, while critical theory seeks to subvert it. However, as Marcuse understood a half century ago, the Establishment, represented in the purest form by the multinational corporation, has a tremendous capacity for folding the contradictions into its own machinery. Corporate executives, sensing the momentum of the critical theories in the universities and the necessity of protecting themselves from the federal civil rights bureaucracy, make concessions to the ideology with the intention of flattening it, co-opting it, and rendering it harmless.

Companies such as Walmart might condemn "objectivity," "individualism," and "power hoarding" as "white supremacy culture" while ruthlessly operating on those principles in the global market. They might lecture minimum-wage store employees about their "white privilege" while hauling in hundreds of millions of dollars in executive compensation.[40] They have paid the tax and believe they can continue on with business as usual.

The result, of course, is critical theory as farce: the ideology of the revolution passed through the human resources department.[41] And while executives might be adopting these programs with cynical motives—to launder their reputations, to protect against frivolous lawsuits, to recast the corporation as an instrument of redemption—the simple fact of hypocrisy does not rule out the damage that can be done. Regardless of their intentions, when corporations submit to the dictates of DEI, the ideology gains power and, through constant repetition, makes an imprint on the mind. The language of the critical theories becomes the new language of access: those aspiring to enter the elite must become fluent in order to establish themselves in the institutions, even the corporation.

Whether they intend to or not, the managers, technicians, and operators become the new foot soldiers in the long march.

*   *   *

Marcuse did not live to see this revolution unfold.

As the drama surrounding his work receded, so did the scrutiny. The chancellor of UCSD, seeking to tamp down criticism, had dismissed Marcuse as a "paper revolutionary";[42] in 1973, the FBI removed him from the active Administrative Index, concluding that Marcuse was "not considered dangerous at the present time."[43] When his students asked him about the height of the New Left, he expressed nostalgia. "That was the heroic age," he said. "You will never see another age like it."[44]

But Marcuse was too modest. He had created an enormous body of work, from his first dissertation on German literature to his final book on Marxist aesthetics. He had built a cadre of intellectuals, activists, and revolutionaries. And, despite the disappointments during his own life, he had laid the ideological foundation for the revolution to come.[45]

Today, his critical theory of society, which he developed in near obscurity, has embedded itself in every major institution, from the Ivy League universities to the Fortune 100 corporations. Marcuse's ideas, although they have often been flattened and euphemized, have risen to an astonishing prominence in public life.

In 1968, at the height of his notoriety, a French journalist accused Marcuse of agitating for a "Platonic dictatorship of the elite." He responded without hesitation: "To be perfectly frank, I don't know which is worse: a dictatorship of politicians, managers, and generals, or a dictatorship of intellectuals. Personally, if this is the choice, I would prefer the dictatorship of the intellectuals, if there is no possibility of a genuine free democracy. Unfortunately, this alternative does not exist at present."[46]

This distinction has now vanished. The lines between academia, media, government, and business are no longer reliable lines of demarcation. The intellectuals have captured the tongues of the politicians, managers, and generals; the vocabulary of the university is now indistinguishable from the vocabulary of the state. The upper half of Marcuse's "new proletariat"— the white, affluent, educated class—now speaks the language of revolution on behalf of the poor, the minority, and the oppressed. The members of this class can move smoothly across geography and institution, secure that their symbolic sophistication, technical knowledge, and right opinion can find a position anywhere.

Marcuse's "dictatorship of the intellectuals" and "dictatorship of politicians, managers, and generals" have now converged. His critical theory has become the normative ideology of the universities and his "counter-institutions" have become, at least as a matter of public affirmation, the dominant institutions across every domain.

This represents a change in regime—a cultural revolution. The victory of the critical theories has displaced the original ends, or telos, of America's institutions. The university no longer exists to discover knowledge, but rather to awaken "critical consciousness." The corporation no longer exists to maximize profit, but to manage "diversity and inclusion." The state no longer exists to secure natural rights, but to achieve "social justice."

The means, too, have changed. As Marcuse predicted, the critical revolution could not win through the democratic process established in the Constitution; rather, it depended upon the mobilization of "extra-parliamentary" forces, the capture of elite institutions, and, when necessary, political violence to advance left-wing ideology "against the will and against the prevailing interests of the great majority of the people."[47]

After the capture of the institutions, however, this method went through an inversion. The descendants of the New Left could use their position in the great bureaucracies to shift the culture from the top down and to exert authority over the "antirevolutionary" masses. They began to wield their own tools of repression. The intellectuals build political narratives at industrial scale. The DEI departments create new codes of speech and behavior. The bureaucrats invent and then punish dissenters for crimes of pure subjectivity, such as "microaggressions," "microassaults," and "microinequities."[48]

The triumph of the long march through the institutions, however, does not represent the ascension of rational, scientific government, nor the arrival of Marcuse's "direct democracy." It represents the extension of bureaucratic power and the creation of a new one-dimensional society. As the activists moved from a position of negation to a position of authority, they slowly undermined their own legitimacy as a movement of subversion and their own rationale as a method for liberation.

The outcome is a revolt of the state against the people. The bureaucracy fortifies its own power and privilege while waging a taxpayer-financed revolution against the middle and lower classes. Liberation becomes the pretext for domination. The counterculture becomes the Establishment. The revolution solidifies into bureaucracy.

In the summer of 1979, while traveling in Germany for a conference, Marcuse suffered a stroke and, after a short struggle in the hospital, passed on. His friends and family organized a small funeral service in the woods near the town of Starnberg that was attended by close colleagues who had helped develop the critical theories; the activist Rudi Dutschke, who had designed the long march through the institutions; and Marcuse's third wife, Erica, who had created the model for modern "diversity and inclusion" programming.[49] Years later, at a ceremony to put his ashes to rest, Marcuse's graduate student Angela Davis commemorated him as the intellectual leader of the New Left's revolution.[50]

Marcuse turned out to be a prophet. In the final months of his life, a young disciple asked him if "his life's project had been to prepare the theory for future revolutionary movements."

Marcuse responded with pleasure: "Yes, you could say that."[51]

PART II

Race

CHAPTER 5

Angela Davis

The Spirit of Racial Revolt

The student radical Angela Davis sat on the floor of a small prison cell in the New York Women's House of Detention. She had received a letter, dated November 18, 1970, from her teacher, Herbert Marcuse, who was overseeing her doctoral thesis on Kant, violence, and revolution.

For Davis, the matter was not merely theoretical; she had put Marcuse's theories into practice. The twenty-six-year-old, whose Afro-and-sunglasses image had been endlessly replicated onto newspaper columns and FBI Most Wanted posters, had become a left-wing icon. She had been arrested on charges of kidnapping, murder, and interstate flight in relation to a botched prison break in San Rafael, California. But to her supporters, Angela Davis was a political prisoner, lashed and chained for the crime of opposing the oppressive American regime.

"Dear Angela," Marcuse's letter opened, "people ask me again and again to explain how you, a highly intelligent, sensitive young woman, an excellent student and teacher, how you became involved in the violent events at San Rafael. I do not know whether you were involved at all in these tragic events, but I do know that you were deeply involved in the fight for the black people, for the oppressed everywhere, and that you could not limit your work for them to the classroom and to writing."

The professor traced Angela's motivations to the world of her childhood—"One of cruelty, misery, and persecution"—and her study of historical oppression. "And you learned something else," he wrote, "namely, that almost all the celebrated figures of Western civilization— the very civilization which enslaved your people—were in the last analysis concerned with one thing: human freedom. Like any good student, you took seriously what they said, and you thought seriously about it, and why all this had remained mere talk for the vast majority of men and women. So you felt that the philosophical idea, unless it was a lie, must be translated into reality: that it contained a moral imperative to leave the classroom, the campus, and to go and help the others, your own people to whom you still belong."[1]

Davis, according to Marcuse, had taken the critical theories to their logical conclusion: violent resistance against the state. She had connected the insights of Western philosophy with the vitalism of the slave revolt—and, in this way, she served as the great symbol of the new proletariat, the synthetic union of the white intelligentsia and the black ghetto. She represented the "new historical Subject of change,"[2] and, as such, she fought for the bound and broken masses, but also for the priests of high culture.

"You fought for us too," Marcuse concluded in his letter. "In this sense, your cause is our cause."[3]

Davis was a devoted follower of Marcuse, having followed him around the globe, from the lecture halls of Brandeis University to the dust-covered stacks of European libraries to the graduate program at the University of California, San Diego. She had absorbed his scholarship on Kant, Hegel, Marx, and the theory of revolution. At the same time, she had become captivated by the black nationalist movement. She had watched the Black Panthers flex their muscles, with berets tilted over their foreheads, bandoliers draped across their chests, and long guns pointed to the sky.[4]

The synthesis of these two ways of being—white philosophy, black power—was explosive.

By her mid-twenties, Angela Davis had become an icon of revolt. She had articulated a vision of total revolution that would turn theory into action. "The revolutionary wants to change the nature of society in a way, to create a world where the needs and interests of the people are responded to," she told the journalist and spiritual adviser Reverend Cecil Williams from her prison cell. "A revolutionary realizes, however, that in order to create a world where human beings can live and love and be healthy and create, you have to completely revolutionize the entire fabric of society. You have to overturn the economic structure where a few individuals are in possession of the vast majority of the wealth of this country, a wealth that's been produced by the majority of the people; you have to destroy this political apparatus which, under the guise of revolutionary government, perpetuates the most incredible misery on the masses of people."[5]

Violence, Davis insisted, was a necessary, if regrettable, step in the revolutionary process. "In the history of revolutions and not only socialist revolutions but bourgeois democratic revolutions such as the American Revolution, you have had the occurrence of violence as a means of seizing power from the oppressor, but why? Because the oppressors have failed to acknowledge that the people were right and that the people had the right to control their destiny,"[6] she said in a calm but insistent voice. "And getting back to the question of what a revolutionary is, a black revolutionary realizes that we cannot begin to combat racism and we cannot begin to effectively destroy racism until we've destroyed the whole system."[7]

Davis had a brilliant sense of the theatrical. Dressed in stylish turtlenecks, leather jackets, and patterned dresses, Davis used her jailhouse interviews and court appearances to craft the image and advance the propaganda of the revolution. She struck a slight, elegant figure and spoke with a dazzling vocabulary, drawn from her years of academic study. Newspaper photographers snapped pictures of her giving the Black Power salute to supporters in the courtroom. Television reporters hung on her every word during her public statements and press conferences.

Davis had earned, in Marcuse's words, "success within the white Establishment"[8]—a scholarship to private school and Brandeis, study-abroad programs in France and Germany, a tenure-track professorship at UCLA—but she extended her life into territory that was unavailable to the white intelligentsia: authentic revolt against the white power structure.

Marcuse theorized about the black revolution. Davis embodied it. She marshalled her own identity—the authority of the black woman, the drama of the fugitive, the small acts of defiance against her enemies—in service of her revolutionary politics.

And it worked. In the months after her capture, Angela Davis transformed herself from a small-time student radical into an international cause célèbre. Left-wing activists established dozens of Committees to Free Angela Davis to agitate on her behalf. The Communist Party, which Davis had joined in 1968, held a press conference announcing "the largest, broadest, most all-encompassing people's movement the country has ever seen to free [their] comrade, Angela Davis."[9] Five thousand people attended a fund-raiser on her birthday at the Manhattan Center in New York City. John Lennon and the Rolling Stones both penned songs of tribute to Davis, "Angela" and "Sweet Black Angel,"[10] calling her a "political prisoner" and demanding her release.

The international Left also rose to her defense. The Soviet Union's political commissars, seeing the persecution of a black female communist as a propaganda opportunity, instructed schoolchildren throughout the empire to flood the United States with letters of support. The messages combined a sense of childhood innocence with the content of state propaganda: "We Soviet students are proud of your struggle for civil rights, of your resilience, and are certain that victory will come for your people"; "We want for you to again fight for the rights of black people, so that people in your country could live the same way we do"; "It is winter here and it snows a lot. The weather is cold and we go to school." The citizens of Latvia, Lithuania, Estonia, Ukraine, and Kazakhstan sent hundreds of thousands of additional letters and the East German government organized an illustrated-postcard-writing campaign to send "a million roses for Angela" on her twenty-seventh birthday.[11]

To both the Left and the Right, the revolution seemed like a viable possibility. The country was on the brink. Young people had been radicalized. Bombs were exploding at police stations. Prisoners threw themselves into a state of revolt.

Angela Davis, with the threat of the gas chamber looming over her head, believed that her revolution was imminent. The brutal murders of prison guards at Attica and San Quentin, she wrote, "evoked visions of the Paris Commune, the liberated areas of pre-revolutionary Cuba, free territories of Mozambique."[12] This was their moment. Their theories, which had languished in the classroom for all those years, were finally yielding fruit. The revolutionaries had slit the throats and shattered the skulls of their immediate oppressors.

Nixon, Reagan, and America were next.

*   *   *

Angela Yvonne Davis was born into a ramshackle housing project in Birmingham, Alabama, at the tail end of the Second World War. Her parents, Frank and Sallye Davis, had risen from impoverished beginnings, earned college degrees, and secured work as schoolteachers. When Angela was a child, Frank bought a gas station and the family moved into the black middle class. They purchased a sprawling two-story Queen Anne–style house on Center Street, with a wraparound porch, high gables, and a turret with small windows; Frank and Sallye rented out an upstairs bedroom to supplement their income. They were not rich, but they had secured a middle-class income and provided a strong foundation for their four children.[13]

The neighborhood, however, was a dividing line. Birmingham city planners maintained the city's segregated zoning laws and designated Center Street as the red line between the races: white families lived on the west side of the street, which they called College Hills; black families moved onto the east side of the street, which they called Smithfield, and developed into a hub for black leaders in the South. Angela's mother was involved with black Communist Party members and the Southern Negro Youth Congress.[14] The National Association for the Advancement of Colored People, or NAACP, had organized the professionals, advocates, and business leaders who lived in the neighborhood. Martin Luther King Jr. huddled in their living rooms as they organized the civil rights movement.[15]

But the red line that ran down the middle of Center Street did not hold back the rising animosity of the enforcers of Jim Crow. Beginning in 1947, the Birmingham chapter of the Ku Klux Klan initiated a terror campaign against the new black residents, targeting the homes of clergy, lawyers, and activists. They detonated dozens of bombs with the hope of forcing the black professional class back into the ghettos on the city's edges.[16] By the time the Davis family had settled into the neighborhood, it was known as "Dynamite Hill."

Angela, a bookish child with a conspicuous gap between her front teeth, was born into the double consciousness of midcentury black America.

On one hand, Davis's parents provided her with the staples of a middle-class Western upbringing: she learned to read before entering school, took music and ballet lessons, and spent hours in the back room of the Birmingham Public Library, where she devoured Booker T. Washington's *Up from Slavery* and Victor Hugo's *Les Misérables*.[17] On the other, she developed her first memories in a world of racial hatred and violence. "At the age of four I was aware that the people across the street were different," Davis wrote in her *Autobiography*. "We were the first black family to move into that area, and the white people believed that we were in the vanguard of a mass invasion."[18] The white families would glare at the black families across the road. Angela would play a game of hurling racial epithets at passing cars full of whites. Her father kept guns tucked away in the house.

Then the bombings began.

"I was in the bathroom washing my white shoelaces for Sunday School the next morning when an explosion a hundred times louder than the loudest, most frightening thunderclap I had ever heard shook our house," Davis recalled. "Crowds of angry Black people came up the hill and stood on 'our' side, staring at the bombed-out ruins of the [neighbor's] house. Far into the night they spoke of death, of white hatred, death, white people, and more death."[19]

Davis's parents met this terror with a quiet, stoic dignity. Her father never admitted to fear and her mother insisted that "the battle of white against Black was not written into the nature of things," leaving open the possibility of reconciliation. Like many middle-class black families of their generation, Davis's parents taught their children to work hard and appreciate what they had. Frank shared stories about walking ten miles to school, while Sallye told stories about her childhood hardships in the Alabama backwoods. At school, which was segregated by race, the teachers taught Angela and the other black students about Frederick Douglass, Sojourner Truth, and Harriet Tubman, and warned them that they would have to steel themselves for "hard labor and more hard labor, sacrifices and more sacrifices," in order to enter the professional class of doctors, lawyers, engineers, teachers, and businessmen.

Since childhood, Angela had told her family that she wanted to become a pediatrician, but as she grew older, she began to feel doubt toward what she later condemned as the "Booker T. Washington syndrome"—the "prevailing myth" that the path to black progress was through individual initiative, rather than changing society as a whole.[20]

This doubt soon blossomed into an ideology. At the age of fifteen, Davis won a Quaker scholarship for black children to attend private school in New York City. Davis packed her bags, left Dynamite Hill, moved into the home of a white family in Greenwich Village, and enrolled in the Elisabeth Irwin High School, nicknamed "Little Red," an experimental educational cooperative that employed teachers who had been blacklisted from the public schools for their radical politics. Her teachers included members of the Communist Party;[21] her classmates included future radicals such as Kathy Boudin,[22] who would later join the Weather Underground and earn a felony murder conviction for her role in an armored car robbery.

There, in the little brick building on Bleecker Street, Angela Davis would have her awakening. The doubts that she had harbored, the pain that she had borne—all of it would be put into perspective by the teachers in the Little Red School House, who taught the history of the communist movement and the ideology of revolution.

Davis found her first inspiration when, sitting in one of the schoolrooms, she opened the pages of Marx and Engel's famous polemic. "The *Communist Manifesto* hit me like a bolt of lightning," she recalled. "I read it avidly, finding in it answers to many of the seemingly unanswerable dilemmas which had plagued me. I read it over and over again, not completely understanding every passage or every idea, but enthralled nevertheless by the possibility of a communist revolution here." She was intoxicated by visions of "how capitalism could be abolished" and make way for "a new society, without exploiters and exploited, a society without classes, a society where no one would be permitted to own so much that he could use his possessions to exploit other human beings."[23]

During this same period, Davis supplemented her book reading by attending meetings with a Marxist-Leninist youth organization and listening to lectures at the American Institute for Marxist Studies. On the weekends, she marched against nuclear weapons and picketed a Woolworth variety store.[24]

By all accounts, Davis was a precocious student. She graduated from Elisabeth Irwin and earned a full scholarship to study French at Brandeis University in Massachusetts. On campus, she immersed herself in the fashionable intellectuals of the era—Camus, Sartre, and the French existentialists—and listened to speeches by James Baldwin and, crucially, Herbert Marcuse. Davis was drawn to the German philosopher and, during her sophomore year, began weekly private discussions with him on Plato, Aristotle, Kant, Hegel, Marx, and the critical theorists. "I read all of Adorno's and Horkheimer's works that had been translated into English or French, in addition to Marcuse's writings. In this way I had acquainted myself with their thought, which was collectively known as Critical Theory," she said.[25]

With Marcuse's encouragement, Davis finished her studies at Brandeis and enrolled in the graduate program at the Institute for Social Research in Frankfurt—the birthplace and spiritual center of the critical theories. In Frankfurt, Davis studied directly under Marcuse's colleague Theodor Adorno, attended communist youth festivals, visited East Germany, and listened to Rudi Dutschke's public speeches.

But her studies in Europe were short-lived. She was following the news back home, watching as Los Angeles erupted in race riots and the Black Panther Party caught the attention of the press. Davis began to feel homesick, submerged in European theory while the American ghettos convulsed with revolutionary action. Her decision was finalized when she opened the international section of the newspaper and saw the iconic images of the Panthers hoisting their rifles into the air on the steps of the California State Capitol.

Davis was studying the old texts on violence and revolution; the black militants were threatening it directly with lead and steel.

Davis packed her bags and, after a short stopover with Marcuse at the Dialectics of Liberation conference in London, followed her teacher back to San Diego to finish her studies there. "I wanted to continue my academic work, but I knew I could not do it unless I was politically involved," she said. "The struggle was a life-nerve; our only hope for survival. I made up my mind. The journey was on."[26]

The following years would become a whirlwind process of radicalization. Davis began by organizing left-wing student groups on the UCSD campus, agitating for the creation of a new Marxist-Leninist college department,[27] and enlisting Marcuse to help break through the doors and occupy the registrar's office.[28]

Meanwhile, in a less public fashion, Davis sought entry into the black militant movements that were bubbling up in Los Angeles, Oakland, and San Francisco. She traveled up and down California's new interstate to meet with the black nationalists, separatists, communists, and revolutionaries, hoping to find her place in the ferment. "There were the severely anti-white factions who felt that only the most drastic measure—elimination of all white people—would give Black people the opportunity to live unhampered by racism. Others simply wanted to separate and build a distinct Black nation within the United States. And some wanted to return to Africa, the land of our ancestors," she wrote. "There were those who felt the most urgent task of the movement was to refine the spirit of confrontation among Black people. They wanted to spark mass uprisings, such as the Watts and Detroit rebellions. Related to them were those who called upon us all to 'pick up the gun' as the major weapon of liberation and transformation."[29]

At first, Davis joined the Black Panther Party, led by Huey Newton, Bobby Seale, and Eldridge Cleaver, and participated in peace negotiations between the Panthers and another militant organization, the Student Nonviolent Coordinating Committee, or SNCC, led by Stokely Carmichael and H. Rap Brown. Shortly thereafter, however, that alliance collapsed and Davis spent brief stints with other revolutionary groups, which, in turn, also fell apart due to internal purges, leadership struggles, enemy infiltration, and conflict with ostensible allies.

Eventually, frustrated with the perpetual infighting of the black militant movements, Davis made up her mind: she would throw in her lot with the Communist Party USA. "I wanted an anchor, a base, a mooring. I needed comrades with whom I could share a common ideology," she wrote. "I knew that this fight had to be led by a group, a party with more permanence in its membership and structure and more substance in its ideology." For Davis, the Communist Party, which ruled the Soviet Union and was establishing tributary states across the globe, offered a viable path to power.

And so, on a summer day in 1968, Davis paid her fifty-cent membership dues and joined the Communist Party's all-black revolutionary cell, the Che-Lumumba Club.[30]

She immediately set to work, opening a school for young revolutionaries on Venice Boulevard in Los Angeles. "No sooner were programs organized than they were bulging with eager young people," she wrote. "From three-thirty in the afternoon, when the junior high school students came in, until ten at night, the office was the scene of meetings, classes and discussions on such topics as the Black Liberation Struggle in the United States, the Movement in the Los Angeles Area, Strategy and Tactics in Community Organizing, and Marxist-Leninist Theory of Revolution."[31]

At the same time, Davis also began teaching revolutionary theory in the state's public university system. In the spring of 1969,[32] the University of California, Los Angeles, philosophy department offered Davis a temporary position as an acting assistant professor while she completed her doctoral thesis, "Kant's Theory of Force."[33]

But Davis's radical teaching was soon disrupted. A whisper campaign began that summer, culminating in newspaper reports, first in UCLA's *Daily Bruin*, then in the *San Francisco Examiner*, that identified Davis as a member of the Communist Party. The establishment powers, represented by Governor Reagan and the Board of Regents, reacted immediately. As it had done with her mentor Herbert Marcuse, the board attempted to strip Davis of her teaching position, citing a state prohibition against employing communists in the universities.

Rather than hide her affiliations, however, Davis turned the tables on the Establishment and proudly declared, "Yes, I am a Communist," and used the controversy to portray herself as a victim of government repression.[34]

To drum up support, Davis gave a series of speeches on public university campuses. She read from the pages of Marcuse's *Essay on Liberation*, accused the university system of "institutional racism," and denounced the Regents for their complicity in "the calculated genocide to the ranks of the Black Panther Party."[35] At another rally, delivered in tandem with Marcuse, Davis encouraged the students to join the revolutionary movements. "We have to go to the streets," she shouted. "We have to talk about a complete and total change in the structures of this society, because that's the only way that a concept like academic freedom is going to be made relevant—we have to go to the streets."[36]

The next year would become a period of acceleration on all fronts. Davis intensified her rhetoric against the universities, deepened her relationships with the militant movements, and launched a campaign to free the black radicals George Jackson, Fleeta Drumgo, and John Clutchette from Soledad State Prison, where they were incarcerated for various street crimes and the murder of a prison guard who had been beaten and throw from a third-floor tier. Davis became a fierce advocate for the three "Soledad Brothers" and began a correspondence, then a love affair, with George Jackson, who had been radicalized at San Quentin State Prison and founded a Marxist-Leninist prison gang called the Black Guerrilla Family.

Davis sent Jackson a string of letters professing her twin ardors: for George and for blood. "George," she wrote, "my feelings for you run very deep. My memory fails me when I search in the past for an encounter with a human being as strong, as beautiful, as you. Something in you has managed to smash through the fortress I long ago erected around my soul."[37] She spent many of her waking hours in fantasies of violence and of liberating her lover from prison: "We have to learn to rejoice when pigs' blood is spilled"; "We must learn to plan the attack, gear it towards the total annihilation of the monster"; "I see myself tearing down this steel door, fighting my way to you, ripping down your cell door and letting you go free."[38]

As the summer of 1970 reached its zenith, Davis received the final word from the University of California—the Regents had decided to let her contract expire without reappointment—and her letters took on an increasingly frenzied tone.

Davis began spending her days with George's seventeen-year-old brother, Jonathan Jackson, and promised that they were making "beautiful plans" for the revolution. "All my life-efforts have gone in one direction: Free George Jackson and the Soledad Brothers. Man, I have gotten into a lot of trouble, but I don't give a damn," she wrote to George. "I love you. I love my people. That is all that matters. Liberation by any means necessary. Those means are determined by the nature and intensity of the enemy's response. The American oppressor has revealed to us what we must do if we are serious about our commitment. If I am serious about my love for you, about my love for Black people, I should be ready to go all the way. I am."[39]

With this in mind, Davis and Jonathan Jackson began assembling an arsenal of weapons. In 1968 and 1969, Davis had purchased a .38-caliber automatic pistol and an M-1 carbine rifle, and then, accompanied by Jonathan in the spring and summer of 1970, purchased another M-1 carbine and 150 rounds of ammunition. Finally, on August 5, Davis and Jonathan visited George at San Quentin, then went to a pawnshop in San Francisco and paid cash for a 12-gauge shotgun and a box of shells.[40]

The word "revolution" was no longer a metaphor. They were preparing for war.

Two days later, on August 7, 1970, these guns became a part of history. Jonathan Jackson rose from his seat in the gallery of the Marin County Hall of Justice, pulled the Browning .38 pistol out of a satchel, threw it to one of the defendants, then pulled the M-1 carbine from his trench coat and yelled to the astonished crowd: "Freeze!"[41]

Three San Quentin inmates and political radicals—James McClain,

Ruchell Magee, and William Christmas—were in court that day regarding McClain's alleged stabbing of a prison guard.[42] After Jackson told the on-lookers to "freeze," the men sprang into action. McClain held the pistol to the head of Judge Harold Haley, Magee freed Christmas from the holding pen, and they lashed together the deputy district attorney and three female jurors with piano wire, taking them as hostages. Jackson then produced the 12-gauge shotgun and the men taped it under the judge's chin. They briefly contemplated taking an infant hostage, but relented after the mother began screaming, "No, don't take my baby!"[43]

Leading the string of hostages, Jackson and his three accomplices an-nounced their demands: they wanted the authorities to release the Soledad Brothers, including Angela's lover George Jackson, by noon that day—or all of the hostages would be killed. They moved through the corridor, tell-ing a photographer "we are the revolutionaries," and climbed into a rented yellow Hertz van with the intention of traveling to San Francisco Interna-tional Airport.[44]

But the quartet never made it past the barricades. As the van approached the perimeter, four San Quentin prison guards exchanged a barrage of bul-lets with the hostage takers. Simultaneously, the deputy district attorney inside the van grabbed McClain's pistol, shot Magee in the stomach, and fired at the other men until the magazine was empty. The entire exchange lasted nineteen seconds.[45]

When the smoke cleared, Jonathan Jackson, James McClain, William Christmas, and Judge Haley were dead. Ruchell Magee and the deputy district attorney were seriously wounded. Miraculously, all of the jurors survived.

Investigators dragged the bodies out of the van with lassos, fearing that they might be booby-trapped with explosives, and began sorting through the materials inside. They discovered that Jonathan Jackson had concealed some of the hostage-taking supplies in two books, *Violence and Social Change* and *The Politics of Violence: Revolution in the Modern World*, both of which were signed and dated on the inside cover by Angela Davis.

In Jonathan's satchel, they found Angela Davis's fingerprints on two more pamphlets, a manual on operating the M-1 carbine and Carlos Marighella's *Minimanual of the Urban Guerrilla*. In his wallet, investigators found a yel-low slip of paper with a telephone number for a public phone booth near the American Airlines ticket counter at San Francisco International Airport. Finally, after running the serial numbers, they learned that all four of the weapons used in the siege traced back to one "Angela Y. Davis."

Meanwhile, as the blood was drying outside the Marin County Hall of Justice, witnesses spotted Davis at the San Francisco airport, where she quickly purchased a Pacific Southwest Airlines ticket to Los Angeles—and went into hiding.[46]

In her *Autobiography*, Davis presents herself as a fugitive slave fleeing the whips and the bloodhounds of the white slave master. "Thousands of my ancestors had waited, as I had done, for nightfall to cover their steps, had leaned on one true friend to help them, had felt, as I did, the very teeth of the dogs at their heels. It was simple. I had to be worthy of them," she wrote.[47]

The reality, however, was less heroic. The FBI had placed Davis on the Most Wanted list for her role in the courthouse siege, and for the next two months the young professor utilized a network of wealthy left-wing benefactors, activists, and militants to disguise her physical appearance, move through a sequence of safe houses, and evade law enforcement.[48] In October, however, the Bureau tracked Davis and a mysterious heir named David Poindexter Jr. to a Howard Johnson Motor Lodge in Midtown Manhattan, where federal agents burst through the door and arrested them.[49]

*   *   *

President Richard Nixon celebrated Davis's arrest on national television, praising FBI director J. Edgar Hoover for capturing his mark[50] and for sending a "warning" to other radicals.[51]

But Davis, despite being bound and shackled, was not powerless. After she was sent to the New York Women's House of Detention, the other prisoners clanged on the doors and chanted Angela's name. Crowds of left-wing supporters assembled on the streets below to offer their support. A network of committees and radical organizations launched a propaganda campaign on her behalf, reaching television screens and newspaper columns around the world.[52]

The most significant writing during this period, however, was Davis's own. In 1971, after she had been transferred to Marin County Jail, Davis edited and contributed to a collection of essays, *If They Come in the Morning*, that featured the key figures in the black militant movement:

Black Panther leaders Huey P. Newton and Ericka Huggins, prison writers George Jackson and Ruchell Magee—both of whom faced murder charges in connection with the Davis case—and an assortment of communists, lawyers, and activists who had committed themselves to the cause.

In the book, Davis carefully constructs her public image and traces the progression of her political awakening. Like Marcuse, she believed that black Marxists, endowed with the spiritual authority of their ancestors and the intellectual power of their ideology, were destined to lead the new proletariat and subvert the ruling order. In her essays, Davis portrayed the United States as a many-tentacled monster, using the arms of the state to manage society and submerge minorities into a life of crime and desperation. She identified the justice system—laws, courts, prisons, and police—as the primary "instrument of class domination" and physical enforcer of America's "racist ideology." For blacks, there was no escape. For Davis, the black underclass was "compelled to resort to criminal acts, not as a result of conscious choice—implying other alternatives—but because society has objectively reduced their possibilities of subsistence and survival to this level."[53]

But there was still hope. Davis saw a new consciousness bubbling up in the ghettos and in the prisons. Through a network of street gangs and Black Power organizations, which had recently captured headlines for violent eruptions from the Watts section of Los Angeles to Newark, New Jersey, the black underclass was beginning to organize and develop an ideology of self-empowerment. The black criminal, who had previously been taught that he was the victimizer of the innocent, was learning that he was, in fact, the victim of an oppressive society. He was not a "prisoner," but a "political prisoner." His crimes—theft, robbery, violence, even rape—were not transgressions, but acts of moral rebellion.

As Davis captured the public imagination with her writing and interviews, her legal team prepared to defend her in court. They pursued a two-part strategy: frame the proceedings as a political persecution and sow doubt about the evidence against her.

Prosecutors had built their case step by step, demonstrating that Davis was committed to liberating her lover George Jackson, had spent the summer with his brother Jonathan Jackson, purchased all of the guns used in the courthouse assault, and had her signature and fingerprints on the violent books and pamphlets discovered on Jonathan's dead body. They also produced dramatic new evidence: eyewitnesses had spotted Davis with the yellow Hertz rental van the day before the siege and, prosecutors alleged, she had planned to be the getaway woman, waiting at the airport public phone booth to coordinate the group's final escape.[54]

But on this final point, the prosecution fell short. The defense admitted that Angela was in love with George, that she was deeply involved with Jonathan, that she had purchased all of weapons, and that she was at the airport the day of the siege—but, because Jonathan and the prisoners never made it to the airport, prosecutors could not prove beyond all reasonable doubt that she was directly coordinating the escape. The evidence was overwhelming, but circumstantial.

Davis and her lawyers imbued the trial with a sympathetic political narrative from the outset. "I stand before this court as a target of a political frame-up which far from pointing to my culpability, implicates the State of California as an agent of political repression," Davis told the court during her arraignment. "In order to ensure that these political questions are not obscured, I feel compelled to play an active role in my own defense as the defendant, as a Black woman and as a Communist. It is my duty to assist all those directly involved in the proceedings as well as the people of this State and the American people in general to thoroughly comprehend the substantive issues at stake in my case. These have to do with my political beliefs, affiliations and my day-to-day efforts to fight all the conditions which have economically and politically paralyzed Black America."[55]

The defense enlisted a team of prestigious attorneys, psychiatrists, psychologists, and a handwriting expert to aid in jury selection, and called in a procession of left-wing activists and Communist Party members to provide alibis for Davis during key moments. These alibis were flimsy—they were from dedicated political allies, often in private spaces that were impossible to corroborate—but ultimately, along with the circumstantial nature of the prosecution's evidence and the political valence of the proceeding, it was enough.

Davis and her attorneys had beguiled the all-white jury, persuading them that the Marin courthouse revolt was a "slave insurrection" and that Angela was a "symbol of resistance."[56] They turned the tables, identifying the state as the victimizer and Davis as the victim. During thirteen hours of jury deliberation, the facts of the case seemed to melt away and the political narrative took hold.

When the judge welcomed the jury back into the courtroom, the clerk read the verdict for each of the three charges. "We, the jury in the above-entitled cause, find the defendant, Angela Y. Davis, not guilty of kidnapping . . . not guilty of murder . . . not guilty of conspiracy."[57]

The courthouse erupted in cheers. One juror flashed the Black Power salute to the audience outside the courtroom and told reporters: "I did it because I wanted to show I felt an identity with the oppressed people in the crowd. All through the trial, they thought we were just a white, middle-class jury. I wanted to express my sympathy with their struggle."[58] Later that evening, a majority of the jurors attended a rock-and-roll festival in celebration of Davis's acquittal.

Four men were dead and one of the hostages had been paralyzed from the waist down, but revolutionary justice had been served. Angela Davis had put American society on trial—and won.

CHAPTER 6

"Kill the Pigs"

The Black Revolution Explodes

Following her acquittal, Angela Davis embarked on a worldwide tour. She spoke to adoring crowds in Los Angeles, Chicago, Detroit, and New York City, then traveled throughout the Soviet Union, with stops in Russia, Central Asia, Bulgaria, Czechoslovakia, Cuba, and Chile.[1]

The state bureaucracies in the communist nations, which had previously sent "a million roses for Angela," assembled the masses in her honor, with fifty thousand welcoming her to East Berlin[2] and hundreds of thousands celebrating her in Havana, where she delivered a speech in tandem with the Cuban dictator Fidel Castro.[3] In Moscow, Davis lavished praise on the Soviet system of government and its treatment of racial minorities. "The possibility of seeing with my own eyes the practical realization of Lenin's ethnic policy will be of tremendous help in our own struggle of resolving the ethnic problem in the United States," she said. "Everything we have seen in the Soviet Union will inspire us in our own struggle. Our devotion to Marxism-Leninism and Communism and our own ideological convictions have been greatly strengthened."[4]

At the same time, Davis had also become a symbol of the left-wing revolution at home. She spoke on college campuses and published a bestselling memoir, *An Autobiography*, which framed her life story as the "neo-slave narrative" of her time.[5] In her lectures to students, she advanced the idea that racism was the great invisible power and warned that the United States was spiraling toward a fascist future. "We can look back over the last four years as we try to predict what we are going to face these next four years. And what I've tried to do is try to understand what happened in Germany prior to the Nazi seizure of power," she said to students at California State

University, Fullerton, in 1972. "And I notice some very, very frightening parallels between the deterioration of the judicial system in pre-Nazi Germany—I'm stressing this, pre-Nazi Germany—before Hitler seized power. There are some very frightening parallels between what was going on there then, and what is going on here now."[6]

For Davis, these dire conditions served as justification for the revolution—and nearly any transgression that carried it forward. She argued that minority criminals, such as the San Quentin Six, who were accused of murdering three prison guards during an escape attempt;[7] Ruchell Magee, who had participated in the Marin courthouse kidnapping-murder;[8] and Ricardo Chavez Ortiz, who had hijacked an airplane to "save America and the whole world,"[9] were driven to commit these crimes by a racist society and should, therefore, be considered "political prisoners"—victims worthy of liberation, rather than perpetrators worthy of condemnation.

At her lecture in Fullerton, Davis illustrated this principle with a story about Emily Butler, a twenty-four-year-old black woman who worked at the Internal Revenue Service office in Atlanta and, after a conflict with her colleagues, retrieved a .22 revolver and shot her white supervisor four times at point-blank range, standing over the dead woman's body and telling her, "I hate you so bad, I hope I killed you."[10] But for Angela Davis, the culprit was not Butler, who had emptied the revolver into her supervisor, but the society that had left her no choice but to kill. "We have to realize that Emily Butler is not guilty," Davis told the cheering students. "It is racism that pulled that trigger. Racism. And if anybody needs to be indicted and imprisoned, it's the reincarnation of racism himself, Richard Nixon."[11]

Despite her appeals to Kant and Hegel, the real ideology of Angela Davis was simple: total war against American society, justifying any atrocity, from the prison camps of the Soviet Union to the cold-blooded murder of an IRS manager—all in the name of the revolution.

And she wasn't alone. There was an entire movement behind her. The Marxist-Leninist prison gangs, the Black Panther Party, and, later, the Black Liberation Army were busy organizing the ghettos, assembling an arsenal of weapons, and, modeling themselves on the Third World liberation armies, preparing for urban guerrilla war.

"America must learn that black people are not the eternal sufferers, the universal prisoners, the only ones who can feel pain," they warned. "The season of struggle is our season."[12]

*   *   *

The person who most embodied the life and spirit of the black Marxist revolution was a man named Eldridge Cleaver.

Cleaver's personal biography contains the entire arc of the revolution: he was radicalized in the California prisons, served as the Black Panther Party's minister of information, and led the movement down its final, apocalyptic path. He was the masculine, hot-blooded complement to Angela Davis's feminine, cold-blooded intellectualism.

He had fought, written, and ravaged with his bare hands.

Like many of the figures in the black liberation movement, Cleaver's awakening began in the prison system. He had spent long stretches of his youth in juvenile detention and, as an adult, was sent to San Quentin after a conviction for rape and assault with intent to murder.

While incarcerated, Cleaver sought his own transvaluation of values, recasting his crimes as a mechanism of liberation. In his bestselling memoir, *Soul on Ice*, he recounted his descent into madness as a young man—"For several days I ranted and raved against the white race, against white women in particular, against white America in general"—and then his rejection of "the white man's law" and creation of his own moral universe, in which all transgressions were permitted.

"I became a rapist," he wrote. "To refine my technique and *modus operandi*, I started out by practicing on black girls in the ghetto—in the black ghetto where dark and vicious deeds appear not as aberrations or deviations from the norm, but as part of the sufficiency of the Evil of the day—and when I considered myself smooth enough, I crossed the tracks and sought out white prey."[13]

But the rape of white women, he insisted, was not personal, but political. Through the act of physical domination, the black man could transform himself from the low-status "supermasculine menial" into a high-status sexual revolutionary.

"Rape was an insurrectionary act," Cleaver wrote. "It delighted me that I was defying and trampling upon the white man's law, upon his system of values, and that I was defiling his women—and this point, I believe, was the most satisfying to me because I was very resentful over the historical fact of how the white man has used the black woman. I felt I was getting revenge. From the site of the act of rape, consternation spreads outwardly in concentric circles. I wanted to send waves of consternation throughout the white race."[14]

Cleaver recanted while in prison, claiming that he had transcended the anti-morality of rape and found salvation in Marxism-Leninism. But these initial themes—violence, revenge, hatred, madness—pervaded Cleaver's life, and the black nationalist movement it represented, from its sordid origins to its catastrophic conclusions.

Angela Davis, who supported Cleaver in the early days,[15] provided the intellectual framework for overthrowing the American state. Cleaver, who had a hot-and-cold opinion of Davis over the years,[16] revealed its depraved and vengeful heart.

After his release from prison, Cleaver joined the Black Panther Party and, working closely with its founder, Huey P. Newton, cobbled together the ideology of the black militant movement. Cleaver was a gifted writer who combined high-minded rhetoric with gangster-style exhortations, publishing a long sequence of essays and articles in the pages of the *Black Panther* newsletter and the *Black Scholar*, a radical academic journal that served as the hub for revolutionary and postcolonial studies. "The ideology of the Black Panther Party is the historical experience of Black people and the wisdom gained by Black people in their 400 year long struggle against the system of racist oppression and economic exploitation in Babylon, interpreted through the prism of the Marxist-Leninist analysis by our Minister of Defense, Huey P. Newton," he wrote. "Essentially, what Huey did was to provide the ideology and the methodology for organizing the Black Urban lumpenproletariat. Armed with this ideological perspective and method, Huey transformed the Black lumpenproletariat from the forgotten people at the bottom of society into the vanguard of the proletariat."[17]

Cleaver's theory represented a departure from orthodox Marxism, which dismissed the lumpenproletariat—the criminal, the vagrant, the drifter, the unemployed—as utterly incapable of revolution. As Marx and Engels described it in *The Communist Manifesto*, the lumpenproletariat was "the 'dangerous class,' the social scum, that passively rotting mass thrown off by the lowest layers of old society" that "may be swept into the movement by a proletarian revolution" but, ultimately, could not achieve the necessary consciousness or sustained action required for overthrowing the ruling class.[18]

Cleaver, on the other hand, arguing that "there is much evidence that Marx and Engels were themselves racists," maintained that the founding fathers of Marxism had put undue faith in the white working class and underestimated the black underclass.[19] Echoing Marcuse's conclusions in *Counterrevolution and Revolt*, Cleaver argued that, in fact, the industrial working classes had become a conservative, even reactionary force—or, in his words, "the House Niggers of Capitalism."[20] Therefore, Cleaver believed that his task as the ideologist of the Black Panthers was to develop a unique dialectic for the black underclass and to "manifest its rebellion in the University of the Streets."[21]

The ultimate goal, he said, was not to achieve "equality in Production, which is the Marxist view and basic error, but equality in distribution and consumption."[22] That is, the black lumpenproletariat might not be able to operate the factories, but it could commandeer a steady stream of material benefits from the men who could.

The Black Panther Party's propaganda and organization-building efforts were built on this ideological foundation. Beginning in the Bay Area and then expanding to dozens of cities across the United States, the Panthers aggressively recruited gang members, pimps, prostitutes, felons, dropouts, and drug dealers, luring them into the party with the glamor of the gun.[23] "To recruit any sizable number of street brothers, we would obviously have to do more than *talk*," Huey Newton wrote in his autobiography, *Revolutionary Suicide*. "We needed to give practical applications of our theory, show them that we were not afraid of weapons and not afraid of death. The way we finally won the brothers over was by patrolling the police with arms."[24]

The Panthers raised money by selling copies of Mao's *Little Red Book*,[25] purchased firearms, and then bought leather jackets, black berets, and ammunition belts to complete the aesthetic. They quickly raised their profile by following, monitoring, and intimidating police officers assigned to black neighborhoods.

The Panthers' manifesto, the "Ten-Point Program," translated Newton and Cleaver's Marxist-Leninist synthesis into a tangible political agenda, demanding that the federal government provide blacks with cash reparation payments, guaranteed monthly income, free high-quality housing, racialist ideology in schools, an end to police brutality, and the immediate release of all black men held in the nation's jails and prisons.[26] The movement's official publication, the *Black Panther*, carried official party proclamations, news of the revolution, and, partly because of low literacy rates in the ghettos, large, graphic illustrations depicting armed urban resistance and the execution of police officers.

Newton and Cleaver returned to these violent themes again and again, revealing an obsession with killing law enforcement officers, which, they believed, could spark the revolution. "When the masses hear that a gestapo policeman has been executed while sipping coffee at a counter, and the revolutionary executioners fled without being traced, the masses will see the validity of this type of approach to resistance," wrote Newton.[27] "A revolution is not a game, it is a war,"[28] echoed Cleaver, who promised in his public speeches to put police officers "against the wall when the shooting starts," to "beat that punk California Governor Ronald Reagan to death," and to burn down the Nixon White House.[29]

Like their comrade Angela Davis, the leaders of the Black Panther Party did not merely talk the talk. They walked the walk of their revolution.

In 1967, during a traffic stop in Oakland, Newton engaged in a shoot-out with police that left two officers wounded and one dead. He was initially convicted of voluntary manslaughter, then, after a court reversal and two hung juries, was freed.[30] The following year, Cleaver and a group of Panthers plotted to ambush the police and, after Cleaver was spotted urinating in the street by a patrol unit, they haphazardly executed the plan and found themselves in a gunfight. Cleaver and the Panthers fired 157 shots through the police cruiser, with a barrage of bullets hitting an officer in the arm and back. Cleaver and his comrade Bobby Hutton fled into the basement of a nearby house and exchanged gunfire with a detachment of police, who eventually flushed them out with tear gas, killed Hutton, and arrested Cleaver.[31]

By 1970, the Black Panther Party's inflammatory rhetoric and low-grade guerrilla war had inspired violence across the country. Police departments in New York, New Jersey, Los Angeles, and Detroit reported massive increases in assaults against officers, which, in the words of one official, were largely driven by the Panthers' "rhetoric of violence" and the "widespread availability" of their newspaper, which "constantly pressed" the incitement to wield "the gun" and "Kill the Pigs." The chief of police in Los Angeles warned that America was facing "a revolution on the installment plan" that threatened to destabilize national government.[32] The Panthers, meanwhile, expanded their operations and bragged publicly that they had assembled an armory with pistols, rifles, explosives, machine guns, and grenade launchers.[33]

But despite the outward bravado, behind the scenes, the black revolutionaries were in disarray. As Angela Davis had observed, the radical organizations were vulnerable to infighting, division, and internal purges. In addition, the FBI was rapidly infiltrating the ranks of the Black Panther Party, which FBI director J. Edgar Hoover had called "the greatest threat to the internal security of the country."[34] By the end of 1969, federal law enforcement agents had raided Panther offices across the country and arrested more than two hundred of its members, including thirty Panthers who faced capital punishment and forty who faced life in prison.[35]

During this period of turmoil, the most significant fissure within the ranks of the Black Panther Party was between the factions of Eldridge Cleaver and Huey Newton.

Following his arrest for the police shoot-out, Cleaver had jumped bail and fled abroad, visiting the friendly left-wing regimes in Cuba, North Korea, and, finally, Algeria, where he set up the international headquarters of the Black Panther Party and ran its American operations from exile.[36] Smoking hashish and working the telephones from a two-story villa in Algiers,[37] Cleaver continued to push the Marxist-Leninist line and encouraged his soldiers to escalate the urban guerrilla war and achieve "revolution in our lifetime."[38] Meanwhile, Newton watched chaos, death, and infiltration decimate his ranks in Oakland and advocated a shift in strategy toward peaceful organizing and political activism.

The FBI, too, played a role, intentionally sowing distrust between the two leaders, who, in 1971, ended their relationship with a vicious public feud, accusing each another of treason and splitting the Black Panther Party in two—the West Coast Panthers remained loyal to Newton, while a smaller contingent of East Coast Panthers pledged allegiance to Cleaver and his vision for total war.[39]

With this, the Black Liberation Army was born. Cleaver gave directions to this new faction and edited its official newspaper from exile. His fifty or sixty followers in New York went underground and began plotting how to secure funds, recruit members, plan operations, and turn the rhetoric about "killing the pigs" into reality.[40]

Cleaver and his men distilled their new ideology to a simple list of negations: "We are anti-capitalist, anti-imperialist, anti-racist, and anti-sexist"; "we must of necessity strive for the abolishment of these systems"; "in order to abolish our system of oppression we must utilize the science of class struggle."[41]

In Algiers, Cleaver's right-hand man, Field Marshal Don Cox, put together a manual for organizing urban guerrilla units, advised the urban revolutionaries to organize into autonomous cells, and offered detailed instructions for the use of pistols, rifles, shotguns, grenades, dynamite, and time bombs. "Since the year 1619 when the first slave ship landed with human cargo from Africa, to toil as slaves in the New World, innumerable methods have been used to gain our freedom and liberation," Cox wrote. "When a guerrilla unit moves against this oppressive system by executing a pig or attacking its institutions, by any means, sniping, stabbing, bombing, etc., in defense against the 400 years of racist brutality, murder and exploitation, this can only be defined correctly as self-defense." As inspiration, it included black-and-white photographs of the Marin courthouse siege and other attacks against law enforcement.[42]

Then the assassinations began.

In the spring of 1971, the BLA launched its first offensive, strafing two New York City policemen with a machine gun, leaving them in critical condition.[43] Later that night, the group sent a communiqué to the *New York Times* and a Harlem radio station claiming credit for the attack and warning "the fascist state pig police" that "the domestic armed forces of racism and oppression will be confronted with the guns of the Black Liberation Army."[44] Two nights later, BLA gunmen ambushed two patrolmen, instantly killing the first, a black man, with a shot to the back of the head, and slowly killing the second, a white man, who was hit with thirteen shots to the body and bled out as a radio car rushed him to the hospital.[45]

Over the next two years, the BLA would unleash a reign of terror: the militants assassinated five more police officers,[46] robbed a series of banks,[47] kidnapped and ransomed a bar owner,[48] orchestrated multiple prison es-

capes,[49] hijacked commercial airplanes,[50] and ran a series of criminal enterprises, ranging from drug-running to street robbery.

Their grisliest crime, however, was the murder of two NYPD officers—
Rocco Laurie, a white man, and Gregory Foster, a black man—in the East
Village neighborhood of Manhattan. On January 27, 1972, as part of their
second "spring offensive," members of the BLA's so-called George Jackson
Squad gunned down the two men at point-blank range, then shot Laurie in
the groin and Foster in the eyes, splattering their genitalia, cranial bones,
and brain tissue across the pavement.[51] After mutilating the bodies, one of
the BLA gunmen performed a Yoruban-style war dance over the corpses.[52]

There was a theory behind the carnage. As its leaders wrote in a series of
newspapers, pamphlets, and communiqués, the Black Liberation Army saw
itself as "an embryonic form" of the National Liberation Armies that had
gained power in Africa and Latin America. Cleaver and his men believed
that they were the "revolutionary class" of fighters and propagandists that
could "lead the masses of black people into a higher degree of revolutionary consciousness" and, catching headlines with audacious robberies and
assassinations, wake the black lumpenproletariat out of its slumber and
into armed revolt against the power structure.

The black ghetto would serve as the initial *foco*, then move outward into
general society. "Once the center of action has been initiated," the BLA
declared, "the theory goes it will be the moving force of the revolution and
the masses of oppressed people will pick up the gun and fight until final
victory."[53]

It was a theory that failed.

The public quickly recoiled from the bloodshed. Even in black
neighborhoods, where the BLA had hoped to build support, the movement
alienated residents. The "revolutionary executions"[54] of black police officers
was met with horror. And although the BLA officially adopted an "anti-
heroin interdiction" policy in black communities,[55] robbing and murdering
drug dealers in a purported effort to protect residents,[56] the group's leaders
often succumbed to addiction and warlordism themselves,[57] replacing,
rather than eliminating, the gangsters on the street corner.

Meanwhile, the FBI's counterinsurgency operation went into high gear.
During the height of the BLA terror campaign, between 1971 and 1973,
law enforcement agencies killed seven suspected BLA fighters and captured

another eighteen of its leaders, reducing the group to a handful of die-hards who retreated to the tenements and back alleys of New York City.[58]

By 1974, the movement was exhausted. The Algerian government had pushed Eldridge Cleaver out of the country[59] and the majority of his soldiers in the United States were dead, strung out, or locked up. Police had captured and indicted a large group of BLA militants involved in the revolutionary violence.[60] Two of the suspects in the murder of Rocco Laurie and Gregory Foster died in shoot-outs with law enforcement.[61] In the final years, some BLA cells were consuming mountains of cocaine, robbing stores, pushers, and banks to feed their habit, which had become insatiable.[62] Their West Coast counterparts returned to a life of petty crime, extortion, pimping, thieving, and violence.[63]

Their political theory had dissipated and their visions of the revolution had collapsed.

Despite all of Eldridge Cleaver's ideological posturing, Marx might have been right after all. The lumpenproletariat—the "thieves and criminals of all kinds living on the crumbs of society"—might have been too undisciplined, violent, hedonistic, and easily manipulated, and, thus, incapable of becoming the true subject of the revolution.[64] As the BLA soldier Sundiata Acoli lamented, the media was able to highlight the movement's "lumpen tendencies," including "lack of discipline, liberal use of alcohol, marijuana, curse words, loose sexual morals, a criminal mentality, and rash actions," in order to discredit the group from the outset. In the words of another soldier, the origins of the BLA were always more criminal than revolutionary. "We went deep off into the ghetto" to find recruits, he said. "Them niggas had been shooting their pistols Friday and Saturday night anyway . . . so we'd get them and politicize them."[65]

But this wasn't enough. Cleaver's original conviction, that "the correct ideology is an invincible weapon against the oppressor in our struggle for freedom and liberation," turned out to be an empty slogan.[66] Shooting a police officer in the back of the head, executing an innocent shopkeeper for thirty dollars,[67] engaging in drug-fueled robberies—these were not the acts of principle, but pathological cruelty, nihilism, and despair.

One by one, the leadership of the black liberation movement succumbed to their vices. Huey Newton fell into a life of addiction, crime, violence, and desperation. He embezzled funds,[68] was suspected in the murder of a prostitute,[69] and spent his time in the crack cocaine dens of the Oakland ghettos. Eventually, a dealer affiliated with the Black Guerrilla Family prison gang shot him in the head outside a drug house and left him to die in a pool of his own blood.[70]

Cleaver contemplated suicide and, with a gun in his hand, had a mystical vision of his face superimposed on the moon, while the faces of his old heroes—Castro, Mao, Marx, and Engels—disappeared into smoke. He abandoned his faith in Marxism-Leninism and dashed through a series of religious conversions, from evangelicalism to Mormonism to doomsday cultism to his own synthetic religion, Christlam, which combined Christianity and Islam.[71] But the demons were always at his heels. Like Newton, he became a crack addict in the gritty neighborhoods of Oakland and, after his health slowly failed, died of a heart attack.[72]

Angela Davis, too, followed the black liberation line to its grim conclusions. Throughout the 1970s, she cheerleaded for the entire lineup of revolutionaries who stood trial for their crimes, including the Soledad Brothers, the San Quentin Six, and Assata Shakur, the "mother hen" of the Black Liberation Army,[73] who was convicted of the murder of the New Jersey state trooper and eventually escaped prison and fled to Cuba. Davis raised funds, wrote pamphlets, and organized rallies for her comrades, insisting that they were "freedom fighters" and "political prisoners."[74] But as the trials dried up and the nation ended its fascination with the urban guerrillas, Davis lost much of her appeal. Her style was passé; her rhetoric had become repetitive; her message fell on deaf ears.

In 1979, when Davis announced her campaign for the vice presidency of the United States on the Communist Party ticket, nobody was listening. The campaign barely registered in the national press and, after the ballots were counted, Ronald Reagan, her old nemesis from the California days, had earned nearly 44 million votes. Davis and her running mate, Gus Hall, had garnered a total of just 45,000.

The revolution, it seemed, was finished.

CHAPTER 7

From Black Liberation to Black Studies

After the collapse of the black radical movement, Angela Davis retreated to the permanent refuge of the failed revolutionary: academia.

Over the years, Davis would serve as a professor and lecturer at UCLA, Rutgers, Claremont, Syracuse, Vassar, San Francisco State University, San Francisco Art Institute, and, most permanently, at the University of California, Santa Cruz. She had a unique talent for securing the support of the institutions she was revolting against: unlike many of her comrades in the black militant movement, who met their end in the graveyard or the prison yard, Davis was able to successfully maintain her reputation in mainstream society and secure a permanent sinecure from the government she had once promised to overthrow.

The influence of Davis's long march through academia is profound. When Davis broke down the door of the UCSD registrar's office as a graduate student, she demanded racial quotas, critical theory, Marxist ideology, and "white studies" to unmask the oppressive nature of European culture, and a general critique of "capitalism in the Western world, including the crucial roles played by colonialism, imperialism, slavery, and genocide." She wanted a reading list of Karl Marx, Vladimir Lenin, Malcolm X, Frantz Fanon, and Che Guevara, and a curriculum designed to "reject the entire oppressive structure of America."[1]

All of this has come into being. Davis's radical curriculum has become the standard humanities program in the American university. Her political program has become the official platform of the progressive Left. The ideology of the old radicals has been translated into academic language, divided up into various subdisciplines, and reprinted as original insight.

From her perch in academia, Davis created a philosophy that laid the groundwork for the "activist-scholars" who would come to dominate intellectual life in the United States. The Weathermen, Panthers, and BLA attacked the physical symbolism of the United States: the Capitol, the Pentagon, the NYPD, Bank of America. But Davis struck much deeper. She sought to scratch out the origins and the legitimacy of Western society altogether.

As it turned out, the failures of the 1970s were not fatal. Davis and the black militant movement were able to reinvent themselves as an intellectual elite. And they became even more dangerous after laying down their arms.

*   *   *

Angela Davis's intellectual conquest began with her first lectures as an assistant professor at UCLA, prior to her incarceration.

The course, which was later published as a pamphlet called *Lectures on Liberation*, established the ideological formula that served as the foundation of her work for the following fifty years: the legitimacy of identity politics, the subversion of the founding myths, and the need for the total deconstruction of American institutions. From the beginning, Davis presented the world as a Hegelian dialectic between master and slave. She wove together the great themes of consciousness, identity, power, and action, and advanced the argument that only the slave could understand freedom. "The slave finds at the end of his journey towards understanding a real grasp of what freedom means," she said. "He understands that the master's freedom is abstract freedom to suppress other human beings. The slave understands that this is a pseudo concept of freedom and at this point is more enlightened than his master for he realizes that the master is a slave of his own misconceptions, his own misdeeds, his own brutality, his own effort to oppress."[2]

In Davis's mind, the master-slave dialectic served as the key to unlocking the principle of equality. She reminded her students that the Greeks invented democracy while also maintaining slavery, a hypocrisy that continued with the American founders. From Athens to Philadelphia, Davis argued, the oppressed, and the black slaves in particular, "have exposed, by their very existence, the inadequacies not only of the practice of freedom, but of its very theoretical formulation."

The slave, whether in the iron chains of the past or the invisible chains of the present, is the only possible means of discovering freedom. Through his identity and through his consciousness, he is uniquely qualified to escape the one-dimensional society and achieve true liberation. And his only viable path, Davis taught, was action. "The slave is actually conscious of the fact that freedom is not a fact, it is not a given, but rather something to be fought for, it can exist only through a process of struggle." Through this struggle, she believed, the slave could finally realize Marx's vision of transforming the "wish-dream of an oppressed humanity" into an immanent, flesh-and-blood reality.[3]

The first objective of Davis's new theory of revolution was to establish racial and sexual identity as the basis for political action. Beginning with her prison writings, Davis presented herself and, by extension, the black woman, as the neo-slave, the maroon, the fugitive wading through the swamps—and, by virtue of her identity, the human embodiment of the quest for freedom.

Davis was one of the first to argue that the fight against oppression must include the fight against racism, patriarchy, and capitalism. "The socialist movement must never forget that while the economic struggle is indispensable, it is by no means the sole terrain of significant anti-capitalist activity," she wrote during her incarceration. The movement must obliterate the entire superstructure that holds the system in place, particularly the architecture of racism and the "family-based structure of oppression." For Davis, just as minorities must be liberated from racial domination, women must be liberated from the "drudgery of full-time child rearing," their "containment within the family," and the "male supremacist structures of the larger society." By dissolving the social bonds that sustain the mode of production, she believed, the revolutionary could begin to undermine the entire capitalist society.[4]

The black woman, because of her position at the lowest point of the social hierarchy, provided the ultimate *foco* for this revolt: she experienced the interlocking oppressions of race, class, and sex all at once, and, as such, was endowed with almost mystical powers of perception, authenticity, and moral standing. For Davis, the fugitive slave women, who "often poisoned the food and set fire to the houses of their masters,"[5] provided the historical inspiration for the war of identity in contemporary society. "We, the black women of today, must accept the full weight of a legacy wrought in blood by our mothers in chains," she wrote. "Our fight, while identical in spirit, reflects different conditions and thus implies different paths of struggle.

But as heirs to a tradition of supreme perseverance and heroic resistance, we must hasten to take our place wherever our people are forging on towards freedom."[6] Davis—as the black woman in leg irons, who would later come out as a lesbian—puts herself at the center. The revolution emanates from her very existence.

Davis's theoretical work on identity had an enormous impact on the development of left-wing politics throughout the era.

In 1977, a group of black lesbian activists working together as the Combahee River Collective followed Davis's lead and published the landmark Combahee River Collective Statement, which gave birth to the term "identity politics" and operationalized Davis's unified theory of oppression. "The most general statement of our politics at the present time would be that we are actively committed to struggling against racial, sexual, heterosexual, and class oppression, and see as our particular task the development of integrated analysis and practice based upon the fact that the major systems of oppression are interlocking," they wrote. "The synthesis of these oppressions creates the conditions of our lives. As Black women we see Black feminism as the logical political movement to combat the manifold and simultaneous oppressions that all women of color face."

Citing Davis's prison essay on black women, the authors advanced the idea that identity is both the source of their oppression and the basis for their resistance against it. Political consciousness, they said, must begin with personal consciousness and recognition of one's place in the social hierarchy. "The psychological toll of being a Black woman and the difficulties this presents in reaching political consciousness and doing political work can never be underestimated," they wrote. "There is a very low value placed upon Black women's psyches in this society, which is both racist and sexist. As an early group member once said, 'We are all damaged people merely by virtue of being Black women.' We are dispossessed psychologically and on every other level."

But this cage of oppression also contained the key. The program of revolution could begin with an excavation of personal complexes, pathologies, and traumas, which can be transformed into emotional weapons, using the status of the oppressed as a means of establishing credibility and a method of organizing resistance. "This focusing upon our own oppression is embodied in the concept of identity politics," they wrote, coining the phrase that would devour American politics for the next half century. "We believe that the most profound and potentially most radical politics come directly out of our own identity."

The Combahee River Collective's goals were unoriginal: they proposed the old tripartite solution of anti-capitalism, anti-racism, and anti-patriarchy. But their means were revolutionary.

The activists eschewed the masculine inclinations toward violence, system-building, physical power, and the seizure of the means of production, and created a uniquely feminine program that marshalled identity, emotion, trauma, and psychological manipulation in service of their political objectives. The Combahee Statement recast left-wing politics as an identity-based, therapeutic pursuit. The language of the document is strikingly modern: the reconceptualization of the activist organization as "an emotional support group"; sentences that legitimize themselves with "as Black women" or "as Black feminists"; gratuitous capitalization of identity markers such as Black and Lesbian; embarrassing neologisms such as "herstory" instead of "history"; emotional references to "pain," "joy," and "sisterhood"; venomous hostility toward white women in particular.[7]

Despite its shortcomings,[8] the Combahee Statement is a triumphant document: a declaration of independence from "white male rule," using a vocabulary and a method of argumentation that would become commonplace in every corner of American society.[9]

The next objective in Davis's project of rationalization was to demolish the founding myths of the United States, which, she believed, would create a predicate for subverting the institutions that maintained the system of racial domination.

Davis's comrade Eldridge Cleaver outlined the intentions of this gambit in a provocative prison essay, "The White Race and Its Heroes," in which he argued that, by the late 1960s, the left-wing effort to revise American history had already drawn blood. Americans, Cleaver said, could no longer look back to Washington, Jefferson, Hamilton, and Lincoln with a sense of innocent patriotism. Their old champions had been exposed as a lineup of criminals; the past had been untethered from the present and could no longer serve as the national myth.

"What has suddenly happened is that the white race has lost its heroes," Cleaver wrote. "The new generations of whites, appalled by the sanguine and despicable record carved over the face of the globe by their race in the last five hundred years, are rejecting the panoply of white heroes, whose heroism consisted in erecting the inglorious edifice of colonialism and imperialism; heroes whose careers rested on a system of foreign and domestic exploitation, rooted in the myth of white supremacy and the manifest destiny of the white race."[10]

Cleaver understood the power of establishing a mythical void. He declared that the great figures of American life—the Founding Fathers who had established the Republic in the name of life, liberty, and the pursuit of happiness—had "acquired new names" and been reduced to a sequence of "slave-catchers, slaveowners, murderers, butchers, invaders, oppressors."[11] Suddenly, Americans who sang the national anthem or stood for the pledge of allegiance began to experience a stirring of doubt. "The racist conscience of America"[12] was beginning to break through the protective layers of denial and hypocrisy.

Cleaver had realized that every society has a pantheon of heroes and, if the radicals could tear it down, the pain would become unbearable and men would rush to find new heroes to replace them. "That growing numbers of white youth are repudiating their heritage of blood and taking people of color as their heroes and models is a tribute not only to their insight but to the resilience of the human spirit," he wrote. "For today the heroes of the initiative are people not usually thought of as white: Fidel Castro, Che Guevara, Kwame Nkrumah, Mao Tse-tung . . . Ho Chi Minh, Stokely Carmichael, W. E. B. Du Bois, James Forman, Chou En-lai."[13]

Davis advanced the same line of attack, presenting slavery as the infinite crucible out of which the United States could never escape. Beginning in her first lectures at UCLA, Davis presented the Founding Fathers as the embodiment of evil, securing their own freedom at the expense of another. "One cannot fail to conjure up the image of Thomas Jefferson and the other so-called Founding Fathers formulating the noble concepts of the Constitution of the United States while their slaves were living in misery," she said.[14]

Even Abraham Lincoln, the Great Emancipator, could not escape this critique. "Lincoln did not free the slaves," she said years later.[15] "Many people are under the impression that it was Abraham Lincoln who played the major role, and he did as a matter of fact help to accelerate the move toward abolition, but it was the decision on the part of slaves to emancipate themselves and to join the Union Army—both women and men—that was primarily responsible for the victory over slavery."[16]

Moreover, Davis claimed, the regime that Lincoln established through the Emancipation Proclamation and the Thirteenth Amendment, which formally abolished slavery, was not an attempt to fulfill the promise of the Declaration of Independence, but a duplicitous scheme to perpetuate the slave system through other means, most notably the prison system. America moved from the "prison of slavery to the slavery of prison," which was designed to control blacks through the demonstration that "incarceration and penal servitude were their possible fate."

According to Davis, the progression of American history was not the incremental realization of American ideals. It was the extension of the slave system, using subtler methods. Washington and Jefferson brought the slave state into being. Lincoln transformed it into "a totalitarian effort to control black labor in the post-Emancipation era."[17] Meanwhile, modern America remained trapped in "the myth that the mid-twentieth-century civil rights movement freed the second-class citizens."[18]

As with Cleaver, Davis's gambit was to strike at the origins of the nation's historical memory, to expose its deepest principles as a pack of lies, and to break apart the cultural foundations that ensure its continuity. She understood that to change a nation's metaphors is to have enormous power over its future. After establishing the premise of American evil, she hoped, the public would be ready to enact its conclusion.

This is the endpoint of Angela Davis's ideological formula: "abolition." If one accepts that the United States is rooted in slavery and oppression, and that modern-day black Americans play the role of "neo-slaves," the only just and reasonable solution is to abolish the social, economic, and political conditions that brought it into being.

It was a shrewd choice of language. By changing the metaphor from "revolution" to "abolition," Davis was able to wrap her political program in the moral authority of the historical abolitionists while continuing to push for the same left-wing vision. The branding of the campaign changed, but the substance remained the same.

The original *foco* of the abolitionist program was the carceral system. In the 1960s and '70s, Davis and Cleaver pursued this policy at human scale.

Davis rallied outside prisons to free a revolving lineup of "political prisoners" and worked with the radicals who led the Marin courthouse siege. Cleaver, meanwhile, stood in front of the crowds and called for emptying the prisons altogether. "I call for the freedom of even those who are so alienated from society that they hate everybody. Cats who tattoo on their chest, 'Born to Hate,' 'Born to Lose' . . . 'Born to Kill,'" he shouted.[19] "Turn them over to the Black Panther Party. Give them to us. We will redeem them from the promises made by the Statue of Liberty that were never fulfilled."[20]

Cleaver's soldiers in the Black Liberation Army put this rhetoric into action. They sent an amphibious escape team to break their comrades out of New York City's Rikers Island jail and tried to cut through the steel doors of the Manhattan House of Detention with an acetylene torch.[21] Later, they succeeded in liberating BLA leader Assata Shakur by smuggling three handguns into New Jersey's Clinton Correctional Facility for Women, holding two guards hostage and escaping in a getaway car.[22]

In retrospect, these tactics seem preposterous, from another era. But the primitive logic of the jailbreak did not disappear with the collapse of the black radical movement—it merely changed shape. The radicals had lost their faith in the lumpenproletariat holding makeshift knives to the throats of prison guards. Instead, they moved the fight onto the respectable terrain of the intelligentsia and reconceptualized their movement in theoretical terms. The prison escape became "criminal justice reform." The act of revolt became "racial justice."

In the hands of the intellectuals, the prison, once the physical recruiting ground for the Black Panther Party, became the metaphor for the broader society and the justification for its destruction.

If anything, the shift from concrete to abstract made the abolitionist program even more ambitious. Davis and her comrades began to call not for the release of individual criminals, but for the abolition of the entire system. "There are vast numbers of people behind bars in the United States—some two and a half million—and imprisonment is increasingly used as a strategy of deflection of the underlying social problems—racism, poverty, unemployment, lack of education," Davis explained.[23] "At this moment in the history of the US I don't think that there can be policing without racism. I don't think that the criminal justice system can operate without racism. Which is to say that if we want to imagine the possibility of a society without racism, it has to be a society without prisons."[24] And once the prisons are eliminated, she believed, the other institutions would follow.

All of this was happening in the shadows. While most Americans considered the black nationalist revolution a dead letter, its leading figures were busy revising their ideology and creating a new ground for revolt. From academia, Angela Davis devised a new formula that transformed the movement's violent impulses into a comprehensive academic theory. All they needed was a method of legitimation—and a new basis for rebuilding their power.

* * *

After the disintegration of their movement during the Nixon years, the black radicals converged on a new strategy: the long march through the universities.

Angela Davis, Eldridge Cleaver, and the Black Panther Party had shaped this movement from the very beginning. In the late 1960s, Davis and Cleaver had both secured teaching positions in the University of California system, despite the efforts of Governor Reagan and the Board of Regents. Davis was a full-time professor, while Cleaver was engaged by UC Berkeley to teach a one-time course called Social Analysis 139X, which christened the birth of the university's "Black Experience" program and served as an initial model for black studies departments, which would soon be established across the country.[25]

At Berkeley, Cleaver lectured on the "roots of racism" and, although he refrained from using his signature expletives, delighted left-wing students with pugnacious rhetoric and situated violence as an element of political expression.[26] "Robbery, Rape, Political Organizing, Escaping, Rebellion, Murder," he wrote on the blackboard.[27]

That same year, Cleaver told students at UCSD and UCLA that their education would have to be demolished down to the foundations.[28] "We have to close the book on every page of American history up until this moment because it is all written in blood, in corruption, in inhumanity, and there are no guidelines to guide us to the future," he said. "The incidents are there, the history is there, but it's not the history of the people. It's the history of the pigs, for the pigs, by the pigs."

The solution, according to Cleaver, was to dust off the books of Karl

Marx—"A smart, smart cat"—and apply the "universal principles of socialism" to the American regime, using any means necessary. "The people have no need to stand in fear and trembling of public servants," he said. "You can kill us, but you'll have to sneak up on us because if you shoot at us, we are going to shoot back."[29]

After gaining this initial foothold, the black radical movement sought to convert the universities into a more durable power center. Rather than individual professorships and one-off lectures, they wanted their own departments, their own curricula, and their own academic programs, which could legitimize and promote black nationalist ideology.

Their first target was San Francisco State University.

In the late 1960s, Cleaver and his comrades in the Black Panther Party helped students at SF State organize as the Black Student Union and the Third World Liberation Front, a nod to the Marxist-Leninist guerrillas in Africa, Asia, and Latin America. These groups hosted rallies, fought with police, occupied campus buildings, went on strike, and released a list of demands to administrators, including the creation of a permanent School of Ethnic Studies, the hiring of fifty left-wing professors, automatic admission for minority students, and the retention of the Black Panther Party's minister of education, George Murray, as a faculty member for minority students.[30]

From the outside, Cleaver rallied students with a call to resist "bone-nosed Nixon, all those jive-assed Regents, [and] all the equivocating pigs of the power structure that need to be in the penitentiary or up against the wall."[31] He told them they needed a "a new history book" that "recognizes that there is a cultural revolution going on in this country."[32]

The campaign was remarkably successful. Within a few years, the coalition opened a student-led Experimental College and, through an agreement with the administration following the strike, secured automatic admission for nonwhite students and established the nation's first ethnic studies and black studies programs, with courses such as "History of the Third World," "Sociology of Black Oppression," and "Black Nationalism."[33]

From the outset, these programs were shaped by the activism and ideology of the Black Panther Party, which skillfully used inside-outside pressure tactics to muscle the universities into submission. "The Black Panthers were a tremendous influence on what happened at San Francisco State, with many of the members of the Black Student Union being early members of the party," explained Jason Ferreira, the current chair of SF State's Race and Resistance Studies Department. "So there's an intimate relationship between the [Black Student Union] and the Black Panther Party."[34]

This movement to connect black nationalist ideology with administrative power in the universities spread rapidly from the campus of San Francisco State.

By the mid-1970s, there were upwards of five hundred black studies programs in universities across the country. Activists had established the technique and replicated it everywhere.[35] As the sociologist Fabio Rojas has documented, once the black militants had realized their campaign for guerrilla warfare was doomed, they shifted with full force to a strategy of institutional capture. "The black studies movement is an example of a social movement targeting bureaucracies," Rojas writes. "The black studies movement proponents clearly understood that inside the university system would allow them to project their message. Using sociologist Ed Shils's phrasing, activists thought 'the power of the ruling class derives from its incumbency of its central institutional system' and acted to appropriate some of that power for themselves."[36]

These departments, however, were not models of academic rigor.[37] According to the black scholar Shelby Steele, who had once worked in the movement to establish black studies departments, the programs were filled were "crooks" and "hustlers" who were more interested in obtaining lucrative sinecures than in doing meaningful academic work. Steele describes a vivid cast of characters that populated the new departments: a street hustler driving to campus in a brand-new Mercedes-Benz; a program administrator who was functionally illiterate but could play the manipulation game; a virulently racist department director who slandered whites as cold, sadistic "ice people."

But the universities, captured by a spirit of "white guilt," rushed to meet their demands. "I came to see that we had no future that way. That we had no respect, we had no methodology, we had no discipline," Steele recalled. "I came to see very quickly that this was an avenue for minorities to gain the economic security of the university professorship. They had no real credentials, so their argument became 'You have to hire me to do this because I'm black.'"[38]

Today, the discipline of black studies has been universalized: 91 percent of public universities have black studies programs and 42 percent have solidified them into full-time academic departments.[39] The black liberation movement may have disintegrated, but over time its ideology has been softened, adapted, and absorbed into the academic bureaucracy.

The concepts for these departments were ready-made. The Combahee River Collective had codified the theory of "identity politics."[40] Black Panther leader Stokely Carmichael had created the concept of "institutional racism."[41] Huey Newton and Eldridge Cleaver had popularized the concept of the "white power structure."[42] Angela Davis popularized the phrases "police brutality," "social inequities," "disproportionate representation," and "prison-industrial complex."[43] Her mentor Herbert Aptheker coined the term "anti-racism."[44] Over the decades, this language escaped from the pages of the *Black Panther* newsletter and the BLA communiqué and legitimized itself through the organs of prestige knowledge-formation.

This set of once-radical ideas has now achieved intellectual mass. The academic journal databases yield 609,000 results for "identity politics," 107,000 results for "anti-racism," 92,000 results for "institutional racism," 72,000 results for "black power," 18,000 results for "prison-industrial complex," 11,000 results for "white power structure," and 4,000 results for "prison abolition."[45] And the popular newspapers and magazines have adopted this language wholesale. The *New York Times* now speaks of the "white power structure." The *Washington Post* contemplates "institutional racism." *Vanity Fair* puffs itself for "prison abolition."[46]

But there is a question that looms underneath the language of the Left: What do they want?

The original black nationalists made their demands explicit: the violent overthrow of the United States; the establishment of a new Marxist-Leninist regime; the execution of law enforcement officers; the creation of a black ethnostate in the American South called the Republic of New Afrika.[47] These elaborate fantasies were ultimately unsustainable. The urban guerrillas' *foco* theory was pulverized by events. Their brightly colored *bubas* and *dashikis* have passed with the change of fashion. Nevertheless, after shedding the trappings of political extremism and symbolic excess, the central preoccupations of the original movement have survived.

In fact, they are more powerful than ever. The demands of the Third

World Liberation Front have become the reality in nearly all of the public universities. The prison breaks and calls for mass decarceration have been formalized as "criminal justice reform." The theory of identity politics has permanently changed left-wing activism.

This transition from "black power to black studies" is best understood as a process of rationalization. The second generation of activists and intellectuals learned from the failures of the past and worked to gain influence within the established institutions. They now wear business casual instead of tribal robes and submit travel reimbursements rather than ransom demands. But the basic ideology, having passed through the process of rationalization, is strikingly consistent over time. When Huey Newton and Eldridge Cleaver laid out the Black Panthers' Ten-Point Program, they demanded affirmative action, universal basic income, racialist ideology in schools, an expansive welfare state, and that the black criminal, once derided as part of "the scum layer of society," become the new moral center.

This remains the functioning ideology of the black studies movement and has been absorbed into the legislative agenda of the Democratic Party's progressive wing. "In many ways, the demands of the BPP's Ten-Point Program are just as relevant—or perhaps even more relevant—as during the 1960s, when they were first formulated," Angela Davis reminisced in 2014. "I think of the Black Power movement—or what we referred to at the time as the Black liberation movement—as a particular moment in the development of the quest for Black freedom."[48]

In one sense, the movement has achieved its goals. The United States has created a sprawling welfare state, with massive outlays for jobs, housing, health, education, and direct support. The universities have installed affirmative action and racialist pedagogy as key pillars of their administrative programs. The largest public school districts have created policies and curricula to advance "anti-racism."[49] Blue cities have turned the black criminal into an object of moral reverence and begun the process of "decarceration, decriminalization, and depolicing."[50]

The goal of substantive equality, however, has remained elusive. The black radicals might have captured the institutions, but they have not yet overturned the basic structures of society.[51]

In a speech at Birkbeck, University of London, in 2013, Davis acknowledged this deficit, reading out the items of the Black Panther

Party's Ten-Point Program and reminding students that it still represented the unfinished work of the revolution. "Number one was 'We want freedom.' Two, full employment. Three, an end to the robbery by the capitalists of our Black and oppressed communities—it was anticapitalist!" Davis exclaimed. "We want an immediate end to police brutality. . . . We want freedom for all Black and oppressed people now held in US federal, state, county, city, and military prisons and jails. . . . We want land, bread, housing, education, clothing, justice, peace, and people's community control of modern technology."[52]

The demands had never changed. The radicals wanted to realize Marcuse's utopia. They wanted to create a world beyond scarcity, abolishing not only racism but the constraints of human nature itself.

The students at Birkbeck could see that Davis was growing old. She had retired from UC Santa Cruz a few years earlier.[53] Her voice had lost the forceful staccato that had characterized her earlier speeches. She contained the entire dialectical transformation within the progression of her own life, from her first demonstration in support of Lumumba-Zapata College at UCSD to the disappointments of the subsequent decades.

But still she believed. She saw the revolution waiting for her at long last. And she was searching for the spark.

CHAPTER 8

BLM

The Revolution Reborn

T he black liberation movement, which had been left for dead in the Nixon era, was reborn in the new millennium with the founding of Black Lives Matter.

The rhetoric, the ambitions, and even the acronym of the movement are identical: although the media and corporate public relations departments have framed the Black Lives Matter movement as an extension of the civil rights movement, the ideology of the organization is, in truth, more in line with the revolutionaries of the Black Panther Party, the Black Liberation Army, and the Marxist-Leninist black liberation movement more broadly. As Black Lives Matter cofounder Alicia Garza summarized it: "BLM, BLM"[1]—in other words, the black liberation movement and Black Lives Matter are one and the same.

And Angela Davis, then as now, is their lodestar.

"Professor Angela Y. Davis—philosopher, Marxist, and former Black Panther whose work on prisons, abolition, and Black struggle has proven relevant over time—has informed our movements and communities for decades," explained BLM cofounder Patrisse Cullors in the *Harvard Law Review*. In fact, as Cullors's essay reveals, the theory and praxis of Black Lives Matter is a basic recapitulation of the Angela Davis oeuvre, beginning with its sweeping historical claims from "the transatlantic slave trade through the prison industrial complex" and calls to "destabilize, deconstruct, and demolish oppressive systems," including prisons, policing, borders, and immigration enforcement.

Likewise, BLM's policy agenda is a simple reprise of the Black Panther Party's Ten-Point Program, demanding "financial restitution, land redistribution, political self-determination, culturally relevant education programs, language recuperation, and the right to return."[2]

The links between the two movements are not merely theoretical—they are deeply personal. Angela Davis herself served as a mentor to Black Lives Matter leaders, sharing the stage with BLM founders Cullors and Garza, making appearances at BLM rallies, and raising the Black Power fist in support of BLM protestors.[3] Cullors spent a year studying Marx, Lenin, and Mao with former Weather Underground member Eric Mann,[4] who described his Labor Community Strategy Center as the "Harvard of revolutionary graduate schools," teaching students how to "take this country away from the white settler state, take this country away from imperialism and have an anti-racist, anti-imperialist and anti-fascist revolution."[5]

The new movement has also absorbed the lessons of the Combahee River Collective Statement and Angela Davis's *Women, Race & Class*, using identity, subjectivity, and emotion as political weapons.

Cullors and Garza have used their status as queer black women to mobilize the entire constellation of oppressed identities. In her *Harvard Law Review* manifesto, Cullors elaborates on her personal trauma—struggling with her brother's mental illness, enduring abuse at the hands of her transgender partner, undergoing "bouts of post-traumatic stress disorder" that led to emotional breakdowns—and projects these personal pathologies onto society, condemning it as racist, oppressive, and cruel.[6] She marshals the language of the therapeutic for political ends, and demands that the society she denounces as evil provide healing and care.

Davis, who came out as a lesbian in 1997 and acknowledged that the movement had failed to include the full range of gender identities in the past, put her stamp of approval on this new, finely tuned form of identity politics.[7] Black lives matter, she told activists in St. Louis, because "Black Women Matter, Black Girls Matter, Black Gay Lives Matter, Black Bi Lives Matter, Black Boys Matter, Black Queer Lives Matter, Black Men Matter, Black Lesbians Matter, Black Trans Lives Matter, Black Immigrants Matter, Black Incarcerated Lives Matter."[8]

If anything, BLM can be best understood as a synthesis of the major lines of the black liberation movement—the racialist dialectic of Angela Davis, the identity-first orientation of the Combahee River Collective, the Marxist-Leninist vision of the Black Panther Party—resurrected for the digital age.

The great coup of BLM was to secure the acceptance of the prestige institutions, but its philosophy, its aesthetic, and its ambitions are unchanged from the earliest days. Fifty years ago, the urban guerrillas of the Black Liberation Army summarized their ideology in a simple formula: "We are anti-capitalist, anti-imperialist, anti-racist, and anti-sexist"; "we must of necessity strive for the abolishment of these systems"; "in order to abolish our system of oppression we must utilize the science of class struggle."[9] The same logic underpins the philosophy of Black Lives Matter. "It's not possible for a world to emerge where black lives matter if it's under capitalism," said Garza, "and it's not possible to abolish capitalism without a struggle against national oppression and gender oppression."[10]

Davis, who had patiently built the intellectual framework for the rebirth of the black liberation movement, put her faith in Black Lives Matter. "I could clearly see that Patrisse and her comrades were pushing Black and left, including feminist and queer, movements to a new and more exciting level, as they seriously wrestled with contradictions that had plagued these movements for many generations," she wrote. "They recognize that universal freedom is an ideal best represented not by those who are already at the pinnacle of racial, gender, and class hierarchies but rather by those whose lives are most defined by conditions of unfreedom and by ongoing struggles to extricate themselves from those conditions."[11]

The dream is still the same dream. Alicia Garza, the BLM cofounder, has adopted as the movement's motto the old chant of Assata Shakur, the Black Liberation Army soldier who was convicted of murdering a police officer and then fled to Cuba after escaping from prison. "When I use Assata's powerful demand in my organizing work, I always begin by sharing where it comes from, sharing about Assata's significance to the Black Liberation Movement, what it's [sic] political purpose and message is, and why it's important in our context," Garza explains.[12]

The chant provides the movement with a political North Star: the sense of forming the conscience of the black proletariat, the commitment to violence as a method of liberation, and a reference to the closing line of *The Communist Manifesto*. "There is, and always will be, until every Black man, woman, and child is free, a Black Liberation Army," Garza reads. "We must defend ourselves and let no one disrespect us. We must gain our liberation by any means necessary. It is our duty to fight for our freedom. It is our duty to win. We must love each other and support each other. We have nothing to lose but our chains."[13]

After its years in the wilderness, the black liberation movement was ready again. They had bided their time in academia and built a new street movement with a more sophisticated message. "We do this work today because on another day work was done by Assata Shakur, Angela Davis, [and] the Black Panther Party," said Cullors.[14]

For this new work to succeed, they needed to lay down a new predicate for revolution.

*   *   *

The great innovation of Black Lives Matter was not political, but linguistic. They did not change the content—anti-racism, anti-capitalism, anti-patriarchy, anti-imperialism—they changed the presentation.

The best way to understand BLM is as a delivery mechanism for Black Panther ideology, passed through a filter of marketing language that makes it palatable to American elites. Just as Marcuse and the critical theorists traded the word "revolution" for the more benign "liberation," the new radicals have wrapped black liberation ideology in the vocabulary of euphemism and social science. They no longer pledge to unleash the "black urban guerrilla" and commit "revolutionary executions."[15] They condemn abstractions such as "systemic racism" and commit to "racial justice." Even the movement's eponymous slogan, Black Lives Matter, follows this shift in tone: the leaders of BLM self-consciously abandoned the masculine notion of Black Power in favor of a more feminine notion of human meaning, which creates a sympathetic, rather than confrontational, frame.

The objective of this approach is to create a new political narrative that legitimizes their ideology and leads automatically to their conclusions. The Black Lives Matter activists have built their argument to orchestrate a precise cascade of human emotions, shocking the conscience with examples of "police brutality," abstracting those rare but salient events as "systemic racism," and leading the public to the morally unopposable cause of "abolition."

The first step in the process is to create the emotional preconditions for their argument. As the Black Panther Party had learned when it was still a small street gang in Oakland, the best recruiting tool for the movement is to whip up anger against the police. And for Black Lives Matter, this method has become even more powerful. Activists now have mobile phone or bodycam video for nearly every police shooting, which can be edited for maximum emotional impact and replicated across social media at a cost and scale that was unimaginable five decades ago.

The media then sears the violent images into the minds of the public and BLM activists read out litanies of the dead—"Say their names"—to establish their moral position and elicit a response in the broader population.[16]

The underlying technique is to drop an emotional anchor with each news cycle and to introduce a closed linguistic universe that can help shape the sequence of events that follows. Unlike their counterparts of the past, Cullors, Garza, and Black Lives Matter leaders seek to engage the emotions of guilt and shame rather than anger and fear, adopting a therapeutic rather than militant tone. The goal is no longer to rouse the fury of the black lumpenproletariat, a strategy that proved to be self-destructive, but to arouse the sentiments of the professional class, including the stratum of liberal white women who now command powerful administrative positions in corporations, philanthropies, universities, and schools, and often mimic the rituals first created by activists.

After a few years of conditioning, most prominently around the police shooting of Michael Brown in Ferguson, Missouri, this technique paid dividends. Affluent suburban women and Fortune 100 executives began speaking the same sanitized language of the activist class, genuflecting to Black Lives Matter, repeating the names of the dead, and posting a black square on social media to pay homage to the movement.

The next step in the process is abstraction, moving from individual incident to general principle. This is the work of theory. In the early days, Angela Davis, Eldridge Cleaver, and the Black Liberation Army identified specific, flesh-and-blood enemies. They made a direct connection between the problem of police brutality and the solution of "killing the pigs." But this approach was a dead end.

The next generation of activists shifted to a more sophisticated strategy. They used individual incidents of police brutality as proof of the existence of "systemic racism." The enemy was no longer the individual police officer, but an abstraction that implicates the entire society. The professional-class activists realized that they didn't need to engage in the messy business of stalking and assassinating NYPD detectives. Instead they could publish reports, replete with color-coded statistical illustrations, that demanded society-wide changes.

Davis had established the basic contours of this approach during her campaign to free the Soledad Brothers in the 1970s. She used the emotional anchor technique, presenting the inmates as "political prisoners" who needed to be saved from "Legal Lynching."[17] But Davis also marshalled the theoretical perspective, assigning the plight of the Soledad Brothers to "the racism securely interwoven in the capitalist fabric of this society"[18] and pointing out that blacks represented 15 percent of the population but 30 percent of those in prison, which, she claimed, was prima facie evidence of institutional racism.[19]

Fifty years later, Black Lives Matter and its allies have perfected the technique. The media lionizes criminal figures such as Michael Brown, who was shot and killed after attacking a police officer and attempting to seize his gun,[20] and Jacob Blake, who was shot after resisting arrest and brandishing a knife.[21] Meanwhile, activists within the universities pump out reams of statistical data, stripped of all confounding variables, that appear to corroborate the narrative of widespread racism. Never mind that the Soledad Brothers, or their modern equivalents such as Brown and Blake, were hardly innocent victims, or that disparities in criminality can explain disparities in incarceration.[22]

Those objections can be brushed aside. The activists had created a narrative weapon that could absorb any incident into its totalizing structure—and they intended to use it.

The final point in the process is the movement's eternal destination: revolution. Since Marcuse, the neo-Marxist theoreticians have tried to divine the phases of American history, grumbling at each other whether the United States was in a pre-revolutionary or anti-revolutionary condition. Marcuse ended his life despairing about the failure of revolutionary politics; Angela Davis and the founders of Black Lives Matter are more optimistic. "Black Lives Matter has always been about much more than police or vigilante violence. . . . It's been about the fact that black people deserve a revolution," said cofounder Garza.[23] "I am very optimistic about Black Power and what I work to do every single day is to train our communities how to wield it."[24]

In a sense, the intellectual and symbolic preconditions had already been set. By 2016, the movement had turned its loaded premise—emotional anchor, statistical rationalization, abstract enemy—into conventional wisdom. Even Davis, reflecting on the progress of Black Lives Matter, admitted some astonishment at how far the language of the revolution had come. "'Structural racism,' 'white supremacy,' all of these terms that have been used for decades in the ranks of our movements have now become a part of popular discourse," Davis told reporters.[25]

She is right. The old vocabulary of the Black Panther Party has become the new vocabulary of the *New York Times*. Between 2010 and 2020, the paper's usage of terms such as "structural racism," "white supremacy," "police brutality," and "antiracism" has exploded.[26] The *Times*, as the guardian of the liberal consensus, accomplished what the Weather Underground and the Black Panther Party could not: persuade millions of Americans that the United States is a white supremacist nation that systematically exploits blacks and other minorities.

According to the Pew Research Center, that narrative has been cemented into the Democratic mind. In 2009, only 32 percent of Democrats believed that racism in the United States was a "big problem"; by 2017, that number had more than doubled to 76 percent.[27]

This dramatic change in public perception seems self-contradictory. Racism, by almost any measure, has declined in the United States from the days of the Black Panther Party. The laws have guaranteed equal treatment since the passage of the civil rights legislation of the mid-1960s. Racist attitudes among whites dropped precipitously following that time period, with virtually no opposition to interracial marriage, integrated schools, and integrated neighborhoods by the mid-1990s.[28] Police killings of black men decreased by 72 percent between 1965 and 2005[29]—and the absolute numbers obscure the fact that the vast majority of these incidents are in response to deadly threats and, therefore, justifiable.[30] Finally, in 2008, the United States elected its first black president, Barack Obama, which, at the time, was heralded as a racial watershed.

But instead of ushering in a new era of racial reconciliation, the country plunged into racial retrograde. According to Gallup, from 2001 to 2013, approximately 70 percent of adults rated black-white relations positively.[31] Then, as the Black Lives Matter narrative began building influence in response to a series of high-profile police shootings, it suddenly collapsed. By 2021, the number of Americans with a positive assessment of race relations plummeted to 42 percent. Among African-Americans, the number fell from 66 percent to 33 percent—the lowest share on record.

The evidence suggests that the Black Lives Matter narrative has succeeded in capturing the American consciousness, and that perception has become stronger than reality.

In 2021, the Skeptic Research Center conducted a survey asking Americans how many unarmed black men they believed were killed by police in 2019. The majority of self-described "very liberal" respondents estimated that the number was at least 1,000, with one-fifth of those respondents estimating that the number was at least 10,000. Even among self-described "moderate" voters, more than one-quarter believed that the police had killed at least 1,000 unarmed black men over the course of the year.[32]

The real number, according to the *Washington Post* database of fatal police shootings, was 14—one-tenth of 1 percent of the highest estimates from the "very liberal" respondents.[33]

In other words, the Black Lives Matter narrative, which had raised the specter of state genocide against blacks,[34] was able to create a free-floating perception that served the movement's political ambitions, even as it became untethered from the facts. The purpose, however, is not accuracy—it is activism. The movement has self-consciously built its support among the 15 percent of Democratic Party voters who describe themselves as "very liberal" and are most amenable to the catastrophic narrative.[35] This is not a trivial faction. It represents more than 7 million American citizens who are committed to politics and bought into the line that the police are systematically murdering unarmed black men on an industrial scale.

For this group, the three-part formula—anchor, rationalization, enemy—proved to be a powerful feedback loop. Every headline reinforced the emotional response. Every op-ed in the *Times* strengthened the movement's mythology. They believed that "white supremacy" is not a metaphor from the past, but an urgent, concrete reality in contemporary America. These are the men and women, predominantly young, white, and highly educated, who are ready to hit the streets.[36]

Following the steadily increasing anxieties of the post-Obama years, they were ready to explode.

*　　*　　*

The fuse was lit on May 25, 2020.

That evening in Minneapolis, Minnesota, a white police officer named Derek Chauvin arrested a black man named George Floyd on suspicion of using counterfeit currency to purchase cigarettes. Floyd, who had a long rap sheet including trespassing, theft, drug possession, and holding a gun to the stomach of a young woman during a home invasion robbery, was acting erratically and asked the officers to lay him on the ground.[37] Chauvin restrained him with a knee to the neck, as Floyd repeatedly told him, "I can't breathe," and then "I'm about to die."[38]

Chauvin did not relent. He kept the pressure on Floyd's neck and, after a gruesome nine and a half minutes, Floyd lost consciousness. He was pronounced dead shortly thereafter.

The killing, which was photographed by onlookers who repeatedly warned the officers that Floyd was in serious distress, sent shock waves through the country. It was the perfect confirmation of the narrative loop established by Black Lives Matter activists over the previous five years: a white police officer extinguishing the life of a poor black man, in full view of the public—brutally, senselessly, without remorse.

The night after Floyd's death, the protests began. First, activists in Minneapolis marched through the streets, threw rocks and bottles at the police, and vandalized the Third Precinct police station.[39] Then they began looting retail stores and burning down entire city blocks.[40] By the following month, protests had erupted in all fifty states, unleashing a wave of riots, violence, and destruction.

The chaos presented an opportunity for a loose but powerful network of left-wing militant organizations. Prior to the riots, the FBI had released a report warning about the rise of "Black Identity Extremists" modeled on the Black Liberation Army. These radicals "have historically justified and perpetrated violence against law enforcement, which they perceived as representative of the institutionalized oppression of African Americans," the Bureau warned.[41] They had not targeted law enforcement officers for decades, but following the death of Michael Brown in 2014, they initiated a three-year violence spree. One extremist ambushed and killed five police officers in Dallas. Another ambushed and shot six cops in Baton Rouge. A third attacked four officers in New York City with a hatchet, promising "mass revolt" against "the oppressors."[42]

In addition, the George Floyd riots provided an entry point for predominantly white anarcho-socialist groups, which used the ongoing disorder to promote their message and attack the symbols of the state. According to a report by the Network Contagion Research Institute at Rutgers, these "anti-fascist," or Antifa, militias used decentralized online communications to recruit new members and organize violent protests. The militant groups, which resemble the Weather Underground movement from the previous era, used digital propaganda to mobilize on-the-ground units in cities such as Seattle and Portland, Oregon, where they laid siege to public buildings, fought against law enforcement, and vandalized private and public property, including historical statues.[43]

Their materials are reminiscent of the old *Prairie Fire* manifesto: the glorification of "revolutionary" violence, photographs of members armed to the teeth, illustrations of pigs with captions urging followers to "kill" and "murder" the police. Their aesthetic, too, is self-consciously derived from the radical movements of the 1960s. The Antifa-affiliated groups photograph themselves in guerrilla training camps, create block prints of Karl Marx and Kalashnikov rifles, and use the old lexicon of the underground, promising to unleash a "revolution" against the "predatory state" and its "fascist hooligans."[44]

At the tactical level, the new white militant groups organized themselves into autonomous cells, or "network-enabled mobs," with an intricate division of labor. There are "shield soldiers," "range soldiers," "medics," "fire squads," "copwatches," "barricaders," "frontliners," "designers," and "online comms" teams.[45]

This is a notable advancement. In 1969, the Weather Underground attempted to rouse the masses in Chicago during the "Days of Rage," but the masses never arrived; the radicals were summarily beaten, humiliated, and arrested by police. In 2020, by contrast, the new left-wing militant groups, armed with bottles, rocks, guns, and bombs, were able to sustain more than one hundred consecutive nights of rioting and destruction in cities such as Portland, dominating the streets and putting the police on the defensive.[46]

As the National Contagion Research Institute noted: "One important feature of the network-enabled mob is its capacity to frustrate the ability of law enforcement to detect directed ideological attacks. A core group of actors are able to mobilize lawlessness and violence. If it becomes wide-spread, the network-enabled mob enables a structure capable of adaptation and evolution especially if it reappears over consecutive days of unrest."[47] The result, according to law enforcement agencies, is that these decentral-ized left-wing groups have initiated an "ongoing low grade insurgency with targeted, ideological attacks by anti-government extremists."[48]

As the rioting spread, it seemed that Marcuse's old two-part proletariat had been revived—and, under the banner of Black Lives Matter, it yielded devastation.

The George Floyd protests were the most widespread since the height of the New Left in 1968. There were more than ten thousand demonstra-tions nationwide, with protestors engaging in violence, looting, arson, and vandalism in all fifty states.[49] Police arrested more than ten thousand pro-testors and recorded twenty-five deaths connected with the unrest.[50] Riot-ers inflicted more than $2 billion in property damage—the single largest insurance loss due to civil disorder on record.[51]

The brute violence and destruction captured headlines in American newspapers, but the patterns and details of the Black Lives Matter riots reveal another layer of interpretation. The physical war was an expression of a deeper symbolic war. The individual acts of violence—the sacking of urban police stations, the Molotov cocktails thrown at police cruisers, the toppling of historical statues, the wholesale looting of big-box stores—were, in fact, the representations of a long-running cultural revolution.

The rioters were unconsciously following the formula Angela Davis had once suggested to students in her first lectures at UCLA: erase the past, demolish the present, control the future. They sought to wage war on the symbols and historical memory of the nation's founding. They vandal-ized and tore down statues of George Washington, Thomas Jefferson, and Abraham Lincoln, spray-painting "slave owner" on Jefferson and "1619" on Washington. "You're doing something by taking down this image," said one man. "I'm just raking in unemployment, so I might as well have the government pay me to dismantle themselves." The authorities, rather than defend the statues, removed them.[52]

Davis, too, saw the power of this narrative reconstruction. As the George

Floyd riots raged, she told *Vanity Fair* magazine that the street demonstrations were "rehearsals for revolution" and praised the destruction of the historical statues. "Those statues are our reminders that the history of the United States of America is a history of racism. So it's natural that people would try to bring down those symbols," she said. "If it's true that names are being changed, statues are being removed, it should also be true that the institutions are looking inward and figuring out how to radically transform themselves. That's the real work."[53]

In other words, the purpose of toppling statues was not simply to exert power in the streets, but to undermine the fundamental myths of the society—or, in the words of Eldridge Cleaver, to turn America's "white heroes" into the "arch-villains" at the root of an oppressive society.[54] When those myths are undone, they believed, the population would seek to fill the void with new ones and the revolution could finally proceed. "The protests offered people an opportunity to join in this collective demand to bring about deep change, radical change. Defund the police, abolish policing as we know it now," Davis concluded. "These are the same arguments that we've been making for such a long time about the prison system and the whole criminal justice system. It was as if all of these decades of work by so many people, who received no credit at all, came to fruition."[55]

For a stretch in the summer of 2020, the Black Lives Matter movement was able to achieve a major tactical victory: street dominance.

In city after city, BLM activists, including its paramilitaries in the black nationalist and anarcho-socialist factions, shut down urban neighborhoods, intimidated residents, and established their ideology as a social requisite. Mobs of BLM supporters marched through the streets and bullied residents and outdoor diners into submission.

In Washington, D.C., dozens of masked activists, with their fists raised in the Black Power tradition, surrounded a woman sitting at a dinner table. They chanted, "No justice, no peace," and shrieked threats within inches of her face. "Are you a Christian?" screamed one. "Raise your fucking fist!" yelled another.[56] In Pittsburgh, black protestors smashed bottles and shouted down white diners: "Fuck [the police] and fuck the white people that built the system set against mine!"[57] In New York, activists stood on top of tables and hurled invective against a white restaurant owner: "We don't want you here! We don't want your fucking taqueria! Owned by fucking white men!"[58]

In all of these cities, the mobs turned violent after sundown: looting, arson, vandalism, and destruction. As these threats escalated, national retail chains began publishing statements of loyalty to the movement and local shopkeepers hung "Black Lives Matter" placards and photographs of George Floyd in their windows—in some cases, out of conviction, but in most cases, out of fear. The message: "We submit. Please do not burn down this establishment."[59]

Meanwhile, the national media adopted the BLM line. Even at the news wires, such as Reuters, reporters mimicked the style and substance of the streets. "Michael Brown. Eric Garner. Freddie Gray," Reuters intoned. "Their names are seared into Americans' memories, egregious examples of lethal police violence that stirred protests and prompted big payouts to the victims' families."

Although some of the reports covering the first days of chaos in Minneapolis were straightforward about the violence—"Protests, Looting Erupt in Minneapolis Over Racially Charged Killing by Police," read one headline—the coverage quickly passed through a filter of ideology and euphemism as the summer progressed. The stories began to frame the unrest as a "new national reckoning about racial injustice" and to describe the protests as "mostly peaceful" or "largely peaceful," despite widespread violence, looting, and crime.

The wire's data-based reporting and "fact checks" did no better, consistently recontextualizing accurate information about racial violence and policing in order to blunt counternarratives and align its coverage with Black Lives Matter rhetoric.[60]

The climax of the riot season occurred on June 6 in Minneapolis. That afternoon, the city's progressive mayor, thirty-eight-year-old Jacob Frey, dressed in a blue and gray Henley shirt and a face mask with the slogan "I can't breathe," arrived at a demonstration in support of abolishing the police. Thousands of protestors lined the streets, with signs reading "Defend Black Lives" and "Police Abolition Now."[61]

The organizers rallied the crowd in call and response: "We are here! We won't leave! We'll build a new state! Defund MPD!" Later, the protest leaders, perched on top of a makeshift stage in the middle of the intersection, summoned Mayor Frey to their feet. The activists below, wearing matching "Stop Killing Black People" masks, surrounded him with their fists raised.[62]

"Jacob Frey, we have a yes-or-no question for you. Yes or no, will you commit to defunding Minneapolis Police Department?" they demanded, as Frey lowered his eyes. "We don't want no mo' police. Is that clear? We don't want people with guns, toting around in our community, shooting us down. You have an answer! It is a yes or a no!" thundered the black woman onstage, with the crowd roaring in a crescendo around her.

Finally, Frey, assuming the posture of a shamed child, whispered into the microphone: "I do not support the full abolition of the police."[63]

The mob erupted. "Get the fuck out of here! You wasted our time!" Then they broke into a chant—"Go home, Jacob, go home!"—and jeered at Frey as he snaked back through the crowd toward the exits. "Shame! Shame! Shame! Shame!" they shouted. "We're not here for police reform bullshit. Abolish the police, then the prisons!"[64]

The entire spectacle was loaded with symbolic significance: the elevation of the mob; the public humiliation ritual; the furious march of the dialectic. For a moment, the activists had reenacted the fabled events of the Paris Commune. They had turned the evanescent spirit of revolt into a moment of flesh. The bodies, pressed together, believed that, after burning down the Minneapolis Police Department Third Precinct, they could "build a new state" in its place.

The presence looming above it all—above the melee of the street demonstrations, above the signs and signifiers of the propaganda war, above the violence unleashed in the name of social justice—was Angela Davis.

After the death of George Floyd, Davis, at seventy-six years old, was resurrected by the press and restored to her position as the conscience of racial revolt. Her photograph graced the pages of *Time* magazine, where she was celebrated as one of the 100 Most Influential People of the year. "She dared to stand against a racist system. She's seen and witnessed it all, and she continues to inspire, educate and resist oppression," remarked one commentator.[65] "An activist. An author. A scholar. An abolitionist. A legend," gushed another.[66]

Like the Soviet news organizations in the old revolutionary time, the American media heralded the Black Lives Matter movement as a march toward liberation. Their transgressions—the burned-out shopping malls, the victims of reprisals, the dead police officers—were to be minimized, papered over, pushed aside. None could be held over the heads of BLM, which, they said, was not an organization, but a movement.

They had adopted the refrain of Assata Shakur, who, standing before a judge on charges of kidnapping and armed robbery, told the courtroom: "The Black Liberation Army is not an organisation: it goes beyond that. It is a concept, a people's movement, an idea. The concept of the BLA arose because of the political, social, and economic oppression of black people in this country. And where there is oppression, there will be resistance. The BLA is part of that resistance movement. The Black Liberation Army stands for freedom and justice for all people."[67]

As Davis had explained many decades before, the revolution would require a certain amount of violence. Back then, her comrade Jonathan Jackson carried the dog-eared and monogrammed pages of Davis's copies of *Violence and Social Change* and *The Politics of Violence* into the Marin County courthouse. Today the young radicals carry the ideas of Davis's *Autobiography* and *Women, Race & Class* into the burned-out buildings of Minneapolis, Portland, and Seattle. The concrete harms perpetrated by her followers—then as now—are subsumed into the narrative of abstract goods. When that fails, the crimes are justified as an automatic reaction to oppression.

For Davis, this was the price of progress. "I've always recognized my own role as an activist as helping to create conditions of possibility for change. And that means to expand and deepen public consciousness of the nature of racism, of heteropatriarchy, pollution of the planet, and their relationship to global capitalism," she told *Vanity Fair*. "And so there has to be a way to think about the connection among all of these issues and how we can begin to imagine a very different kind of society. That is what 'defund the police' means. That is what 'abolish the police' means."[68]

For a moment during the summer of 2020, it appeared that she could finally turn this long-stalled dream into a reality.

CHAPTER 9

Mob Rule in Seattle

The city of Seattle was ground zero for the George Floyd revolution. The spectacular looting and violence in Minneapolis and Portland might have dominated the headlines, but under the surface, activists in Seattle launched an unprecedented campaign to turn the street protests into a new political regime. They had perfected the Angela Davis–style narrative about the "prison-industrial complex," rallied thousands of militants to the streets, and made the case for overthrowing the three pillars of the traditional justice system—the police, the prisons, and the courts—and replacing them with a new conception of law and order based on the principles of social justice.

This campaign was decades in the making. In the years leading up to 2020, the city's radical-progressives had slowly gained control over the entire apparatus of local politics, from the media to the academic institutions to the philanthropic foundations to the city council to the public bureaucracy. There was, however, one notable exception: the criminal justice system. Activists believed that the police, prisons, and courts were the final remnant of an oppressive society and the last remaining bulwark against total control.

If they could dismantle the institution of criminal justice, they believed, they could finally begin to establish the new society that has escaped their grasp.

During the George Floyd protests, rather than resist, the city's political establishment joined the activist campaign to dismantle the justice system. Following the activist line, elected officials in Seattle and King County announced their intentions to simultaneously defund the Seattle Police Department, permanently close the county's largest jail, and gut the municipal court system. They made the case that traditional law enforcement should be replaced by what could be described as a "shadow justice system" of ideologically aligned nonprofit programs. They believed they could replace the carceral state with a new therapeutic state, under the assumption that, when the oppression of the justice system is lifted, the new society could be guided through psychotherapy, criminal diversion, and tribal-style justice rituals.

The theoretical underpinnings of this movement were straight from the handbook of black liberation ideology. Nikkita Oliver, the self-described "abolitionist" who became the figurehead of the movement to dismantle Seattle's justice system, self-consciously modeled her politics and aesthetics on Angela Davis, shouting to the crowds that they must join the struggle to overthrow "racialized capitalism" and smash "patriarchy, white supremacy, and classism" once and for all.[1] During the uprising of 2020, thousands of left-wing activists heeded Oliver's call, pouring into the streets, smashing store windows, and seizing control of a police precinct in the city's Capitol Hill district. For a brief moment, they established their own Paris Commune—the Capitol Hill Autonomous Zone, or CHAZ—and attempted to create a system of self-government beyond the reaches of the American oppressor.

The activists, who deemed themselves the "new abolitionists," were willing to play the dangerous game. They saw the chaos as the necessary price—and the accelerant—for their revolution. Their agenda was lifted nearly verbatim from the pages of the Black Panther Party. "Honoring the long history of abolitionist struggle," they said, "we join in their efforts to divest from the prison industrial complex, invest in our communities, and create the conditions for our ultimate vision: a world without police, where no one is held in a cage."[2]

But, unlike the Black Panther Party, which had been dissolved into history, the young revolutionaries in Seattle believed that they had the organs of the state on their side. The highest officials in the region knelt to their demands, mimicked their language, joined them at the barricades, and pledged to "defund the police" and transform the criminal justice system according to the principles of "anti-racism."

During this period, the city, it seemed, was coming apart at the seams. Crime exploded in the downtown corridor; businesses barricaded their windows; citizens started to fear that the city would collapse into prolonged disorder. Yet the activists and political class moved forward with their experiment in "abolition" at an astonishing rate of speed. They elevated a series of three commandments—"Abolish the police," "Abolish the prisons," "Abolish the courts"—into a new holy trinity. They transformed "burn it down" from a street slogan into a real political platform.

They believed their time had finally come.

*   *   *

The first commandment of the new abolitionists is to "abolish the police."

In the activist narrative, American police forces were first established to catch fugitive slaves and have served as the guardians of white supremacy ever since. As the Decriminalize Seattle Coalition has argued: "The police have never served as an adequate response to social problems. They are rooted in violence against Black people. In order to protect Black lives, this moment calls for investing and expanding our safety and well-being beyond policing."[3]

The solution, then, can never be reform: the system of policing must be demolished. During the rioting following the death of George Floyd, this line of thought gained currency with the local government. The Seattle City Council responded to activist pressure by releasing draft legislation that suggested a path for abolishing the police department and replacing it with a new civilian-led "Department of Community Safety & Violence Prevention." The plan was predicated on the idea that "institutional racism" and "underinvestment in communities of color" were the cause of crime, and, once the police department was abolished and its budget redistributed to communities of color, social workers and nonprofit organizations could keep the peace with "trauma-informed, gender-affirming, anti-racist praxis" and "the immediate transfer of underutilized public land for BIPOC community ownership"[4]—which, in effect, means government by activism.

Meanwhile, in order to increase the pressure from the outside, a roving mob of activists patrolled the streets of residential neighborhoods and paid midnight house calls to wavering public officials. The group, which called itself Every Day March, assembled groups as large as three hundred people and descended upon the personal residences of Seattle mayor Jenny Durkan, Seattle police chief Carmen Best, and nearly all of the city council members. They banged drums, chanted slogans, terrorized neighbors, and left threatening messages on the driveways and doors of their perceived enemies: "Liberate oppressed communities," "Don't be racist trash," "Guillotine Jenny."[5]

In one incident, the mob marched to the home of Councilman Andrew Lewis and roused him out of bed past midnight. When Lewis arrived at the entrance of the building, the ringleader, Tealshawn Turner, demanded that the councilman verbally commit to "defunding the police." Lewis, standing alone at the gate, was visibly frightened—and relented. He promised to cut the police budget by 50 percent, to fire officers who had citizen complaints filed against them, and to redirect millions of dollars in public funding to "communities of color." Turner, having extracted his demand, left with a threat: "If you don't keep your promise, we're for sure coming back."[6]

Despite, or perhaps because of, these threats, the government weighed in on behalf of the mob. At the same time that the demonstrators were extending their control of the streets, the city council passed legislation to deprive the police department of essential crowd control tools, such as pepper spray, tear gas, blast balls, and stun grenades.[7] In a desperate letter to residents, Chief Best warned that officers would have "no ability to safely intercede to preserve property in the midst of a large, violent crowd"[8]—in essence, announcing the potential end of law and order within the city limits.

Although the riot control ordinance was blocked by a judge hours before taking effect, one veteran police officer said the activists had adopted a bare-knuckled strategy: reduce police power enough to achieve "mob rule" in the streets, then press the politicians for more. If they could defund the police and deprive officers of crowd control weapons, they could end the state's monopoly on violence. Whenever its leaders could mobilize a large crowd, they could dominate the physical environment and establish a new standard of public order that conformed to their principles of social justice.

Incredibly, in the midst of rising street disorder and intimidation of public officials, a majority of Seattle voters supported the plan to "defund the police." In a telephone poll, more than half supported the plan to "permanently cut the Seattle Police Department's budget by 50% and shift that money to social services and community-based programs."[9]

According to sources in the police department, officers found themselves in a state of "disbelief." They were besieged on two fronts—in the streets and in the corridors of City Hall. The black-clad mobs smashed the windows of banks and storefronts with impunity, the city council voted for an initial set of budget cuts that set the stage for "abolition," and the activists successfully waged a campaign of legislative humiliation and political intimidation against Police Chief Best, who eventually resigned.

"Our leadership is in chaos," said one frontline officer. "The mayor has made a decision to let a mob of 1,000 people dictate public safety policy for a city of 750,000."[10]

* * *

The second commandment of the new abolitionists is to "abolish the prisons." This has long been a motif for radical movements, from the storming of the Bastille during the French Revolution to the jailbreak of Kresty Prison during the Russian Revolution.

In modern-day Seattle, however, the revolution is happening from within. According to a trove of leaked documents from the King County Executive's Office, during the season of George Floyd, policymakers were busy laying out the rationale for permanently closing the region's largest jail and ending all youth incarceration—including for minors charged with serious crimes such as rape and murder.

The official documents cast the prison system as an institution of "oppression based on race and built to maintain white supremacy." In a pyramid-shaped graphic, policymakers claimed that crime and incarceration were merely expressions at the "tip of the iceberg"; on a deeper level, however, the justice system is rooted in "white supremacist culture," "inequitable wealth distribution," "power hoarding," and the belief that "people of color are dangerous or to be feared." After establishing this premise, the conclusion is foregone: white supremacy cannot be reformed, it must be abolished.[11]

To this end, the King County executive, Dow Constantine, released a plan for permanently terminating youth detention and shuttering the downtown Seattle jail, which represented approximately two-thirds of the county's total jail capacity. And, contrary to the rhetoric about releasing "non-violent offenders," more than half of all inmates in the King County system are incarcerated for violent crimes—so the plan would, by simple arithmetic, release violent criminals to the streets.[12]

County corrections officers, who had not been consulted on the executive's surprise announcement, were horrified. One senior manager said that "activists [are] seeking to rewrite the narrative of society" and, if the shutdowns were to pass, "the ones who will suffer in the end are [racial minorities], as crime skyrockets and lawlessness becomes the norm." According to the manager, following the announcement, frontline correctional officers and medical staff within the jails were in a state of "chaos" and bracing for "mass layoffs."[13]

But rather than accommodate these concerns, the county executive decided it was simply the price of progress: according to the internal documents, he warned his team to expect "stress, confusion, and a sense of overwhelm" within the department, but said it should not impede the work to create a "shift in power structure" and counseled his employees to let "internal discrimination and racism come to the surface," so it could be suppressed.[14]

The question facing these officials was obvious: What will replace the jails in this new regime? The leading coalition of the progressive reform movement in the region, Budget for Justice, had an answer: the government should "transfer resources from formal justice systems to community-based care" programs that are "rooted in restorative justice practices that are trauma-informed, human rights–, and equity-based." The activists highlighted three nonprofit programs as models for the new justice system—Community Passageways, Creative Justice, and Community Justice Project—that offer programs such as "healing circles," "narrative storytelling," art-based therapy, and community organizing.[15]

All three providers share a common philosophical foundation: they are predicated on the assumption that poverty, racism, and oppression force the dispossessed into a life of crime and violence. Their programs are explicitly designed to deconstruct how "systems of power create conditions that perpetuate violence in our homes and daily lives" and help offenders "reimagine a society in which their liberation is not only possible, but sustainable by the community itself." They embodied the heart and spirit of the revolution—but were a disaster in practice and could not develop the capacity to serve as practical replacements for the "formal justice system."[16]

In one high-profile case, prosecutors diverted a youth offender named Diego Carballo-Oliveros into a "peace circle" program, in which nonprofit leaders burned sage, passed around a talking feather, and led Carballo-Oliveros through "months of self-reflection."[17] According to one corrections official with knowledge of the case, prosecutors and activists paraded Carballo-Oliveros around the city as the "shining example" of their approach.[18] However, two weeks after completing the peace circle program, Carballo-Oliveros and two accomplices lured a fifteen-year-old boy into the woods, robbed him, and then slashed open his abdomen, chest, and head with a retractable knife. The boy placed a desperate phone call to his sister and a passerby called an ambulance, but the boy bled out and later died at the hospital.[19]

Despite these public setbacks, however, County Executive Constantine plowed forward with his plan to permanently close the downtown jail and end all youth incarceration. And the activists on the outside worked to speed up the process. During the riots, they dispatched a mob to Constantine's home in the darkness of night to demand that he shut down the jail immediately. They shouted him down and shook cans of spray paint, calling on Constantine to release all youth prisoners, including minors charged with murder, because "the police are murderers all the time."

Constantine, standing under a streetlamp with his arms crossed, nodded his head blankly and tried to placate the mob.[20]

* * *

The third commandment of the new abolitionists is to "abolish the courts." In simple terms, the modern revolutionaries want to destroy the existing conception of "justice" and replace it with a new regime of "social justice."

In the historical imagination of the radical Left, American courts are not the impartial and public forum described in the Sixth Amendment, but an extension of a brutal, racist, and punitive state apparatus. In Seattle, activists have long sought to limit the scope and authority of the municipal courts. For years, influential organizations such as Budget for Justice and the Public Defender Association have advocated eliminating cash bail, decimating the probation department, reducing the number of municipal judges, and softening sex offender registration requirements—all under the rubric of "ongoing, real and progressive policy and system change."[21]

However, with the rise of the Black Lives Matter movement providing an even more favorable political ground, the activist coalition mobilized behind a much more ambitious agenda: abolishing the municipal court altogether and transferring authority to a shadow court system administered by ideologically aligned nonprofit organizations such as Law Enforcement

Assisted Diversion, or LEAD, which provides "crisis response, immediate psychosocial assessment, and long term wrap-around services including substance use disorder treatment and housing"[22]—that is, an effort to replace the punitive state with a therapeutic process.

Unfortunately, the sociopolitical regime that emerged following these initial "reforms" didn't usher in utopia—it devolved into anarchy. In the years leading up to 2020, Seattle became a haven for tent encampments, public drug use, and street disorder, and boasted one of the highest property crime rates in the nation. The LEAD program, which received millions in annual city funding, had repeatedly failed to produce results. In its original "scientific study," when controlling for old warrants, LEAD had no statistical effect on new arrests—in other words, participation in LEAD was as effective as doing nothing.[23]

In 2019, following a series of high-profile "repeat offender" cases, Seattle Municipal Court judge Ed McKenna tried to raise the alarm about the city's failure to prosecute career criminals such as Francisco Calderon, a homeless man who had garnered more than seventy criminal convictions but continued to secure jail-free plea deals from the prosecutor and public defender's offices.[24] McKenna's call to restore public order caused an uproar. The Calderon story was widely covered in the media and dovetailed with an explosive report about the city's "prolific offenders" who had been terrorizing residents and businesses with little consequence.[25]

But McKenna's public stand caused an even more powerful backlash. Almost immediately, the leaders of the progressive-justice movement—City Attorney Pete Holmes, Public Defense Director Anita Khandelwal, and LEAD cofounder Lisa Daugaard—waged a merciless public relations war against the judge and successfully pressured him to retire two years before the completion of his term.

After moving out of state, Judge McKenna warned the public that the progressive-justice coalition was perilously close to establishing a shadow court system. He argued that the leaders of the government-and-nonprofit criminal justice coalition were becoming "modern-day lords and landowners," with the power to dispense justice outside the constitutional framework. McKenna explained that nonprofit diversion programs, which exist beyond the confines of the state and are not subject to meaningful public oversight, were potentially violating the Sixth

Amendment, which guarantees the right to a public trial before a jury of one's peers.

"In [pretrial diversion schemes], potential defendants are contacted by prosecutors and told that if they 'voluntarily' participate in specific programs, criminal charges will not be filed against them," McKenna said. "The ethical concern, however, is whether accused persons are waiving their rights 'knowingly and voluntarily' or whether accused persons feel compelled to waive those rights under threat of prosecution and jail."[26]

However, despite these ethical concerns, the campaign to replace justice with activism continued apace. After the George Floyd riots, dozens of King County prosecutors, organized as the "Equity & Justice Workgroup," issued a letter encouraging their office to stop filing charges for assault, theft, drug dealing, burglary, escape, fare evasion, and auto theft—in effect, moving all but the most serious crimes into the nonprofit-diversion process.[27]

Meanwhile, the architects of LEAD, sensing the opportunity to extend their power, formally declared its intention to move the city "beyond police" and serve as the centerpiece of the new progressive-justice complex.[28]

The officials in the municipal courts sensed their vulnerability. They feared that their entire branch of government, designed to provide an open forum for justice and a bulwark against tyranny, could be obliterated by the new abolitionists. "The system does not wish to be remade and it resists remaking," LEAD cofounder Daugaard told reporters. "And there's no doubt that we would not be having anything like the scale of a redesigned conversation that is occurring if not for the top-line demands of people in the street."[29]

Suddenly the activists who had patiently built their movement had the upper hand. Seattle found itself in the midst of a remarkable moment: the movement to abolish the police, prisons, and courts was no longer the dream of marginalized radicals and utopianists; it had been adopted at the highest levels of the state itself.

"We are preparing the ground for a different kind of society," declared socialist city council member Kshama Sawant at the height of the unrest. "We are coming to dismantle this deeply oppressive, racist, sexist, violent, utterly bankrupt system of capitalism—this police state. We cannot and will not stop until we overthrow it and replace it with a world based instead on solidarity, genuine democracy, and equality—a socialist world."[30]

*   *   *

The new abolitionists' Paris Commune moment came during the long and tumultuous afternoon of June 8, 2020.

Protestors had been relentlessly attacking the city's East Precinct police headquarters, barraging the line of officers protecting the building with bottles, fists, rocks, and explosives. Then, suddenly, the police disappeared. The mayor had made the decision to abandon the precinct to the mob. Officers boarded up the building, moved the barricades, and retreated into the city, leaving demonstrators to make the bewildering transition from protest to conquest.

That evening, groups of armed men associated with Antifa, the John Brown Gun Club, and other left-wing militant organizations established a new security perimeter around the neighborhood and declared the territory the Capitol Hill Autonomous Zone, or CHAZ, and promised to govern it according to the principles of social justice. Overnight, the CHAZ turned into a small-scale laboratory experiment for the ideological commitments of the modern Left and, they hoped, proof of concept for a new system of governance beyond the police, prisons, and courts.[31]

The results of this experiment in abolition are deeply illuminating. Almost immediately, activists established the basic social structure of the CHAZ, following the theory of identity politics formulated in the Combahee River Collective Statement. Black, indigenous, and trans women were elevated into the highest authority; identity determined social rank; whites were called to perform rituals of atonement. Through a series of speeches and meetings, the leaders of the commune sought to implement the social practice of "decolonization," doling out favorable treatment for racial minorities, "centering" black and indigenous women in all public meetings, and encouraging whites to "move past guilt or fragility" and "commit to long-term action and accountability."

At one evening event, an indigenous rights activist with a purple bandana wrapped around his face announced a campaign for immediate small-scale reparations: "I want you to give ten dollars to one African-American person from this autonomous zone," he said to the crowd. "White people, I see you. I see every one of you, and I remember your faces. You find that African-American person and you give them ten dollars."[32]

The practice of racial distribution was a recurring theme. The leaders of the CHAZ adopted policies of explicit racial segregation, with some spaces reserved exclusively for BIPOC, or "Black, Indigenous, and People of Color." Activist Marcus Henderson, a black urban farmer with an engineering degree from Stanford, created a shared agricultural project in the neighborhood park with a sign announcing: THIS GARDEN IS FOR BLACK AND INDIGENOUS FOLKS AND THEIR PLANT ALLIES.[33] As Henderson told reporters, the urban garden was a response to "the question of how Black people have been disenfranchised for so long"[34] and a demonstration of "collective land ownership, taking back property and really making it work for the people."[35]

A few days after CHAZ declared independence, activists began to consider formalizing the governance of the autonomous zone.[36] Although the protestors were unified in opposition to the Seattle Police Department, a number of competing factions emerged within CHAZ—and engaged in an intra-party struggle to represent the movement.

Black Lives Matter activists, led by Nikkita Oliver, wanted the new microstate to focus on racial inequality and defunding the police. Socialist and anti-fascist groups emphasized the radical political nature of the protests, with socialist city councilwoman Kshama Sawant insisting that the occupation must be oriented toward the "dismantling of capitalism itself" and the progression of the "socialist revolution." A third faction of predominantly white bourgeois youth wanted to transform the CHAZ into a block party, with muralists, musicians, and small vendors providing Woodstock-style handicrafts and entertainment.[37]

On June 10, with the goal of building consensus and designating leadership for the movement, protestors organized the first CHAZ People's Assembly. After setting up a stage and PA system, one of the speakers introduced the question of legitimate authority, asking the audience: "What's the structure, how are we going to achieve some sort of communal hierarchy that we all feel comfortable with?" In response, the audience booed and insisted that the movement should remain leaderless and horizontal. At the end of the People's Assembly, one of the activists conceded that no leadership had been established, but maintained that the group had settled on the ideological principles of an "abolitionist framework" and "commitment to solidarity and accountability to Black and Indigenous communities."[38]

This vacuum of legitimate authority, however, did not last.

Within days of the People's Assembly, the most heavily armed and aggressive factions in the CHAZ started to exert dominance over the neighborhood and became the de facto police power. A revolving group of vigilantes armed their followers with semiautomatic rifles and took up positions at the barricades. These soldiers forcibly removed journalists from the autonomous zone and beat up dissenters who opposed their rule. In one incident, masked Antifa militants violently confronted a Christian street preacher and provocateur, choking him unconscious and dragging him through the streets. In another, a large mob hunted down a man who had allegedly stolen items from a local automotive shop before setting the building on fire. The police, having ceded control of the CHAZ to activists, did not respond to any calls for service.[39]

Then the killings began. The first homicide victim was killed in an outburst of gang violence. The second, who was reportedly unarmed and joy-riding in a stolen car, was gunned down by CHAZ paramilitary forces. In the autonomous zone's brief history of independence, there were two murders, four additional shootings, and an overall homicide rate that turned out to be nearly fifty times greater than the city of Chicago's.[40] In a cruel irony, all of the identified victims were black men—precisely the demographic for whom Black Lives Matter and the leaders of the CHAZ had claimed to offer protection.

After the killings, activists lost confidence in their revolutionary project and the mayor moved to retake the territory. Early on the morning of July 1, a phalanx of Seattle police officers, armed with long batons and semiautomatic rifles, cleared out the Capitol Hill Autonomous Zone for good. As officers and public works teams cleared the barricades and washed away the graffiti, the true legacy of CHAZ was revealed: two black youth, Lorenzo Anderson Jr., nineteen, and Antonio Mays Jr., sixteen, had died under the false promise of utopia.[41]

The truth is politically impolite but factually unassailable: the real problem in America, from the Black Panther Party to Black Lives Matter, is not police brutality, but the brutality of the American streets. By instituting a "police-free zone," the CHAZ did not become peaceable; it became lawless, brutish, and violent. The rule of the margins is not automatically better, but often worse, than the rule of the center.

As the national media conducted its final autopsy of the CHAZ, there was one tragic detail that escaped notice. The Seattle Police Department East Precinct building, which radicals believed to be a symbol of "white supremacy," was originally constructed under the leadership of Seattle's first African-American city councilman, Sam Smith, who wanted to provide faster response times to the city's Central District, where black residents had demanded greater police protection.[42] The irony is cutting: Smith, who grew up in the Deep South during Jim Crow, saw policing as a public service; sixty years later, college-educated radicals saw it as a force for evil that must be abolished.

The consequences of this movement have been devastating. The activists of Black Lives Matter have yielded the same results as the black liberation movement before them: violence, instability, chaos, death. Following the George Floyd riots, the United States witnessed the greatest single-year rise in homicides since record keeping began in 1960: a total of 21,500 people shot, stabbed, poisoned, beaten, and bludgeoned to death;[43] social scientists have attributed thousands of excess murders to the unintended consequences of Black Lives Matter.[44]

In Seattle, the same story holds. During the riot year, police recorded the largest number of homicides in a generation, with the highest rates of violence concentrated in black communities.[45] The victimized often became victims again. Horace Lorenzo Anderson Sr., for example, the father of one of the teenagers killed at CHAZ, was shot in the face, but fortunately, and unlike his son, survived.[46]

The failure of the CHAZ, however, like the failure of the Paris Commune, will not stop the revolution.

Like their historical predecessors, the new abolitionists are not seeking to achieve reforms within the given social order; they are seeking to overturn that social order altogether. Marx, and later Herbert Marcuse and Angela Davis, saw the short-lived Paris Commune as a small-scale model for their larger project of moral and political revolt. The Capitol Hill Autonomous Zone serves the same function, updated for the digital age—and, as in the past, the emergence of violence and instability is seen as an accelerant, rather than a deterrent, for social change. The revolution is, after all, the relentless application of the negative dialectic: to subvert, to shift, to unmask, to destroy.

In Seattle, the revolutionary mood has created a sense of danger. Building owners have fortified entire city blocks. Groups of vagrants have established large open-air drug markets. Dealers ply heroin, fentanyl, and methamphetamine in broad daylight. Addicts collect cash by emptying corner stores and smashing car windows.[47] Meanwhile, the professional-class revolutionaries use the image of the oppressed to justify deeper action and to wage their own symbolic war. They use their vast informational apparatus to shape the perception of reality toward revolution.

The ultimate goal is to achieve the impossible: to bring the promise of heaven down to earth. "Karl Marx [once] said that religion is the wish-dream of an oppressed humanity," Angela Davis once told her students. "Real wants, needs and desires are transformed into wish-dreams via the process of religion, because it seems so hopeless in this world: this is the perspective of an oppressed people. But what is important, what is crucial is that those dreams are always on the verge of reverting to their original status—the real wishes and needs here on earth. There is always the possibility of redirecting those wish dreams to the here-and-now."[48]

PART III

Education

CHAPTER 10

Paulo Freire

Master of Subversion

I n the fall of 1969, a Brazilian Marxist educator named Paulo Freire arrived on the Harvard University campus with a suitcase full of clothes and a Portuguese-language manuscript of a book he called *Pedagogy of the Oppressed*. He arrived as an exile, forced out of Brazil following a right-wing military coup, and soon became enmeshed in radical political circles in Cambridge, Massachusetts. As the weather turned cold, Freire grew a beard and adopted the appearance of a guru—the Third World theoretician with the keys to subversion.

During Freire's short stay at Harvard, where he served as a research associate at the Center for Studies in Education and Development, Freire and his colleagues translated the manuscript of *Pedagogy of the Oppressed* into English, which, over the subsequent decades, helped transform American education. The book sold more than one million copies[1] and is now the third-most-cited work in the social sciences.[2] It has become a foundational text in nearly all graduate schools of education and teacher training programs. Although Freire only spent six months in Cambridge, he departed as a prophet of the intellectual Left and identified the education system as a vehicle for the revolution.

As a book, *Pedagogy of the Oppressed* is a Rorschach test. At one level, it presents a simple, even uncontroversial lesson: children must be invested in their own education and engage in creative problem-solving, rather than be subjected to rote learning and top-down control. This insight is packaged in American schools today as "critical pedagogy" and "culturally responsive teaching," with Freire playing the role of the kindly, bearded teacher who wants to cultivate the spirit of social justice.

But underneath the surface, there is a deeper, troubling current that runs all the way through *Pedagogy of the Oppressed*. Freire bases his pedagogy on the political belief that capitalism has enslaved the population and "anesthetized" the world's oppressed with a series of myths: "the myth that the oppressive order is a 'free society'"; "the myth that all persons are free to work where they wish"; "the myth that this order respects human rights"; "the myth of private property as fundamental to personal human development"; "the myth of the charity and generosity of the elites."[3]

Freire stands ready to offer the solution. Through his work, he reveals a vision of an ideal education system that deconstructs society's myths, unmasks its oppressors, and inspires students to "revolutionary consciousness."[4] Freire's language—liberation, revolution, struggle—is not merely symbolic. The most-cited political figures in the *Pedagogy* are Lenin, Mao, Guevara, and Castro, all of whom mobilized violence to advance their political cause.

The revolution might begin in the classroom, Freire told his students, but it would end in the streets. He worshipped the decisive action of the Third World militants and saw the education system as the ideal recruiting ground for a cultural revolution that would overturn the world. "'Cultural revolution' takes the total society to be reconstructed," he thundered. "As the cultural revolution deepens [critical consciousness] in the creative praxis of the new society, people will begin to perceive why mythical remnants of the old society survive in the new. And they will then be able to free themselves more rapidly of these specters."[5]

Paulo Freire imagined himself an oracle: a man who had demythologized the oppressions of his time. But he was, in truth, a man who would unleash unimaginable cruelties in the name of justice. "The ideal lies in punishing the perverse—the killers of popular leadership, of country folk, and forest people—here and now," he thundered.[6]

The smiling, bearded teacher was not so much a guru as a fanatic. Even as the Marxist-Leninist regimes revealed themselves as purveyors of great barbarism, he refused to abandon the faith. He clung to his idols—Che, Lenin, Mao—even as their own societies repudiated them. But despite the failure of his ideology everywhere it was attempted, his influence took root in an unlikely place: the United States of America.

That is where he would become a prophet.

*   *   *

Paulo Reglus Neves Freire was born in the fall of 1921 in the city of Recife, Brazil. The city, which was once the first slave port in the Americas, had remained poor, backward, and crowded onto the Atlantic shoreline. As other regions of Brazil began to industrialize, the Northeast remained stagnant: the economy persisted in the colonial mold, with sprawling farms and a primitive railroad system that supplied sugarcane to the world market.[7] At the time of Freire's youth, the region had the lowest per capita income in Latin America and some of the highest rates of illiteracy, malnutrition, and tropical disease.[8]

The Freire family was suspended precariously between the middle and lower classes. Paulo's father, Joaquin, was an officer in the military police, but was forced into early retirement due to a heart condition and never managed to find steady work again. He eventually passed away when Paulo was a teenager, plunging the family into dire circumstances. Paulo's mother maintained some of the trappings of the middle class—clothes, neckties, a piano in the living room—but the children often went without food.[9]

Freire traced the origins of his political thought to the deprivations of his childhood. "My lived experiences as a child and as a man took place socially within the history of a dependent society in whose terrible dramatic nature I participated early on," he recalled in his memoirs. "I should highlight that it was this terrible nature of society that fostered my increasing radicality."[10] As an example of his political education, Freire recounts a story in which he and a group of friends, worn down and hungry, wandered into an orchard to steal papayas, only to be caught by the landowner. "I must have turned pale from surprise and shock. I did not know what to do with my shaking hands, from which the papaya fell to the ground," Freire wrote. "At that time, stealing the fruit was necessary but the man gave me a moralistic sermon that had little to do with my hunger."[11]

This symbolic world of Freire's childhood—part recollection, part allegory—provided the human ground for the philosophy that emerged in Freire's adulthood. In a real sense, Freire's feelings of betrayal and outrage at the conditions in Recife were justified. The former colonial territory was structured into rigid hierarchies and countenanced immense suffering of the poor. The latifundia system, in which large landowners sent the mass of laborers into the sugar fields, still bore the stigma of feudalism. The peasants were bound to the land and worked to the bone; they were bound to the land and, as illiterates, barred from voting in democratic elections. They lived at the mercy of domestic plantation owners and foreign commodities markets, which had always been brutal masters.[12]

Politics provided a path out of this nightmare.

After finishing high school, Freire went to the University of Recife, earned a law degree, and joined the Social Service of Industry (SESI), where he started working as an educator for the region's poorest citizens. He began his career as a modernist and a reformist, believing that "progressive education" could bring literacy to the masses and incorporate their interests into the governing system. As a young man, he traveled through the city's slums and rural backwaters preaching the value of a "democratic education" and the "work of man with man."[13]

At SESI, he conceptualized the practice of "culture circles," in which participants engaged in an active dialogue with their instructors, seeking to understand their historical-political position as well as the mechanics of literacy. This was the period of Freire the humanist, driven by the conviction that "human beings, by making and remaking things and transforming the world, can transcend the situation in which their *state of being* is almost *a state of non-being*, and go on to a state of being, in search of *becoming more* fully human."[14]

Over time, however, Freire became disillusioned with this model. He came to see his work at SESI as serving the "interests of the dominant class," and criticized the institution for abandoning its utopian purpose and devolving into "a paternalistic, bureaucratic service."[15] The institute, he believed, presented the values of humanism, but was ultimately designed "to ease class conflict and stop the development of a political and militant consciousness among workers." It was an attempt by the industrial powers to "domesticate" the men who populated the sugar fields and the factory floors.[16]

As a reaction, Freire sought out a new theory that would meet the radical nature of class conflict with an equally radical political philosophy. He immersed himself in the Marxist literature, which provided the utopian impulse and the vision of a classless society, as well the means for achieving it: revolution. Freire described this as a spiritual conversion that brought together Christian humanism with dialectical Marxism. "It was the woods in Recife, refuge of slaves, and the ravines where the oppressed of Brazil live coupled with my love for Christ and hope that He is the light, that led me to Marx," he wrote. "The tragic reality of the ravines, woods, and marshes led me to Marx."[17]

Freire's conversion was fast and deep. By the mid-1960s, as Marxist revolutionaries had begun to seize power in Asia, Africa, and Latin America, Freire began to think of education as a means for driving and supporting the "cultural revolution" that provided the intellectual basis for transforming the political, economic, and social order in the Third World. "Revolution is always cultural," he wrote, "whether it be in the phase of denouncing an oppressive society and proclaiming the advent of a just society, or in the phase of the new society inaugurated by the revolution."[18]

During this period, the reformist pedagogy of Freire's early years turned into a Marxist pedagogy aimed at nothing less than the complete transformation of society. In *Pedagogy of the Oppressed*, he describes this new method: "The pedagogy of the oppressed, as a humanist and libertarian pedagogy, has two distinct stages. In the first, the oppressed unveil the world of oppression and through the praxis commit themselves to its transformation. In the second stage, in which the reality of oppression has already been transformed, this pedagogy ceases to belong to the oppressed and becomes a pedagogy of all people in the process of permanent liberation."[19]

How should one interpret this new pedagogical approach? First, it must be recognized that, throughout his life, Freire played a double game: he used abstractions such as "liberation" that could be interpreted through the lens of humanism or radicalism. "Liberation" meant a personal process of attaining *conscientização*, or "critical consciousness," that frees the pupil from illiteracy, helplessness, and ignorance. But "liberation" also meant a revolutionary struggle to overthrow a given political regime and install Marxism-Leninism as the new state ideology.

In order to soften his image, Freire's disciples have consistently emphasized his humanist mission, portraying the man as a wise, peaceful presence. In a typical portrayal, Freire translator Donaldo Macedo and Freire's second wife, Ana Maria Araujo-Freire, declared that Freire "never spoke, nor was he even an advocate, of violence or of the taking of power through the force of arms. . . . He fought and had been fighting for a more just and

less perverse society, a truly democratic one, one where there are no repres-
sors against the oppressed, where all can have a voice and a chance."[20]

But this softening, which attempts to make Freire's work palatable to
modern audiences, is preposterous.

Freire explicitly rationalized violence in *Pedagogy of the Oppressed* and
defended violent revolutionaries such as Lenin, Stalin, Castro, and Mao,[21]
who left behind them a trail of up to 90 million dead.[22] "Violence is initiated by those who oppress, who exploit, who fail to recognize others as
persons—not by those who are oppressed, exploited, and unrecognized,"
Freire wrote. "Consciously or unconsciously, the act of rebellion by the
oppressed (an act which is always, or nearly always, as violent as the initial
violence of the oppressors) can initiate love. Whereas the violence of the
oppressors prevents the oppressed from being fully human, the response
of the latter to this violence is grounded in the desire to pursue the right to
be human."[23]

Even after the atrocities of Freire's heroes were revealed, he continued to
idealize them. In 1974, he called China's Cultural Revolution—which led to
the death, starvation, and persecution of millions of innocent people—"the
most genial solution of the century."[24] In 1985, he described Che Guevara
as the incarnation of "the authentic revolutionary utopia" who "justified
guerrilla warfare as an introduction to freedom."[25] Revolutionary violence,
Freire maintained, was best understood as "an act of love."[26]

The Brazilian military, however, took a different interpretation. In the
1960s, Freire had expanded his "culture circles" throughout Northeast
Brazil and led a pilot program in Angicos, Rio Grande do Norte, with the
support of left-wing president João Goulart, who had laid out an ambitious
policy agenda called the Basic Reforms, including higher taxes on business,
large-scale land redistribution, the extension of the franchise to illiterates,
and investments in national education. Goulart attended a ceremony at
one of Freire's culture circles in Angicos, during which Freire proudly announced that the movement was creating "a people who decides, a people
that is rising up, a people that has begun to become aware of its destiny
and has begun to take part in the Brazilian historical process irreversibly."[27]

That same year, Goulart hired Freire to build out the federal
government's national literacy campaign,[28] which, together with the Basic
Reforms, they hoped would finally usher in the "Brazilian Revolution."[29]

The Brazilian Communist Party put its full weight behind the effort, convinced that Goulart's "structural reforms of society" would provide "a link in the revolutionary process which will culminate with the advent and the construction of socialism."[30]

With such rhetoric, Goulart, Freire, and the communists put themselves directly in the crosshairs of the Brazilian military and the American presidents John F. Kennedy and Lyndon Johnson. In 1963, American diplomats and Brazilian allies furiously exchanged messages warning of "an extremely grave process of institutional subversion" that "might require removal of threat through military action." One message described Goulart and Freire's literacy program as a "brainwashing" campaign that used the same techniques as the Chinese communists.[31]

In the spring of 1964, the Brazilian military pulled the trigger. The generals toppled Goulart, shut down the literacy programs, and jailed suspected communists and subversives. Military officials denounced the national literacy campaign as an attempt to "communize" Brazil and create "five million electoral robots for the populist parties, including the communists."

Within months, the military had dismantled the structure of Freire's campaign. Soldiers seized troves of documents, detained cultural circle leaders, and even set fire to some school buildings. The new regime accused Freire and his comrades of leading "the most subtle and efficient work of subversion yet realized in Brazil," with the ultimate aim of transforming the "illiterate masses into an instrument of the peaceful conquest of power by the Communist Party."[32] By summer, the government had arrested Freire in his home and transferred him into a prison cell in Recife. "Another one for the cage," said the security officer.[33]

For the next seventy days, interrogators questioned Freire about his techniques of subversion, support for communist revolution, relationship with Cuba and the USSR, and an alleged weapons cache discovered in the headquarters of Freire's popular culture movement.[34] Freire denied the charges, dismissing them as "hallucinations."[35]

Finally, the military released him. Freire, fearing that he might be arrested again, sought asylum in the Bolivian embassy and, from there, went into exile.

For the next sixteen years, Freire would wander around the globe, from the United States to Latin America to postcolonial Africa, seeking to turn his theories of liberation into practice. The coup, Freire said, had radicalized him.[36] The mild-mannered humanist from Recife had transformed into the pedagogist for the global revolution. He had abandoned hope in reformist politics and, by the time he went into exile, had become a committed Marxist, believing that only the total transformation of society would be sufficient to end the dehumanization of the laboring classes.

Although his project had failed in Brazil, he believed it could succeed in the Third World nations where the communists had secured power, such as Chile, Nicaragua, El Salvador, Angola, Mozambique, Tanzania, Cape Verde, São Tomé and Príncipe, and a small country on the west coast of Africa: Guinea-Bissau.

*   *   *

The coastline of Guinea-Bissau cuts into the Atlantic Ocean like a set of shark's teeth. The series of islands, bays, and inlets once provided protected sailing for Portuguese colonial ships, which used Guinea-Bissau as a transit center for sending African slaves to their territories in Brazil. The Portuguese had dominated Guinea-Bissau for nearly five centuries, although they never ventured far into the territory, limiting their colonial enterprise to the coastline and small urban centers along the shores. Until late in the twentieth century, most of the nation's interior was untouched by the modern world.

When Freire arrived in the capital city, Bissau, in 1975, the colonial backwater had just won its independence from Portugal and had established a revolutionary Marxist-Leninist regime under the leadership of the African Party for the Independence of Guinea and Cape Verde, or PAIGC. Freire arrived at the invitation of President Luís Cabral, half brother of and successor to revolutionary leader Amílcar Cabral, who had been assassinated at the tail end of the war. Luís Cabral and his state education commissioner, Mario Cabral, had invited Freire into the country with the hope that the Brazilian could use his pedagogical techniques to help carry the government from the stage of military revolution, which Freire described as "the taking of power," to cultural revolution, which he described as "inaugurating a society of women and men in the process of continuing liberation."[37]

The task of educating the masses was a daunting one. The country had just emerged from a violent decade-long war and only 10 percent of Guinea-Bissauans were literate.[38]

In a series of letters to education minister Mario Cabral, Freire lavished praise on the guerrilla fighters and conceptualized the national education program as an extension of the revolution, combining his literacy campaign with central economic planning, collectivist agricultural policy, and political indoctrination. "If the society, in remaking itself, moves toward socialism," Freire wrote, "it needs, on the one hand, to organize its methods of production with this objective in mind, and, on the other, to structure its education in close relation to production, both from the point of view of the understanding of the productive process and also the technical training of the learners."[39]

The new regime, Freire argued, must "see literacy education of adults as a political act, coherent with the principles of PAIGC,"[40] which, in accordance with Marxist doctrine, would lead to a society in which "economic productivity will increase to the degree that the political consciousness of the popular masses becomes clarified."[41]

In practice, Freire and his colleagues designed a literacy campaign that can only be described as propaganda. The content of the program focused on eight "national themes," including production, defense, education, culture, and labor, weaving in Amílcar Cabral's revolutionary slogans and lessons aimed at instilling "political clarity" among the masses. Freire imagined transforming teachers into a cadre of "militants" through "a permanent revision of [their] ideological class conditioning."[42]

Following the revolutionary theory of Amílcar Cabral, Freire argued that the nation's *assimilados*, urban residents, and tiny bourgeoisie should commit "class suicide" and go to the farms in order to transcend the boundaries of city and countryside, mind and body, rich and poor.[43] Freire's ambition was not only to build a Marxist-Leninist society, but to create "the new man and the new woman." He argued that Guinea-Bissau's native population might be "illiterate, in the literal sense of the term," but was "politically highly literate" because of their experience with the war of liberation.[44]

But Freire and the regime made a series of fatal mistakes. First, they based their entire political and cultural project on a set of economic ideas that was bound to fail. At the first Popular National Assembly after the nation achieved independence, the PAIGC abolished private property, nationalized all land, mandated collectivized agriculture through Village Committees, and decreed a state monopoly on basic goods through government-run People's Stores.

The *Black Scholar*, one of the preeminent journals of black radicalism in the United States, described Guinea-Bissau's program in a 1980 dispatch: "The leaders have chosen to base the economy on agriculture in which 86 percent of the population is engaged. The government is gradually introducing mechanized and diversified production in the traditional farming areas. It sees the key to economic progress through a collectivist system of some type. The small land holding peasants are encouraged to adopt the cooperative mode. State farms are operational wherever possible. . . . Experimental farms have been established by the state; some in the interior where large farms abandoned by the Portuguese had existed."[45]

Second, despite Amílcar Cabral's vision of a distinctly African Marxism predicated on the "the re-Africanization of minds," the education ministers chose Portuguese as the national language of instruction.[46] The decision was bewildering: they were adopting the language of the colonial power, but, more importantly, they were adopting a language that almost nobody in the country could understand. At the time, only 5 percent of Guinea-Bissauans could speak Portuguese; the rest of the country, meanwhile, spoke a mix of tribal and indigenous languages.[47]

Amílcar Cabral had dreamed of the revolution as a campaign to "mentally decolonize" the native population, but by selecting Portuguese as the national language, the regime extended the colonial language deeper into the country than ever before.[48] And by inviting Freire, the regime layered in another irony: the educator arrived in Africa as a self-described liberator, but carried with him the tongue and the mind of a European—after all, he was the descendant of Portuguese settlers in the metropole's most important colony.

Finally, Freire's vision for Guinea-Bissau was modeled on the Chinese Cultural Revolution, which would prove to be an economic and human disaster. As Freire explained in the memoir of his work in Guinea-Bissau, *Pedagogy in Process*, his model was the Dazhai agriculture commune in Shanxi Province, China, which Chairman Mao heralded in the "Learn from Dazhai" campaign as having perfected communist economic development, crop production, and mass education.

Although the Chinese Cultural Revolution was on the verge of collapse when Freire arrived in Guinea-Bissau, he still believed it was the key to the country's future. "The new climate created by liberation enables the people to become involved in a literacy campaign and in agrarian reform," he wrote. "A program linked to production that seeks to build such social incentives as cooperative work and concern for the common good places its faith in human beings. It has a critical, not ingenuous, belief in the ability of people to be remade in the process of reconstructing their society." For Freire, Mao's collective work program in Dazhai was proof that revolutionary Marxism had made possible "the dynamic of transforming reality," which could be applied directly to the situation in Guinea-Bissau.[49]

There was one problem: despite Freire's insistence that he could see through the "myths" of capitalist societies, he was seduced by the even more dangerous myths of communist societies.

Dazhai, in reality, was a disaster. Chairman Mao had forced the peasants through brutal work routines, laboring day and night to the point of exhaustion, and the government had fabricated the harvest numbers: the commune was not self-reliant, but received enormous subsidies from the state. Meanwhile, Dazhai's great construction projects, leveling mountains down to the bedrock and filling ravines with earth, were economic sinkholes; none led to greater prosperity or agricultural productivity.[50] As one scholar of the Dazhai campaign concluded: "Rarely has there been a historical moment in which political repression, misguided ideals, and an absolutist vision of priorities and correct methods coincided to achieve such concentrated attacks on nature, environmental destruction, and human suffering."[51]

Freire should have known better. In 1975, when he arrived in Guinea-Bissau, China's Cultural Revolution was less than a year away from total collapse—and Dazhai's collective agricultural system would be officially repudiated shortly thereafter.[52]

But Freire was still under the spell of the Cultural Revolution. He ignored the horrors, brutalities, famines, slaughter, and mass deaths that had accumulated over the course of the revolution. He betrayed no skepticism of Dazhai's propaganda campaign and fantastical slogans, such as "move the mountains to make farm fields" and "change the sky and alter the land."[53] Even in 1985, when the violence and destruction of the Chinese revolution were known to the world, Freire refused to acknowledge his errors. He continued to tout the "great merits" of the Cultural Revolution[54] and praised Chairman Mao as a model of "tolerance," "humility," and "patience."[55]

This blindness—the denial of the old myths and the certainty in the new ones—doomed the efforts in Guinea-Bissau.

In 1977, the country's Third Party Congress enacted a national agricultural policy that was nearly identical to the old Soviet policy of "primitive socialist accumulation."[56] As a result, food production plummeted. Guinea-Bissau went from being a net exporter of rice to being dependent on foreign aid. Food shortages, hunger, smuggling, graft, and corruption were rampant. Freire's national education program devolved into pure illusion.

When the Brazilian lectured to young educators at Guinea-Bissau's Maxim Gorki Center for the Formation of Teachers, he insisted that any failure in education was a failure in politics. "Militancy teaches us that pedagogical problems are, first of all, political and ideological," he said. "Therefore we insist increasingly, in the qualifying seminars, on analysis of national reality, on the political clarity of the educator, on the understanding of ideological conditioning, and on the perception of cultural differences. All this must begin long before discussion of literacy techniques and methods."[57]

The results of Cabral's economic program and Freire's education program were identical: abject failure.

For years, Guinea-Bissau's official newspaper, *Nô Pintcha*, tried to prop up Freire's literacy campaign with optimistic headlines.[58] But in the most comprehensive study of Freire's program in Guinea-Bissau, scholar Linda Harasim discovered that, for all the fanfare, Freire's project was utterly fruitless.[59] According to official records, Guinea-Bissau's Department of Adult Education found that, of the 26,000 participants in Freire's program over three years, almost none had achieved basic literacy.[60]

The pedagogy, the codifications, the pamphlets, the teachers college, the mass mobilization, the call for class suicide—none of it taught the Guinea-Bissauans how to read. "The activities envisioned and eventually implemented were inappropriate, unrealistic, and beyond the capacities of the country," Harasim concluded. "[Freire's] strategy was more concerned with orchestrating the 'class suicide' of the [literacy teachers] than with such concrete tasks as teaching the population to read and write."[61]

Freire concluded his work in Guinea-Bissau in 1977, leaving it, by almost any measure, worse off than when he arrived.

Over the next three decades, Guinea-Bissau ricocheted through a series of elections, coups, assassinations, and a civil war; the country's failed collectivist economic policies gave way to scattershot reforms, then to the rule of the black market and recurring bouts of inflation.[62] In 1990, Pope John Paul II visited Guinea-Bissau and prayed for the nation to move beyond violence and corruption. The pope encouraged then-president João Bernardo Vieira to reform the national curriculum, which, according to Vatican officials, was still shot through with Marxist propaganda. "I pray that educative programs enjoy full success, beginning with genuine literacy," he said, encouraging Guinea-Bissauans to resist "all that would seek to crush the individual or cancel him in an anonymous collectivity by institutions, structures, or a system."[63]

Today, Guinea-Bissau is a failed state. South American drug cartels use the islands along the nation's coastline as a drug transit point, smuggling up to one thousand kilograms of cocaine into the territory each night. Guinea-Bissau's sprawling and corrupt military leases airstrips and naval facilities to the cartels, which paper their way through the bureaucracy with drug dollars.[64]

Meanwhile, the population suffers. Guinea-Bissau is one of the poorest nations on earth: nearly 70 percent of residents live on less than two dollars per day and large swaths of the population depend on foreign aid for basic survival.[65] The territory is plagued by slavery, child labor, forced marriage, female genital mutilation, and the torture of political opposition.[66] And, despite the regime's ambitions, Guinea-Bissau remains an illiterate society: 54 percent of adults cannot read, including 69 percent of all women.[67]

In retrospect, Freire had made a tragic mistake. He had identified a constellation of monsters—colonialism, capitalism, ignorance, oppression—but put too much faith in the revolution. In Guinea-Bissau, Freire and Cabral had followed their theory to its limits, expelling the colonial power, dismantling the market economy, and establishing the one-party state that would, through *conscientização* alone, "transform reality."[68] But after they vanquished the old constellation of monsters, they unleashed another one: violence, barbarism, precarity, and disillusionment.

The Portuguese, who had never extended their influence beyond the coastline, provided a convenient foil. But after their departure, the revolutionaries had to grapple with the complex tribal, economic, linguistic, and cultural realities in the country's tangled interior. For this task, Freire's theories proved insufficient. Wherever he went—Angola, Mozambique, Nicaragua, El Salvador, Guinea-Bissau—the system of colonialism gave way to a system of poverty, repression, illiteracy, mass murder, and civil war.

Yet, despite this string of failures, Freire's image as the wise, peripatetic guru persevered. His practical work might have been a supreme disappointment—he enabled tyranny more than he taught literacy—but his theoretical project would soon be resurrected in an unlikely place: the United States of America.

CHAPTER 11

"We Must Punish Them"

Marxism Conquers the American Classroom

For Paulo Freire, America was the ultimate oppressor—and for that reason, he accepted a position at Harvard University, in order to study the enemy from within. "I thought that it was very important for me as a Brazilian intellectual in exile to pass through, albeit rapidly, the center of capitalist power," he said. "I needed to see the animal close on its home territory."[1]

Between 1969 and 1970, Freire spent six months as a research associate at the Harvard Graduate School of Education, hosting seminars, writing articles, and haunting left-wing bookstores with other teachers and activists. His work, despite being anti-capitalist, was funded by two of the great titans of American industry: the Carnegie Corporation and the Ford Foundation. The months in Cambridge were extremely productive. He worked with a colleague to translate *Pedagogy of the Oppressed* into English and wrote two essays for the *Harvard Education Review*, which, as the historian Isaac Gottesman has documented, helped introduce "critical Marxism" into the field of American education.[2]

More importantly, Freire established two crucial relationships—first, with the education reformer Jonathan Kozol, then, in subsequent trips, with the professor Henry Giroux—that would, over time, embed his ideas throughout the American public education system. Kozol became one of Freire's first American champions, publishing a letter in the *New York Review of Books* promoting the Brazilian's theories and making the argument that his ideas were "directly relevant to the struggles we face in the United States at the present time, and in areas far less mechanical and far more universal than basic literacy alone."[3]

Giroux proved to be an even more important ally. Freire had exchanged correspondence with Giroux for a number of years and, after his work with the Marxist-Leninist regimes in Africa and Latin America, finally met the American academic in the early 1980s.[4] Giroux was immediately seduced by Freire's ideas. Giroux had immersed himself in the intellectual milieu of "critical Marxism," drawing inspiration from the critical theorists such as Herbert Marcuse and the critical pedagogists led by Paulo Freire.[5]

After establishing a relationship, Giroux and Freire initiated a long collaboration, co-editing an influential series called Critical Studies in Education, which began the process of popularizing their radical pedagogical theories. Giroux dedicated the first book of the series to his master, calling Freire the "living embodiment of the principle that underlies this work: that pedagogy should become more political and that the political should become more pedagogical."[6]

Although Freire's work had failed in the Third World, he sought to revive it in the First World.

Freire believed that the United States was a key source of the world's problems, projecting war, racism, imperialism, domination, and oppression across the globe. He also believed that the country projected these forces within. Although Freire initially refrained from explicit political activism during his time at Harvard—he was, after all, a political exile—he quietly developed his own theories about the United States in collaboration with his American counterparts.[7] As Giroux explained in an article for *Curriculum Inquiry*, Freire's analysis needed to take into account the nature of domination in North America, which was more subtle than in the postcolonial societies: "The fact of domination in Third World nations, as well as the substantive nature of that domination, is relatively clear. . . . The conditions of domination are not only different in the advanced industrial countries of the West, but they are also much less obvious, and in some cases, one could say more pervasive and powerful."[8]

Freire's basic theory of oppression in the First World was that capitalism "uproots" the poor and working classes, then "domesticates" them through a series of "myths" that seek to legitimize and manufacture support for the system of private property, individual rights, and human initiative.[9] This liberal-democratic order creates the superficial appearance of freedom and prosperity, but upon deeper analysis serves the interests of economic elites and subjugates the masses to a form of psychological slavery. "Perhaps the greatest tragedy of modern man is his domination by the force of these myths," Freire explained in his book *Education for Critical Consciousness.* "Gradually, without even realizing the loss, he relinquishes his capacity for choice; he is expelled from the orbit of decisions. . . . And when men try to save themselves by following the prescriptions [of the elites], they drown in leveling anonymity, without hope and without faith, domesticated and adjusted."[10]

During his travels to the United States throughout the 1970s, Freire spent much of his time helping organize poor and minority communities,[11] believing that the revolution must begin with what he called "the Third World in the First World."[12] The FBI closely tracked Freire's movements and affiliations. The Bureau's declassified files describe Freire as an "intellectual radical revolutionary" who, according to confidential informants, was working to organize a leftist school in Bridgeport, Connecticut, and giving lectures to young militants, including members of the Black Panther Party.[13]

But the Brazilian educator encountered a double frustration in the American slums. After working with radical groups composed of "negroes, indians, chicanos, puerto ricans and whites," Freire privately concluded in a letter to a friend that the American revolutionaries suffered from the "lack of ideological and political clarity, the paroquial vision of reality [and] the lack of dialectical thought."[14] Additionally, Freire began to see the limitations of working with elites, who funded his work at Harvard and, subsequently, at the Geneva, Switzerland–based World Council of Churches, but were ultimately shaped by the interests of capitalist society. "We cannot expect the ruling classes to commit suicide," he confided. "They cannot really permit us to put into practice a kind of education that will lay them waste, once the raison d'être of the oppressive reality is revealed."[15]

This insight, originally applied to the Third World, held even stronger for the First World. If the small and fragile elite of Guinea-Bissau could not be persuaded to commit "class suicide," how could one persuade the enormous middle and upper classes in the United States to do the same?

The answer to this question, Freire hoped, was through the education system. Since *Pedagogy of the Oppressed*, Freire had argued that traditional schools were designed for "changing the consciousness of the oppressed, not the situation which oppresses them";[16] or, in modern terms, that the focus of education was individualistic rather than systemic. Freire proposed turning this model upside down: "The solution is not to 'integrate' [students] into the structure of oppression, but to transform that structure so that they can become 'beings for themselves.'"[17]

This political strategy, Freire believed, was universal. "In metaphysical terms, politics is the soul of education, its very being, whether in the First World or in the Third World," Freire said.[18] "Education must be an instrument of transforming action, a political praxis at the service of permanent human liberation. This, let us repeat, does not happen only in the consciousness of people, but presupposes a radical change of structures, in which process consciousness will itself be transformed."[19]

In the 1980s, Freire's American disciples, led by Henry Giroux, began translating Freire's visions into reality. The first step, a book series in direct collaboration with Freire, would lay out their "critical theory of education" and establish a base of support in academia. This effort was explicitly neo-Marxist. As Giroux explained: "The neo-Marxist position, it seems to us, provides the most insightful and comprehensive model for a more progressive approach for understanding the nature of schooling and developing an emancipatory program for social education." Giroux believed that public schools served as "agents of ideological control" on behalf of the oppressor class—which, he hoped, the circle of intellectuals around Paulo Freire could demystify and subvert from within.[20]

The next step, according to Giroux, was to launch a "political intervention" within the university and work to secure tenure for one hundred radical intellectuals. He believed that, if they could reshape the concepts in academia, they would eventually trickle down to the classroom.[21] Thus, with Freire as the guru and Giroux as the tactician, the project was born: the critical theorists of education began methodically deconstructing the existing curricula, pedagogies, and practices, and replacing them, brick by brick, with the ideology of revolution.

What followed is nothing short of a coup. Over the course of forty years, Giroux's initial cadre of one hundred bespectacled and shabbily dressed academics expanded their influence, recruited followers, and achieved dominance in the field of education. They pumped out papers, secured tenure, marginalized rivals, and transformed scholarship into activism. *Ped-*

agogy of the Oppressed became the bible of teachers colleges throughout the United States[22] and created a cottage industry in academic publishing.[23]

In total, Freire's oeuvre has generated nearly 500,000 academic citations and his disciple, Henry Giroux, has generated another 125,000.[24] Freire's concepts—"Mythologization," "cultural invasion," "codification-decodification," "critical consciousness"—have reshaped the language of pedagogical theory and dominated the discourse in the academic journals. Over time, these ideas have become part of the official architecture of higher education: UCLA sponsors an official Paulo Freire Institute; Chapman University hosts an annual Paulo Freire Democratic Project Awards; McGill University runs a Paulo and Nita Freire Project for Critical Pedagogy; and similar initiatives have been established in Spain, Portugal, Ireland, Germany, Finland, Austria, England, and Brazil.[25]

As the historian of education Isaac Gottesman has documented, the field of education went through a "critical turn" that radicalized the discipline, from the university to the primary school. "The turn to critical Marxist thought is a defining moment in the past 40 years of educational scholarship, especially for educational scholars who identify as part of the political left," Gottesman explains. "It introduced the ideas and vocabulary that continue to frame most conversations in the field about social justice, such as hegemony, ideology, consciousness, praxis, and most importantly, the word 'critical' itself, which has become ubiquitous as a descriptor for left educational scholarship."[26] The Brazilian educator stands at the center of this change: "Freire is the touchstone voice—scholarship espousing social justice is almost always in conversation with his critical educational approach."[27]

Over time, the scholarship that began in the universities trickled down to the primary and secondary education systems. The result is that thousands of public schools are now training American schoolchildren, explicitly or implicitly, to see the world through the lens of critical pedagogy.

In California, America's vanguard state, Freire's ideas have reshaped the curriculum entirely. In 2021, the state Board of Education approved a sweeping Ethnic Studies Model Curriculum, with the goal of transforming education in ten thousand public schools, serving a total of 6 million students. The curriculum, which is based in large part on Freire's framework of critical consciousness, decolonization, and revolt, begins with the assumption that students must learn how to "challenge racist, bigoted, discriminatory, imperialist/colonial beliefs" and critique "white supremacy, racism and other forms of power and oppression." Teachers are then encouraged to drive their pupils to participate in "social movements that struggle for social justice" and "build new possibilities for a post-racist, post-systemic racism society."[28]

R. Tolteka Cuauhtin, the original cochair of the Ethnic Studies Model Curriculum, developed much of the material regarding early American history. In his book *Rethinking Ethnic Studies*, cited in the state's official reference guide, Cuauhtin argues that the United States was founded on a "Eurocentric, white supremacist (racist, anti-Black, anti-Indigenous), capitalist (classist), patriarchal (sexist and misogynistic), heteropatriarchal (homophobic), and anthropocentric paradigm brought from Europe." Cuauhtin claims that whites began "grabbing the land," "hatching hierarchies," and "developing for Europe/whiteness," which created "excess wealth" that "became the basis for the capitalist economy." The result was a system of white "hegemony" that continues to the present day, in which minorities are subjected to "socialization, domestication, and 'zombification.'"

The solution, according to Cuauhtin, is to "name, speak to, resist, and transform the hegemonic Eurocentric neocolonial condition" in a posture of "transformational resistance." The ultimate goal is to "decolonize" American society and establish a new regime of "countergenocide" and "counterhegemony," which will challenge the dominance of white Christian culture and lead to the "regeneration of indigenous epistemic and cultural futurity."[29]

In pursuit of this goal, the state curriculum encouraged teachers to lead their students in a series of indigenous songs, chants, and affirmations, including the "In Lak Ech Affirmation," which appealed directly to the Aztec gods. Students clapped and chanted to the deity Tezkatlipoka—whom the Aztecs traditionally worshipped with human sacrifice and cannibalism— asking him for the power to become "warriors" for "social justice." As the chant came to a climax, students performed a supplication for "liberation, transformation, [and] decolonization," after which they asked the gods for the power of "critical consciousness."[30]

This is pure Paulo Freire. According to the "vision statement" prepared by the Board of Education, the purpose of the curriculum is not to assist students in achieving literacy or competency, but to provide a "tool for transformation, social, economic, and political change, and liberation."[31] The curriculum writers have deliberately recast the United States as an oppressor nation that must be "decolonized" through politics. They unabashedly elevate the Aztecs—who brutally sacrificed thousands of innocent men, women, and children—into religious symbols of California's state-approved ideology.

As Cuauhtin tells it, white Christians committed "theocide" against indigenous spirituality.[32] Those deities must be resurrected and restored to their rightful place in the social justice cosmology. It is, in a philosophical sense, a revenge of the gods.

This curriculum is already transforming local districts into centers for left-wing political activism.

In 2020, the Santa Clara County Office of Education held a series of teacher-training sessions on how to deploy ethnic studies in the classroom. As state ethnic studies advisor Jorge Pacheco explained, the model curriculum is based on the "pedagogy of the oppressed," and although the Marxist underpinnings of the theory might "scare people away," he insisted that teachers must be "grounded in the correct politics to educate students."

During the training sessions, Pacheco told the teachers that the United States is a political regime based on "settler colonialism," which he described as a "system of oppression" that "occupies and usurps land/labor/resources from one group of people for the benefit of another." The settler colonialist regime, Pacheco continued, is "not just a vicious thing of the past, but [one that] exists as long as settlers are living on appropriated land."

What is the solution? Pacheco told the teachers they must "awaken [students] to the oppression" and lead them to "decodify" and eventually "destroy" the dominant political regime. The first step in this process is to help students "get into the mind of a white man" such as Christopher Columbus and analyze "what ideology led these white male settlers to be power and land hungry and justify stealing indigenous land through genocide." Pacheco described this process as transforming students as young as six years old into "activist intellectuals" who "decodify systems of oppression" into their component parts, including "white supremacy, patriarchy, classism, genocide, private property, and God."

It's "never too young" to begin the process of conversion, Pacheco said, telling educators they should be "cashing in on kids' inherent empathy" in order to reshape their ideological foundations.[33]

The method of critical pedagogy is now mandatory statewide. After releasing the model curriculum, the California state legislature quickly passed a bill making ethnic studies a graduation requirement for all high school students, which will make the "pedagogy of the oppressed" the official ideology in every school district in the state.[34]

The ethnic studies activists grasp the destabilizing nature of their project—but they believe it provides them leverage for their broader political ends. During the Santa Clara presentation, the instructors provided the audience a handout with a quote from Paulo Freire: "Critical consciousness, they say, is anarchic. Others add that critical consciousness may lead to disorder. Some, however, confess: Why deny it? I was afraid of freedom. I am no longer afraid!"[35] They seek, at a minimum, a moral revolution—and, out of such tumult, the political revolution that might follow.

The critical pedagogists foreground ideology, but there is another, deeper force at play: the cold and calculated expansion of the public school bureaucracy. Implicit in every step in the process of "decolonization" is a transfer of power from parents, families, and citizens to the bureaucratic class: administrators, counselors, consultants, specialists, advisors, and paper-pushers.

Following the model of the universities, the largest school districts have all begun to entrench the critical pedagogies into the bureaucracy under a variety of names, such as "Diversity and Inclusion," "Racial Equity," and "Culturally Responsive Programs." These departments fulfill a dual purpose. First, they serve as a mechanism for ideological enforcement. Second, they serve as a jobs program for college graduates with degrees in the critical theories. Contrary to many skeptics who have argued that students in the fields of race, gender, and identity would have difficulty finding employment, these ideologically trained graduates have found rapidly expanding opportunities in the educational bureaucracy.

The statistics reveal the extent of this shift in power. Between 1970 and 2010, the number of students in American public schools increased by 9 percent, while the number of administrators increased by 130 percent. In total, half of all public school employees are now nonteaching administrators, bureaucrats, and support workers.[36] According to the US Department of Labor, there are now hundreds of thousands of public school managers making an average wage of $100,000 per year, which is significantly more than classroom teachers and the median American household.[37]

This fifty-year experiment has yielded virtually no improvement in academic outcomes—the test scores for American high school students have flatlined since the federal government began collecting data in 1971[38]—yet the expansion of the bureaucracy continues, with recent growth driven by "diversity and inclusion" divisions in the largest school districts. As the Heritage Foundation discovered, 79 percent of school districts with more than 100,000 students have hired a "chief diversity officer" and implemented university-style "diversity, equity, and inclusion" programming.[39]

Seattle Public Schools provides a model for how deeply the bureaucracy can entrench itself. The district, which has a $1 billion annual budget for 52,000 students, has created a Department of Racial Equity Advancement; a Division of Equity, Partnerships, and Engagement; a Department of Ethnic Studies; Office of African American Male Achievement; and an Equity and Race Advisory Committee. The district's race and identity programs receive at least $5 million in dedicated annual funding and involve hundreds of school employees, who design the policies at the central offices and implement them as part of school-level "Racial Equity Teams."[40]

These positions are purely ideological: as part of the Department of Racial Equity Advancement, for example, the district employs a full-time director for building "Black liberation movements," a full-time program manager for "actively dismantling the systems of oppression," and a full-time "critical race theorist" for "building leadership racial capacity."[41]

The narrative of these programs is a familiar one: in its teacher training materials, Seattle Public Schools explains that the United States is a "race-based white-supremist society," that public schools are guilty of "spirit murder" against minorities, and that white teachers must confront their "thieved inheritance"; in order to rectify these injustices, school employees must embrace "anti-racist pedagogy," support the "current social justice movements taking place," and work toward the "abolition" of whiteness.[42] The lesson planners in the central office are busy designing a "liberatory curriculum for grades K–5 that embeds Black Studies across all subjects

[and] a district-wide Black Studies course for middle and high school students that will be required for graduation."[43]

Even math and science have been captured. According to the district's Math Ethnic Studies Framework, students must learn to reject "'Western' mathematics," which has been used to "oppress and marginalize people and communities of color," and adopt the superior theory of "ethnomathematics," developed by the Brazilian postmodernist and student of Paulo Freire, Ubiratan D'Ambrosio.[44] The district spins the postcolonial myth that mathematical theory "is rooted in the ancient histories of people and empires of color," whose accomplishments were then stolen, subverted, and obscured by white Europeans. Students, therefore, must decolonize mathematics and, following Freire, learn how to "decode mathematical knowledge," "advocate against oppressive mathematical practices," and "change mathematics from individualistic to collectivist thinking."[45]

The real innovation in Seattle, however, is beyond content and curriculum. The district's planners have begun an unprecedented campaign to encrust every subdivision of the school system with a layer of racial bureaucracy. It begins, as in the universities, with an endless rotation of lectures and training programs, but concludes with the deployment of ideologically driven "Racial Equity Teams" to every campus in the district.[46] The program, which currently operates in forty-nine schools, seeks to create "racialized educators," implement critical pedagogy "in every classroom," deconstruct "whiteness [and] privilege," and engage in "anti-racism advocacy in schools."[47] These teams are composed of one administrator and four teachers at each school, who meet regularly, undergo extensive critical pedagogy training, and enforce the ideology across the campus.[48]

They are the eyes and ears of the bureaucracy, in the same way that political officers in the postcolonial regimes monitored and regulated the practices of local schools. The ideology is the weapon, the bureaucracy is the authority, and the revolution is the goal.

The grounds have already shifted within Seattle Public Schools. In meetings, teachers identify themselves by race and gender identifiers—"Brandon, He/Him, White," "Nichole, She/Her, Black"—and engage in elaborate rituals and repetitions of the faith. They confess their status as colonizers, promise to "bankrupt their privilege," and orient their classrooms toward "abolition."[49] They also accumulate power. The bureaucracy subsidizes and rewards individuals who enforce the orthodoxy and, in turn, reinforce the bureaucracy. From ethnomathematics to mandatory "racial equity audits," education is passed through the filter of politics—and there is no limiting principle.

During his lifetime, Freire had a certain ambivalence about pure identity politics, which had been gaining ground in academic circles. Toward the end of his life, in his book of correspondence to his niece, *Letters to Cristina*, he bowed to the identity categories of "class, gender, race, and culture," but warned that "the fight for liberation" could never be "reduced to the fight of women against men, of blacks against whites." In his rhetoric, Freire strove to provide a basis for unity, prioritizing human universals over fragmented identity categories. "The fight is one of all human beings toward being more," he wrote. "It is a fight to overcome obstacles to the humanization of all. It is a fight for the creation of structural conditions that make a more democratic society possible."[50]

But, at the same time, he could not resist the temptations of sweeping explanations and racial reductionism. When asked why "students of color" had failed to achieve strong educational outcomes even in "so-called progressive societies," he responded: "The failure of students of color represents the success of a dominant racist power. . . . The failure of black students is not their responsibility, but that of the policies discriminating against them." That is, the complex reasons for educational disparities—including formative influences such as family, culture, and study habits—could be reduced a priori to a single variable: racism. The problem was that the progressive societies might have adopted a regime of legal equality but had "not yet died to their racist selves or experienced their rebirth as democratic selves."

Freire's answer, as always, was more revolution. He believed that left-wing activists must not only seize the "infrastructure" of state institutions but also must continuously work to change the "superstructure" of culture, which inevitably lags behind.[51]

In practice, however, this process always ends in disappointment: from Guinea-Bissau to the California ghetto, Freire's theories have never resulted in the meaningful improvement of practical skills, such as reading and writing. They provide a relentless critical function, but not a substantive alternative. But rather than confront these failures on their own terms, the critical pedagogists use them as justification for a permanent revolution against the "cultural invasion" of the dominant class.[52] As the ideology exhausts itself logically and empirically, the humanism falls away and vengeance reveals its hideous face.

In the final stretch of his life, Freire recounted in his letters that his vision was still influenced by the ghost stories he had heard as a child, in which God would send the spirits of the oppressors wailing into the darkness of the sugarcane fields. But, as a man, he believed that this retribution must be made real in the world of the flesh. "The ideal is to punish them in history, not in the imagination," he wrote. "The ideal is in overcoming our weakness and impotence by no longer concerning ourselves with punishing the souls of the unjust, by 'making them' wander with cries of remorse. Precisely because it is the live, conscious body of the cruel person that needs to weep, we must punish them in society."[53]

This—idealism that has devolved into revenge—is where his revolution would turn.

* * *

Paulo Freire died in 1997 at the Albert Einstein Hospital in São Paulo, Brazil.[54] He died a hero of the global Left. In the last stretch of his life, he had traveled the world collecting the accolades of the liberal intelligentsia: the UNESCO Prize for Education for Peace, the King Balduin African Development Prize, and twenty-seven honorary doctorates from institutions scattered across the earth.[55]

Freire's legacy is, in some ways, a surprise. History should have reduced *Pedagogy of the Oppressed* into an ideological curiosity. The revolutionary figures he idealized—Lenin, Stalin, Mao, Castro, Guevara—turned out to be monsters. Lenin, Stalin, and Mao laid waste to their own societies in the name of the revolution. Castro and Guevara's Cuba still clings to state-run communism, but it is a poor, isolated, authoritarian nation. And all of the regimes that Freire advised—Angola, Mozambique, Tanzania, Cape Verde, São Tomé and Príncipe, and El Salvador—abandoned Marxism-Leninism and have sought, sometimes furtively, to make the transition to a market economy and democratic system of government.

And yet, Freire remained unrepentant until the end. The old man, having watched his revolutions fail across the globe, having seen the mass deaths unleashed in the name of utopia, wanted to try once more. In his final works, there is no sign of guilt or introspection, no trace of regret about the regimes he had guided and rationalized.

Long after the fall of the Berlin Wall in 1989, Freire still railed against "the intrinsic evil of capitalism" and "bourgeois democracy." He insisted, just before his death, that "the proclaimed triumph of capitalism and death of socialism actually just underlines the perversity of capitalism on the one hand and the enduring socialist dream on the other, if it is purified, with sacrifice and pain, from authoritarian distortion."[56] He downplayed the atrocities under Stalinism as "historical, philosophical, and epistemological errors," not intrinsic flaws of state communism. He insisted that his "dream," his "utopia," was still possible—it just needed to be purified, purged, reimagined.[57]

But while Freire failed to institutionalize his ideas in the Marxist-Leninist nations, his work has had a profound influence in the United States—the beating heart of global capitalism.

For the men and women of the Third World, where poverty, hunger, disease, and corruption reigned, Freire's abstractions offered little sustenance; his call for "committing suicide as a class" was madness.[58] But in the First World, insulated from the concrete miseries of the postcolonial societies, Freire's abstract appeals to liberation, revolution, and socialism have found a receptive audience. American intellectuals took Freire's concepts as a metaphor, believing that the slums of the "Third World in the First World" provided a justification for, at minimum, a cultural revolution. These writers and activists, maintained by the university system and celebrated in the public schools, imagined themselves as a new vanguard that could finally correct the unfinished business of the twentieth century.

The grave diggers of São Paulo might have buried Paulo Freire's body,[59] but nothing, it seems, could adequately shake the world of his ideas. America might have vanquished the revolution abroad, only to find itself in the midst of a revolution at home.

CHAPTER 12

Engineers of the Human Soul

The Soviet dictator Joseph Stalin raised his glass to a group of artists assembled at the home of famed writer Maxim Gorky in 1932. "The 'production' of souls is more important than the production of tanks," he said, explaining that the communists desired not only to remake the world of politics and economics, but to reshape human nature according to the dictates of left-wing ideology. "And so," he continued, "I raise my glass to you, writers, the engineers of the human soul."[1]

This concept—the ruthless application of politics to the most intimate recesses of the human spirit—would drive the communist regimes for the middle part of the twentieth century. The Soviets had their artists. The Chinese had their propagandists.[2] The Third World armies had their pedagogists. All were committed to the creation of the New Man.

The Marxists in the West, such as Paulo Freire, held the same philosophy. Freire and his disciples believed that the critical pedagogies could reengineer the human soul and inspire a revolution from the bottom up. But in contradiction to their counterparts in the East, the dividing line between oppressor and oppressed in the West was not social class, but racial identity.

"Although [Freire]'s early work was understandably rooted in an almost exclusive concern with class, many of us realized that it had theoretical shortcomings in dealing with the central issues shaping the multicultural debate," explained Freire's closest American collaborator, Henry Giroux. "Many of us began to expand the notion of social justice to include a discourse about racial justice. That is, justice could not be taken up solely in terms of the ownership of the means of production, or strictly around questions of labor or the division of wealth. These were very important issues, but they excluded fundamental questions about racism, colonialism, and the workings of the racial state."[3]

Echoing Marcuse's redefinition of the proletariat—the white intellectuals united with the black underclass—Freire's American disciples developed an elaborate framework for categorization and subversion of the ruling order. Their primary pedagogical strategy was to pathologize white identity, which was deemed inherently oppressive, and radicalize black identity, which was deemed inherently oppressed. In the academic literature, this technique is sometimes referred to as "revolutionary pedagogy," "critical multiculturalism," or "decolonization," which entails ridding the education system of the repressive influence of "whiteness" and infusing it with the liberating influence of "blackness."

Peter McLaren, another Freire disciple who worked in tandem with Henry Giroux, laid out the mechanics of how this new pedagogy of revolution would work in practice. American teachers and students, McLaren argued, must "[break] the imaginary power of commodified identities within capitalism" and "construct sites—provisional sites—in which new structured mobilities and tendential lines of forces can be made to suture identity to the larger problematic of social justice."[4]

Appealing directly to figures such as Che Guevara and Vladimir Lenin, McLaren contended that the ultimate end of critical pedagogy was to use the power of identity politics in order to "gain control of the production of meaning"[5] and to usher in a "democratic socialist society" that combined the identity-based "struggle over cultural meanings" with the traditional Marxist "redistribution of material resources."[6] For McLaren and the critical pedagogists, this movement of decolonization was already gathering at the margins in the 1990s as the influence of Freire's theories began to expand in academia and school administration. "Decolonized spaces are forming in the borderlands," McLaren predicted a quarter century ago. "And these will affect the classrooms of the future."[7]

That future has already arrived. Public school districts across the country have begun to apply the principles of critical pedagogy in the classroom. The practice follows a recurring pattern: teachers set an emotional anchor by framing the United States as an oppressive society, separate individual students into the categories of "oppressor" and "oppressed," and direct the group toward prearranged political conclusions. As the diversity czar and activist teachers at Buffalo Public Schools recently explained, school districts that follow the "pedagogy of liberation" begin "preparing [students] at four years old," train them to achieve "critical consciousness," and transform them into "activists for antiracism."[8]

And just as it was for the revolutionaries in the Third World, the goal for Giroux, McLaren, and the second-generation critical pedagogists is always the same: dismantling the criminal justice system, disrupting the nuclear family, overthrowing the system of capitalism, and, in the words of Freire, turning the schools into "an extraordinary instrument to help build a new society and a new man."[9]

The critical pedagogists of today have combined that long-standing vision with the latest techniques of the social and behavioral sciences. Freire's techniques have been adapted, merged, and combined with a range of other educational approaches, including critical social justice, critical ethnic studies, critical whiteness studies, culturally responsive teaching, antiracist pedagogy, and social-emotional learning. The theoreticians divide the world into identity hierarchies; the teachers engage in the work of decolonization; the students become entries in sprawling databases; the bureaucracies process human data into social change.[10]

"It's important to recognize that now is the time to brush hard against the grain of teaching until the full range of revolutionary pedagogical options are made available in the public schools of the nation," says the pedagogist McLaren. "Part of the task is ethical: to make liberation and the abolition of human suffering the goal of the educative enterprise itself. Part of the task is political: to create a democratic socialist society in which democracy will be called upon daily to live up to its promise."[11]

When Stalin toasted the artists of postrevolutionary Russia as "engineers of the human soul," he was speaking metaphorically, imagining the day that artists could create new men with scientific precision. That time, the critical pedagogists believe, has now come. The cherished goal of liberation through education, emblazoned in the sky by Guevara and implanted in the soul by Freire, might finally be within reach. After students are primed emotionally, categorized individually, and mobilized collectively, they can set about doing the work of revolution.

*   *   *

The "pedagogy of liberation" is, in practice, composed of two parallel pedagogies: one for the oppressor, another for the oppressed.

The dominant method, given the racial demographics of the United

States, could be described as the "pedagogy of whiteness." The foundation of this approach is the reification of white identity, which is reduced and hardened into an essentialist category—"Whiteness"—then loaded with negative connotations. Barbara Applebaum, a leading scholar in the field of "critical whiteness studies," describes this racialist metaphysics in her book *Being White, Being Good*: "Critical whiteness studies begins with the acknowledgement that whiteness and its concomitant privileges tend to remain invisible to most white people. In order to dislodge whiteness from its position of dominance, whiteness must be studied in order to 'make visible what is rendered invisible when viewed as the normative state of existence.' From this perspective, racism is essentially a white problem. . . . For white people then, it is impossible to gain an understanding of systemic racism without naming whiteness and understanding how whiteness works."[12]

Applebaum argues that all white people are "infected" by a cluster of psychological evils: "white ignorance," "white complicity," "white privilege," "white denial," and "white supremacy."[13] Individual whites might insist on their own moral goodness, but, in truth, "all whites, by virtue of systemic white privilege that is inseparable from white ways of being, are implicated in the production and reproduction of systemic racial injustice"—in other words, as Applebaum summarizes, "'all whites are racist,'" or, at minimum, complicit, no matter their individual behavior, character, or beliefs.[14] Racism is baked into the very ontology of whiteness. It is a collective psychological condition that emanates through and upholds the oppressive structures of society.

Within such a system, what can be done? For Applebaum and the critical pedagogists, it begins with confession. One pair of theorists describes it simply: "A big step would be for whites to admit that we are racist, and then to consider what to do about it."[15]

The San Diego Unified School District provides a concrete example of this process of renunciation. In a district-wide training program, administrators delivered the blunt commands of the pedagogy of whiteness, telling white teachers: "you are racist"; "you are upholding racist ideas, structures, and policies"; "confront and examine your white privilege." It is the pedagogical equivalent of shock therapy: stun the subject, send him into emotional disarray, and purge the sickness from the body. The administrators concede that this technique will likely cause "guilt, anger, apathy, frustration, closed-mindedness, [and] defensiveness."[16] But that is part of the process: teachers should recoil in horror at their whiteness.

The running theme of this pedagogy is the production of guilt. In another training, a consultant for San Diego Unified explained that white teachers were guilty of "spirit murdering" black children and that their "whiteness reproduces poverty, failing schools, high unemployment, school closings, and trauma for people of color." The cure, according to the district, is racial renunciation and "antiracist therapy for White educators," who must "acknowledge," "confront," and "use" their whiteness for the cause of "antiracism"[17] and, in the words of one school official, "racial healing."[18] Such is the tenor of the critical pedagogy in practice: whiteness is seen as a malevolent, invisible force that shapes the material world and manifests as a sickness within an entire race.

While this confessional method could theoretically solve whiteness as a psychological problem, it does not solve "whiteness" as an economic and political problem. Here one must turn to another theorist, Noel Ignatiev, who was the first activist, then scholar, to elaborate the theory of "white-skin privilege."

Ignatiev was a man who bridged the old and the new Left: he had worked in the steel mills and organized for the Communist Party USA before pursuing a doctorate at the Harvard Graduate School of Education. In an influential 1967 pamphlet, *White Blindspot*, Ignatiev laid out his theory that American capitalists and labor leaders had struck an unholy bargain, dispensing racial privileges to the white working class in order to appease them with material comforts, divide them from oppressed minorities, and prevent the development of a class-based socialist revolution.[19]

"The U.S. ruling class has made a deal with the misleaders of American labor, and through them with the masses of white workers," Ignatiev wrote. "The terms of the deal, worked out over the three hundred year history of the development of capitalism in our country, are these: you white workers help us conquer the world and enslave the non-white majority of the earth's laboring force, and we will repay you with a monopoly of the skilled jobs, we will cushion you against the most severe shocks of the economic cycle, provide you with health and education facilities superior to those of the non-white population, grant you the freedom to spend your money and leisure time as you wish without social restrictions, enable you on occasion to promote one of your number out of the ranks of the laboring class, and in general confer on you the material and spiritual privileges befitting your white skin."[20]

For Ignatiev, whites must shed this "white-skin privilege" in order to create cross-racial solidarity and then subvert the system of capitalism. Thus, the renunciation of "whiteness" becomes more than a personal act of purification. It becomes a political act against the entire racial and economic order. Just as Freire urged the bourgeoisie to commit class suicide in Guinea-Bissau, Ignatiev urged whites to commit race suicide in America—all, of course, to advance the revolution.

"Communists," Ignatiev pleaded, "must go to the white workers and say frankly: you must renounce the privileges you now hold, must join the Negro, Puerto Rican and other colored workers in fighting white supremacy, must make this the first, immediate and most urgent task of the entire working class, in exchange for which you, *together with* the rest of the workers will receive all the benefits which are sure to come from one working class (of several colors) fighting together."[21]

Decades later, after earning his PhD from Harvard and becoming a whiteness studies professor, Ignatiev founded the magazine *Race Traitor* and intensified his rhetoric: "abolish the white race"; "treason to whiteness is loyalty to humanity"; "we intend to keep bashing the dead white males, and the live ones, and the females too, until the social construct known as 'the white race' is destroyed—not 'deconstructed' but destroyed."[22] As one of Ignatiev's collaborators put it, the new radicals must see "the attack against white supremacy as the key to strategy in the struggle for socialism in the United States."[23]

Ignatiev's worldview, as radical as it was, was not limited to the confines of academia. His concepts and rhetoric, which serve as the crucial link between individual and collective action, have made their way into the public education system.

At the East Side Community School in New York City, for example, principal Mark Federman sent a letter encouraging white parents to become "white traitors" and advocate for "white abolition"—the precise terminology developed by Ignatiev decades prior. The letter included a graphic outlining eight stages of white identity development—from the lowest form, "white supremacist," to the intermediate forms of "white confessional" and "white traitor," to the highest form, "white abolitionist."[24]

The goal of this process, according to the graphic's creator, Northwestern University professor Barnor Hesse, is to challenge the "regime of whiteness" and eventually to "subvert white authority" and "not [allow] whiteness to reassert itself."[25] For Hesse, the Western concepts of "'rationality,' 'liberalism,' 'capitalism,' 'secularism,' [and] 'rule of law'" are "white mythologies" that are used to justify, extend, and perpetuate white domination.[26] Hesse's theoretical work buries itself in dense critiques of Kant, Hegel, Marx, Weber, and Foucault, but his "8 white identities" schematic is easily digested by schoolteachers and left-wing activists. Hesse describes his method as creating a "shock to the system" that can begin to prepare the grounds for "abolishing white institutions that rest on the authority of structural racism and white supremacy."[27]

The ambition of the pedagogy of whiteness is sweeping: from the initial changes to "white identity," to the condemnation of "white mythologies," to the subversion of the entire "regime of whiteness," the critical pedagogists see the manipulation of racial identity as a key mechanism for advancing the left-wing revolution. American parents might wince at submitting their children to "white privilege" exercises, but they are often reassured by the soft, therapeutic language of many educators. "It's just acknowledging that some people start life with more advantages than others," a teacher might say. Or, if there is resistance, school officials can use harder tactics of guilt and shame: as the East Side Community School told parents, white people who hesitate in "owning [their] privilege" are upholding white supremacy itself. "Racism and hate [are] the underlying cause fueling their beliefs."[28]

But underneath the rhetoric, the critical pedagogists are playing a serious game. They want to dismantle the pillars of Western society—rationalism, individualism, capitalism, natural rights, the rule of law—and usher in a post-liberal, or post-whiteness, political order. This process begins with the engineering of the human soul: the educator can reshape the psychology of the child, then lead him down the path of political activism.

Although it might be translated into brightly colored illustrations for kindergartners, the beating heart of the pedagogy of whiteness is to enact a revolution of values against the West and install another set of values that will lead, they hope, to the realization of Paulo Freire's elusive dream: the suicide of the bourgeoisie.

*   *   *

The pedagogy for minority students—the true "pedagogy of the oppressed"—is the mirror image of the pedagogy of whiteness.

Freire and his disciples conceptualized minority communities in America as "the Third World in the First World": the ruling power has created a web of structures and mythologies that secure the interests of white elites and submerge the consciousness of the oppressed.[29] Like the native populations in Mozambique or Guinea-Bissau, racial minorities in the United States must fight to decolonize their communities and liberate themselves from their oppressor.

For Freire, liberation cannot be achieved through individual cultivation, but requires the transformation of society as a whole. "The relationship between the metropolitan society and the dependent society [is] the source of their respective ways of being, thinking, and expression," he wrote in *The Politics of Education*. "Both the metropolitan society and the dependent society, totalities in themselves, are part of a greater whole, the economic, historical, cultural, and political context in which their mutual relationships evolve."[30]

Therefore, Freire says, the oppressed must learn how to "read the world" in order to "read the word."[31] That is, the starting point of education is to gain political consciousness, rather than basic literacy. He poses his ideal as "a society that is increasingly decolonized, that increasingly cuts the chains that made it, and that make it remain the object of others, which they are subjected to."[32]

In the American context, the relationship between colonizer and colonized takes on an explicit racial dimension: the social categories of oppressor and oppressed can be neatly transposed onto the racial categories of "whiteness" and "blackness." While white children are directed to dismantle "whiteness" as an internalized psychological phenomenon, black children must dismantle "whiteness" as externalized social structures that imprison, denigrate, and repress their "blackness."

This interpretation can be either literal or figurative. In Freire's time, the decolonizers fought physical wars to banish whites from Africa, Asia, and Latin America. In the current day, the decolonizers fight symbolic wars to banish "whiteness" from American institutions, beginning in the classroom and ending, they hope, with the institutions of culture, economy, and law. The enemy is dispersed through the superstructure—and "blackness" is seen as the antidote to "whiteness."

Freire's disciple Peter McLaren makes the point explicit. "Blackness and whiteness are not symmetrical; rather, they exist in society within a dependent hierarchy, with whiteness constraining the social power of blackness: by colonizing the definition of what is normal; by institutionalizing a greater allocation of resources for white constituencies; and by maintaining laws that favor Whites," he says. Consequently, society must free itself from "the shackles of whiteness," engage in "antiwhite struggle," and adopt the politics of "blackness" and the "Reason of the Other"—an entirely separate epistemological framework that negates Western rationality and opposes the "violent, coercive, genocidal reason" of whiteness.

"I call for the denial, disassembly, and destruction of whiteness as we know it," McLaren declares. "Revolutionary multiculturalism is not limited to transforming attitudinal discrimination, but is dedicated to reconstituting the deep structures of political economy, culture, and power in contemporary social arrangements. It is not about reforming capitalist democracy but rather transforming it by cutting it at its joints and then rebuilding the social order from the vantage point of the oppressed."[33]

How does the "pedagogy of blackness" work in practice? It begins with teaching minority students how to "read the world" through the lens of critical pedagogy.

Buffalo Public Schools provides a vivid illustration. The district, which serves a student population that is 45 percent black and 80 percent minority,[34] has adopted a "pedagogy of liberation" that follows the principles of Paulo Freire. Instead of focusing on improving academic achievement—dismissed as a myth used to perpetuate whiteness—school administrators have adopted the full suite of fashionable, left-wing methods: "culturally responsive teaching," "equity-based instructional strategies," "Black Lives Matter at School," and an "emancipatory curriculum."[35] As the district's diversity czar, Fatima Morrell, explained to teachers, the solution to the challenges facing American society is to "be woke, which is basically critically conscious."[36]

The predicate to Buffalo's "pedagogy of liberation" is to establish the narrative that the white power structure in the United States systematically oppresses minorities—in other words, to establish the conditions from which students must be liberated. During an all-hands training session for teachers introducing the new curriculum, Morrell explained that America "is built on racism" and that all Americans are guilty of "implicit racial bias." She argued that "America's sickness" leads some whites to believe that blacks are "not human," which makes it "easier to shoot someone in the back seven times if you feel like it."[37]

The curriculum constantly reprises these themes. In kindergarten, teachers ask students to compare their skin color with an arrangement of crayons, which establishes their position in the racial hierarchy, and then play a video that dramatizes dead black children speaking to them from beyond the grave, warning black students they could be killed by "racist police and state-sanctioned violence" at any moment. By fifth grade, students are taught that America has created a "school-to-grave pipeline" for black children and that, as adults, "one million Black people are locked in cages."

In middle and high school, students learn the theory of "systemic racism," which teaches that America was designed for the "impoverishment of people of color and enrichment of white people." Students are told that "all white people play a part in perpetuating systemic racism" and that white elites, in particular, "work to perpetuate racism through politics, law, education, and the media." By the end of high school, the predicate is firmly established: the regime of whiteness, from epistemology to economics to criminal justice, is the omnipresent force that has reduced minorities to a life of misery, failure, and oppression.[38]

What then? The pedagogy of blackness. Buffalo's curriculum is explicitly opposed to Western epistemology, values, and institutions. Schools are instructed to promote the fourteen "Black Lives Matter principles," which teach students to disrupt "Western nuclear family dynamics," dismantle "structural racism and white supremacy," challenge "cisgender privilege," break "the tight grip of heteronormative thinking," and abolish "sexism, misogyny, and male-centeredness." In their place, schools must become "unapologetically Black," support "Black villages," create "queer-affirming network[s]," embrace "Black families," uplift "Black trans folk," and hire "more Black teachers."[39]

In a series of lessons on government, the district encourages students to imagine replacing the white European system of justice with a traditional African system of justice. According to the materials, whites have created a "retributive," "merit-based" justice system, which relies on harsh punishment and creates inequalities. Traditional Africans, on the other hand, rely on a "restorative," "need-based" justice system focused on healing, prioritizing "collective value" over individual rights, prohibiting ownership of private property, and providing for each according to his needs—a primitive communism that preceded European contact.[40]

The district utilizes Chancellor Williams's 1971 book *The Destruction of Black Civilization*, which argues that ancient black civilizations had superior constitutions and systems of government, which, following colonization, "all Africans lost and of which their descendants do not have even a memory." Williams proposes rediscovering this tradition of blackness, summoning the power of the ancient civilizations, and reconquering white institutions in their image. "The re-education of Blacks and a possible solution of racial crises can begin, strangely enough, only when Blacks fully realize this central fact in their lives: the white man is their bitter enemy," Williams writes. "For this is not the ranting of wild-eyed militancy, but the calm and unmistakable verdict of several thousand years of documented history."[41]

The pedagogy of blackness quickly becomes naked political activism, which is often smuggled under the label of "anti-racism."

In the School District of Philadelphia, for instance, administrators, unions, and teachers have all converged on racial politics as the new North Star. Following the George Floyd riots, the district superintendent released an Antiracism Declaration promising to dismantle "systems of racial inequity"[42] and circulated a memo recommending racially segregated training programs for white and black educators. Meanwhile, the local teachers' union produced a video denouncing the United States as a "settler colony built on white supremacy and capitalism" that has created a "system that lifts up white people over everyone else."[43] The solution, according to the union, is to overthrow the "racist structure of capitalism," provide "reparations for Black and Indigenous people," and "uproot white supremacy and plant the seeds for a new world."[44]

At Philadelphia's William D. Kelley elementary school, which is 94 percent black and 100 percent poor,[45] administrators have overhauled the school's programming to focus on political activism. As part of the social studies curriculum, for example, the school's fifth-grade teacher created a unit celebrating Angela Davis, praising the "black communist" for her fight against "injustice and inequality." At the end of the lesson, the teacher led the ten- and eleven-year-old students into the school auditorium to "simulate" a Black Power rally to "free Angela Davis" from prison, where she had once been held while awaiting trial on charges of conspiracy, kidnapping, and murder.

The students marched on the stage, holding signs that read "Black Power," "Jail Trump," "Free Angela," and "Black Power Matters." They chanted about Africa, appealed to their tribal ancestors, then shouted "Free Angela! Free Angela!" as they stood at the front of the stage.[46] Even the school's public artwork illustrates this shift: administrators painted over a mural of Martin Luther King Jr., Nelson Mandela, and Barack Obama and replaced it with the iconography of Davis and Huey P. Newton.[47]

The theory in Buffalo, Philadelphia, and other majority-minority districts is that, by focusing on the development of racial and political consciousness, schools can prepare students to reshape the world. Paulo Freire believed the schools could "extroject" the oppressor ideology and establish a new method of liberation on the grounds of indigenous knowledge. But this is an illusion. The call to abandon Western epistemology and retribalize Marcuse's "ghetto population" is a dead end. The appeal to tribal ancestors or the primitive communism of ancient black civilizations cannot provide a stable foundation for success in the modern world.

The schoolhouse protests can provide psychological compensation— the fantasy of liberation and revenge—but, after the crowds disperse and the cardboard signs are broken down, they offer nothing for the future. As one William D. Kelley School teacher remarked, "One of the saddest things about [the] Angela Davis assignment is that most of the children in the class are either barely literate or functionally illiterate."[48]

And this is the problem. The pedagogy of liberation in America functions about as well as Freire's pedagogy of the oppressed in Guinea-Bissau—that is to say, not much at all. Buffalo Public Schools and the School District of Philadelphia have annual budgets of more than $30,000 per child,[49] significantly higher than the average educational expenditure of every other nation on earth, including rich countries such as Denmark, Norway, and

Sweden.[50] Yet the results are dismal. In Buffalo, only 18 percent of black students reach basic proficiency in English and 13 percent reach basic proficiency in math.[51] In Philadelphia, only 27 percent of black students reach basic proficiency in English and 11 percent reach basic proficiency in math.[52] In other words, the majority of these children enter the modern world functionally illiterate and innumerate.

They are condemned: not by "Western nuclear family dynamics" and "heteronormative thinking," but by the heartbreaking pathologies in their communities and the immense failures of the institutions that are supposed to serve them. The gap between rhetoric and reality is almost beyond comprehension. The ten- and eleven-year-olds at William D. Kelley march for the utopia of "black communism," but they are unable to read and write. School officials promise to transform society, but they can barely teach rudimentary skills.

In Freire's case, one might have some sympathy: Guinea-Bissau was a desperately poor nation, emerging from a bloody war, unable to produce enough food for its own citizens. But the same is not true for the "Third World in the First World." The internal colonies of Buffalo, Philadelphia, Baltimore, Detroit, and other majority-minority cities have large budgets at their disposal, as well as an ostensibly "postcolonial" leadership class of black mayors, council members, police chiefs, and district attorneys, many of whom preach the gospel of liberation. That students in these cities could leave school virtually bereft of basic literacy is a tragedy for them and a shame for the political and educational leaders promising to "plant the seeds for a new world."[53]

Sadly, administrators have chosen to double down. As Freire said of his efforts in Guinea-Bissau, they believe that "their methodological errors have ideological roots,"[54] and, consequently, they focus even more on political activism. They conduct lengthier self-criticisms, seek greater ideological purity, and blame any failures on a lack of commitment.

In Buffalo, according to a veteran teacher, the district's "pedagogy of liberation" has, in practice, become a series of "scoldings, guilt-trips, and demands to demean oneself simply to make another feel 'empowered.'" Teachers must submit to "manipulative mind games" and express support for the administration's left-wing politics, or else risk professional retaliation.[55]

In Philadelphia, rather than come to terms with the pedagogical failure of the public schools, educators shift the blame to "systemic racism" and make renewed promises of "racial justice." Meanwhile, the activists and the teachers' union intensify their commitment to racial politics and create new lists of demands, including "eliminating inherently biased practices like standardized testing," "ongoing antiracist training for all school and district staff," and "firing of racist teachers and administrators."[56]

The solution for the failure of the revolution, they believe, is more revolution. As in Guinea-Bissau, the Freirean method promises to rebuild the social structure in the image of the oppressed, but in practice it offers a cheap simulation of political power that cannot provide a viable substitute for the achievement of competency.

*   *   *

What do the critical pedagogists want? There are many names for their desires—decolonization, liberation, equity, anti-racism—but the most revealing is "abolition."

The phrase has a double meaning. On the surface, it appeals to the cachet of the anti-slavery movement. Beneath this linguistic shell, however, it is pure critical theory, operating on a ruthless dialectic of negation.

As Bettina Love, the most prominent advocate of abolitionist education, explains in her book *We Want to Do More Than Survive*, the program of abolition is a totalizing one. America, she says, is a "superpredator" that systematically "spirit-murders" minority children and "has a long history of passing laws that protect Whites when they kill, torture, and displace dark people."[57] In order for the oppressed to emerge from these eternal cruelties, Love argues, activists must abolish the entire range of American institutions, down to the foundations. The demolition list includes tangible institutions such as traditional schools, prisons, immigration enforcement, gun ownership, drug laws, cash bail, and standardized testing, as well as deep abstractions such as rationality, whiteness, and capitalism, which perpetuate "dark suffering" and ensure that "the rich get richer and the poor get disposed of."[58]

Love would destroy all of these. She believes that rationality should be suspended in favor of imagination, whiteness should be eradicated in favor of blackness, and capitalism should be destroyed in favor of collectivism. "Dark folx," Love argues, have access to secret knowledge that can transform societies beyond the restrictions of the white oppressor. Quoting the historian Robin D. G. Kelley, Love suggests that "any revolution must begin with thought, with how we imagine a New World, with how we reconstruct our social and individual relationships, with unleashing our desire and unfolding a new future on the basis of love and creativity rather than rationality."[59]

This process, for Love, can be initiated by administrators and teachers in the public school system, which is a scale-model representation of the larger society. "We like to think that education is untouched by White supremacy, White rage, and anti-Blackness, that educators are somehow immune to perpetuating dark suffering," she writes. "Education from the outset was built on White supremacy."[60] Therefore, the work of abolition begins with the elimination of white pathologies such as "White privilege," "White fragility," "White emotionality," "White violence," and "White rage."[61]

Love tells white teachers that they must constantly interrogate themselves and relinquish authority to "dark folx," who can provide the "collective vision and knowledge" that is required to build the new society.[62] "White folx have to get well on their own terms before they engage with abolitionist teaching. More than just attending antiracist workshops and culturally relevant pedagogy professional developments, they need to come to terms with what Whiteness is, how violence is needed to maintain it, and how their successes in life are by-products of Whiteness," Love explains. "White folx cannot lose their Whiteness; it is not possible. But they can daily try to deal with and reject the Whiteness that is obsessed with oppressing others, centering itself, and maintaining White supremacy through White rage. Being well and White is rejecting Whiteness for the good of humanity."[63]

From there, Love believes, the revolution can proceed. Educators can work to excavate America's rotten roots and smash them into dust. Again quoting Robin D. G. Kelley, Love argues that the solution to America's problems "cannot be traced to the founding fathers or the Constitution or the Declaration of Independence. Instead, it is manifest in the struggles of the dispossessed to overturn the Eurocentric, elitist, patriarchal, and dehumanizing structures of racial capitalism and its liberal underpinnings."[64]

Whatever one calls it—"Abolitionist," "decolonizing," "liberatory"—

the new pedagogy marks a significant advancement from Freire's original pedagogy of the oppressed. The second generation of theorists has retained the basic structure of his revolutionary neo-Marxism, then burrowed into the soft ground of identity and learned how to manipulate the primal emotions of guilt, shame, envy, and pride. They have taken Freire's analysis of "capitalism as the root of domination"[65] and added a racial politics that can guide students into identity-driven activism.

And their ambitions are just as strong. As Love told an audience of teachers and US Department of Education officials, whites must sacrifice their wealth, privilege, and power. Activists must lay waste to the prisons, the schools, capitalism, and the constitution. Minorities must be ready to receive their due. "If you've been oppressed for 400 years, you'd want to start over," she said, according to notes from the seminar. "This world was not set up for people of color, so [we] need to tear [it] down."[66]

For the critical pedagogists, nothing can be left standing. The endpoint of abolition is, ultimately, the abolition of America itself.

CHAPTER 13

The Child Soldiers of Portland

There are few places on earth where political radicals and their children ritualistically burn the American flag and chant "Death to America"—Tehran, Baghdad, Beirut, Kabul, Ramallah, and Portland, Oregon.

The city of Portland, a grim and cloud-covered metro on the south bank of the Columbia River, has developed a reputation for the colorful sloganeering of its political protestors. Anarchists, communists, ecofascists, and a variety of other agitators regularly denounce the police, politicians of both parties, and the American state itself; flag-burning has become part of the regular syntax of the protest movement.

During the summer riots in 2020, teenagers associated with the Youth Liberation Front escalated the rhetoric with chants of "Death to America" and months of violence to avenge the death of George Floyd.[1] Children as young as three or four years old marched with the crowd to the federal courthouse, raising the Black Power fist and chanting "Fuck the Police! Fuck the Police!"[2]

The irony isn't difficult to identify: Portland is famously the "whitest city in America," and yet it has become the headquarters of race radicalism in the United States. The city has elevated white guilt into a civic religion. Its citizens have developed an elaborate set of rituals, devotions, and self-criticisms to fight the chimeras of "systemic racism" and "white supremacy." The ultimate expression of this orthodoxy is violence: street militias, calling themselves "anti-racists" and "anti-fascists," are quick to smash the windows of their enemies and burn down the property of anyone who transgresses the new moral law.

It might be easy to dismiss this as the work of a few harmless radicals who are "keeping Portland weird" and, for the most part, represent a minority coalition of the malcontent and the mentally deranged—a quick glimpse through the Antifa mug shots released by the Portland Police Department will confirm this impression. But in recent years, the underlying ideology of Portland's radicals has become institutionalized. The city government has adopted a series of Five-Year Plans for "equity and inclusion," shopkeepers have posted political slogans in their windows as a form of protection, and local schools have designed a program of political education for their students that resembles propaganda.

The schools of Portland have self-consciously adopted Paulo Freire's "pedagogy of the oppressed" as their theoretical orientation, activated it through a curriculum saturated in critical theory, and enforced it through the appointment of de facto political officers within individual schools under the cover of "equity and social justice." The internal documents from three local districts—Tigard-Tualatin School District, Beaverton School District, and Portland Public Schools—reveal this revolutionary shift. Administrators and teachers have combined theory, praxis, and power in service of left-wing political activism.

The results are predictable. By perpetuating the narrative that America is fundamentally evil, steeping children in the doctrine of critical pedagogy and lionizing the rioters in the streets, the schools have consciously pushed students in the direction of revolution. In the language of the Left, the political education program in Portland-area school districts could be described as a "school-to-radicalism pipeline"—or, more provocatively, as a training ground for child soldiers.

This is not hyperbole: some of the most violent anarchist groups in Portland are run by teenagers. Dozens of minors were arrested during the long stretch of the George Floyd riots. They have attached their political cause to climate change, anti-capitalism, anti-fascism, and Black Lives Matter—whatever provides the pretext for violent "direct action."

The movement is unmistakable: out of the schools and into the streets. And contrary to those who believed that the end of the Trump presidency would usher in a "return to normalcy," the social and political revolution in Portland has not stopped with the ascendance of President Biden—it has only accelerated. On the day of Biden's inauguration, teenage radicals marched through the streets of Southeast Portland, smashing the office windows of the state Democratic Party, and unfurling large banners with their hand-painted demands: "We don't want Biden, we want revenge"; "We are ungovernable"; "A new world from the ashes."[3]

The children of Portland, intoxicated by revolution and enabled by their elders, have escaped the chain.

*   *   *

Tigard, Oregon, is a placid suburban city southwest of Portland. The city's historic main street is a pastiche of coffeehouses, boutiques, repair shops, and small-town restaurants. Historically, the city's political squabbles have been focused on zoning and land use issues, with developers fighting the city, preservationists fighting developers, and neighbors fighting one another—in other words, the typical political patterns of an affluent, predominantly white American suburb.

Nevertheless, the educators at the Tigard-Tualatin School District have gone all in on radical pedagogy and the social justice trinity of "diversity, equity, and inclusion."

In 2020, at the height of the George Floyd riots, Tigard-Tualatin superintendent Sue Rieke-Smith and board chair Maureen Wolf signed a proclamation "condemning racism and committing to being an anti-racist school district." The preamble to the document recited the names of George Floyd, Breonna Taylor, and Ahmaud Arbery, which has become a penitential rite in social justice circles, then confessed that the district's "students of color, and Black students in particular, still regularly experience racism in [their] schools." To rectify this situation, the superintendent pledged to become "actively anti-racist," "dismantle systemic racism," implement a "collective equity framework," establish "pillars for equity," deploy "Equity Teams" within schools, create racially segregated "Student Affinity Groups," and use "an equity lens for all future curriculum adoptions."[4]

The following month, the district announced the creation of a new Department of Equity and Inclusion and installed left-wing activist and critical pedagogist Zinnia Un as its director.[5] Un quickly created a blueprint for overhauling the curriculum at Tigard-Tualatin schools. The document explicitly called for adopting Freire's "pedagogy of the oppressed." Following Freire's categorizations, Un argued that the Tigard-Tualatin School District must move from a state of "reading the world" to the phase of "denunciation" against the revolution's enemies and, eventually, to the state of "annunciation" of the liberated masses, who will begin "rewriting the world." For Un, the first-order targets of denunciation were not capitalism and colonialism, as they were for Freire, but the new set of targets for the modern West: "whiteness," "colorblindness," "individualism," and "meritocracy."[6] These are the values of capitalist society, to be sure, but more deeply, they are the values of white society, which, to the second-generation critical pedagogists, is the primary axis of oppression.

What is the solution to pathological whiteness? According to Un and the Tigard-Tualatin School District, the answer lies with a new form of "white identity development." In a series of "antiracist resources" provided to teachers, the Department of Equity and Inclusion circulated a handout of strategies for "white identity development," which were designed to "facilitate growth for white folks to become allies, and eventually accomplices, for anti-racist work." The process, which is couched in the language of personal development, begins with the assumption that all whites are born "racist," even if they "don't purposely or consciously act in a racist way." In order to move beyond this state, white students must do the work of reformulating their identities according to the dictates of "anti-racist" ideology.

The first step is "contact," in which white students are confronted with "active racism or real-world experiences that highlight their whiteness." The goal is to provoke an emotional rupture that brings the subject to the next step, "disintegration," in which he or she feels intense "white guilt" and "white shame," eventually admitting: "I feel bad for being white." Once the emotional hooks have been established, the training outlines a process of moving white students from a state of "reintegration" to "pseudo-independence" to "immersion" to "autonomy," in which whites can finally serve as "allies" for the oppressed.

This is an explicitly political project: at the early stages, the district encourages students to participate in activities such as "attending a training, joining an allies group, participating in a protest." Later, white students are told to analyze their "covert white supremacy," host "difficult conversations with white friends and family about racism," and use their "privilege to support anti-racist work." At the final stage, the trainers plumb the depths of the students' individual psychology to ensure that pathological "whiteness" has been banished from their psyches. Students must answer a series of questions to demonstrate their final commitment: "Does your solidarity make you lose sleep at night? Does your solidarity put you in danger? Does your solidarity cost you relationships? Does your solidarity make you suspicious of predominantly white institutions? Does your solidarity have room for Black rage?"[7]

This is not a pedagogy of education; it is a pedagogy of revolution.

The "identity development" program also follows the textbook cult indoctrination process: persuade initiates of their fundamental guilt, present a remedy through participation in the group, manipulate the emotions to achieve compliance, identify an amorphous scapegoat, demand total loyalty to the new orthodoxy, proselytize through personal circles, isolate from old friends and family, and keep the ultimate solution always out of reach.

One veteran teacher, who requested anonymity out of fear of reprisals, said the new movement led by Un and the Department of Equity and Inclusion led to a "big change" in the district. The focus shifted immediately from academics to politics—and employees were expected to fall in line with the new ideology. The veteran teacher described one professional development training that left some of her colleagues in a neighboring school devastated: "They had teachers actually crying because of their 'whiteness.'"[8]

Which leads to the final plank in Tigard-Tualatin's new pedagogy: enforcement. As soon as Zinnia Un ascended to the position of director of equity and inclusion, she formulated a new "hate speech" policy designed to prevent legitimate discriminatory speech—and to pathologize any political opposition to the new regime. In an internal memo sent to teachers, the district outlined a clear policy that right-wing symbols and opinions were forbidden, while left-wing symbols and opinions were tacitly encouraged. As an example, the document described the "Make America Great Again hat" as a "symbol of hate or oppression" and recommended that teachers explain to students that the hat "makes [students] feel afraid" and "causes a substantial disruption to the learning environment."[9]

This is deliberate. The district requires teachers to celebrate one political movement and condemn another. "I almost feel like we're walking around on eggshells. You have to be careful what you say," the veteran teacher said. "I'm afraid of speaking up for fear I might lose my job. . . . I mean, what would happen if I said I'm a conservative Republican Christian? How would that go? How would that slide?" When asked how the new political education program had affected her personally, her voice broke and she said quietly: "I don't want to go back to work. I don't believe in this. It goes against my faith system. It's downright wrong. We're all created as equals in God's sight and this is just wrong, the way we're teaching our children. I don't have to be embarrassed because of my skin color."[10]

*   *   *

The city of Beaverton was born with the arrival of the Oregon Central Rail Road in 1868. Since then, the small farming community has transformed into a busy and affluent suburb. Commuters fight their way to the Nike corporate headquarters on Southwest Murray Boulevard and through traffic to the Intel research laboratories in nearby Hillsboro. Like Tigard, which borders the city to the south, Beaverton is a predominantly white and Asian-American community; just 2 percent of the city's population is black.[11]

Beaverton shares another important similarity with Tigard: its public schools were consumed by the racial panic following the death of George Floyd. Following the same educational theories as in Tigard, Beaverton teachers designed and began implementing a new curriculum for every grade level, beginning in kindergarten. The general language for these lessons seemed innocuous—"Diversity," "empowerment," "change-making," "culturally responsive teaching"—and most parents, busy with the demands of everyday life, would normally glance at the syllabus during parent-teacher night and forget about them.

In 2020, however, many parents had been keeping closer tabs on their children's education because of the coronavirus lockdowns and remote learning requirements. The curriculum, they discovered, revealed its radicalism in the details.

One family, which had moved to Beaverton in part for the city's highly rated public schools, collected a folder of lessons being taught to their third-grade child. The social studies module on race began innocently enough: the teacher asked the eight- and nine-year-old students to think about their "culture and identity" and join her in "celebrating diversity," set alongside pictures of a world map and cartoons of smiling children. The subsequent lessons, however, became more pointed. The teacher explained to students that "race is a social construct" created by white elites, who use those categories "to maintain power and control of one group over another." This, the teacher said, is "racism," which "can determine real-life experiences, inspire hate, and have a major negative impact on Black lives."

The next module focused on "systemic racism" and the history of the

United States. The teacher told the students that racism "infects the very structure(s) of our society," including "wealth, employment, education, criminal justice, housing, surveillance, and healthcare." To accompany the lesson, the teacher included a video presentation in which the speaker directly accused the children of being racist themselves: "Our society speaks racism. It has spoken racism since we were born. Of course you are racist. The idea that somehow this blanket of ideas has fallen on everyone's head except for yours is magical thinking and it's useless." The speaker then told the students that if they did not convert to the cause, they would "affirm the status quo of certain bodies being allowed resources, access, opportunities, and other bodies being literally killed."

The final modules presented the solution: students must embrace the principles of "revolution," "resistance," and "liberation." The teacher introduced these principles through a series of photographs of child activists, the Black Power fist, and Black Lives Matter demonstrations, as well as protest signs reading "White Silence = Compliance," "Black Lives > Property," "AmeriKKKa," and "Stop Killing Us." The goal, according to the curriculum, was for students to become "change-makers" and "antiracist in all aspects of [their] lives." They must actively fight "white supremacy, white-dominated culture, and unequal institutions," or else they would be upholding these evils. In the final lesson, the curriculum instructed third graders to "do the inner work to figure out a way to acknowledge how you participate in oppressive systems," "do the outer work and figure out how to change the oppressive systems," and "learn how to listen and accept criticism with grace, even if it's uncomfortable."[12]

Families who learned about the curriculum were outraged.

One mother, who originally emigrated from Iran to the United States, said the lessons were "absolutely unacceptable" and reminiscent of the political indoctrination in the Islamic Republic. "I moved here because this is America, because of the rights and the opportunities that we have. And this is not where I want my country to go," she explained. When asked about her own childhood in Iran, she broke down in tears. "I remember when we would line up in the morning in an assembly. We had to chant 'Death to America.' I remember being in elementary school and thinking, 'I don't want to chant this. I have aunts and uncles in America. I don't want them to die.'"

Her husband immediately sent a letter to the Beaverton School District blasting the curriculum as "presenting racist material under the guise of 'antiracism.'" He said the district was trying to conceal the materials from families. "They're trying to indoctrinate the children," he said. "And they're doing it very carefully and very slowly." He believed the ultimate intention of the new pedagogy was to turn child against parent. After the lessons began, his own child became torn between the word of the school and the word of the family, sometimes crying out of confusion. "They're slowly going to get behind their defenses, get behind the parents' defenses, and create little social justice warriors," the father said. "They're trying to hyper-empathize and hyper-emotionalize the children in order to get them to be more receptive to . . . some sort of revolution."

Eventually, the mother and father decided to pull their child from the social studies program and made plans to transfer to another school the following year. Although they were able to opt out of the program temporarily, they feared that, left unchecked, the campaign to turn children into the "pointed sword for revolution" could lead to wider social consequences.

The mother pointed out that many Iranians initially supported the Islamic Revolution in 1979 in order to depose the shah and usher in a better world, only to be bitterly disappointed. The revolutionaries promised a new utopia but ended up transforming their country into a bone-breaking tyranny. "They have absolutely zero rights," she said. "They hang people in the streets. They make them disappear. Not only them, but their families. They are for months tortured in the political prisons and then killed."

And, she believed, it could happen in America: "I'm fighting this at the school and even at my work, because I see this country going that way."[13]

Unfortunately, the kind of teaching in Beaverton is no longer the exception in the state of Oregon—it is fast becoming the rule. In 2017, Oregon state legislators passed a bill that overhauled the state curriculum and installed a mandatory "ethnic studies" program that reflects the emergent racial orthodoxy,[14] which, in the language of the Critical Ethnic Studies Association, promises to deconstruct, dismantle, abolish, eradicate, resist, and interrupt the component parts of the liberal order.[15]

According to drafts of the new Oregon state curriculum standards, kindergartners will be required to learn the "difference between private and public ownership" of goods and capital, and "develop understanding of identity formation related to self, family, community, gender, and disability."

In first grade, they will learn how to "define equity, equality, and systems of power," "examine social construction as it relates to race, ethnicity, gender, disabilities, and sexual orientation," and "describe how individual and group characteristics are used to divide, unite, and categorize racial, ethnic, and social groups." By third, fourth, and fifth grade, students will learn to deconstruct the US Constitution, uncover "systems of power, including white supremacy, institutional racism, racial hierarchy, and oppression," and "examine the consequences of power and privilege on issues associated with poverty, income, and the accumulation of wealth."

If the elementary school curriculum sets the premise—the United States is the great oppressor—the middle and high school curricula deliver the conclusion. The learning standards read like an old left-wing pamphlet. Students must internalize the principles of race-based "subversion, resistance, challenge, and perseverance." They must fight against the "structural and systemic oppression" of capitalism, authority, religion, and government. They must commit to the "pursuit of social justice."[16]

As the internal documents from the Oregon Department of Education make clear, the point of ethnic studies is not academic achievement, but "social change"[17]—education is the means, politics is the end.

*   *   *

If the cities of Tigard and Beaverton represent the categories of theory and praxis, the city of Portland represents their conclusion: power.

In recent years, Portland has emerged as the leading hub of America's left-wing radical movements. The city's loose network of Marxist, anarchist, and anti-fascist groups has turned the street riot into an art form. After the death of George Floyd, Portland's radicals attacked police officers and laid siege to federal buildings for more than one hundred consecutive nights; they armed themselves with rocks, bottles, shields, knives, guns, bricks, lasers, boards, explosives, gasoline, barricades, spike strips, brass knuckles, and Molotov cocktails.[18] Following the chaos, many downtown businesses closed their doors and insurance companies began to raise premiums or refuse to issue policies because of the risk of ongoing property destruction.[19]

The same philosophy that animates the street radicals also animates the bureaucrats at Portland Public Schools, who have institutionalized the philosophy of social justice and incorporated political activism into every aspect of the education system. In recent years, administrators have pledged to make "antiracism" the district's "north star," promising to build "an education system that intentionally disrupts—and builds leaders to disrupt—systems of oppression." The superintendent reorganized the bureaucracy around these goals, hiring a new equity czar and announcing a "Five-Year Racial Equity Plan," which promises a dizzying sequence of acronyms and academic catchphrases such as "intersectionality" and "targeted universalism."[20]

It's hard to overstate how deeply left-wing political ideology has been entrenched in all aspects of the Portland public school system.

According to one veteran elementary school teacher, who describes herself as a longtime liberal, the district's "antiracist journey" began with good intentions a decade ago but, over time, hardened into a suffocating dogma. Today this teacher must submit to mandatory anti-racism trainings each week and toe the party line in all of her instruction and communications. "From the beginning, we were told that we couldn't question [the antiracism program]," the teacher said. "I called human resources and asked them if I needed to profess that I believe this and if I had to teach from this perspective. And I was told that I need to understand it, I need to know all about it, [and] you could probably lose your job if your principal is super into making sure that you're using this lens as you teach."

At one anti-racism session, this teacher was required to participate in a "line of oppression" exercise. The trainers lined up a group of educators and shouted out various injustices—racism, sexism, homophobia, etc.—then asked the teachers who would suffer from these harms to step forward. The room was then divided into the oppressors and the oppressed, with straight white men and women forced to reckon with their identity as oppressors. The objective, according to the teacher, was to consolidate ideological power and intimidate white teachers into submission through collective guilt and fear of being labeled racists.

The anti-racism program "was the battering ram," but the ultimate goal, according to the teacher, is the "dismantling of Western culture" and the ushering in of a new left-wing utopia. "I have no doubt that that's exactly what they want," the teacher said. "And dismantling means just picking it apart until there's nothing to hold it up anymore, and then they can replace it."[21]

Today, the ideology of "anti-racism" has permeated every department in the district.

Even the educators in the English as a Second Language program have begun teaching the principles of critical pedagogy to immigrants and refugees. According to internal documents, ESL teachers are told to develop "counterstories" to the dominant American culture and focus their instruction on "advocacy for racial equity for emergent bilingual/multilingual students." As part of the curriculum, they are asked to teach immigrants that "racism in the USA is pervasive and operates like the air we breathe" and that "civil rights gains for people of color should be interpreted with measured enthusiasm."

In order to combat the pernicious influence of their own "Whiteness," the district recommends that teachers adopt a series of affirmations, beginning with "getting to know myself as a racial being" and then "[deconstructing] the Presence and Role of Whiteness in my life and [identifying] ways I challenge my Whiteness." Finally, after shedding their racial limitations, the teachers can begin the work of "interrupting institutional racism" and "the perpetuation of White Supremacy."[22]

This is a bewildering curriculum decision. Portland has a significant population of immigrants and refugees from countries such as Somalia, Ethiopia, Eritrea, Guatemala, and El Salvador. These families have escaped some of the most nightmarish conditions in the world, including civil war, genocide, starvation, and grinding poverty. The city of Portland is not perfect, but it is certainly, by comparison, a haven of peace and opportunity for the foreign-born. Yet Portland schools are intent on teaching the children of immigrants and refugees that they should tear down the very country that provided them safe harbor.

How does this regime of teacher training translate in the classroom? In all the ways one would expect.

At Forest Park, Whitman, and Marysville elementary schools, a teacher named Sarita Flores, who runs the information technology program, has transformed her role into that of a political inquisitor. According to leaked internal documents and whistleblower accounts, Flores holds weekly "anti-racism" sessions in which white teachers are asked to remain silent, "honor the feelings of BIPOC," and "make space for and amplify BIPOC educators." In a series of presentations resembling a twentieth-century struggle session, Flores instructs teachers that they must "deepen [their] political analysis of racism and oppression" and "start healing with public apologies about [their] racism and then go back and apologize through an audit through an anti-racist lens."[23]

During one of these sessions, according to a whistleblower, Flores denounced one of her white female colleagues by screaming "you make me feel unsafe, you make me feel unsafe" over and over for ninety seconds.[24]

For Flores and other teachers in the social justice wing of Portland Public Schools, the only solution is revolution. During one presentation to teachers, Flores claimed that "an educator in a system of oppression is either a revolutionary or an oppressor." In a folder hosted on the district website, Flores shared an illustration with teachers that justified the ongoing political violence in Portland: "The root cause of every riot is some kind of oppression. If you want to end the riots, you have to end the oppression. If you want to end a riot without ending its root cause, your agenda isn't about peace and justice—it's about silencing and control."

Flores's message to students was similar. In a series of video lessons delivered to her elementary school students, Flores declared that "Black people were used as slaves in the US" and, therefore, students must become "justice fighters." At the height of the protests in Portland, Flores released another video lesson telling the children that "protesting is when people hold up signs and march for justice. You've trained for this moment all year: the fight for justice."[25]

By high school, the basic education about "skin color" and "justice fighters" turns into advanced ideological training and live-action street protesting. The curriculum is saturated with critical pedagogy. At Lincoln High, a wealthy public school with only 1 percent black student enrollment, some students take two full years of "critical race studies." The course, taught by Jessica Mallare-Best, begins with training on racial identity, white supremacy, institutional racism, and racial empowerment, with the goal of providing "methods in which students can begin to be activists and allies for change." During the second year, students devote two semesters to studying "white fragility," "whiteness as property," "the permanence of racism," "collective organizing," and "being an activist" in order to prepare themselves to "do [their] part in dismantling white supremacy."[26]

The next step is obvious. The abstract becomes concrete. Theory leads to action. The students, steeped in the logic of racial revolution, go from the classroom into the streets.

This happened all over the city. At Sabin Elementary School, children as young as five held a mock protest and raised the Black Power fist alongside their teachers.[27] At Ockley Green Middle School, the "police abolitionist" Teressa Raiford held an assembly on social justice and led hundreds of students into the streets to perform a "die-in" in the middle of an intersection—without the permission or notification of their parents.[28]

During the George Floyd riots, these teacher- and student-led protests accelerated. Middle school students in Northeast Portland led a public march advocating for defunding the police.[29] High school students in Southwest Portland marched through the neighborhood demanding that white residents provide "reparations" to black people. Other schools held simulated rallies, demonstrations, protests, and activist campaigns, all in service of the district's official ideology.[30]

This is the endpoint of critical pedagogy: the students have reached "critical consciousness" and readied themselves to take their revolt into the world.

*   *   *

The consequence of Portland's educational program is a grim one: political violence. During the long summer of the George Floyd riots, Portland-area students and teachers engaged in widespread rioting, vandalism, and destruction.

The Youth Liberation Front, which was founded by teenagers and recruited heavily from Portland-area high schools, was one of the most active and violent organizations in the city. The group's leaders divided the group into autonomous cells to avoid law enforcement infiltration and armed its members with shields, weapons, gas masks, and explosives. Following the death of George Floyd, the group organized a walkout of high school students and then rioted for more than three months straight. "We are a bunch of teenagers armed with ADHD and yerba mate," they declared on social media. "We can take a 5 a.m. raid and be back on our feet a few hours later. We'll be back again and again until every prison is reduced to ashes and every wall to rubble."[31]

Over the course of the summer, the YLF led a youth revolt that rocked the city. Portland-area law enforcement arrested dozens of minors and young adults for protest-related crimes, including rioting, burglary, property destruction, throwing rocks and bottles at police officers, brandishing a fake handgun at a crowd, setting fire to the police union headquarters, and stomping a man unconscious.[32]

Portland's teachers, too, immersed themselves in the chaos. During the same period, police arrested at least five teachers for riot-related crimes, including felony riot, disorderly conduct, interfering with police officers, and assaulting a federal officer. All except one were released immediately without bail[33] and at least two of the Portland Public Schools teachers were still employed by the district a year later.[34]

None of this should come as a surprise. For years, administrators, teachers, and political leaders in Portland had been playing with fire. They filled the heads of the young with nightmarish visions of America and then promised fulfillment through revolution. But as the destruction following the death of George Floyd revealed, that revolution was devoid of positive values. The child soldiers of Portland had been promised "a new world from the ashes," but the real outcome, if they get their way, will be a world of rubble—cold, empty, and salted over.

It is difficult not to see this as a cynical game: teachers and administrators, ensconced in the public bureaucracy and secured by the public trust, engage in an absurd theater of cultural Marxism, spinning stories about "the pedagogy of the oppressed" to their privileged, suburban, predominantly white students. But for all the talk about "liberation" and "critical consciousness," they are, in truth, condemning these children to a profoundly pessimistic worldview in which racism and oppression have pervaded every institution, with no recourse but violence.

The governing institutions in Portland have reached the strange paradox in which the state, through the organs of education, is agitating for its own destruction. They have condemned the entire structure of the social order and celebrated the figures who would tear it down. They might get what they wish for, although not in the way they imagine. As the historians have warned since ancient times, democracy can easily degenerate into mob rule, which occurs when the populace loses faith in the governing system and the rule of law. The result is not utopia, but anarchy.

In Portland, they are shaping the character of the young into this regime of disorder and may not be able to withstand the consequences when the story turns. When the city's rioters chant "Whose streets? Our streets!" in call and response, one should heed them—and beware of what's to come.

PART IV

Power

CHAPTER 14

Derrick Bell

Prophet of Racial Pessimism

Derrick Bell remained a pessimist until the bitter end. He had risen from humble origins to become the first black professor at Harvard Law School. He had published bestselling books and won the praise of the national media. And he had been a mentor to a promising young student named Barack Obama, who would later win the presidency.

But in 2010, the year before his death from carcinoid cancer, Bell reaffirmed his basic principle: progress was an illusion, a myth, a false hope. "Barack is a brilliant politician, a very smart man, had a great campaign," he said. But the reason that whites had cast their vote for him was not to heal the wounds of racism but to secure their own interests through a cynical political calculus. Bell did not see the election of America's first black president as a transcendent moment, but as another pathway for the eternal recursion of American racism. "We are now not in the post-racism era, but rather in an era in which racism has been resurrected," he said. "The truth is that we are still in a racist society."[1]

Derrick Bell was a radical, but he was not a radical in the traditional mold. He was a soft-spoken academic who wore oversize black glasses and neat wool suits. He had a gentle courtroom demeanor and had written a dense, thousand-page casebook called *Race, Racism, and American Law.*[2] At the same time, he was intimately connected to the left-wing radical milieu: Bell had provided legal support to Angela Davis at her murder trial, studied the critical pedagogy of Paulo Freire, and maintained a close relationship with Black Panther Party members such as Kathleen Cleaver, the wife of Eldridge Cleaver.

But he was playing a different game than his contemporaries: Bell had seen the limitations of the Left's militant turn in the 1970s and wanted to bring the fight out of the streets and into the faculty lounge. The black lumpenproletariat had revealed the ultimate impotence of Third World–style revolution. The superior gambit, Bell understood, was to rationalize those ideas and carry them through the elite institutions.

At this task, Bell was a master. He had a brilliant strategic vision and a surprising personal magnetism. During his long career at Harvard, Bell cultivated a cadre of young intellectuals beneath him—law students who would go on to establish the discipline of critical race theory—and encouraged them to challenge the institutions from within. In his own activism, he deftly manipulated the logic of affirmative action and the emotion of white guilt in order to achieve his political objectives within the academy. And, most importantly, he laid out a grand theory of racial pessimism that became the dominant tone for left-wing racialist ideology, moving it from the rhetoric of Marxist-Leninist revolution to the rhetoric of elite grievance.

It is not an overstatement to say that Derrick Bell set the stage for the racial politics of our time. Through a combination of legal and creative writing, Bell recast the American story in a sinister light. He argued that Washington, Jefferson, and Lincoln were the cynical authors of a "slave history of the Constitution,"[3] that "racism is an integral, permanent, and indestructible component of this society,"[4] and that the contemporary regime of colorblind equality was, in fact, an insidious new form of racism that was "more oppressive than ever."[5]

In Bell's fictional stories, which allowed him to transgress polite expectations with plausible distance between his characters and his own opinions, Bell filled his pages with spleen and paranoia. In his view, white society fed blacks with myths, symbols, and a national holiday, but would never provide them with real recognition. The stories in his most famous book, *Faces at the Bottom of the Well*, featured "far-right paramilitary types"[6] hunting down blacks in the woods and raised the specter that whites might exterminate their darker-skinned countrymen in a "black holocaust."[7] In Bell's fantasies, whites traded blacks to space aliens, assassinated all of the black employees at Harvard, and paid license fees in order to practice open discrimination. Bell believed that progress was an illusion, telling his readers matter-of-factly that "black people will never gain full equality in this country."[8]

Despite this posture of fatalism, however, Bell also demonstrated a method for achieving power. He staged protests, strikes, and denunciations. His cadre of student activists engaged in pressure campaigns under the banner of "diversity." He embarrassed colleagues in public and threatened his resignation in the national press.

Bell was not a Huey Newton–style revolutionary, but something much more dangerous: an institutional player who understood how to use the politics of race to manipulate the bureaucracy. His most enduring accomplishments were grounded in his writings but became real through his disciples, who cobbled together his racial predicates with a substantive demand to deconstruct the constitutional order. These students, calling themselves "critical race theorists," would throw acid on the founding principles of the country, making the argument for dismantling colorblind equality, curtailing freedom of speech, supplanting individual rights with group-identity-based entitlements, and suspending private property rights in favor of racial redistribution.[9]

The professor was not a doctrinaire Marxist himself—he admitted that he never had time to read Marx's original texts[10]—but his students supplemented their legal education with a stew of critical theory, postmodernism, black nationalism, and Marxist ideology.[11] And following the strategy of their master, Bell, the student-activists-cum-critical-race-theorists carefully cultivated their résumés for elite influence, not violent rebellion. They did not want to assemble bombs and set them off in the US Capitol or assassinate police officers. They wanted to create a theoretical basis for undermining the American regime as a whole by attaching their ideas to real administrative power in government, education, and law.

Now, a decade after Bell's death, their blitz through the institutions has succeeded. Critical race theory, whether by name or through the euphemism of "diversity, equity, and inclusion," has become the default ideology of the universities, the federal government, the public schools, and the corporate human resources department. It is a stunning coup that began with the vision of one brilliant but troubled man.

* * *

The roots of Derrick Bell's pessimism were planted in the clay shales of Pittsburgh, Pennsylvania. His father, Derrick Sr., was born in the cotton and peanut fields of Alabama, dropped out of school in sixth grade, and emigrated to the North to work in the steel mills. The family survived the Great Depression and Derrick Sr. eventually found work as a porter in a department store, earning a respectable nineteen dollars a week. His son, Derrick Jr., was small, bookish, and timid. The black children in the neighborhood terrorized him and ran him through the streets. "I was very small, couldn't fight worth anything," Bell recalled.[12]

Then the family's fortunes changed. Bell's father hit the numbers with the local bookmaker, earning a seven-hundred-dollar windfall, and Bell's mother, Ada, insisted that the family put the money toward buying a three-bedroom house in a mostly white section of the city's Hill District. Bell Sr. was proud of the home—they had a view over the entire city from their back window—and the fact that he earned enough for his wife to stay home with the children.[13]

Beginning in junior high school, Derrick took on a paper route, serving the homes of the neighborhood's black professional class. He witnessed a remarkable tableau of black success—doctors, ministers, businessmen, lawyers, and judges—in spite of the ugly regime of racial segregation.

Two men along Bell's route, Judge Homer Brown and attorney Everett Utterback, sensed a restless intelligence in the boy and encouraged him to consider a career in law. "[They] virtually adopted me. They invited me in for tea, to visit on holidays, and were always ready with advice that in short let me know that 'we made it and so can you,'" Bell wrote.[14] It was an era of unconscionable racial subordination, but Bell had seen the possibility of dignity and hope for the future. "My family enjoyed what was, by black folks' standards, a middle-class life," he recalled. "My parents encouraged and paid for my college education and that of my brother and two sisters."[15]

Although Bell describes his white neighbors on the Hill as friendly and respectful, there was an undercurrent of racial tension in the Bell household. Derrick Sr. had grown up in the backwaters of the Deep South and had faced the cruelty of white racism, once getting whipped, bloodied, and humiliated by a group of white teenagers at the county fair. He taught his son to maintain an understandable suspicion of whites. "Neither of my parents hated whites. They simply dealt realistically with race issues as they found them," Bell wrote years later. "My father often cited from a mental collection of racial assertions. Example: 'Son, you must work hard because white folks are planning and scheming while we Negroes are eating and sleeping.'" He told his son that he could invite whites into their home, but "as for me, I never trusted them."[16]

At the same time, Derrick Sr. taught his son how to be strong. When he worked as a porter and, later, after he started a business running sanitation trucks, Bell the father always demanded the respect of whites—and they gave it to him. As he told his son, after getting whipped by the white teenagers at the county fair, he tracked them down to a deserted stretch of road and pummeled them into the ground.

As he turned into a man, Bell Jr. was an immense success. He earned a bachelor's degree from Duquesne University, served a stint in the US Air Force, and then, in 1954, following the encouragement of the black law-yers on his old paper route, enrolled at the University of Pittsburgh Law School. It was a buoyant year for black expectations. The Supreme Court had struck down racial segregation and the civil rights movement was be-ginning to deliver meaningful victories. Bell was the only black student at Pitt Law and, through his involvement with civil rights organizations, met the greatest black legal minds of the era: Charles Houston, Thurgood Mar-shall, William Hastie.

After graduation, he secured a job with the Department of Justice, then with the NAACP in Pittsburgh, and finally with the NAACP's central office in New York City. The attitude at the time was unadulterated optimism. Hastie, the first black federal judge in the United States, told young Bell that his interest in civil rights law was admirable but that he "was born fifteen years too late to have a career in civil rights"—in other words, the fight for racial equality was nearly won.[17]

Still, Bell poured himself into civil rights work with courage and gusto.

Between 1960 and 1966, he supervised or litigated nearly three hun-dred school integration cases in the Deep South.[18] "During the early 1960s, I doubt that I was the only civil rights lawyer who saw him- or her-self as the briefcase-carrying counterpart of the Lone Ranger," he wrote. "We flew into Southern cities and towns, prepared our hearings with lo-cal counsel, and spoke out fearlessly in courtrooms often filled with hos-tile whites on one side, and hopeful blacks on the other. Whatever the outcome, we were the heroes to our black clients and their friends and supporters. 'Lawyer,' they would tell us admiringly, 'you sure did stand up to those racists.' We were, we thought, breaking down the legal barriers of racial segregation and opening a broad new road toward freedom and justice."[19]

While pursuing this work, Bell married and started a family, which, due to the hectic pace in the office and on the road, he sometimes neglected.[20] But he believed that he was serving the greater, maybe the greatest, cause of his time. And, by all accounts, he was a remarkable lawyer. He argued in the courts on behalf of James Meredith, who would become the first black student at the University of Mississippi, and crisscrossed the rural counties helping local blacks fight for school integration.

Over the summer of 1964, the *New York Times* dispatched a reporter to cover Bell's campaign for school integration. He had his work cut out for him. White residents were busy changing boundary lines, rezoning school districts, and harassing local black families in order to undermine the desegregation effort. Bell told the *Times* that black residents of Leake County, Mississippi, faced threats of violence, eviction, and economic ruin, and had become afraid. One family, however, summoned the courage to send their six-year-old daughter for enrollment at a previously all-white school. Bell himself flew down from New York, took the child under his wing, and walked her to the schoolhouse on the first day, under the protection of fifty policemen, eighteen federal marshals, and nine FBI agents.[21]

In the courtroom, despite skepticism and outright hostility from many judges, Bell proved to be a persuasive litigator. Over the course of the summer, he won a series of victories in Clarksdale, Biloxi, and Jackson. The headlines in the *Times* captured the spirit of the moment: "Rural School in Mississippi Enrolls One Negro Girl Under Heavy Guard";[22] "Grade Schools in Mississippi Are Integrated";[23] "Integration Ordered by U.S. Judge Who Deplores It."[24] Mississippi had been the last holdout on desegregation—and Bell, the precocious child from Pittsburgh, helped force the state into compliance.

It was a remarkable triumph. The civil rights movement was changing the legal regime in the United States, down to the sprawling cotton country of the Mississippi Delta. There was a sense of optimism that pervaded all of the literature of the era. The courts had decided *Brown v. Board of Education* in 1954 and the legislature had passed the Civil Rights Act and Voting Rights Act in 1964 and 1965. Figures such as William Hastie believed that legal equality was the end of a long road—once blacks had attained full citizenship, they would finally reach the Promised Land.

But this turned out to be a false hope. As the 1960s came to a close, many activists felt the creeping realization that equality under the law would not lead easily to the equality of human conditions.

Bell, perhaps a bit dour by nature, began to see the entire enterprise as a bitter disappointment. In his memoirs, he recalls one moment in a courtroom in the Deep South, watching a judge treat Bell's black clients with contempt and then, in the next breath, cheerily administer the oath of citizenship to a group of European immigrants. This was, in his own words, a "courthouse epiphany" that slashed down his faith in the movement.

"[The judge] asked the newly minted citizens to gather around the bench to be sworn in, then welcomed them to the country in tones of sweetness and warmth that were the Dr Jekyll opposite of the Mr Hyde treatment he'd been giving my clients for seeking the relief to which the Supreme Court had said they were entitled a decade earlier," Bell recalled. "But that wasn't what surprised me. What froze me in my seat, dumbfounded, was this realization: The moment these people became citizens, their whiteness made them more acceptable to this country, more a welcome part of it, than the black people I was representing would likely ever be. The realization pushed me to a moment of existential doubt: What was the point? Why was I trying to get children admitted to schools where they were not wanted and where—unless they were exceptional—they would probably fare poorly? Chances were good that they would drop out or be expelled for responding with anger or violence to the hostile treatment they were sure to receive."[25]

These questions would haunt him for the rest of his life. The optimistic child who delivered the newspaper to the black professionals in his neighborhood had taken a tremendous blow. A new Derrick Bell, battered by experience and shorn of his youthful illusion, was born in the Mississippi floodplains. Years later, he returned to Leake County and visited a pair of sisters who had fought side by side with Bell during the struggle for integration and now felt the same underlying pessimism. "Looking back, I wonder whether I gave you the right advice," Bell told them. "I also wondered whether that was the best way to go about it," one responded. "It's done now. We made it and we are still moving."[26]

Bell, too, kept moving through his professional career. He had spent nearly a decade traveling through the Deep South and working in the trenches of civil rights law. Then, as the 1960s came to an end and his disillusionment with trial work reached its conclusion, he seized a new opportunity. A number of law schools, feeling pressure to recruit racial minorities onto the faculty, had reached out to Bell with offers of a teaching position. Soon enough, the golden ticket arrived: Harvard Law School wanted to make Bell its first full-time black professor.

He was, by his own admission, unqualified according to traditional standards. "When in the Spring of 1969 I accepted the Harvard Law School's offer to join its faculty, both the school and I had reason to recognize that mine was a pioneering appointment, a mission really, that would mark a turning point in the school's history," he wrote in his memoirs. "The break in tradition was twofold. First, I would become the first full-time black teacher in Harvard's one-hundred-fifty year history. Second, unlike virtually all of the faculty at that time, my qualifications did not include either graduation with distinction from a prestigious law school or a judicial clerkship on the Supreme Court. I had not, moreover, practiced with a major law firm where a well-known partner, himself a Harvard alumnus, was urging my appointment."[27]

Bell understood the politics of racial hiring in elite institutions—a kind of proto–affirmative action—and saw it without illusion. "We must not forget, particularly those of us who are 'first blacks,' that our elections, appointments, and promotions were not based solely on our credentials, ability, or experience," he said. "As important—likely more important—than merit is the fact that we came along at just the right time."[28]

At Harvard, Bell worked to transform his disillusionment with the civil rights movement into a cohesive theory of race and power.

In 1973, he published his landmark casebook, *Race, Racism, and American Law*. The political orientation of the book was unmistakable: on the opening page, Bell reproduced the famous photograph of the two black sprinters raising the Black Power fist at the 1968 Olympics. The book, originally published for a limited audience of legal scholars, contained the entire seed of what would become known as "critical race theory." Bell argued that race is "an indeterminate social construct that is continually reinvented and manipulated to maintain domination and enhance white privilege." His goal was to examine "the law's role in concretizing racial differences, maintaining racial inequality, and reifying the status quo"—and then to change it through the application of political power.[29]

Bell was dissatisfied with the regime of legal colorblindness and began searching for more radical solutions. He devoured the works of the Italian communist Antonio Gramsci[30] and Paulo Freire[31]—the latter of whom, by coincidence, was working at the Harvard Graduate School of Education at the same time that Bell was working at Harvard Law School—seeking to understand how societies replicate social control and how one could subvert those forces through institutional capture and radical education. Gramsci provided him with a theoretical framework for explaining how civil rights law, while appearing to help minorities, actually served the interests of white elites. Freire provided Bell with a theoretical justification for infusing his teaching with political activism.

In addition, Gramsci and Freire both validated Bell's reflexive anti-capitalism. Since he was a child in Pittsburgh, Bell had always seen racism and capitalism as mutually interconnected. "Racism is more than just bad white folk hating black folk. It is the major underpinning of this capitalist society, of control of both blacks and whites," he believed.[32] This simplistic formulation would remain Bell's basic political ideology for the rest of his life. "We live in this capitalist society," he reiterated decades later, "that, by definition, means that some people are going to make a whole lot of money, gain a whole lot of power, by the exploitation of a whole lot of other people."[33]

After years of this ferment, absorbing the radical literature and adapting to the privileges of tenure, Bell cobbled together a series of law review articles and fictional short stories that would coalesce into a grand theory of racial pessimism and mark the completion of Bell's arc of disillusionment. "For many civil rights participants the decision in *Brown* represented not simply the fatal blow to Jim Crow statutes, but also a prescription for healing the racial wounds of the society," Bell wrote.[34] But that vision, he concluded, was an illusion. Whites could no longer maintain the structures of overt racism, but they had kept them alive through great cunning and subtlety, using ostensibly "colorblind" institutions to invisibly reproduce white domination.

"I contend that the decision in *Brown* to break with the court's long-held position on these issues cannot be understood without some consideration of the decision's value to whites," Bell wrote, "not simply those concerned about the immorality of racial inequality, but also those whites in policy making positions able to see the economic and political advances at home and abroad that would follow abandonment of segregation."[35]

Bell believed that white elites committed to civil rights in order to shore up their moral credibility against the Soviet Union, to appease black soldiers who expected equality after their service in the Second World War, and to accelerate the South's transition from an agricultural to an industrial economy. He called this phenomenon "interest convergence": whites heralded advancements for blacks but, beneath their superficial appeals to freedom and equality, always secured their own material desires first. The superficial elements had changed over time, but the power structure remained the same.[36]

Bell came to see the entire post-*Brown* legal regime as a work of profound racial cynicism. After a generation of integration efforts, public schools had started to revert back to de facto racial separation, with black schools falling further and further behind.[37] Whites could offload their guilt by pointing to civil rights legislation and de jure legal equality without having to sacrifice any of their economic or political privileges. As he later wrote, white elites had "rewir[ed] the rhetoric of equality"[38] in order to preserve the substance of white supremacy.

Also, in Bell's interpretation, blacks provided America with an eternal scapegoat. As he developed his theory over the years, Bell went so far as to argue that American democracy itself was predicated on maintaining capitalist domination through racial control. "Racism is not an anomaly, but a crucial component of liberal democracy in this country," he wrote. "The extreme inequality of property and wealth in America is the direct result of the historic and continuing willingness of a great many, perhaps most, white people to identify with and attempt to emulate those at the top of the economic heap while comforting their likely permanent lowly state by disidentifying and refusing to join with blacks and other people of color."[39]

The mark of Bell's full conversion came in the mid-1980s. He had been putting together the premise of his argument since his first years at Harvard Law School. But the culmination of his intellectual transformation came with a surprising twist: he abandoned the conventions of legal academic writing and embraced creative fiction as a new method of argumentation.

The catalyst for Bell's narrative turn was an invitation to write the foreword to the *Harvard Law Review*'s 1984 Supreme Court volume, the most prestigious page-space in the academic legal world. Bell felt anxious about writing a scholarly article. Instead, he proposed writing four fictional stories on the theme of race and the law. "I wanted to write about race, but to write about it in the strictly legal stuff with thousands of footnotes was just going to be boring. And the editors said, 'You know, if you did one of those kinds of things, it would be mediocre, but it wouldn't matter,'" he recalled. "'But if you're going to write this fiction, we [would be very excited about that].' They helped me and we worked very hard and that was the beginning, because it was [the] first time ever—and probably the last time ever—that the *Harvard Law Review* Foreword would be basically four allegorical stories."[40]

The editors, including future Supreme Court justice Elena Kagan,[41] helped Bell deliver on his desire to "appraise the contradictions and inconsistencies that pervade the all too real world of racial oppression" using "the tools not only of reason but of unreason, of fantasy."[42] Through these stories, Bell was able to dispatch with academic requirements and present his theory of racial pessimism in raw, emotionally loaded narratives.

The stories themselves—"The Chronicle of the Celestial Curia," "The Chronicle of the DeVine Gift," "The Chronicle of the Amber Cloud," and "The Chronicle of the Slave Scrolls"—were simple racial allegories: the spirits of three mystical black women explain how the liberal welfare state will never lead to substantive equality; a black hair product executive provides funding for minority law professors, but white administrators refuse to hire beyond a token population; a mysterious cloud infects white children with the social pathologies of the black ghetto, but white legislators refuse to provide the cure to black children; a pastor discovers magical scrolls in Africa that will lift American blacks out of poverty, but jealous whites force him to burn the scrolls in the bottom of a wooden ship.

The didactic lessons are anything but subtle. Bell portrays whites as ruthless exploiters who take pleasure in the permanent subordination of black America. After the fall of slavery and segregation, Bell contends, whites have cynically used civil rights laws, welfare policies, affirmative action, and colorblindness to create a "mirage" of equality, while secretly doing "all in their power to ensure their dominion and maintain their control."[43] The standard narrative of racial progress, Bell claimed, was little more than a racial myth designed to absolve whites of historical responsibility and to lull blacks into present-day complacency. Meanwhile, the actual behavior of whites was as vicious as ever. They would gleefully withhold, delay, and burn any mechanism for black progress.

As he wrote in his Chronicles, the promise of equality was always a ruse. The real history of the United States was one long parade of horrors from the origins of the country to the present day. In Bell's historical revision, the framers of the Constitution "were unable to imagine a society in which whites and Negroes would live together as fellow-citizens," "the Emancipation Proclamation was intended to serve the interests of the Union, not the blacks," "the Civil War amendments [to the Constitution] actually furthered the goals of northern industry and politics far better and longer than they served to protect even the most basic rights of the freedmen," and the social movement that achieved the Civil Rights Act and the Voting Rights Act "must be seen as part of the American racial fantasy."[44]

Bell's political vision was an infinite recursion: whiteness was the invisible poison that turned every victory into defeat. His stories were loaded with bitterness, and yet, because of their placement in the *Harvard Law Review*, they sparked immediate controversy and interest.

Despite his lifelong insistence that he did "not care to write in ways that whites can vindicate,"[45] Bell suddenly became a star among the white intelligentsia, which has always had an affinity for messages of white racism and American evil. He went on radio and television expounding his unitary theory of racial catastrophe. A major publisher bought the rights to Bell's Chronicles and asked him to expand them into a series of books that would become *And We Are Not Saved* and *Faces at the Bottom of the Well*. Both would become *New York Times* bestsellers, and the latter included a story that was optioned and turned into a film by the premium cable outlet HBO.

Bell's relentless pessimism was turned into a brand—and he chased it for the rest of his life. He had become the great misanthropist, the great prophet of doom, and, completing the reversal from his younger life, abandoned all hope in "the nation's long-held myth of equality."[46] Thus the pattern was set: the gloomier his work, the greater his influence; the more apocalyptic his conclusions, the greater his prestige.

"Racism is an integral, permanent, and indestructible component of this society," he thundered. "The racism that made slavery feasible is far from dead in the last decade of twentieth-century America."[47] Indeed, Bell warned, it could return. American whites were so depraved, they might even put people like him back in chains. "Slavery is, as an example of what white America has done, a constant reminder of what white America might do."[48]

There was no turning back. Bell had created a nightmare that captured the imagination of the Left. He was moving toward the height of his power—his fame and his cynicism were growing in tandem—and he wanted to exert it. He looked around him, seething at the state of the nation and the complicity of the institutions, and prepared himself to achieve, if not equality, then revenge.

CHAPTER 15

"I Live to Harass White Folks"

The Politics of Eternal Resentment

Derrick Bell had all the trappings of academic success—a tenured professorship at Harvard, publications in the prestigious law reviews, a coterie of students at his feet—but he wanted more. By his own description, Bell was not a traditional scholar, but an activist with an eye toward real-world application.

Bell had spent the 1980s in a state of restlessness, building his ideology, experimenting with activist campaigns, and refining his techniques. He left Harvard in 1980 to become dean of the University of Oregon Law School, then quit after the university refused to hire an Asian-American woman. Next he taught for a year at Stanford Law School, where students complained that his courses were steeped in ideology rather than constitutional theory,[1] and, finally, he rejoined the faculty of Harvard Law School in 1986. He had grown disillusioned with the possibility of reform through the democratic process, but he had discovered the potential for a new strategy: reshaping the manners and mores of elite institutions.

The revolution did not run through the streets, Bell concluded, but through the faculty meeting and the seminar room.

Over the years, Bell had fashioned himself into a Paulo Freire–style "liberationist teacher"[2] who recruited students into campus politics. According to one of Bell's disciples, the law professor Charles Lawrence III, Bell and his students imagined that they were the modern equivalents of the "field hands, blacksmiths, and conductors on the Underground Railroad"[3] and had a duty to subvert the "traditional white-male model"[4] of education and begin "replacing those ideologies and practices with ones that liberate us."[5] Student radicals followed him wherever he went and solicited his involvement in campus protests, sit-ins, and demonstrations. "For [Bell] the classroom is not just a stage or podium, it is a place to tell and listen to stories, a spawning ground for new ideas, a laboratory, a workshop for theory building," recalled Lawrence. "Derrick Bell's classes are 'healing groups,' where Black minds, and the minds of those who choose to join our cause in solidarity, are 'decolonized.' They are 'war rooms' where the strategies for the struggle are conceived and from whence political battles are launched. As a 'first' at Harvard, it has fallen to Professor Bell to frame a paradigm for liberationist pedagogy, a methodology for we teachers of color who find ourselves thrust by necessity into the vanguard of the struggle."[6]

The other left-wing faculty in Bell's orbit soon joined in the fight. In a feature-length essay for *City Journal*, the writer Heather Mac Donald captured a sense of how this vaunted "liberationist pedagogy" expressed itself in the classroom. These theorists, Mac Donald observed, followed the line of argument that "law is merely a mask for white male power" and attacked what they saw as "illegitimate hierarchies," which included nearly every facet of the liberal order, including legal neutrality, limited government, and private property. In practice, the professors of this new approach, which went by the name "critical legal studies" before getting absorbed into "critical race theory," turned their classes into a "forum for white-bashing," unleashing tremendous personal hostility toward white students under the pretext of legal criticism.

"I was going home crying every day," said one white female student. "No matter what I said, the response was: you don't know because you're white. Some students wouldn't speak to me after class. It scared me, because I thought I was this big liberal, and I was treated like the devil."[7]

Relations between faculty members were no better. As the critical legal scholars and their allies made their initial blitz, one professor began to describe Harvard Law as "the Beirut of legal education," with rival factions seeking to undermine one another. The critical legal theorists and, after them, the critical race theorists were the ones who had the upper hand. They understood the power of racial politics and knew that capturing prestige institutions such as Harvard would set the precedent for elite discourse down the line. "There's a peculiar kind of vanity or megalomania at Harvard, that the place is the soul of the American ruling class," one professor told the *New York Times* during the conflict. "Whoever wins in local institutional battles there thinks they will control America's cultural and institutional destiny."[8]

Bell was ready to lead the effort.

When he returned to Harvard in 1986, Bell's primary demand was that the university hire additional left-wing racialists onto the faculty.[9] He made public appeals to "diversity" and "affirmative action," but the unspoken gambit, which was obvious to outside observers at the time, was to stack the faculty with ideological allies who would help Bell collapse the foundations of traditional legal theory and replace them with the tenets of what would become known as critical race theory. He staged protests, directed student demonstrations, and sought additional leverage by threatening to quit if his demands were not met. He calculated that, as the first affirmative action hire at Harvard Law School, he had significant symbolic power and, by creating a scene, he could damage the university's reputation. As his wife reminded him, "Harvard needs us more than we need Harvard."[10]

In 1987, Bell announced a four-day sit-in to support two critical race scholars who had been denied tenure. Then, three years later, he took his strategy to the brink, writing a letter to the administration and the faculty announcing that he was going on strike until the law school hired and tenured a black woman. He worked with student activists to organize rallies and negotiate exclusive coverage in the *New York Times*.

Bell and his students demanded that the university hire visiting professor Regina Austin, a critical race theorist who was known for writing inflammatory polemics, denouncing the "white man's racist, sexist comic imagination," celebrating the stereotype of the "Black Bitch," and telling her black female colleagues that "the time has come for us to get truly hysterical."[11]

These qualities were rare among legal scholars, but they made Austin the perfect candidate for Bell's activism. Austin brought with her a reputation of being a strict enforcer of racial politics. She knew how to wield the concept of "diversity" as both a shield and a sword, coming down hard on colleagues and students who dissented from her views. "The problem is, you can't tell the truth around here anymore without being accused of being a racist," one of her students told the *Times*.[12]

During this period, Bell also used his writing to ratchet up the pressure on the administration. He argued that the tenure process at Harvard was a racist system, selecting for the status quo and excluding most black candidates.

In his fictionalized writing, he pushed the boundaries even further. As the faculty wars heated up, Bell wrote a long story for the *Michigan Law Review*, later republished in *Faces at the Bottom of the Well*, that began with the explosion of a "huge, nuclearlike fireball"[13] on the Harvard campus, killing the university president and all 196 of the university's black faculty and staff. In the story, many whites assumed that black faculty members, desperate at the slow pace of affirmative action, had enacted a "bizarre murder-suicide pact"[14] to become martyrs for the cause. Blacks, on the other hand, were convinced that "ultraconservatives, possibly acting with government support,"[15] had detonated the bomb in a racial assassination plot. Investigators sifted through the ashes and found a diversity report, revealing the dismal whiteness that continued to reign among Harvard faculty.

The lesson of the story, according to Bell, was that the university was a racist institution that had formalized a "black tokenism policy" that amounted to: "Hire one if you must, but only one."[16] The purpose of his writing, he suggested, was to "shame those high-level white folks"[17] into expanding diversity hiring—which, in the fictional narrative, they did.

But in reality, the story caused frustration among Bell's colleagues at Harvard. Bell had called the university a "plantation"[18] and directly fantasized about the murder of the university president—a crude and vengeful representation of Bell's own vitriol toward his colleagues.

This time, Bell had gone too far. After his strike on behalf of Regina Austin and lurid assassination fantasies, the administration decided that it would no longer submit to the professor's racial blackmail campaign. The university dispatched Professor Roger Fisher, who led the Harvard Negotiating Project and had brokered complex peace agreements in the Middle East,[19] but the negotiations went nowhere.[20] Bell was intransigent. He was at the height of his fame and power and, playing into the role of the martyr, he refused to budge.

And so, the administration iced him out. Law school dean Robert Clark would not to concede to Bell's pressure campaign and university president Neil Rudenstine refused to meet directly with Bell during the negotiations. Bell spent the next two years on unpaid leave, continuing his demands and rallying students who took over the dean's office and denounced administrators as complicit in racism and sexism.[21]

But after a few months of theatrics, the public lost interest. Bell had been using these tactics for a decade and the university finally called his bluff. Harvard's policy at the time was that professors could not take more than two years of unpaid leave. As the timeline expired, Bell made last-minute demands to meet with the university's governing board.

The administration summoned Bell to an appeal hearing at 17 Quincy Street. "The University did not relish a hearing at which students might mount protests. Instead, the president's office arranged for a small group of the members of the Corporation and the Board of Overseers to meet with me in late July," Bell wrote in his memoirs. "Ironically, this was the same building that, in my fictional protest story, was mysteriously blown up, killing the university president and all the black faculty members and finally inspiring the school to launch a major effort to recruit minority candidates. Perhaps University officials remembered my story, for on the morning of the hearing, uniformed and plainclothes security personnel were visibly present around the building."[22]

Bell made his case, but administrators were unmoved. They attended the meeting, processed the paperwork, and fired him. Shortly after he was let go, Bell sat for a profile in the *New York Times*, which called him a "devoutly angry man" who had nothing but contempt for Harvard and all that it represented. Bell blamed administrators and his former colleagues, including the five black law school professors who failed to support his one-man suicide mission. He also confided that he had launched his protest as his wife, Jewel, was dying of breast cancer and conceded, with a tinge of shame, that he had doubts that his "protests were entirely praiseworthy."[23]

The only consolation, Bell later wrote, was that he had caused distress for his white colleagues. "I was disappointed, but also amused—as blacks are from time to time—when we recognize how easy it is to frighten whites, notwithstanding the fact that they hold all the power."[24]

After this progression of tragedy, failure, and disruption, Bell's pessimism hardened. During his leave of absence, Bell had secured another professorship at New York University. His writing and teaching became even more cynical, advancing the arguments that America is an irredeemably racist nation, that whites are carriers of immense evil, and that blacks in America risk genocide and extermination.

In an acidic mixture of revisionism and personal grappling, Bell sought to rewrite American history as a long sequence of gloom and oppression. He wrote fictional stories attacking Thomas Jefferson and George Washington as racist hypocrites.[25] He made the case that the Constitution was not a "hallowed document,"[26] but a self-serving compact that protected the interests of whites who controlled massive "investments in land, slaves, manufacturing, and shipping."[27]

In his lectures at NYU, Bell told students that the Constitution was a useless document, because the Supreme Court would always manipulate the law to serve elite interests, then appeal to the Constitution after the fact. "When I was a kid, we had cockroaches in the house, but we didn't have roach powder," Bell told his students. "So we killed the roaches by stomping on them. What the Justices do is stomp on the roaches, and then spray them with roach powder. The Constitution is like the roach powder."[28]

For Bell, the real story of American history was that of a racial conspiracy, with white elites manipulating racial hatred to maintain their monopoly on wealth and power. This dynamic was established at the Founding and has continued without deviation ever since. "The involuntary servitude of black rights to white property interests is the basic explanation for the slavery of the past and the continuing subordinate status of black people today," Bell wrote.[29]

Bell believed that the entire arc of America's racial history—from the Declaration to the Emancipation to the Fourteenth Amendment to the Civil Rights Act—appeared to be in the service of freedom for blacks but, in actuality, served the self-interest of elite whites. The Founders signed the Declaration of Independence not to establish the grounds of universal freedom, Bell argued, but to use the profits of slavery to enrich themselves at the direct and conscious expense of blacks.[30] Lincoln issued the Emancipation Proclamation not to free the slaves, but "to win the war and preserve the Union."[31] Legislators enacted the Fourteenth Amendment not to extended citizenship and equal protection under the law, but as a mechanism to secretly protect the fortunes of the great robber barons of the railroads, utilities, banks, and vested interests.[32] Even the Civil Rights Act, in Bell's revisionist history, provided only a fig leaf of colorblind equality while, in truth, entrenching and legitimizing existing racial inequalities.[33]

Bell argued that American blacks in the modern era were worse off than at any other time since slavery. "From the very beginning of this nation, blacks have been the exploited, the excluded, and often the exterminated in this society," says one of Bell's fictional characters in *And We Are Not Saved*. "For most of that time, racial policies were blatant, vicious, and horribly damaging, leaving most of us in a subordinate status when compared with all but the lowest whites. And now that the Court has, as a result of our ceaseless petitions, been forced to find that overt discrimination is unconstitutional, we are for all intents and purposes still maintained in a subordinate state by the so-called neutral policies of a still-racist society because—for God's sake—we are not white!"[34]

Bell made no attempt to conceal his own racial animosity. In fact, as his notoriety grew, he expressed it in more direct and cutting terms. His two most famous texts, *Faces at the Bottom of the Well* and *And We Are Not Saved*, can, to a certain extent, be described as book-length fantasies of white depravity. In Bell's imagination, whites are uniformly cruel, selfish, sadistic, exploitative, and evil. In one of his stories, he wrote that many whites would gladly pay a 3 percent income tax for a "racial preferences license" that allowed them to openly discriminate against blacks and resegregate their neighborhoods, businesses, and schools.[35] In another, he wrote that whites secretly enabled black crime in order to profit from the management of prisons, courts, and law enforcement, using the "fear of black crime" to provide a stabilizing mechanism for society.[36]

From his perch at NYU, Bell even endorsed the notorious anti-Semite and Nation of Islam leader Louis Farrakhan. "Minister Farrakhan is perhaps the best living example of a black man ready, willing, and able to 'tell it like it is' regarding who is responsible for racism in this country," Bell said. "In this regard, he's easily a match for all those condescending white talk-show hosts who consider themselves very intelligent, certainly smarter than any black man. . . . Minister Farrakhan, calm, cool, and very much on top of the questions, handles these self-appointed guardians with ease. I love it!"[37]

Bell's most famous story, "The Space Traders,"[38] contains the cynical heart of his new politics. The narrative begins on the first day of the year 2000 as a flotilla of glimmering spaceships arrives along the Atlantic coastline from Massachusetts to North Carolina. The leader of the alien force descends from the bow of one of the ships and speaks to the American people in a voice simulating Ronald Reagan. He offers a deal to the human delegation: the aliens will provide America with enough gold, anti-pollutant chemicals, and nuclear fuel to clear the national debt and provide a permanent source of clean energy; in exchange, the aliens want to take all of the country's black citizens back to their home star.

In Bell's story, the racial politics of American society had grown dire. Laissez-faire economics, welfare dependency, AIDS, and rampant crime had devastated the black community. The white power structure had put blacks in inner-city concentration camps, with high walls and armed guards controlling the entrances and exits. "Young blacks escaped from time to time to terrorize whites. Long dead was the dream that this black under-class would ever 'overcome,'" Bell wrote.[39] The American public was split into two camps. White conservatives warmed to the deal because it would cut government costs. The business lobby opposed it, as "most business leaders understood that blacks were crucial in stabilizing the economy with its ever-increasing disparity between the incomes of rich and poor."[40]

Ultimately, legislators came to a consensus, passing a constitutional amendment to authorize the trade and sending it to the people for a refer-endum vote. "The Framers intended America to be a white country," the pro-trade group told the public. "After more than a hundred and thirty-seven years of good-faith efforts to build a healthy, stable interracial na-tion, we have concluded—as the Framers did in the beginning—that our survival today requires that we sacrifice the rights of blacks in order to protect and further the interests of whites. The Framers' example must be our guide. Patriotism, and not pity, must govern our decision. We should ratify the amendment and accept the Space Traders' proposition."[41]

On voting day, 70 percent of Americans cast their ballots in favor of sending the black population into the void.

At dawn on Martin Luther King Day, the alien ships unloaded their trea-sures and opened their hatches for boarding. "Crowded on the beaches were the inductees, some twenty million silent black men, women, and children, including babes in arms," Bell wrote. "As the sun rose, the Space Traders directed them, first, to strip off all but a single undergarment; then, to line up; and finally, to enter those holds which yawned in the morning light like Milton's 'darkness visible.' The inductees looked fearfully behind them. But, on the dunes above the beaches, guns at the ready, stood U.S. guards. There was no escape, no alternative. Heads bowed, arms now linked by slender chains, black people left the New World as their forebears had arrived."[42]

The most profitable interpretation of Bell's work is not as literature, but as psychodrama. He did not have the mind of a novelist—his themes and characters were polemical, rather than human, representations—but the mind of a lawyer who had fallen into despair. The most compelling characters in Derrick Bell's stories are not the Founding Fathers or the Space Traders, but Derrick Bell himself. The blizzard of dark emotions in his fiction—the hatred, pessimism, inferiority, terror—are inseparable from the biographical details of the author. The underlying theme of all of his stories—the innate and unchangeable corruption of white America—represents the writer's deepest conclusion about the country of his birth.

In his memoirs, Bell revealed the psychological motivation behind his work as an author and an activist. "At its essence, the willingness to protest represents less a response to a perceived affront than the acting out of a state of mind," he wrote. "Often, the desire to change the offending situation which is beyond our reach may be an incidental benefit and not the real motivation. Rather, those of us who speak out are moved by a deep sense of the fragility of our self-worth. It is the determination to protect our sense of who we are that leads us to risk criticism, alienation, and serious loss while most others, similarly harmed, remain silent. Protest that can rescue self-esteem is of special value to black Americans in a society where overt discrimination and unconscious acts of racial domination pose a continual threat to both well-being and mental health."[43]

On the surface, Bell had reached the height of professional achievement. He was a successful civil rights lawyer and the first tenured African-American professor at Harvard Law School. But he was plagued with self-doubt. He once confided to his second wife, Janet Dewart Bell, that he "had a lot of nerve to think that he could be the first tenured black professor at Harvard."[44] He was deeply self-conscious about his lack of traditional legal credentials[45] and told the New York Times he never felt accepted by his peers.[46]

This contradiction led to a bipolar reaction. Bell retreated into racial pessimism at the same time that he lashed out in symbolic rage. He sought validation from the same institutions that he despised. He fantasized about the murder of his colleagues and was outraged that they rejected him. "Being black in America means we are ever the outsiders," he wrote. "As such, we are expendable and must live always at risk of some ultimate betrayal by those who will treat such treachery as a right."[47]

The conservative black economist Thomas Sowell, whom Bell had attacked as a race traitor,[48] offered an explanation of Bell's predicament. "Derrick Bell was for years a civil-rights lawyer, but not an academic legal scholar of the sort who gets appointed as a full professor at one of the leading law schools. Yet he became a visiting professor at Stanford Law School and was a full professor at Harvard Law School. It was transparently obvious in both cases that his appointment was because he was black, not because he had the qualifications that got other people appointed to these faculties," Sowell said. "Derrick Bell's options were to be a nobody, living in the shadow of more accomplished legal scholars—or to go off on some wild tangent of his own, and appeal to a radical racial constituency on campus and beyond. His writings showed clearly that the latter was the path he chose."

And this path, in Sowell's view, was a tragic turn. Bell's "previous writings had been those of a sensible man saying sensible things about civil-rights issues that he understood from his years of experience as an attorney. But now he wrote all sorts of incoherent speculations and pronouncements, the main drift of which was that white people were the cause of black people's problems."[49]

Seen through this lens, Bell's bluster was a cover for his self-doubt. His assault on colorblindness, meritocracy, and tenure was a justification for his own position. His hatred for his colleagues was a preemption against personal rejection. The problems of Derrick Bell were not the problems of the black ghetto—they were the problems of the affirmative action hire in the elite institution.

Yet, in a cruel irony, the very structures that Bell condemned incentivized his pessimism. His stories served an important political function: Bell was a high-prestige black intellectual who sold a narrative of white evil, which delighted left-wing audiences, especially white liberals in positions of influence, who rewarded Bell with fame, wealth, and prestige. His bipolar reaction—attack and retreat, fury and resignation—built into a tremendous tension. He hated them as much as he needed them. He sought rejection as much as he sought approval.

Bell never escaped this negativity spiral. As the 1990s turned to the 2000s, his signature pessimism devolved into paranoia. He developed a verbal tic, often prefacing his sentences in media interviews with variations on the phrase, "Maybe I'm getting a little racially paranoid."[50]

He was. Bell's worldview had grown darker and darker as the years passed. His characterizations descended into caricature. His insights turned into clichés.

As the demand for his pessimism grew, the lines of his thought terminated on a preposterous judgment: whites in America were so hateful and sadistic, Bell believed, that they were on the verge of exterminating blacks altogether. He fantasized that heavily armed white supremacists were hunting him down in the woods. "What do I find? A nigger and his nigger-lovin' white woman," said one of Bell's fictional characters, a "far-right paramilitary type" who threatened to march Bell and his companion to his command outpost, where they would be imprisoned, tortured, or killed.[51] Blacks were at such great risk of persecution, Bell wrote, that there was a growing movement to build a "nationwide network of secret shelters to house and feed black people in the event of a black holocaust or some other all-out attack on America's historic scapegoats."[52] His language verged into the catastrophic: "holocaust," "genocide," and "extermination."[53]

These apocalyptic views cannot be dismissed as mere fictionalizations. Bell truly believed—or, at least, had convinced himself to believe—that, given the opportunity, whites would enact unimaginable brutalities against blacks. In an interview on NPR's *Fresh Air* shortly after "The Space Traders" was published, Bell told host Terry Gross he believed that, in real life, Americans would vote to permanently expel blacks from the universe, just as they had in his stories. "Civil rights measures always go down to defeat in popular referenda," he said matter-of-factly, pointing out that, during his public lectures, most whites and virtually all blacks told him that their communities would vote for the space trade.[54] In a law review article published in response to critics, Bell speculated that the United States might even commit "racial genocide" and eliminate blacks on a mass basis.[55]

Bell had long insisted that American society was a wasteland that forced blacks into unemployment, poverty, addiction, broken homes, and social anarchy. Their only function was as a scapegoat that stabilized relations between the white socioeconomic classes. But in the modern economy, he feared, even this function might not be necessary anymore.

Following the publication of *Faces at the Bottom of the Well*, Bell engaged in a dialogue with another professor, Sidney Willhelm, who suggested that blacks had become economically superfluous and, therefore, faced an "ever-growing danger of genocide."[56] Slaves had been necessary for their labor, Willhelm reasoned, but now that regular work had disappeared from the inner cities, the black underclass did not even serve as exploitation. Bell sympathized with this line of thought and linked it with his long-standing belief in the permanence of racism.

"Are African Americans locked into a permanently racist society and can developments in that society be leading toward their extermination?" Bell asked. "I cannot answer either question with proof that would satisfy you. Nor can I convince you that past experience leads me, without more, to know that I am right about racism and right to fear that Professor Willhelm is right as well. What is clear is that black Americans are now, as were our forebears when they were brought to the New World, objects of barter for those who, while profiting from our existence, deny our humanity."[57]

Bell was ready to make the final leap. He peered over the precipice, saw nothing but racism, carnage, and destruction—and jumped.

For the last decades of his life, Bell frequently told a story that illustrated the endpoint of his philosophy. "The year was 1964. It was a quiet, heat-hushed evening in Harmony, a small, black community near the Mississippi Delta. Some Harmony residents, in the face of increasing white hostility, were organizing to ensure implementation of a court order mandating desegregation of their schools the next September. Walking with Mrs. Biona MacDonald, one of the organizers, up a dusty, unpaved road toward her modest home, I asked where she found the courage to continue working for civil rights in the face of intimidation that included her son losing his job in town, the local bank trying to foreclose on her mortgage, and shots fired through her living room window," Bell recalled. "'Derrick,' she said slowly, seriously, 'I am an old woman. I lives to harass white folks.'"[58]

This simple phrase became Bell's personal motto. "Mrs. MacDonald did not say she risked everything because she hoped or expected to win out over the whites who, as she well knew, held all the economic and political power, and the guns as well. Rather, she recognized that—powerless as she was—she had, and intended to use, courage and determination as weapons 'to harass white folks,'" he wrote. "Mrs. MacDonald did not even hint that her harassment would topple whites' well-entrenched power. Rather, her goal was defiance and its harassing effect was more potent precisely because she placed herself in confrontation with her oppressors with full knowledge of their power and willingness to use it. . . . Mrs. MacDonald understood twenty-five years ago the theory that I am espousing in the 1990s for black leaders and civil rights lawyers to adopt. If you remember her story, you will understand my message."[59]

The story contains the basic themes of Bell's work: the retreat into fatalism, the symbolic lashing out. But, seen from another angle, the story also illustrates Bell's own tragic shortcomings. Mrs. MacDonald was a poor black woman born into the segregated South; Derrick Bell was a Harvard professor at the height of legal and professional power. The old woman's noble dignity becomes, in the hands of Derrick Bell, an abdication. The professor refused to acknowledge any progress. He imagined himself no better off than Mrs. MacDonald and explained away all black success as ultimately serving the interests of white elites.

Bell had made a fetish out of white evil and black despair. He turned his provocative theory of racial pessimism into a bottomless pit of racial nihilism. The young lawyer, fighting against Jim Crow in a pressed suit, had succumbed to his own cynicism and paranoia. He could not prove that racism was eternal or that black genocide was imminent, but his fears provided enough justification to believe it.

In the epigraph to *Faces at the Bottom of the Well*, Bell summarized his ultimate vision of society. "Black people are the magical faces at the bottom of society's well," he wrote. "Even the poorest whites, those who must live their lives only a few levels above, gain their self-esteem by gazing down on us. Surely, they must know that their deliverance depends on letting down their ropes. Only by working together is escape possible. Over time, many reach out, but most simply watch, mesmerized into maintaining their unspoken commitment to keeping us where we are, at whatever cost to them or to us."[60]

No hope, no progress, no transcendence.

The economist Thomas Sowell described Bell's philosophical descent in blunt terms. "He's turned his back on the ideal of a colorblind society and he's really for a getting-even society, a revenge society," Sowell said. "It's particularly ironic in the case of Bell because, at one point in his career, he fought against racism. And now he seems to have metamorphosed into someone who thinks that racism should not be eliminated, but simply put under new management."[61]

Sowell was right. Bell had abandoned the idea that the United States could transcend racism. He was focused entirely on attacking that society, undermining its self-confidence, and exacting psychological revenge. This question—what should be done with the eternally racist system of the United States—was Bell's final contribution to the history of American legal theory. Although he did not provide a comprehensive answer himself—he was, after all, a critic rather than a builder—he created the space for his students to follow.

In time, a small group of Bell's disciples, moving from a circle at Harvard into positions at legal academies across the country, would turn their master's insights into a working program of scholarship and activism. They would call their project "critical race theory"—and change the face of American society in the new century.

CHAPTER 16

The Rise of Critical Race Theory

In the summer of 1989, Derrick Bell and a small group of his disciples assembled at the St. Benedict Center, a convent turned retreat destination outside Madison, Wisconsin.[1]

The meeting gathered together many of the key figures of the new racialist legal movement that Bell had cultivated as a teacher. Bell had always felt alienated from his colleagues at Harvard and spent much of his time with his students, particularly racial minorities, who affirmed his worldview and participated in his activism. He had raised the fundamental question—what to do in the face of permanent racism and the failures of legal equality—and his young students, most of whom came of age in the post–civil rights era, sought to answer it.

Kimberlé Crenshaw, the lead organizer of the conference, tells the story of planning for the Wisconsin "summer camp" and coining the term for the new intellectual movement that followed. "I began to scribble down words associated with our objectives, identities, and perspectives, drawing arrows and boxes around them to capture various aspects of who 'we' were and what we were doing," Crenshaw recalled. "We settled on what seemed to be the most telling marker for this peculiar subject. We would signify the specific political and intellectual location of the project through 'critical,' the substantive focus through 'race,' and the desire to develop a coherent account of race and law through the term 'theory.'"[2] Or, as Crenshaw summarized later, in a nod to Marcuse: "We discovered ourselves to be critical theorists who did race, and we were racial justice advocates who did critical theory."[3]

And thus the new discipline of "critical race theory" was born.

Crenshaw and the other student organizers eventually persuaded twenty-four legal scholars—all racial minorities, as whites were officially barred from participation[4]—to submit papers, give presentations, and attend the summit. The contrast between the ideology and the setting of the first summit, an old Catholic convent, did not escape the participants of the new group. "I was a member of the founding conference," recalled Richard Delgado, who would become the key chronicler of the movement. "We gathered at that convent for two and a half days, around a table in an austere room with stained glass windows and crucifixes here and there—an odd place for a bunch of Marxists—and worked out a set of principles."[5]

They imagined themselves as outsiders, relegated to the margins of academia, coming together out of necessity. Derrick Bell provided their anchor, but the young scholars dreamed of moving beyond critique and establishing a method for surpassing the regime of colorblind equality. They saw the new discipline as a way to revitalize the study of law and infuse it with a pastiche of critical theory, racialist ideology, and Marxist politics. They hoped to transform the American constitution to achieve, if not justice, then retribution.

Although they were grasping at the time, worried that they were academic impostors,[6] their theories would travel far beyond the confines of their small group of minority law professors. "At the outset," Delgado said many years later, "I had no idea that critical race theory would become a household word."[7]

In the years following the conference, the newly minted critical race theorists published a burst of academic papers that solidified the discipline. This work was collated, condensed, and contextualized in two books, *Critical Race Theory: The Cutting Edge* and *Critical Race Theory: The Key Writings That Formed the Movement*, both of which were published in 1995 and, together, comprised the core of the new philosophy. The self-described "misfits"[8] and "outsiders"[9] had put together an intellectual stew, combining elements of critical theory, critical legal studies, postmodernism, radical feminism, black nationalism, and neo-Marxism.[10] They mixed-and-matched the most acidic parts of modern thought, beginning from the assertion that "objective truth, like merit, does not exist,"[11] continuing to the Derrick Bell–style posture of "deep dissatisfaction with traditional civil rights discourse,"[12] and ending with a call for a "war of position"[13] against whiteness, colorblindness, private property, and traditional constitutional theory.

The critical race theorists did not pretend to be dispassionate scholars in pursuit of knowledge. They saw themselves as political activists in pursuit of change.

In the early years, the critical race theorists imagined their academic theories serving the same function as Marxist ideology, with race replacing class as the key axis of oppression and resistance. "By legitimizing the use of race as a theoretical fulcrum and focus in legal scholarship, so-called racial-ist accounts of racism and the law grounded the subsequent development of Critical Race Theory in much the same way that Marxism's introduction of class structure and struggle into classical political economy grounded subsequent critiques of social hierarchy and power," wrote Kimberlé Cren-shaw and her co-editors in *Critical Race Theory: The Key Writings That Formed the Movement*.[14] "We have shown that the putatively neutral base-line [of colorblind legal equality] is in fact a mechanism for perpetuating the distribution of rights, privileges, and opportunity established under a regime of uncontested white supremacy. Critical Race Theory recognizes accordingly that a return to that so-called neutral baseline would mean a return to an unjust system of racial power."[15]

The elements of critical race theory are, in fact, a near-perfect transposi-tion of race onto the basic structures of Marxist theory. "White supremacy" replaces "capitalism" as the totalizing system. "White and black" replaces "bourgeoisie and proletariat" as the "oppressor and oppressed." "Aboli-tion" replaces "revolution" as the method of "liberation."

This is not a mere metaphor or post hoc comparison. The critical race theorists appeal directly to Marxist theoreticians and the Marxist-Leninist figures of the black liberation movement. Although in subsequent years they sought to downplay or deny their Marxist lineage—Crenshaw fa-mously refused to answer whether critical race theory was "Marxism" on national television[16]—one can uncover the entire intellectual genealogy in the paragraphs and footnotes of the discipline's original texts, which appeal to Marx, Davis, Freire, and the Marxist-Leninist revolutionary movements.

These beliefs were fundamental. Even after the collapse of global com-munism, the critical race theorists continued to believe that the essential thrust of Marxian theory, translated into praxis, was correct. They sought to reprise the old dialectical unity of Herbert Marcuse and Angela Davis and apply it directly to the realm of the law, waging a self-conscious intel-lectual war against "the very foundations of the liberal order, including equality theory, legal reasoning, Enlightenment rationalism, and neutral principles of constitutional law."[17]

The young scholars had a driving ambition and, following the model of Derrick Bell and playing the game of elite institutional politics, had earned the academic credentials to ensure that their ideas would be heard.

*   *   *

Since the beginning, critical race theory was designed to be a weapon. The critical race theorists spent years building an ideology they believed could undermine the authority of the "white male voice"[18] and disrupt the certainties of the "white academy."[19] They built an intellectual system that promised to replace Western rationality with a racialist alternative, dramatically expand their coalition with a new concept of political identity, and, from their base in academia, devise a strategy for capturing America's elite institutions.

The first key element of critical race theory is the discipline's reconceptualization of the truth. By the mid-1990s, the young law professors who were affiliated with the movement had absorbed a thoroughly postmodern epistemology, arguing that Western rationality was a mask for power and domination. They followed the fashionable line of French post-structuralist philosophers Jacques Derrida and Michel Foucault, arguing that "truth is a social construct created to suit the purposes of the dominant group"[20] and casting skepticism on traditional notions of knowledge, justice, and freedom. They began their political project with the ambition of exploding the epistemology of natural rights, which would make way for a radical reinterpretation. They wanted to replace the old system of colorblindness, equality, and individual rights with a new system one might call a theory of "racial reasoning."

The initial task was to attack the idea of rationality itself. In *Critical Race Theory: The Key Writings That Formed the Movement*, law professors Gary Peller and Charles Lawrence III made an aggressive case for demolishing the existing conceptions of knowledge, which, Peller suggested, serve as a form of "academic colonialism" that placed white cultural norms over minority alternatives.[21] Following the radical critique of black nationalist sociologists, Peller proposed that "objective reason or knowledge could not exist because one's position in the social structure of race relations influenced what one would call 'knowledge' or 'rationality.'" In other words, there is no neutral frame for interpreting society, but rather a plurality of racially contingent frames based on one's position as either "the oppressed or the oppressor, either African-Americans or whites, either the sociologist or the subject."

Therefore, Peller argued, the "knowledge" and "rationality" that underpinned the dominant liberal order—everything from constitutional law to the capitalist economy to the school curriculum—provided a pretense of universalism that, in practice, served to subordinate racial minorities. "There could be no neutral theory of knowledge" in the black nationalist critique, Peller maintained. "Knowledge was itself a function of the ability of the powerful to impose their own views, to differentiate between knowledge and myth, reason and emotion, and objectivity and subjectivity."[22]

Charles Lawrence III took the logic of racial reasoning to its conclusion by offering a racialist alternative to the "the colonizer's canon."[23] He called this system "the Word," drawing on the tradition of African mystical healing and Paulo Freire's "pedagogy of the oppressed."[24] Lawrence's epistemology prioritizes racial subjectivity, narrative, emotion, and revisionism, uniting Marxian theory and praxis toward the goal of "liberation."[25] He embraced a "positioned perspective" and told his colleagues they must "learn to privilege their own perspectives and those of other outsiders," self-consciously elevating the "victim perspective" over the "perpetrator perspective."[26] This functioned as a reversal: knowledge is reduced to power, and provides the critical race theorists with a new basis for overturning the existing hierarchy. In practice, the victim becomes the new source of authority—and his subjective feelings must be validated.

Lawrence illustrated this principle with an example that has now become a cliché. He recounts the story of a black female colleague who complained about an assigned reading, telling him: "I am offended. Therefore, these materials are offensive." For Lawrence, this was a revelation. "It is these words that are revolutionary," he wrote. "The [colleague] has done much more than offer a different perspective on the materials. She has given her/our perspective authority, and in doing so she has shown us that we can do the same. . . . By embracing a positioned perspective, this gifted practitioner of the Word reallocated the power to define what is real."[27]

This is the nebulous epistemological foundation of critical race theory:

personal offense becomes objective reality; evidence gives way to ideology; identity replaces rationality as the basis of intellectual authority.

Lawrence concluded his theory of knowledge with a reprise of the Marxist dictate that the proper measurement of an activist philosophy is not whether it approaches the truth, but, in Lawrence's phrase, "the degree to which the effort serves the cause of liberation."[28] In other words, in a world where truth does not exist, all that is left is power—and the critical race theorists intended to take it.

The second key element of critical race theory, which builds on the foundation of racial reasoning, is the concept of "intersectionality." The simplest way to explain intersectionality is that it expands the Marxist oppressor-oppressed binary into a finely graded, multivariate hierarchy of oppression. The concept had already been formulated in rudimentary terms by Angela Davis in *Women, Race, & Class*, which sought to address overlapping systems of oppression, but the critical race theorists took it a step further. In a pair of essays, "Demarginalizing the Intersection of Race and Sex: A Black Feminist Critique of Antidiscrimination Doctrine, Feminist Theory and Antiracist Politics" and "Mapping the Margins: Intersectionality, Identity Politics, and Violence Against Women of Color," Kimberlé Crenshaw turned Angela Davis's original insight into a multisyllabic Latinate term—intersectionality—which provided a single point of reference and gave it the perception of intellectual heft.

Crenshaw begins by inviting the reader to contemplate the full hierarchy of oppression through metaphor. "Imagine a basement which contains all people who are disadvantaged on the basis of race, sex, class, sexual preference, age and/or physical ability. These people are stacked—feet standing on shoulders—with those on the bottom being disadvantaged by the full array of factors, up to the very top, where the heads of all those disadvantaged by a singular factor brush up against the ceiling," she wrote. "In efforts to correct some aspects of domination, those above the ceiling admit from the basement only those who can say that 'but for' the ceiling, they too would be in the upper room. A hatch is developed through which those placed immediately below can crawl. Yet this hatch is generally available only to those who—due to the singularity of their burden and their otherwise privileged position relative to those below—are in the position to crawl through. Those who are multiply-burdened are generally left below unless they can somehow pull themselves into the groups that are permitted to squeeze through the hatch."[29]

For Crenshaw, the figure hovering above the basement ceiling—the affluent, able-bodied, heterosexual, white male—is the ultimate oppressor, who has the power to admit and to exclude those below him. He has created a system of laws, norms, and values that pit the black woman at the bottom of the heap of human bodies. This presents the black woman with a gauntlet of hardships, from racial discrimination to sexual violence, but also gives her a near-magical status within the discipline of critical race theory. Following critical race theory's elevation of the "victim perspective" as a source of authority, the doctrine of intersectionality gives the marginalized black woman the ultimate authority: her word is "the Word."

The goal for Crenshaw was to create a more durable basis for political action, turning intersectionality into a more sophisticated method of identity politics. "Identity continues to be a site of resistance for members of different subordinated groups," Crenshaw wrote. "At this point in history, a strong case can be made that the most critical resistance strategy for disempowered groups is to occupy and defend a politics of social location rather than to vacate and destroy it."[30] In practice, the critical race theorists did not want to transcend identity in pursuit of universal values. They wanted to wield identity in pursuit of left-wing political power.

For Crenshaw, the lodestar for this new politics was the marginalized black woman, who represents a unitary embodiment of the oppressed—and, by the logic of intersectionality, a formula for restructuring society along every axis of oppression. For the marginalized black woman, antiracism was insufficient, because it did not address her sex. Feminism was insufficient because it did not address her race. And anti-capitalism was insufficient because it did not address her identity at all. Unlike the older theories of identity politics, Crenshaw's unitary theory of oppression required a unitary method of revolt, liberating the marginalized black woman along each axis of identity simultaneously.

Politically, Crenshaw's innovation was that her theory of intersectionality provided the basis for a new revolutionary Subject, far beyond Marx's white male proletariat and Marcuse's white-students-and-black-ghetto coalition. In Crenshaw's vision, the new constellation of oppressions—the woman, the minority, the homosexual, the disabled—could be aggregated into a political majority, which, despite superficial differences, represented the crush of flesh at the bottom of the basement, teeming with grievances and ready to revolt.

The final key element of critical race theory is critical race praxis, or the application of the theory to practical politics. Crenshaw and her colleagues explicitly adopted Marx's famous dictum in the Eleventh Thesis on Feuerbach that the purpose of philosophy is not to interpret the world, but to change it.[31] "Unlike some academic disciplines, critical race theory contains an activist dimension. It tries not only to understand our social situation but to change it," Richard Delgado and Jean Stefancic announced in the opening pages of *Critical Race Theory: An Introduction*.[32] "Street activists, for their part, need new theories to challenge a social order that treats minority communities and the poor so badly. By the same token, theorists need the infusion of energy that comes from exposure to real-world problems, both as a galvanizing force for scholarship and as a reality test for their writing. As for criticizing the existing system, the crits respond that they are indeed at work developing a vision to replace it."[33]

The critical race theorists based their political strategy on the work of Antonio Gramsci, the Italian communist who pioneered the concept of "cultural hegemony" and argued that modern left-wing revolutions could succeed through a "war of position" against the establishment. "Critical scholars derive their vision of legal ideology in part from the work of Antonio Gramsci," wrote Crenshaw in *The Key Writings That Formed the Movement*. "In examining domination as a combination of physical coercion and ideological control, Gramsci articulated the concept of hegemony, the means by which a system of attitudes and beliefs, permeating both popular consciousness and the ideology of elites, reinforces existing social arrangements and convinces the dominated classes that the existing order is inevitable."[34]

In the United States, Crenshaw continued, the existing hegemony was the regime of "white supremacy," which, even after the fall of slavery and Jim Crow, had "been submerged in popular consciousness," but still provided the basic structure of racial domination.[35] According to the narrative of critical race theory, American institutions perpetuated this invisible white supremacy while mystifying it through appeals to merit, neutrality, colorblindness, and equal protection under the law—all of which were illusions designed to protect the "racist ideology" and material interests of the ruling class.[36]

The solution, for Crenshaw, was not to engage in direct revolution against the state, as the black militant movement had attempted to do in the previous generation, but to subvert the culture-forming institutions from within. In other words, the ideology of Eldridge Cleaver had a better chance at success with the strategy of Derrick Bell, who had gained the prestige of elite institutions and manipulated their internal logic to suit his political objectives.

"The struggle of blacks, like that of all subordinated groups, is a struggle . . . to manipulate elements of the dominant ideology in order to transform the experience of domination," Crenshaw explained. "Gramsci called this struggle a 'war of position' and he regarded it as the most appropriate strategy for change in Western societies."[37] This strategy, for Crenshaw, provided the most powerful method for seeding critical race theory into the American regime and creating a "counterhegemony" within the American power structure. And the critical race theorists, who by the mid-1990s had secured professorships at prestigious law schools around the country, were in the perfect position to execute it.

Mari Matsuda, another law professor who attended the founding conference on critical race theory, proposed the tactical methods for waging the "war of position."

In an essay for *The Key Writings That Formed the Movement*, Matsuda rallied the entire intellectual substructure of critical race theory—from the logic of the racial reasoning to the authority of the intersectional Subject to the Gramscian war of position—in service of this political vision. She called on the critical race theorists to "[look] to the bottom," adopt "the perspective of those who have seen and felt the falsity of the liberal promise," and rely on the marginalized to "[define] the elements of justice." She believed that the new representatives of the oppressed, which Gramsci had called "organic intellectuals," had the power to subvert the existing legal and political order that "serves to legitimate existing maldistributions of wealth and power" and to rebuild society according to "the actual experience, history, culture, and intellectual tradition of people of color in America."[38]

For Matsuda and the critical race theorists, the endpoint of the law was not to achieve universal equality, which they dismissed as an abstraction, but to orient the machine of the state toward the benefit of the particular flesh-and-blood communities that comprised the intersectional coalition. The ideal outcome, Matsuda wrote, was for "the victim's interpretation" of the Constitution to achieve hegemony, so that "the promise of liberty" would mean "freedom from public and private racism, freedom from inequalities of wealth distribution, and freedom from domination by dynasties."[39] From the beginning to the beyond, critical race theory represented the next turn in the dialectic, promising a process of "fundamental change" that could, at last, usher in "a utopian conception of a world" liberated from past oppressions.[40]

In a remarkably short time period, the critical race theorists had cobbled together their ideology, which they saw as "fuel for social transformation"[41] that began in the university and moved outward through elite activism. As their master Derrick Bell had once observed: "Critical race theory recognizes that revolutionizing a culture begins with the radical assessment of it."[42] The young scholars were ready to commit to "a program of scholarly resistance" that, they hoped, would finally "lay the groundwork for wide-scale resistance."[43]

*　　*　　*

The critical race theorists had set their initial plans in private, but as soon as they began publishing, their movement came under immediate fire from prominent scholars. Critics on the Right and the Left attacked the critical race theorists' victim epistemology, unwarranted pessimism, and partisan political strategy.

The most withering critiques, however, came from black scholars and civil rights leaders.

The first shot came from one of Derrick Bell's colleagues at Harvard Law School, Randall Kennedy, who wrote a highly critical 1989 essay in the *Harvard Law Review* questioning the intellectual foundations of the new discipline.[44] Kennedy argued that the critical race theorists had failed to substantiate their claims of representing the "victim perspective" in academia and of producing racially distinctive scholarship. The critical race theorists had attempted to bolster their "standing" by claiming the mantle of oppression, but, according to Kennedy, a closer examination of the evidence suggested that minority scholars did not suffer meaningful exclusion at law schools. Their limited representation could be better explained, among other reasons, by the limited pool of qualified candidates.

Furthermore, Kennedy attacked the notion that "because of their minority status and the experience of racial victimization that attaches to that status, people of color offer valuable and special perspectives or voices, that, if recognized, will enrich legal academic discourse."[45] In reality, the critical race theorists "[failed] to show the newness of the 'new knowledge' and the difference that distinguishes the 'different voices.'"[46] Kennedy argued that skin color alone was not an automatic indicator of wisdom or an entitlement to special standing. The critical race theorists had attempted to reduce the world into a crude racial binary, which collapsed meaningful distinctions between individuals who might share the same racial ancestry. As Kennedy pointed out, their analysis "wraps in one garment of racial victimization the black law professor [and] the black, unemployed, uneducated captive of the ghetto" and, even worse, assumes that all members of a racial category must hold the same opinion.[47]

Kennedy had laid bare an embarrassing truth: the critical race theorists crusaded for "diversity" but treated racial groups as monoliths. The discipline did not transcend racial stereotypes, it simply inverted them: minorities were assumed to be wise, disadvantaged, and deserving; whites were assumed to be sterile, imperial, and oppressive. Race became a proxy for worth and group identity became the new criterion of moral and intellectual evaluation.

Kennedy flatly rejected this logic of racial standing—and, along with it, the logic of racial reasoning—as poisonous to academia and, by extension, to society. "Widespread application of [the critical race theorists'] concept of standing would likely be bad for minority scholars," he wrote. "It would be bad for them because it would be bad for *all* scholars. It would be bad for all scholars because status-based criteria for intellectual standing are anti-intellectual in that they subordinate ideas and craft to racial status."[48]

At its inception, Kennedy saw the ambitions of the new discipline—to establish a method of obtaining institutional power through racial manipulation—and warned against it.[49] He viewed the reduction of individuals to racial categories as an ugly resurrection of the notion that "race is destiny."[50] And he considered the concepts of "whiteness" and "blackness" as hopelessly vague, ill-motivated, and hostile to the individual and to universal values.

Kennedy's work caused immediate conflict. While Kennedy was working on a draft of the essay, Derrick Bell personally intervened, telling his younger colleague that he should not publish it because it would betray his obligation to his racial and ideological tribe. When Kennedy ignored him and published the critique in the *Harvard Law Review*, Bell exploded with acrimony. He attacked Kennedy publicly, saying that his colleague served "the role of academic minstrel" and that the positive reception to Kennedy's work demonstrated that "the media is ready to accord Kennedy that special celebrity status available to any black willing to speak for whites . . . who are unwilling to criticize blacks for the record."[51]

Other scholars took note. To question the logic of racial reasoning would invite accusations of racism, professional ostracism, and a campaign of character assassination—even if those scholars were black. Years later, after Bell's death, Kennedy acknowledged this dynamic in a retrospective, which offered a grudging respect to Bell, but concluded that he "was drawn to grand generalities that crumple under skeptical probing" and, ultimately, was consumed by his anger, bitterness, and disappointments.[52]

The second significant broadside against Bell and his students' theory of racial pessimism came from another one of his colleagues, Leroy Clark, who worked as a civil rights attorney for the NAACP Legal Defense Fund, collaborated with Martin Luther King Jr. on the Poor People's Campaign, and then became a law professor at Catholic University of America.[53] Whereas Randall Kennedy attacked the intellectual foundations of racial reasoning and victim epistemology, Clark attacked Bell's historical account of racism in America, which, he argued, was detached from the facts and harmful to black self-improvement.

Having observed Bell's bitter reaction to criticism, Clark opened his critique with a note of caution. "I write this article in ambivalence, but with a sense of urgency. The ambivalence comes from criticizing the work of a one-time working colleague, who gained my sincere respect because of his unquestioned concern for the black plight," he wrote. "I do not doubt that Professor Bell has written, as he always does, with honesty. But it is precisely because he is a man of profound integrity, a man labeled the 'founder of Critical Race Theory,' that his pronouncements may have an unprecedented powerful influence, especially on developing minority scholars. . . . The urgency, therefore, comes from my sense that Professor Bell's work propagates a damaging and dampening message which must be confronted and rejected if we are to fashion our future creatively."[54]

After graciously setting the stage, Clark went after Bell's relentlessly negative perception of American history and his argument that racism is permanent, indestructible, and all-powerful in society. The truth, Clark pointed out, was that, throughout American history, many whites fought selflessly for racial equality. In the antebellum period, white abolitionists fought to prohibit slavery out of moral and religious conviction. During the civil rights movement, white activists worked hand in hand with black activists to end the practice of segregation and state-sanctioned racism.

Bell had attempted to explain away any expression of white virtue as cloaked self-interest, but, according to Clark, a basic historical study of the Civil War and of the civil rights movement, in which both he and Bell had participated, left no doubt: white Americans could transcend their own narrow interests and contribute toward the realization of black freedom. Contrary to Bell's dismal characterizations, Clark maintained that "white abolitionists saw the Confederates as the 'Space Traders' of their day" and that, when he and Bell were colleagues at the NAACP Legal Defense Fund, at least one-third of the lawyers on their team were white.[55]

Likewise, Clark rejected Bell's insistence that contemporary blacks were worse off than at any time since slavery.

Blacks, Clark argued, had, in fact, made a "profound qualitative leap toward freedom" at each stage of American history, from abolition to Reconstruction to the Great Migration to the civil rights era.[56] He pointed to a range of historical evidence that contradicted Bell's theory of permanent racism and, instead, made the case for continued progress. In their lifetime, Clark wrote, black poverty had declined by 60 percent, three-fifths of blacks had moved into the middle class, black women had arrived at income parity with white women, and the number of black elected officials had grown from a few dozen in 1940 to 6,800 in 1988. Quoting the economist Peter Drucker, Clark summarized the case for racial optimism: "In the fifty years since the Second World War the economic position of African-Americans in America has improved faster than that of any other group in American social history—or in the social history of any country."[57]

This is not to say that Clark was a Pollyanna. He acknowledged the persistent challenges for black Americans, but maintained that they could not be attributed to racism as an all-powerful and unitary cause. As Clark observed, many of the social problems that were most pronounced in poor black communities had also spread to poor white communities. The cause of social disadvantage could not be reduced to the single variable of race, but must include the full range of economic and cultural factors that lead to inequalities both across and within racial groups.

There is a sense of personal anguish in Clark's writing. He was pained by the fact that his old comrade had lost his way, allowing himself to drift into the paranoid fantasy that contemporary whites were busy plotting "a future holocaust for African-Americans."[58] Clark saw something deeper: Bell's "racial realism" was, in truth, a form of racial nihilism. His protests were not a demonstration of moral heroism, but a form of narcissism and moral grandstanding.

Clark respectfully chastised his former colleague for abandoning the key lesson of the civil rights era—that broad-based, multiracial coalitions were essential for black progress—in favor of a selfish and self-fulfilling attitude of pessimism. "Professor Bell does not offer a single programmatic approach toward changing the circumstance of blacks. He presents only startling, unanalyzed prophecies of doom, which will easily garner attention from a controversy-hungry media," Clark wrote, barely concealing his frustration.[59] "Bell's 'analysis' is really only accusation and 'harassing white folks,' and is undermining and destructive. There is no love—except for his own group—and there is a constricted reach for an understanding of whites. There is only rage and perplexity. No bridges are built—only righteousness is being sold."[60]

The final critique of critical race theory during its initial formation came from Henry Louis Gates Jr., a professor of African-American studies who arrived at Harvard in 1991, as Derrick Bell was engaging in his academic strike. Gates, who would later become the much-celebrated chair of Harvard's Afro-American Studies Department, attacked Bell from the outset. He said that Bell's protest was "a very courageous and dramatic thing to do,"[61] but condemned Bell's endorsement of Louis Farrakhan and hinted that Bell might be enabling the "black demagogues and pseudo-scholars" who refused to clearly condemn anti-Semitism within the black intelligentsia.[62]

Bell, in turn, was furious. He lashed out at Gates in the *New Republic* and the *New York Times*,[63] saying that his Harvard colleague was the equivalent of men such as Clarence Thomas, Shelby Steele, and Thomas Sowell, who criticized left-wing black intellectuals in order to enhance their standing and "serve as a comfort to whites who are upset."[64]

But Gates was just getting started.

Later that year, Gates penned an essay for the *New Republic* that leveled an even more serious criticism against the professor and his young disciples. Gates blasted the ideology of critical race theory, drawing a sharp contrast between the civil rights movement, which regarded civil rights and civil liberties as mutually beneficial, and critical race activism, which had abandoned faith in the principles of the Constitution and argued in favor of the government regulating, restricting, and punishing individuals for vague notions of "hate speech." The critical race theorists, Gates observed, imagined themselves the victims of institutional racism, pervasive bias, academic exclusion, and subtle oppression. But this was an illusion.

In truth, Gates argued, the critical race theorists—law professors in elite universities—were not members of a persecuted class. They were members of a privileged class with significant institutional support. They could appeal to the institutions for protection against "hate speech" because they knew the institutions were likely to side with them. The critical race theorists used their identity as the "victim" in order to exploit the moral power of the oppressed minority, while in reality they represented an ideological majority that sought to cement its own power. "Why would you entrust authority with enlarged powers of regulating the speech of unpopular minorities, unless you were confident that the unpopular minorities would be racists, not blacks?" Gates asked rhetorically.[65]

One by one, Gates cataloged the flaws in the critical race theorists' ideology and the problems that would emerge from their ideal regime. He argued that their political project, which would involve regulating expressions of speech, would replace politics with an unstable form of psychotherapy. The critical race theorists had based their theory of knowledge on the shaky ground of radical subjectivity, which elevated their perspective as the only valid point of judgment and then demanded that it be turned into positive law.

Gates predicted that this approach would lead to absurd inquisitions, empower the most hysterical and punitive elements of the bureaucracy, and enthrone "a vocabulary of trauma and abuse, in which the verbal and physical forms are seen as equivalent." He cited an example from the University of Connecticut, which had banned individuals from "actions that undermined the 'security or self-esteem' of persons or groups" and, at the same time, also banned "attributing objections to any of the above actions to 'hypersensitivity' of the targeted individual or group." In other words, a catch-22: the enforcers of the victim perspective determine guilt and any attempt at defense is considered further proof of wrongdoing.[66]

More importantly, Gates argued that the critical race theorists would turn racism into a mirage. The critical race theorists had focused all of their attention on the preoccupations of academia and abstract condemnations of elite speech and behavior while offering very little to say on the real-world plight of the black underclass. "The problem may be that . . . the continuing immiseration of large segments of black America cannot be erased simply through better racial attitudes. Poverty, white and black, can take on a life of its own, to the point that removing the conditions that caused it can do little to alleviate it," Gates wrote. "Rather than responding to the grim new situation with new and subtler modes of socioeconomic analysis, [the critical race theorists] have finessed the gap between rhetoric and reality by forging new and subtler definitions of the word 'racism.' Hence a new model of institutional racism is one that can operate in the absence of actual racists. By redefining our terms, we can always say of the economic gap between black and white America: the problem is still racism . . . and, by stipulation, it would be true. But the grip of this vocabulary has tended to foreclose the more sophisticated models of political economy that we so desperately need."[67]

The critical race theorists had substituted verbalism for meaning, and symbolism for substance. If they were to attain power, Gates warned, they would sacrifice liberty for a phantom notion of equality, which, in the end, might end up destroying both. Contrary to the activists of the civil rights movement, the aim of the critical race theorists was "not to resist power, but to enlist power."[68] The result would be a system of manipulation that uses guilt, shame, and intricate linguistic and psychological traps to maintain social control.

These three critiques—from Kennedy, Clark, and Gates, all published by 1995—represented a significant intellectual challenge to critical race theory. They did not, however, represent a significant political challenge.

One by one, Bell and his disciples dispatched their black critics through smears and character assassination. Bell called his black opponents "minstrels" and accused them of participating in "the slave masters' practice of elevating to overseer and other positions of quasi-power those slaves willing to mimic the masters' views."[69] His students reproduced this strategy in subtler therapeutic language, diagnosing black critics as suffering from the disease of "internalized racial inferiority."

The critical race theorists had built their philosophy on the unstable foundation of postmodernism, designated themselves the avatars of the oppressed, and created a manipulative political praxis in search of a nebulous and always-failing utopia. All of this was obvious to the early critics. Yet, despite these glaring flaws, the critical race theorists managed to vanquish their opposition one by one and begin the process of installing their ideology in elite enclaves. The real brilliance of critical race theory was not intellectual, but tactical. The "activist scholars" learned how to wield the politics of race in elite milieus and use it as a fulcrum for accumulating power.

After the ideological foundations were set, the critical race theorists turned to the next phase of their campaign: conquering the institutions.

CHAPTER 17

DEI and the End of the Constitutional Order

Critical race theory was never designed to reveal truth—it was designed to achieve power. The real history of the discipline is not a story of its intellectual discoveries, but of its blitz through the institutions.

Over the course of thirty years, the critical race theorists and their allies in left-wing social movements seeded this ideology in nearly every elite knowledge-making institution in America, from the university academic department to the Fortune 100 corporation. They synthesized, reduced, and euphemized the intellectual work of Derrick Bell and his disciples for mass adoption in school curricula, government bureaucracies, and diversity training programs. Over time, the ideology transformed itself from the abstract principles of the academic theory into the concrete policies and practices of "diversity, equity, and inclusion."

This move was inevitable—and brilliant. In order to achieve hegemony within the institutions, the critical race theorists had to create a means of attaching their ideology to administrative power. They first developed these techniques in the confines of the university, then moved laterally through weak points in the bureaucracies of other institutions, most notably the federal diversity apparatus, corporate human resources departments, and the sprawling administration of the public schools. They created a circular, self-reinforcing system that created its own demand and installed a new, universal class of "diversity officials" across the institutions, which seeks to break down the old protections of individual rights, colorblind equality, and private property and replace them with a substitute morality and system of government based on the principles of critical race theory.

In a way, critical race theory has become the überdiscipline of the critical theories. It has harnessed the essential frame of Marcuse's critical theory, absorbed the strategy of Angela Davis's critical praxis, merged with the application of Paulo Freire's critical pedagogy, and combined them all into a formidable, if largely invisible, political movement, which has moved from the margins to the center of American power. Their theory—that the Constitution upholds the regime of white supremacy and must be superseded by a regime of "racial equity"—has become dominant across the entire range of elite institutions.

Their praxis—the Gramscian war of position, supplemented by the tactics of identity politics—has been astonishingly successful in advancing their ideology into power.

*   *   *

The first step for the critical race theorists was to devise a rhetorical strategy for expanding their power within the universities.

From the beginning, the critical race theorists constructed their argument like a mousetrap. They used their epistemology of the oppressed to justify their claims on the grounds of identity, rather than reason, evidence, and rationality, which they dismissed as the logic of the oppressor. From there they were able to use the premise of historical racism to raise sympathies, then pressure the listener into affirming their conclusions, whether or not they were logically or historically justified. By using this technique, the critical race theorists could reinterpret even the highest points in American history, such as the signing of the Emancipation Proclamation or the passage of the Fourteenth Amendment, as a racial conspiracy to subordinate blacks. If anyone disagreed, the critical race theorists had a battery of explanations: the black critic was suffering from "internalized racial oppression"; the white critic was suffering from "white fragility," "unconscious bias," and "internalized white supremacy." They used the emotions of guilt and shame to bludgeon their enemies into accepting their conclusions.

This tactic worked perfectly in the universities. The methods of critical race theory served as high-concept, easy-to-use rationalizations for the practices of denunciation, vendetta, and moral posturing. One simply has to deploy them to gain professional status within elite institutions, where the accusation of racism is enough to transform a member in good standing into an intellectual leper. Left-wing academics could experience the moral thrill of accusation at little cost for error—an attractive calculus for intellectuals to bolster their reputation as brave truth-tellers while never assuming any real personal or professional risk.

The broader goal, from the outset, was conquest. The critical race theorists deployed these techniques of manipulation, subversion, and status games with the goal of embedding their ideology "so thoroughly in academic scholarship and teaching that its precepts became commonplace, part of the conventional wisdom."[1] Their first beachhead was the law school, but the principles of critical race theory—victim epistemology, intersectionality, systemic racism, affirmative action—proved irresistible to other scholars, who used them to advance their own politics and career advancement.

In the face of this new politics, the universities immediately buckled. As the economist Thomas Sowell noted in 1990, administrators seemed powerless to resist the racial hostage-taking of Derrick Bell and his imitators. The universities had "perfected the technique of pre-emptive surrender," Sowell said.[2] "At the very time that there's all this mouthing of the word 'diversity,' there is this extremely narrow ideological conformity that is being enforced wherever people have the power to enforce it."[3]

The defenses continued to fail through the subsequent decades. Critical race theory, which claimed to represent the decolonial impulse, colonized discipline after discipline. The "activist scholars," moving outward from the law schools, quickly established footholds in ethnic studies, women's studies, social sciences, public health, philosophy, and education.

The rise of critical race theory can only be described as an intellectual coup. From its beginning in the late 1980s to the present, the theory has become pervasive in virtually every discipline in the universities. Their output has been enormous: the academic databases yield 390,000 results for "critical race theory," including thousands of papers, reviews, articles, studies, books, and conference presentations. The movement's key figures—Derrick Bell, Kimberlé Crenshaw, Richard Delgado, Jean Stefancic, Mari Matsuda, and Gloria Ladson-Billings, who founded critical race theory in education—have notched nearly 200,000 citations in a broad range of academic journals.[4] There are now entire departments, majors, and minors in critical race theory at dozens of American universities.[5] "The name Critical Race Theory," said Crenshaw, began as an aspiration but, within a decade of the discipline's founding, was "used as interchangeably for race scholarship as Kleenex is used for tissue."[6]

In a way, the critical race theorists achieved victory through volume. In the education field alone, the critical race theorists have published an avalanche of materials and nested their ideas into the architecture of the education departments, which train the teaching force for American primary and secondary schools. By conquering these departments over a period of thirty years, the critical race theorists built a powerful transmission belt for their ideology, moving it from the universities into the public school system. "We didn't set out to colonize, but found a natural affinity in education," said critical race theorist Richard Delgado. "Seeing critical race theory take off in education has been a source of great satisfaction."[7]

Today, critical race theory has achieved hegemony in the educational systems in many blue enclaves. The states of California, Oregon, and Washington have all incorporated the principles of critical race theory into the official state curriculum.[8] Children as young as kindergarten are studying the theories of "systemic racism," "white privilege," and "intersectionality," whether directly or through euphemism.[9]

In Detroit, the superintendent of schools said that his district's "curriculum is deeply using critical race theory" in all of its humanities and social science courses.[10] In Seattle, administrators have hired a full-time critical race theorist, endorsed critical race theory as part of its black studies curriculum, performed "racial equity training" using "critical race theory tenets" for teachers, and deployed more than two dozen "racial equity teams" that practice critical race theory in individual schools across the district.[11] At the national level, the National Education Association, which represents more than 3 million public school teachers and employees, has explicitly endorsed critical race theory and pledged to promote it in all 14,000 local school districts.[12]

But the capture of the classroom was hardly the greatest prize. During this same period, the discipline underwent an even more significant transformation: from critical race theory to "diversity, equity, and inclusion."

From the beginning, the critical race theorists understood that hegemony is achieved not through ideological debate, but through administrative power; the intellectual coup must be followed by the bureaucratic coup. This is where critical race theory has been most successful. The "activist scholars" and their allies—an entire professional network of social justice activists, diversity trainers, philanthropic foundations, affirmative action administrators, and left-wing human resources professionals—adapted the rhetorical strategies from the universities and turned them into a standardized administrative program that would lend legitimacy, power, financing, and status to their ideology.

The process began with simplification: the academics provided the concepts; the professionals translated them into bureaucratic language. The symmetry between the two expressions—in other words, between theory and praxis—is revealed through a careful reading of the basic terms that compose the acronym of DEI.

First, "diversity." The term appeals to the verbal connotation of demographic representation. But at a deeper level, the euphemism of "diversity" is built on the intellectual foundations of intersectionality, which argues that the individual represents not only a demographic reality, but a political imperative—that person must check the boxes of identity and also advance the "victim perspective" as an ideology. As Derrick Bell once explained: "The goals of diversity will not be served by persons who look black and think white."[13] The practical outcome of this policy is the deliberate inversion of the hierarchy of oppression: the "victim perspective" is raised above the "perpetrator perspective" within the institution, and the supposedly "marginalized" individual who represents the favored ideology moves to the center.

Next, "equity." If diversity is the framework, equity is the method. The word is a deliberate obfuscation. It is a near homonym to the word "equality" but carries an entirely different meaning. The American principle of equality was first proclaimed in the Declaration of Independence, consecrated in blood with the Civil War and the Fourteenth Amendment, and codified into law with the Civil Rights Act, which attempted to create a colorblind system that treated individuals equally under the law. But for the critical race theorists, these documents provided a fig leaf of equality that disguised the reality of continuing racial domination.

The critical race theorists explicitly rejected the American standard of colorblind equality, arguing that equal treatment under the law represents "mere nondiscrimination" and serves as a mask for white supremacy and capitalist oppression. Equity is the other side of the coin. It would replace the regime of individual rights with a regime of group entitlement, calling for "*equalizing treatment* by redistributing power and resources in order to rectify inequities and to achieve real equality."[14]

Finally, "inclusion." Again, the signifier and the signified are in opposition. The word "inclusion" has the surface meaning of tolerance for a wide range of people and opinions. But, following the epistemology of the oppressed, the true meaning of "inclusion" is the regulation of speech and behavior to protect the subjective well-being of the intersectional coalition. Anything that is deemed "exclusive," or representing the interests of the oppressor, is excluded; anything that is deemed "inclusive," or representing the interests of the oppressed, is included. This is the logic of racial reasoning, turned into a tautology, managed from above by the bureaucracy. Since the beginning, the critical race theorists argued that the restriction of "racist" and "sexist" speech and behavior was essential to the governance of the university and, by extension, to the governance of society.[15] The bureaucracies internalized this philosophy and used the language of critical race theory—"microaggressions," "microinequities," "unconscious bias," "hate speech"—to construct policies that replaced the rule of free expression with the rule of limited expression.

Together, the acronym for "diversity, equity, and inclusion" represents a new mode of institutional governance. Diversity is the new system of racial standing, equity is the new method of power transfer, inclusion is the new basis of enforcement. All of this could be presented to institutional leadership in a language that appears to be soft, benign, tolerant, and open-minded—something that, combined with the threat of accusation, elite administrators were culturally incapable of resisting.

After establishing this method of colonization in the universities, the critical race theorists and their administrative counterparts extended into the bureaucracies of other institutions. The first and most natural extension was the government, which functioned much the same way as the university: subsidized by taxpayers, layered with administration, operating on a prestige economy, and existing outside the discipline of the free market. As such, the ideology and tactics of critical race theory, adapted into the professionalized language of diversity and inclusion, were easily transposed onto the agencies of the federal government.

The blitz was made even easier by the federal government's existing civil rights apparatus—the various offices of equal opportunity, minority programs, and legal compliance—which was easily captured and converted from the ideology of colorblindness to the ideology of color-consciousness.

In quick succession and, in most cases, without any explicit mandate from Congress, the federal agencies converged on the principles of critical race theory in their internal programs. The bureaucracies retooled their civil rights offices to replace the old lodestar of "equality" with the new objective of "equity." The pattern of conquest was perfectly circular: the intellectuals provided the ideology, the administrators captured the infrastructure, and private diversity contractors attached themselves to a new source of financing and distribution.

Over the past decade, the entire range of federal agencies, from the Environmental Protection Agency to the Federal Bureau of Investigation, has adopted critical race theory as an in-house ideology. In quick succession, these departments created new programming that condemned the United States as "systemically racist," interrogated employees for their "whiteness," and demanded loyalty to government by "anti-racism," or, more accurately, government by the principles of critical race theory.[16]

This formula was repeated across the federal apparatus. In the wake of George Floyd, the National Credit Union Administration told employees America was founded on "white supremacy."[17] The Department of Homeland Security told white employees they have been "socialized into oppressor roles."[18] The Centers for Disease Control and Prevention hosted a thirteen-week training program denouncing the United States as a nation dominated by "White supremacist ideology."[19]

The agencies then told employees to abandon their historical commitment to neutrality and engage in explicit, left-wing political activism. The EPA told workers to internalize the principles of "anti-racism, white fragility, microaggressions, white privilege, and systemic racism" in order to become "allies" for the cause. The State Department organized a three-week anti-racism "habit building challenge" and asked employees to sign a "pledge" in "the pursuit of racial equity." The Department of Veterans Affairs hosted a series of "Race Cafés," with administrators signing an "equity pledge" in front of employees.[20]

When investigators at the Office of Personnel Management conducted an inquiry into critical race theory in the federal government, they discovered an avalanche of ideological materials across the federal agencies. "The first thing I remember was the sheer volume of the material," recounted one official. "A single agency produced nearly 1,000 pages of documents on 'unconscious bias' training alone. We had to hire additional staff just to get through all the material. Another agency had several in-person seminars on 'whiteness' which cost tens of thousands of dollars scheduled for that month alone."[21]

Even federal defense contractors have submitted to the new ideology.

Lockheed Martin, the nation's largest defense firm, sent white male executives on a mission to deconstruct their "white male privilege." The instructors told the men that "white male culture" and the values of "rugged individualism," "hard work," and "striving towards success" were "devastating" to minorities.[22]

Raytheon, the second-largest defense firm, followed suit. The company launched an "anti-racism" program, teaching the principles of "intersectionality" and instructing employees to recognize "interlocking systems of oppression" and "break down power into privilege and marginalization." Whites, according to Raytheon's diversity consultant, "have the privilege of individuality" and must silence themselves in front of minorities. Finally, following the logic of critical race theory to its conclusion, the firm told employees to reject the principle of equality outright. The colorblind standard of "equal treatment and access to opportunities" is not enough; the company must instead strive for "equity," which "focuses on the equality of the *outcome*."[23]

The training program at the Department of the Treasury is representative of the increasing bureaucratization of critical race theory in the federal government. As part of the Dodd-Frank Wall Street Reform and Consumer Protection Act, the Obama administration created Offices of Minority and Women Inclusion in all of the federal financial agencies and Federal Reserve banks across the country. According to multiple federal employees, who agreed to speak on condition of anonymity, the leaders of the Offices of Minority and Women Inclusion serve as political commissars, promoting the official ideology and enforcing orthodoxy. One Treasury employee said that the office bombards staff "almost daily" with racially and politically charged content. Conservative employees are "terrified," anticipating that "managers within the federal government [will] start coercing federal employees into repeating [anti-racist] slogans."[24]

The Treasury Department's programming followed a familiar narrative: America is a racist one-dimensional society, the country's institutions are mechanisms of oppression, and white citizens, in particular, must atone for their collective guilt and renounce their "whiteness."

In 2020, Treasury hired a pair of outside consultants, Howard Ross and Johnnetta Cole, to conduct a series of training programs for thousands of workers in the financial agencies.[25] Together, Ross and Cole reprise the two roles of Marcuse's new proletariat: the white bourgeois and the black militant. Ross is a white, college-educated activist turned "diversity consultant" with a long history with the federal government: across a fifteen-year time span, he billed American taxpayers more than $5 million for racial training programs, including dozens of programs on "diversity," "unconscious bias," and "privilege," at federal agencies including the Departments of Justice, Energy, Veterans Affairs, and Health and Human Services, and NASA.[26]

Cole, on the other hand, is a Marxist "scholar-activist" with a distinguished pedigree in black militancy. In the 1970s, Cole was a leader in multiple communist-supported organizations, including the pro-Castro Venceremos Brigade,[27] the Marxist-Leninist Angola Support Conference,[28] a Soviet front group called the US Peace Council,[29] and the Weather Underground–aligned July 4 Coalition.[30] She repeatedly denounced the United States for "genocidal practices against peoples of color around the world" and the desire to "destroy all enemies of corporate America." Cole celebrated the communist victory in Vietnam, even endorsing the new government's "reeducation camps," and argued that the Castro regime could provide the model for "eliminating institutional racism"[31] in the United States. As the revolution faded, Cole continued to work in academia as a professor and college administrator, then began to join corporate boards and consulting firms, including Cook Ross Inc., led by her co-lecturer Howard Ross.

At the Treasury Department, Ross and Cole began their presentation to 8,500 employees with a short history of the United States, filtered through the counternarrative of critical race theory. "We have a system that is built on race," Ross began. "And one of the core flaws, the original sin of this country, is that it was built on the backs of people who were enslaved, and in order to keep that structure in place, we've had to form systems and structures . . . for hundreds and hundreds of years." Whites, Ross continued, bear special responsibility for these historical crimes, because they are complicit in "a system that's based on racism," and perpetuate that system "not necessarily by choice, but by automatic response to the ways we're taught." Even "good and decent [white] people" uphold "systemic racism" unless they are "actively engaged in trying to dissemble the system." Blacks, Cole added, have endured a four-hundred-year reign of "racial terrorism" that continues "to this very day."

The solution, according to Cole, was for federal employees, especially "White folk" who have an obligation to do serious "inner work," to become "activists" and advance the agenda of "racial equity."

In a follow-up, the Office of Minority and Women Inclusion circulated a document outlining the expectations for the federal financial agencies and their 100,000 employees: they must adopt the language of critical race theory—"Whiteness," "white privilege," "institutional racism," "unconscious bias"—"sit in the discomfort that these notions could cause," and recruit "everyone in the federal government" into "the dismantling of systemic racism." Blacks, who suffer from "post-slavery traumatic syndrome" and the "deep emotional and physiological toll of racism," should undergo therapy, meditation, journaling, and healing in order to overcome their "oppression." Members of both groups, Cole concluded, can then begin the work of political activism and "make policy changes" in local, state, and federal government, in the interest of overturning existing institutions.[32]

The reversal is dramatic. Cole had once promoted her radical ideology as a fellow traveler of the Soviet Union and editorial board member of the journal *Rethinking Marxism*. Now she was promoting it as an official contractor of the United States government. After fifty years, the long march had been completed. The radical Left had finally won its Gramscian "war of position" and attained ideological power within the American state.

* * *

The ambition of the critical race theorists and their confederates in "diversity, equity, and inclusion" is not simply to achieve cultural hegemony over the bureaucracy, but to use this power to reshape the structures of American society. But in the miasma of mystical reasoning and therapeutic language, it is sometimes easy to lose sight of the critical question: What specifically do they want?

The answer is to be found in the original literature of critical race theory, which, before its transformation in the euphemisms of "diversity, equity, and inclusion," was remarkably candid about the discipline's political objectives. They had abandoned the Marxist-Leninist vocabulary of their precursors, such as Angela Davis and the Black Panther Party, but the critical race theorists imagined a revolution that struck just as deeply. They cobbled together a strategy of revolt against the Constitution, using the mechanisms of institutional power to change the words, meanings, and interpretations that provide the foundation of the existing order.

"The Constitution is merely a piece of paper in the face of the monopoly on violence and capital possessed by those who intend to keep things just the way they are," said Mari Matsuda.[33] Tearing it down was not a transgression; it was a moral obligation. When necessary, Matsuda argued, the critical race theorists could appeal to the Bill of Rights and the Constitution to advance their interests, but ultimately, they believed, "rights are whatever people in power say they are."[34] The point was not to uphold the principles of the Constitution, but to wield them as a weapon for securing authority.

In place of the existing interpretation, the critical race theorists proposed a three-part overhaul of the American system of governance: abandoning the "colorblind" notion of equality, redistributing wealth along racial lines, and restricting speech that is deemed "hateful."

To begin, following the line of Derrick Bell, the critical race theorists made the case that "color-blind constitutionalism" functions as a "racial ideology" that "fosters white racial domination"[35] and advances an implicit form of "cultural genocide."[36] The system of individual rights and equal protection, they argued, provided an illusion of equality that failed to address the history of racial injustice. The way stations of "multiculturalism," "tolerance," and "diversity" were inadequate substitutions for "legitimate governmental efforts to address white racial privilege."[37] To rectify this deficiency, the critical race theorists proposed a new interpretation of the Fourteenth Amendment that moves from a system of negative rights—or, protection against state intrusion—to a system of positive rights, or an entitlement to state action.

As Bell explained, the remedy for the limitations of the Fourteenth Amendment, which had failed to achieve substantive racial equality, was to "broaden the Constitution's protections to include economic rights" and an "entitlement to basic needs—jobs, housing, food, health care, education and security—as essential property rights of all individuals."[38] In practice, the implementation of this view would require a system of affirmative action, racial quotas, reparations, and group-based rights. The Constitution would thus become "color-conscious" and the state would treat individuals differently according to race, deliberately reducing privileges for whites and securing privileges for minorities. "The only substantive meaning of the equal protection clause," explained Mari Matsuda, "mandates the disestablishment of the ideology of racism."[39]

There is no bottom to this line of thinking. For the critical race theorists, the word "racism" included everything from explicit discrimination to unconscious bias to unequal outcomes of any kind. And, as Bell insisted, it had an eternal, indestructible power over American society. As a consequence, the critical race theorists abandoned the hope of racial integration and equality under the law, which was deemed naïve, and would replace it with a permanent machine of racial reasoning and reapportionment.

At the abstract level, this would mean foreclosing the promise of the Declaration, the Emancipation, and the Fourteenth Amendment. At the practical level, it would mean permanently categorizing, ranking, sorting, rewarding, and punishing individuals on the basis of identity, rather than character, merit, or individual accomplishment. For the critical race theorists, the question was how, not if, racism has occurred, and any alternate explanations for disparities, such as family, culture, and behavior, were dismissed as rationalizations for white supremacy.

How could this system of white supremacy be corrected? First and foremost, through the equalization of material wealth through racial redistribution.

The key justification for this policy came from UCLA law professor Cheryl Harris, who wrote an influential *Harvard Law Review* paper called "Whiteness as Property," which was celebrated by Derrick Bell and republished as one of the founding texts in *Critical Race Theory: The Key Writings That Formed the Movement*. In the essay, Harris argued that property rights, enshrined in the Constitution, were in actuality a form of white supremacy and must be subverted in order to achieve racial equality.

"The origins of property rights in the United States are rooted in racial domination. Even in the early years of the country, it was not the concept of race alone that operated to oppress blacks and Indians; rather, it was the interaction between conceptions of race and property which played a critical role in establishing and maintaining racial and economic subordination," Harris wrote. "Only white possession and occupation of land was validated and therefore privileged as a basis for property rights. These distinct forms of exploitation each contributed in varying ways to the construction of whiteness as property."[40]

Harris thus established the emotionally loaded premise—whiteness and property are inseparable from slavery—that she then projected onto modern society. "Whiteness, initially constructed as a form of racial identity, evolved into a form of property, historically and presently acknowledged and protected in American law,"[41] she wrote. But this had been mystified by the racial ideology of the Constitution. "Although the existing state of inequitable distribution is the product of institutionalized white supremacy and economic exploitation, it is seen by whites as part of the natural order of things that cannot legitimately be disturbed. Through legal doctrine, expectation of continued privilege based on white domination was reified; whiteness as property was reaffirmed."[42]

Harris, however, believed that this system was not inevitable and, through the process of demystification, could be overthrown. She argued that the basic conceptual vocabulary of the constitutional system—" 'rights,' 'equality,' 'property,' 'neutrality,' and 'power' "—are mere illusions used to maintain the white-dominated racial hierarchy. In reality, Harris contended, "rights mean shields from interference; equality means formal equality; property means the settled expectations that are to be protected; neutrality means the existing distribution, which is natural; and, power is the mechanism for guarding all of this."[43]

The solution for Harris was to replace the system of property rights and equal protection, which she described as "mere nondiscrimination," with a system of positive discrimination tasked with "redistributing power and resources in order to rectify inequities and to achieve real equality."[44] To achieve this goal, she advocated large-scale land and wealth redistribution, inspired in part by the African decolonial model. Harris envisioned a temporary suspension of existing property rights, followed by a governmental campaign to "address directly the distribution of property and power" through property confiscation and race-based reapportionment.

"Property rights will then be respected," Harris noted, "but they will not be absolute and will be considered against a societal requirement of affirmative action."[45]

In Harris's formulation, if rights were a mechanism of white supremacy, they must be curtailed; if property was "racialized property,"[46] it was the legitimate subject for racialist reconquest. And the state is justified in pursuing a regime of "affirmative action," which Harris defined broadly as "equalizing treatment,"[47] including South Africa–style wealth seizures, which, she said, were "required on both moral and legal grounds to delegitimate the property interest in whiteness—to dismantle the actual and expected privilege that has attended 'white' skin since the founding of the country."[48]

The next question facing the critical race theorists was more practical: How would this proposed system of group-based rights and racialist redistribution be enforced? The answer was clear: through the regulation of "harmful" speech.[49]

In a book titled *Words That Wound*, Mari Matsuda, Charles Lawrence III, Richard Delgado, and Kimberlé Crenshaw laid out the case for dramatically restricting the First Amendment in order to suppress individuals and institutions that represent the forces that would "advance the structure and ideology of white supremacy."[50]

The foundation of their argument was that speech can be a form of violence and, as such, must be restricted by the state in a similar manner. "This is a book about assaultive speech, about words that are used as weapons to ambush, terrorize, wound, humiliate, and degrade," they write in the book's opening paragraph.[51] As with private property and colorblind equality, the critical race theorists proposed that the First Amendment was not designed to protect individual speech, but to cynically enable "racist hate speech" and protect the system of white supremacy.[52]

Freedom of expression, they argued, does not serve citizens equally; in fact, it is both a means and a mask for the subordination of minorities. When the state permits harmful speech, which ranges from subconscious racial messaging to explicit racist polemics, it threatens the physical and psychological safety of racial minorities. "We are not safe when these violent words are among us," Matsuda wrote.[53] "Victims of vicious hate propaganda experience physiological symptoms and emotional distress ranging from fear in the gut to rapid pulse rate and difficulty in breathing, nightmares, post-traumatic stress disorder, hypertension, psychosis, and suicide. Patricia Williams has called the blow of racist messages 'spirit murder' in recognition of the psychic destruction victims experience."[54]

In order to adjudicate guilt, the critical race theorists argued that the concept of "harmful speech" must be interpreted through the lens of intersectionality, with the victim-perpetrator distinction offering a rubric for culpability. The writers of *Words That Wound* were explicit in their argument that whites, and whites only, had the capability of committing speech violence.

Racist language used by minorities against whites, such as Malcolm X's famous tirades against the "white devil," would be exempted from restrictions. "Some would find this troublesome, arguing that any attack on any person's ethnicity is harmful," Matsuda argued. "In the case of the white devil, there is harm and hurt, but it is of a different degree. Because the attack is not tied to the perpetuation of racist vertical relationships, it is not the paradigm worst example of hate propaganda. The dominant-group member hurt by conflict with the angry nationalist is more likely to have access to a safe harbor of exclusive dominant-group interactions. Retreat and reaffirmation of personhood are more easily attained for members of groups not historically subjugated."[55]

In addition to racial speech, the critical race theorists would also regulate political speech. Under their ideal regime, Marxist speech would be protected by the First Amendment; "racist," "fascist," and "harmful" speech would not.[56]

This simple binary described in *Words That Wound* was a basic reformulation of Marcuse's "liberating tolerance," using the black-white and left-right distinctions as crude sorting mechanisms. But unlike Marcuse, whose critique was general and philosophical in nature, the critical race theorists, as law professors, created a detailed framework for the regime of speech suppression. They linked the subtlest expression of "racist speech," from the emanations of unconscious bias to academic research with politically damaging conclusions, to the larger "structure of racism,"[57] which, they claimed, should be regulated, shaped, and confined by the state in order to make free expression "a vehicle of liberation" rather than "an instrument of domination."[58]

In practice, the critical race theorists would institute a system of speech codes, behavior regulation, bias detection, and reshaping of the subconscious in order to produce a predetermined outcome of "anti-racist" speech, behavior, and culture. The justification, following the example of Cheryl Harris's treatment of private property, was that speech power must be redistributed in order to dismantle the institutions and ideologies that prop up the racist system. Speech that embodies "whiteness" must be suppressed; speech that embodies "blackness" must be supported. The content of speech, beginning with "unconscious racism"[59] and ending with the "fighting words" of racial threats,[60] must be reordered and redirected toward the substantive goal of overturning the existing system.

Taken together, the three pillars of the critical race theorists' ideal system of governance—the replacement of individual rights with group rights, the race-based redistribution of wealth, the suppression of speech based on a racial and political calculus—constitute a change in political regime.

Under the ideology of the critical race theory, the meaning of the First Amendment, the Fourteenth Amendment, and the protections of private property would be demolished. The result would be a form of tyranny: the state would not only control the distribution of material resources, as in a collectivist economic regime, but would also extend its domain over individual psychology, speech, expression, and behavior. These twin goals—material and nonmaterial reapportionment—would be achieved through the heavy hand of the state, which would be granted unprecedented intrusion into public and private life.

As the ideologists and bureaucrats of critical race theory entrenched themselves in the institutions, they worked to turn these concepts into policy. They believed their ideas were ready to see the light of day.

*   *   *

The rise of the DEI regime is no longer an academic exercise.

In recent years, left-wing bureaucracies have proposed and enacted a range of policies predicated on the logic of critical race theory. For example, during the coronavirus pandemic, some states created a race-conscious formula for distributing vaccinations that would deny treatment to whites in order to achieve "racial equity."[61] On the West Coast, some cities have created income transfer programs exclusively for racial and sexual minorities.[62] In government, some agencies have started to mandate separate employee training programs for "whites" and "people of color" so that whites can "accept responsibility for their own racism" and minorities can insulate themselves from "any potential harming [that] might arise from a cross-racial conversation."[63] Some public schools have followed suit, segregating students by race for field trips and extracurricular activities, which are, according to school officials, designed to "create a space of belonging," which, they say, without a hint of irony, is "about uniting us, not dividing us."[64]

At the federal level, Massachusetts senator Elizabeth Warren has introduced an "Anti-Racism in Public Health Act" that seeks to use the theory of "intersectionality" to direct resources to favored racial-political factions and to embed the monocausal "racial disparities" doctrine into every appendage of the federal government.[65] Likewise, on his first day in office, President Joseph Biden issued an executive order seeking to nationalize the approach of "diversity, equity, and inclusion" and "embed equity principles, policies, and approaches across the Federal Government." In business, every Fortune 100 corporation in America has submitted to the ideology of "diversity, equity, and inclusion."[66]

This is only the beginning. This movement seeks to establish itself in every layer of the public and private administration, which will be refitted to advance the substitute morality of critical race theory and replace governance by the Constitution with governance by the bureaucracy. The strategy is not to amend the Constitution through the democratic process—which, the critical race theorists concede, would be an impossibility—but to subvert it through a thousand administrative cuts. Their gambit is to normalize the regime of group-based rights, active discrimination, speech suppression, and racialist redistribution of resources through small administrative decisions, which can, over time, legitimize broader policies.

The critical race theorists' ultimate ambition is to establish these principles as state orthodoxy from the top down. In an essay for *Politico Magazine*, Boston University professor and bestselling popularizer of critical race theory Ibram Kendi unveiled his proposal for an "anti-racist amendment" to the Constitution.[67] "The amendment would make unconstitutional racial inequity over a certain threshold, as well as racist ideas by public officials," Kendi explained. "It would establish and permanently fund the Department of Anti-racism (DOA) comprised of formally trained experts on racism and no political appointees. The DOA would be responsible for preclearing all local, state and federal public policies to ensure they won't yield racial inequity, monitor those policies, investigate private racist policies when racial inequity surfaces, and monitor public officials for expressions of racist ideas. The DOA would be empowered with disciplinary tools to wield over and against policymakers and public officials who do not voluntarily change their racist policy and ideas."[68]

In other words, the scope and power of the new "Department of Antiracism" would be nearly unlimited. In effect, it would become a fourth branch of government, unaccountable to voters, that would have the authority to veto, nullify, or suspend any law in any jurisdiction in the United States. It would mean an end to the system of federalism and to the lawmaking authority of Congress. Furthermore, under the power to "investigate private racist policies" and wield authority over "racist ideas," the new agency would have unprecedented control over the work of lawmakers, as well as auxiliary policymaking institutions such as think tanks, research centers, universities, and political parties.

Although Kendi's proposal—a crude translation of the policies intimated in *Words That Wound* and *The Key Writings That Formed the Movement*—is framed as an amendment to the American constitutional order, it is better described as an end to the constitutional order. In the name of racial justice, the critical race theorists and their fellow travelers would limit, curtail, or abolish the rights to property, equal protection, due process, federalism, speech, and the separation of powers. They would also replace the system of checks and balances with an "anti-racist" bureaucracy with nearly unlimited state power—and every other institution would be forced to fall in line.[69]

If critical race theory should succeed as a system of government, it is easy to imagine the future: an omnipotent bureaucracy that manages transfer payments between racial castes, enforces always-shifting speech and behavior codes through bureaucratic rule, and replaces the slogan of "life, liberty, and the pursuit of happiness" with the deadening euphemism of "diversity, equity, and inclusion."

This is not yet the regime in America, but unless there is a reversal within the institutions, the slow, hulking machine of critical race ideology will continue to accumulate power and marginalize democratic opposition. Once the public has been sufficiently alienated from the Constitution of 1789—when its heroes have been destroyed and its memories severed from their origins—the Constitution will finally become "merely a piece of paper," a palimpsest to be written over in pursuit of the "total rupture" with the past. It will become, in the words of Derrick Bell, nothing but "roach powder" used to suffocate and destroy American liberty.

The triumph of the new ideological regime would mean the end of a society oriented, however imperfectly, toward the eternal principles, and the installation of society of racial score-settling and bureaucratic leveling, abandoning the individual to his fate.

The Counter-Revolution to Come

The story of America's cultural revolution is one of triumph. The critical theories have become the dominant frame in the academy. The long march through the institutions has captured the public and private bureaucracy. The language of left-wing racialism has become the lingua franca of the educated class.

But underneath these apparent victories, there is a darkness—a moral void that threatens to reverse these triumphs and turn the revolution into a monster.

The warning signs were there from the beginning. As a historical matter, the cultural revolution has been a failure everywhere it has been tried. During the rise of the New Left, Marcuse, Davis, and Freire all expressed unalloyed support for the communist revolutionary movements, which were putting their theories into practice. They heaped praise on Lenin, Mao, Che, Castro, and Cabral. But this dream quickly changed into a nightmare. Within a few years of the emergence of the New Left, the cultural revolutions from Beijing to Havana to Bissau devoured themselves. Mao's government annihilated millions of its own citizens in pursuit of cultural revolution. Castro's regime degenerated into state tyranny. Cabral's state fell into a decades-long pit of stagnation, failure, and dependency.

Yet the critical theorists were unrepentant. Marcuse defended his support for violent revolution until his death, arguing that "there is a difference between violence and terror."[1] Freire never disavowed the regimes of Lenin, Mao, and Castro, even as their atrocities had long been a matter of public record. Angela Davis never relented in her support for global communism, claiming that, despite the collapse of the USSR, "the Russian Revolution will always retain its status as a monumental historical moment" and "Marxism will continue to be relevant" as long as capitalism survives.[2]

These theorists were simultaneously wrong and prescient. Their revolution failed in the Third World only to succeed in the First World. Although communism has all but vanished from modern life, the theories that justified it have taken power in the heart of capitalism. In the United States, Marcuse's critical theory has dissolved the national narrative down to the foundations. Angela Davis, Eldridge Cleaver, and their imitators have recast the country's "greatest heroes as the arch-villains."[3] The followers of Paulo Freire and Derrick Bell have ensured that the institutions repeat these themes ad nauseam and transmit them to the next generation.[4]

The administrators of this movement—the intellectuals, bureaucrats, experts, activists, and social engineers—are approaching the status of the "universal class," in which Hegel and, in modified form, Marx had put their hopes.[5] In their own minds, the members of this class represent the omniscient point of view. They can survey society as a whole, diagnose its problems, and administer the cure through the bureaucracy. They have turned Marcuse's "society of total administration"[6] into a virtue. They can achieve human perfectibility using the methods of revolution and social science.[7]

But this, too, as it did in the Third World, has turned out to be an illusion. The bitterest irony of the critical theories is that they have attained power but have not opened up new possibilities; they have instead compressed the prestige institutions of society with a suffocating new orthodoxy. The revolution along the axes of identity has proven unstable, alienating, and incapable of managing a complex society, much less improving it. As it moves into the position of governance, the universal class reveals itself to be more parochial, partisan, and inept than the modernist administrators whom they replaced.

From one perspective, the current battlefield may appear overwhelming. The Left has achieved cultural dominance over the entire range of prestige institutions. But from another, there is the possibility of reversal. Beneath the appearance of universal political rule, their cultural revolution has an immense vulnerability: the critical ideologies are a creature of the state, completely subsidized by the public through direct financing, university loan schemes, bureaucratic capture, and the civil rights regulatory apparatus. These structures are taken for granted, but with sufficient will they can be reformed, redirected, or abolished through the democratic process. What the public giveth, the public can taketh away.

The most urgent task for the enemies of the critical theories is to expose the nature of the ideology, how it operates within the institutions, and devise a plan for striking back. The opposition must ruthlessly identify and exploit the vulnerabilities of the revolution, then construct its own logic for overcoming it. The critical theories have proven immensely seductive, but as they have proceeded along the dialectic and manifested themselves within the institutions, they have revealed a series of insurmountable flaws. The "critical theory of society" collapses when it is put into practice. The racial revolution devolves into nihilism when it unleashes violence. The bureaucracies of "diversity, equity, and inclusion" cannot improve conditions for the common citizen.

The opposition must stand in the breach between the cultural revolution's utopian abstractions and concrete failures. It must devise a strategy for laying siege to the institutions, severing the link between ideology and bureaucracy, and protecting the common citizen from the imposition of values from above. The task is to meet the forces of revolution with an equal and opposite force, creating new ground for the nation's common life and reorienting the institutions toward the nation's eternal principles.

The task is, in short, counter-revolution.

*   *   *

The cultural revolution's first vulnerability is philosophical.

The New Left's house philosopher, Herbert Marcuse, created a dazzling theoretical system, but once it made contact with reality, it began to fall apart. As Marcuse rose to prominence, even left-wing academics began to cast doubts on his theory of revolution. The Marxist philosopher Alasdair MacIntyre, for example, eviscerated the underpinnings of Marcuse's political vision, denouncing his "dictatorship of the intellectuals" as elitist, authoritarian, and irredeemably naïve. "One cannot liberate people from above; one cannot re-educate them at this fundamental level. As the young Marx saw, men must liberate themselves," MacIntyre scolded. "To make men objects of liberation by others is to assist in making them passive instruments; it is to cast them for the role of inert matter to be molded into forms chosen by the elite."[8]

Marcuse's old colleague Theodor Adorno, who had broken with him over the student riots, turned away from practical politics entirely. "When

I made my theoretical model, I could not have guessed that people would try to realize it with Molotov cocktails," he said.[9]

But the dialectic had already been unleashed. As the critical theory of society conquered institution after institution, these more careful scholars watched in horror as its fundamental limitation was revealed: the dialectic had a tremendous power of disintegration, but it was incapable of establishing a new ground of truth and, consequently, building a real-world alternative to the liberal society. Marcuse had sold his Great Refusal as an act of heroism, but after the initial thrill of the counterculture dissipated, it revealed itself as a form of emptiness—a rejection of society without a corresponding positive function.[10]

The result of Marcuse's critical revolution was not the creation of a multidimensional society, but a one-dimensional society in reverse. The bureaucracy simply co-opted the ideology and turned it into a standard for the new "one-dimensional man": the manipulative, guilt-ridden, security-seeking functionary, feigning revolution more than waging it.

The members of this new elite might lambaste individualism, hard work, silent strength, and striving toward success as features of "white supremacy," but they are unable to propose anything but platitudes in their place. Privately, they know there is no practicable way to make ancient West African spirituality or lost Aztec rituals the basis for governing a modern university or school system, but publicly they continue producing boilerplate, pretending to be in opposition while abdicating any responsibility over the institutions they now control.

Marcuse and Rudi Dutschke both feared this outcome. In the 1950s, Marcuse had warned about the "centralized bureaucratic communist"[11] organization of society that had turned the Soviet Union into a tyrannical regime.[12] Dutschke was even more prescient: he worried that the middle-class white revolutionaries would become "parasites of the system" and use elite institutions to lavish themselves with "a certificate of independence and elite-security."[13] He cautioned against turning the universities—and, by extension, other domains of white, middle-class intellectualism—into a "fetish." He desperately wanted to believe that the radical movement could shatter the entire "state-social bureaucracy" and bring down "the whole way of life of the authoritarian state as it has existed up to now."[14]

But this was an impossibility. Contrary to Marcuse and Dutschke's desires, the New Left was never able to transcend, in Marx's phrase, the "abominable machine of class rule"—they simply replaced the management. The descendants of the New Left have done nothing but extend the "state-social bureaucracy" into new territories, where they fight endlessly about language, symbols, and ephemera, and their relationship to the institutions becomes purely parasitical.

There will be a reckoning. The simple fact is that the ideology of the elite has not demonstrated any capacity to solve the problems of the masses, even on its own terms. The critical theories operate by pure negation, demolishing middle-class structures and stripping down middle-class values, which serves the interest of the bureaucracy but leaves the society in a state of permanent disintegration.

Ultimately, critical theory will be put to a simple test: Are conditions improving or not improving? Are cities safer or less safe? Are students learning to read or not learning to read? The new regime can only suppress the answers for so long. The average citizen will be able to feel the truth intuitively, even if he is temporarily deprived of the language for articulating it.

This realization cannot be stopped. The working class is more anti-revolutionary today than at any time during the upheaval. The common citizens have seen the consequences of elite ideology as public policy. Their family structures have been destabilized. Their culture of self-reliance has been usurped by state dependence. Their quality of life has plummeted into a revolving nightmare of addiction, violence, and incarceration.[15] Marcuse's vision of liberated eroticism and the infinite malleability of human nature resulted not in utopia, but in catastrophe for those with the least capacity to resist it.

Even Marcuse, the brilliant prophet of the critical theories, conceded again and again that he could not see beyond the abyss. He blindly hoped that the "total rupture" would lead to a world beyond necessity. But his descendants—all of them lesser minds than their master—have proved that the destruction of the old values is not automatically followed by the creation of new ones. To the contrary, when the philosophy of negation prevails, it can succeed only in shredding the social fabric within which the common citizen must survive.

* * *

The racial revolution follows a similar line of development. The activists of the black liberation movement summoned the romantic spirit of the revolutionary and used sophisticated continental theories to legitimize their use of violence. They believed that "violence is a cleansing force" that "frees the native from his inferiority complex and from his despair"[16] and, ultimately, serves as a catalyst for meaningful progress.

Their theory, however, was bunk. The truth is that their cultural revolution could only exist in a state of disintegration. As the opposition, they could tear away the masks, dispel the great myths, and humiliate the old heroes—but after the bombs detonated and the blood dried, they were left with nothing but an immense and overwhelming void.

Rather than freeing the black militant from his "inferiority complex and from his despair," the racial revolution cemented his feet into those exact psychological conditions. In truth, the praxis of the black liberation movement was not an expression of liberation, but a death wish. The militants, following Eldridge Cleaver, had internalized the image of the black lumpenproletariat, demonstrating little confidence in its ability to achieve productive self-determination, and instead relied almost exclusively on its capacity for violence and destruction. "We take a revolutionary position against every organized structure that exists in the world," Cleaver wrote.[17] These are the words of a madman, a thrower of dynamite, a human kamikaze, and, ultimately, an incantation of self-destruction.

The true heart of the quest for liberation—the driving force behind its theory and praxis—is nihilism. Cleaver believed that raping white women was "freedom." Angela Davis believed that taping a shotgun to the neck of a county judge was "justice." Black Lives Matter activists believed that looting and burning down shopping malls was "reparations." But all of these are, in truth, pure resentment. The black liberation movement rationalized violence, first dressing it up in Kant and Hegel, and then, in the contemporary period, using it as a method for extorting corporate and public support. But this method of liberation is ultimately a dialectic of destruction.

In the end, the "abolitionists," who seek nothing less than the "total rupture" of society, cannot fill the void with anything but abstractions: "justice," "liberation," "freedom." But their policies—defunding the police, closing the jails, relieving the prosecutors—do not produce justice. They produce disorder. Each transgression of the law reveals the emptiness of those abstractions; each spasm of activism unleashes a new wave of violence in poor neighborhoods.

The ugly secret is that the radical Left cannot replace what it destroys. The peace circle and the synthetic tribal ritual are no substitute for the existing architecture of social institutions. When the left-wing activists control the moment of decision, it becomes clear that they do not have an agenda to transform their sweeping visions into a stable reality. Instead, chaos becomes the highest value. They believe they are succeeding because there is a frenzy of activity. Destruction begins to provide a sense of meaning in and of itself.

Then the vultures swoop in. The new revolutionaries pretend they are striking at the foundations of the capitalist order, but when their campaign inexorably fails, they simply want their cut. The looters get a box of sneakers and a flat-screen television. The intellectuals get permanent sinecures in the universities. The activists get a ransom payment, disguised as a philanthropic contribution, from the corporations and the local government. The revolution becomes a pose, a reenactment of the 1960s on the stage of the present.

And the leading actors are well compensated. After their summer of revolution, Black Lives Matter cofounder Patrisse Cullors signed an entertainment deal with Warner Bros. and spent $3.2 million on four high-end homes across the country.[18] The other cofounders, Alicia Garza and Opal Tometi, signed entertainment deals with marquee Hollywood talent agencies[19] and the group secretly bought a $6 million mansion in Southern California.[20] Meanwhile, their organization descended into outright graft: one leader allegedly stole $10 million in donations.[21] Others transferred millions to family members through shadowy consulting firms and nonprofit entities.[22] Massive sums of money went missing altogether.

BLM activists were never a threat to capitalism—they were its beneficiaries. The wave of chaos they unleashed was never a viable path to liberation; it was an accelerant for destruction.

*   *   *

The ultimate tragedy of the critical theories is that, as a governing ideology, they would trap the United States in an endless loop of failure, cynicism, and despair.

There is a profound irony that haunts all the leading figures of the movement: the solution was always within their sight. Herbert Marcuse admitted that the United States was among the freest countries in the world, but still argued that it must be destroyed in order to achieve true liberation.[23] Paulo Freire spent decades searching for the secret to literacy, but fell to the myth that education must begin with the suicide of the middle class, blind to the evidence that the opposite is true. Angela Davis succumbed to the illusion that violent revolution was the only path to liberation, while millions of Americans fought for and achieved substantive freedoms by appealing to the Declaration and utilizing the democratic process. Derrick Bell surrendered to pessimism in an era of undeniable progress, forgetting the lessons of his own rise, which was made possible by parents and neighbors who prioritized merit, education, family, and hard work while fighting to eliminate all-too-real barriers and injustices.

Looking back at his life, Bell described being trapped in "the protestor's dilemma," a feeling that each righteous action had the potential for unintended consequences, eternal regressions, and the alienation of allies as well as enemies.[24] He was a man captured by his premises. For decades, he had argued that racism was permanent, indestructible, and essential. He could not deviate from its inevitable conclusion without invalidating his life's work. He believed that he was "imprisoned by the history of racial subordination" and, like the slaves before him, was fated to exist in the netherworld between the abstract understanding of freedom and the concrete existence of the bound and shackled man. His lasting conviction was that "racism lies at the center, not the periphery; in the permanent, not in the fleeting; in the real lives of black and white people, not in the sentimental caverns of the mind."[25]

There is a seductive romanticism to Bell's prose, but, in the final judgment, his philosophy is better understood as nihilism in the mask of the tragic hero.

Derrick Bell burned bridges, nursed miseries, diminished victories, and failed to recognize authentic progress in America's past and present. His disciples—Crenshaw, Harris, Delgado, Matsuda, Lawrence—carried on the contradictions of their master and added the striving inauthenticity of the precocious student. They entered adulthood in a different world, after the hard-won victories of equal rights and the regime of affirmative action, yet they imagined themselves as the avatars of the oppressed. They populated elite institutions and wielded the politics of position while ignoring the masses of the black underclass, who, despite the achievement of equal rights, continued a long slide into social pathology.[26]

For all of their faults, Davis, Cleaver, and black revolutionaries at least grappled with and appealed to the black lumpenproletariat. The critical race theorists, on the other hand, treat them like lepers—the lumpen class is nowhere to be found in their work, except as symbolic justification for their abstractions.

This is where the critical race theorists reach the final impasse. Their program has become a form of empty professional-class aestheticism, designed for manipulating social status within elite institutions, not for alleviating real miseries or governing a nation.

The critical race theorists pretend to reveal a deeper understanding of racism in the United States, but by reducing the complex phenomenon of inequality to a single causal variable—racism—their theory is dangerously incomplete. Their policy of "anti-racism"—the destruction of middle-class norms and the construction of a racial patronage machine—would deepen racial divisions, not transcend them. Even worse, it would undermine the very institutions that are essential to addressing inequality in America.[27]

The critical race theorists, who claim to represent the oppressed, exist outside the class system altogether: they represent a new bureaucratic class that exists outside the demands of labor and capital, with permanent sinecures in the institutions and total protection from the constraints on either side of the private market. They think of themselves as Gramsci's organic intellectuals but are, in actuality, paper tigers.

This is not to say that they are not powerful. The opposite is true: they have seized the means of cultural production and, through the cynical games of elite social status, launched a supremely ambitious bureaucratic coup.

But now, as the ideology is identified not as an insurgent force but as an arbiter of the status quo, they will have to confront a series of difficult questions. What do they have to offer the oppressed? How does their revolution move beyond the cultural superstructure? How will their proposals achieve better results than the Great Society's "health, education, and welfare" programs, which have ballooned to more than one trillion dollars in annual public spending but have failed to stop the rise in social pathologies among poor populations of all racial backgrounds? How will they address the catastrophic cultural conditions in poor communities that are the greatest barrier to substantive equality in America?

There are no good answers in the literature of critical race theory. For all its pretensions, it provides nothing more than a repetition of the vague formulas of the black liberation movement that had exhausted itself a generation prior. They would rather reenact the fantasies of past revolutions than grapple with the intractable truth that the only viable answer to inequality is to strengthen the very institutions that they have helped to dissolve.

Critical race theory is, at heart, pseudo-radicalism. Professors at Harvard, Columbia, and UCLA are not guerrilla fighters with their chests wrapped in bandoliers. They are not a threat to the system; they are entirely dependent on the system. Their ideology is not revolutionary; it is parasitic, relying on permanent subsidies from the regime they ostensibly want to overthrow.

The critical race theorists and their allies have turned resentment into a governing principle. But this is also a trap: resentment is a tool for obtaining power, not of wielding it successfully. One can almost imagine a cinematic sequence, in the style of the old Soviet propaganda films, in which the new professional-class proletarians seize the means of elite cultural production and then, shocked and bewildered at their arrival, look at one another with an immense fear spreading across their faces. The revolution was a pretension, a posture of opposition; they never intended to wield the machines; it was not supposed to work this way.

This fear, this hesitation, provides the space for another reversal. It provides the opportunity to face the revolution, on its own terrain, with an equal or greater force of counter-revolution. The critical theories might have taken hegemony over elite institutions, but their grip over the superstructure might not be as strong as it appears. Through a mobilization of the physical classes against elite abstraction, it can—and it must—be broken.

*　　*　　*

The revolution of 1968, although it seems to have captured the edifice of America's elite institutions, might not be as strong as it appears. It has created a series of failures, shortcomings, and dead ends—and in this gap of contradiction, a counter-revolution can emerge.

The fear of counter-revolution has haunted every revolution since the beginning. Marx saw the counter-revolutionaries—the monarchy, the church, the bourgeoisie—as an overwhelming threat and watched them defeat all of the left-wing political movements of his time.[28] This recursion would repeat itself throughout history: the French Revolution fell to the forces of Thermidor,[29] the Revolutions of 1848 fell to the bourgeoisie,[30] the Bolshevik Revolution fell to internal tyrants. Karl Korsch, a colleague of Herbert Marcuse at the Institute for Social Research, believed that the twentieth-century revolutions were doomed along a similar line. "More than any preceding period of recent history, and on a much vaster scale, our period is a time not of revolution but of counter revolution."[31]

The urgent task for the political Right is to correctly understand the contours of the current revolution and create a strategy for defeating it on real political grounds: revolution against revolution, institution against institution, negation against negation. This new counter-revolution will not take the form of the counter-revolutions of the past: it is not a counter-revolution of class against class, but a counter-revolution along a new axis between the citizen and the ideological regime.

Despite the success of the long march through the institutions and the capture of the "technology of liberation,"[32] the new elite has failed to extinguish the bourgeois desires for property, family, religion, and democratic representation. The intellectuals and, following them, the institutions have spent decades disparaging these desires as racist, exploitative, and illusory, but quietly, in the tract homes and small churches in the American interior, they have proven remarkably durable, even as their tangible expression has degraded.

The great weakness of the cultural revolution is that it negates the metaphysics, morality, and stability of the common citizen. As it undermines the institutions of family, faith, and community, it creates a void in the human heart that cannot be filled with its one-dimensional ideology.

The counter-revolution must begin at that exact point: to reestablish the basic human desires, to redraw the boundaries of human nature, and to rebuild the structures for the fulfillment of human meaning, which cannot be engineered by the critical theories and must go "beyond politics"[33] into the realm of ethics, myth, and metaphysics. The truth is that, despite a half century of denigration, most Americans still believe in the Declaration and the promise of liberty and equality. The statues of America's Founders might have been toppled, spray-painted, and hidden away. Their principles might have been deconstructed, denigrated, and forgotten. But the vision of the Founders strikes at something eternal.

The common citizen understands this intuitively, down to his bones, but he must be guided through a process of recollection. The theorists of the counter-revolution must breathe new life into the American myth and mobilize the tremendous reservoir of public sentiment toward a project of restoration. The critical theories work via negation, but the counter-revolution must work as a positive force. While the revolution seeks to demolish America's founding principles, the counter-revolution seeks to restore them. While the revolution proceeds by a long march through the institutions, the counter-revolution proceeds by laying siege to the institutions that have lost the public trust.

In historical terms, the counter-revolution can be understood as a restoration of the revolution of 1776 over and against the revolution of 1968. Its ambition is not to assume control over the centralized bureaucratic apparatus, but to smash it. It is a revolution *against*: against utopia, against collectivism, against racial reductionism, against the infinite plasticity of human nature. But it is also a revolution *for*: for the return of natural right, the Constitution, and the dignity of the individual.

For this movement to be successful, the architects of the counter-revolution must develop a new political vocabulary with the power to break through the racialist and bureaucratic narratives, tap into the deep reservoir of popular sentiment that will provide the basis for mass support, and design a series of policies that will permanently sever the connection between the critical ideologies and administrative power.

The counter-revolution must be understood not as a reaction or a desire to return to the past, but as a movement with the intention of reanimating the eternal principles and reorienting the institutions toward their highest expression. The foundations of the counter-revolution are thus moral in nature, seeking to guide the common citizen toward what is good and to rebuild the political structures so that his moral intuitions can be realized in society.

If the endpoint of the critical theories is nihilism, the counter-revolution must begin with hope. The principles of the society under counter-revolution are not oriented toward sweeping reversals and absolutes, but toward the protection of the humble values and institutions of the common man: family, faith, work, community, country. The intellectuals and activists of the counter-revolution must arm the population with a competing set of values, spoken in language that exposes and surpasses the euphemisms of the left-wing ideological regime: excellence over diversity, equality over equity, dignity over inclusion, order over chaos.

The counter-revolution must also restore a healthy sense of historical time. The past must be remembered not as a procession of horrors, but as a vast spiritual tableau for mankind, in which his greatest cruelties and his greatest triumphs are revealed. History must once again serve as nourishment for society, and its highest symbols—the Founders, the Constitution, the Republic—must inspire a renewed and unashamed defense. The critiques of the critical theories, insofar as they reveal injustice, must be absorbed into the narrative of the counter-revolution and serve as a reminder of human limitation, which has been gradually and steadily overcome through the unfolding of the principles of the American Republic.

The ultimate objective of this campaign must be the restoration of political rule. The deepest conflict in the United States is not along the axis of class, race, or identity, but along the managerial axis that pits elite institutions against the common citizen. The revolution, which seeks to connect ideology to bureaucratic power and to manipulate behavior through the guise of expertise, is ultimately anti-democratic.

The counter-revolution, on the other hand, seeks to channel public sentiment and restore the rule of the legislature, executive, and judiciary over the de facto rule of managers and social engineers. It must reanimate the instincts of self-government among the people and mobilize an organic movement of citizens that will reassert its power in the institutions that matter: the school, the municipality, the workplace, the church, the university, the state. The anti-democratic structures—the DEI departments and the captured bureaucracies—must be dismantled and turned to dust. The counter-revolution must work not to seize the centralized institutions, but to disrupt and decentralize them in the interest of small, textured, and differentiated communities.

In the end, America under counter-revolution will return to being a patchwork republic: local communities will have the autonomy to pursue their own vision of the good, within the framework of the binding principles of the Constitution. The common citizen will have the space for inhabiting and passing down his own virtues, sentiments, and beliefs, free from the imposition of values from above. The system of government will protect the basic dignity and political rights of the citizen while refraining from the hopeless and utopian task of remaking society in its image. The promise of this regime lies in the particular, rather than the abstract; the humble, rather than the grandiose; the limited, rather than the limitless; the shared, rather than the new sensibility.

Under the cultural revolution, the common citizen has been shamed, pressed, and degraded. His symbols have been subverted and buried below the earth. But he still retains the power of his own instincts, which orient him toward justice, and the power of his own memory, which makes possible the retrieval of the symbols and principles that contain his own destiny.

The partisans of the counter-revolution must provide a clear vision of this process, so that the common citizen can begin to see the source of the nihilism that threatens to bury him, too. The counter-revolutionaries must put themselves in the breach, so that the common citizen can finally look up, with his worn and weary face, toward that eternal and unchanging order that will put him at peace and allow him to finally escape the emptiness and desolation that surrounds him.

From that humble beginning, America's cultural revolution can be overcome. The American public can restore the mechanisms of democratic rule, reform the institutions that have compromised public life, and revive the principles of the revolution of 1776. And, unlike their enemies, whose promises always vanish into the ether, they can make them real. They can re-secure the rights of the common citizen, allowing him to live as an equal, raise a family, participate in the Republic, and pursue the good, the true, and the beautiful.

ACKNOWLEDGMENTS

I was with my family at the Blue Lagoon in Grindavík, Iceland, when I signed the contract to write this book. It was an auspicious beginning. My wife, Suphatra, deserves eternal gratitude. She has been by my side for everything, lifting me through difficult times and always challenging me to follow the call of the true, the good, and the beautiful. She saw me through the writing process and served as a constant source of love, companionship, and inspiration. Our sons, Milo, Matteo, and Massimo, are my other inspiration. They have shown me the meaning of family, community, and country—all of which are being threatened by the ideological capture described in this book.

Over the past five years, I've had the good fortune of working with a number of conservative research centers, which have provided the stimulation and support that made this book possible. I acknowledge a great debt to Bruce Chapman, George Gilder, and Steve Buri of Discovery Institute, who offered the encouragement I needed to make the transition from filmmaking to politics. My friends in the Claremont Institute circle have provided me with a sense of brotherhood and challenged me to think more radically about philosophy, governance, and action. Finally, Reihan Salam, Ilana Golant, Brian Anderson, Paul Beston, and Brandon Fuller of Manhattan Institute have given me the opportunity to live out my dreams: producing journalism, working in politics, and helping shape the culture. It is the highest honor to work for Manhattan Institute and its in-house publication, *City Journal*, which is, in my opinion, the best political magazine in the United States.

The writing process for *America's Cultural Revolution* was simultaneously a solitary work—many hours spent alone reading, writing, and editing—and a collaborative effort. Michael Young was a diligent researcher for this project, combing through hundreds of books, papers, and miscellany, searching for the crucial ideas and the perfect details. His passion for understanding left-wing ideology was a constant inspiration to keep digging, keep thinking, and keep pushing. Bernadette Serton, who runs the book program at Manhattan Institute, provided crucial support, helping me conquer the anxiety of beginning the book and giving notes for every draft. Joshua Moro was a champion at the end of the process, organizing my chicken scratch into comprehensive endnotes.

My agent, Jonathan Bronitsky, has the rare combination of business acumen and political principle; he believes in the mission of his authors and is an advocate without peer. Last but not least, Eric Nelson at HarperCollins has been an expert guide through the process of writing and publishing, taking a risk and maintaining his patience with a first-time author. His composure, respect for the author, and dry sense of humor make working with him a great pleasure.

On my team at American Studio, Maggie Roberts-Kohl and Armen Tooloee both helped me stay organized with the book and provided critical support. Armen expertly juggled working on a huge number of projects and did everything from transcribing pages from paper books to leading the process of compiling footnotes. He deserves immense credit for all of the journalism, activism, and media I've been able to do in the past two years. My board members at American Studio—Marshall Sana, Nathan Rimmer, and Pratik Stephen—have been extremely supportive of my vision and provided great fellowship at our annual fly-fishing retreat on the Hood Canal.

Lastly, I want to thank some of the established figures who publicized my early work and helped me enter the public debate, including Tucker Carlson, Laura Ingraham, Jordan Peterson, Ben Shapiro, Dave Rubin, Glenn Beck, Dennis Prager, and many others.

I hope this book does all of these friends, colleagues, and contributors justice.

NOTES

Introduction: America's Cultural Revolution

1. Aleksandr I. Solzhenitsyn, *Solzhenitsyn: The Voice of Freedom*, pamphlet (Washington, DC: American Federation of Labor and Congress of Industrial Organizations, 1975), PDF, https://history.fee.org/media/3686/134-solzhenitsyn-the-voice-of-freedom.pdf.

Chapter 1: Herbert Marcuse

1. David Cooper, ed., *The Dialectics of Liberation* (Baltimore: Penguin, 1968), 7–11.
2. Peter Davis, Jacky Ivimy, and Martin Levy, "Memories of the Congress," Dialectics of Liberation, accessed November 21, 2022, https://web.archive.org/web/20220516123118/http://www.dialecticsofliberation.com/1967-dialectics/memories/.
3. Cooper, *The Dialectics of Liberation*, fourth cover.
4. Herbert Marcuse, *The New Left and the 1960s: Collected Papers of Herbert Marcuse*, vol. 3, ed. Douglas Kellner (New York: Routledge, 2005), 85, Kindle.
5. Marcuse, 81.
6. Davis, Ivimy, and Levy, "Memories of the Congress."
7. Marcuse, *The New Left and the 1960s: Collected Papers of Herbert Marcuse*, vol. 3, 81–83.
8. "Interview with Lowell Bergman," Maximum Crowe, maximumcrowe.com, 2000, accessed October 31, 2022, https://web.archive.org/web/20040624230852/http:/www.geocities.com/Hollywood/Cinema/1501/maxcrowe_lowellbergman.html.
9. Marcuse, *The New Left and the 1960s: Collected Papers of Herbert Marcuse*, vol. 3, 35.
10. Marcuse, 59.
11. Douglas Kellner, "Western Marxism," in *Modern Social Theory: An Introduction*, ed. Austin Harrington (Oxford: Oxford University Press, 2005), 154–74.
12. Patrick O'Brien, "Herbert Marcuse: Liberation, Domination, and the Great Refusal" (master's thesis, Lehigh University, 2014), https://preserve.lib.lehigh.edu/islandora/object/preserve%3Abp-7256446; "Haters of Herbert Marcuse," Marcuse Family Website, accessed November 1, 2022, https://www.marcuse.org/herbert/booksabout/haters/haters.htm.
13. George Katsiaficas, "Marcuse as an Activist: Reminiscences of His Theory and Practice," *New Political Science* 36, no. 7 (Summer/Fall 1996): 1; Judith Moore, "Marxist Professor Herbert Marcuse's Years at UCSD: Angel of the Apocalypse," *San Diego Reader*, September 11, 1986, https://www.sandiegoreader.com/news/1986/sep/11/angel-apocalypse/.
14. *Herbert's Hippopotamus: Marcuse and Revolution in Paradise*, documentary, 1997, https://www.youtube.com/watch?v=gbzhmMDFcFQ.
15. "Pontiff Assails Eroticism Again; Scores Freud and Marcuse in Homily at Basilica," *New York Times*, October 2, 1969, sec. Archives, https://www.nytimes.com/1969/10/02/archives/pontiff-assails-eroticism-again-scores-freud-and-marcuse-in-homily.html.
16. Lowell, "Maximum Crowe."
17. Moore, "Marxist Professor Herbert Marcuse's Years at UCSD."
18. Herbert Marcuse, *An Essay on Liberation* (Boston: Beacon Press, 1971), 50–51, Kindle.
19. Herbert Marcuse, *Marxism, Revolution and Utopia: Collected Papers of Herbert Marcuse*, vol. 6, ed. Douglas Kellner and Clayton Pierce (New York: Routledge, 2017), 95, Kindle.
20. Herbert Marcuse, "A Note on Dialectic," in *The Essential Frankfurt School Reader*, ed. Andrew Arato and Eike Gephardt (New York: Continuum, 1978), 444.
21. Marcuse, *An Essay on Liberation*, 4–5.

22. Marcuse, *The New Left and the 1960s: Collected Papers of Herbert Marcuse*, vol. 3, 77.

23. Javier Sethness Castro, *Eros and Revolution: The Critical Philosophy of Herbert Marcuse* (Leiden: Brill, 2016), 20.

24. Sethness Castro, 20.

25. Stephen Kalberg, *Max Weber: Readings and Commentary on Modernity* (Hoboken, NJ: Wiley-Blackwell, 2008).

26. Marcuse told a colleague that he had rarely experienced overt anti-Semitism while growing up in Germany. This, of course, took a turn as the Nazis gained power. Douglas Kellner, *Herbert Marcuse and the Crisis of Marxism* (London: Macmillan, 1984), 379, https://doi .org/10.1007/978-1-349-17583-3.

27. Theresa MacKey, "Herbert Marcuse: Biographical and Critical Essay," in *Dictionary of Literary Biography*, vol. 242, *Twentieth-Century European Cultural Theorists, First Series*, ed. Paul Hansom (Washington, DC: Gale, 2001), 315–29.

28. Kellner, *Herbert Marcuse and the Crisis of Marxism*, 14–17.

29. Marcuse, *Marxism, Revolution and Utopia: Collected Papers of Herbert Marcuse*, vol. 6, 428–29.

30. Herbert Marcuse, *Five Lectures: Psychoanalysis, Politics and Utopia* (Boston: Beacon Press, 1970), 102–3.

31. Marcuse, *Marxism, Revolution and Utopia: Collected Papers of Herbert Marcuse*, vol. 6, 428.

32. Herbert Marcuse, *The Essential Marcuse: Selected Writings of Philosopher and Social Critic Herbert Marcuse*, ed. Andrew Feenberg and William Leiss (Boston: Beacon Press, 2007), Introduction, Kindle.

33. O'Brien, "Herbert Marcuse: Liberation, Domination, and the Great Refusal," 15, 56.

34. Marcuse, *The Essential Marcuse: Selected Writings of Philosopher and Social Critic Herbert Marcuse*, Introduction.

35. Martin Jay, *The Dialectical Imagination: A History of the Frankfurt School and the Institute of Social Research, 1923–1950* (Berkeley: University of California Press, 1996), 44, Kindle.

36. Marcuse, *The New Left and the 1960s: Collected Papers of Herbert Marcuse*, vol. 3, 161.

37. Marcuse, 161.

38. Herbert Marcuse, *One-Dimensional Man: Studies in the Ideology of Advanced Industrial Society*, 2nd ed. (Boston: Beacon Press, 2012), Kindle.

39. Marcuse, 18.

40. Marcuse, *An Essay on Liberation*, 65.

41. Marcuse, *One-Dimensional Man*, 7–8.

42. Marcuse, 32.

43. Marcuse, 188.

44. Marcuse, 23–24.

45. Marcuse, 8.

46. Marcuse, *An Essay on Liberation*, 64.

47. Marcuse, 65–66.

48. Marcuse, *One-Dimensional Man*, 39–40.

49. Marcuse, *The New Left and the 1960s: Collected Papers of Herbert Marcuse*, vol. 3, 114.

50. To a certain extent, Marcuse's pessimism about the Great Society would be vindicated by history. Anti-discrimination has been law for two generations and anti-poverty spending now exceeds $1 trillion per year, and yet poverty and social pathologies are as entrenched as ever. President Johnson's promises on domestic policy, like the war in Vietnam, would end in exhaustion and defeat.

51. Marcuse, *One-Dimensional Man*, 256–57.

52. "Race Troubles: 109 U.S. Cities Faced Violence in 1967," *U.S. News & World Report*, July 12, 2017, https://www.usnews.com/news/national-news/articles/2017-07-12/race-troubles -109-us-cities-faced-violence-in-1967.

53. Arnold Farr, "Herbert Marcuse," in *The Stanford Encyclopedia of Philosophy*, ed. Edward

N. Zalta (Metaphysics Research Lab, Stanford University, 2019), https://plato.stanford.edu /entries/marcuse/.

54. Herbert Marcuse, *Negations: Essays in Critical Theory*, ed. Steffen G. Bohm, trans. Jeremy J. Shapiro (London: MayFly Books, 2009).

55. For a selected bibliography of the most significant lectures, see Kellner, *Herbert Marcuse and the Crisis of Marxism*, 491–95.

56. Marcuse, *The New Left and the 1960s: Collected Papers of Herbert Marcuse*, vol. 3, 57.

57. Marcuse, 59.

58. Marcuse, 68.

59. Stephen J. Whitfield, "Refusing Marcuse: Fifty Years after One-Dimensional Man," *Dissent* 61, no. 4 (2014): 102–7, https://doi.org/10.1353/dss.2014.0075.

60. Herbert Marcuse, Bernardine Dohrn, and Jamil Al-Amin, "Radical Perspectives," speeches, December 5, 1968, New York, NY, Radio Free People audio recording, Carl Oglesby Papers (MS 514), Special Collections and University Archives, University of Massachusetts Amherst Libraries, https://credo.library.umass.edu/view/full/mums514-b080-i006.

61. Tom Bourne, "Herbert Marcuse: Grandfather of the New Left," *Change* 11, no. 6 (1979): 36–64; Michael Horowitz, "Portrait of the Marxist as an Old Trouper," *Playboy*, September 1970.

62. Marcuse, *The New Left and the 1960s: Collected Papers of Herbert Marcuse*, vol. 3, 77, 81.

63. Marcuse, *An Essay on Liberation*, 5.

64. Marcuse, 3.

65. Marcuse, 4, 87.

66. Marcuse, 54, 51, 35.

67. Marcuse sought to explain that the deviation from Marxism was not a deviation at all, but part of its historical development. "For Marxian theory, the location (or rather contraction) of the opposition in certain middle-class strata and in the ghetto population appears as an intolerable deviation," Marcuse explained. "But, in the advanced monopoly-capitalist countries, the displacement of the opposition (from the organized industrial working classes to militant minorities) is caused by the internal development of the society; and the theoretical 'deviation' only reflects this development." Marcuse, *An Essay on Liberation*, 51.

68. Marcuse, *An Essay on Liberation*, Preface.

69. Marcuse, 58, 57.

70. Marcuse, 56.

71. Marcuse, 34–36.

72. Marcuse, 53.

73. Herbert Marcuse, *Marxism, Revolution and Utopia: Collected Papers of Herbert Marcuse*, vol. 6, ed. Douglas Kellner and Clayton Pierce (New York: Routledge, 2017), 299, Kindle.

74. Marcuse, *An Essay on Liberation*, 53.

75. Herbert Marcuse, *The Essential Marcuse: Selected Writings of Philosopher and Social Critic Herbert Marcuse*, ed. Andrew Feenberg and William Leiss (Boston: Beacon Press, 2007), 33–35, Kindle.

76. Marcuse, 51.

77. Marcuse, 41.

78. Marcuse, 48–50.

79. Marcuse, 44–45.

80. Marcuse, 50–51.

81. Marcuse, 46.

82. Marcuse, 54–55.

83. Marcuse, 46.

84. See, for example, Robyn Meredith, "5 Days in 1967 Still Shake Detroit," *New York Times*, July 23, 1997, https://www.nytimes.com/1997/07/23/us/5-days-in-1967-still-shake-detroit .html.

85. Marcuse, *An Essay on Liberation*, 19.

Chapter 2: The New Left

1. Tamara Chaplin and Jadwiga E. Pieper Mooney, eds., *The Global 1960s: Convention, Contest, and Counterculture* (New York: Routledge, 2017), 274.

2. Barbarella Fokos, "The Bourgeois Marxist," *San Diego Reader*, August 3, 2007, https://www.sandiegoreader.com/news/2007/aug/23/bourgeois-marxist/.

3. Herbert Marcuse, *The New Left and the 1960s: Collected Papers of Herbert Marcuse*, vol. 3, ed. Douglas Kellner (New York: Routledge, 2005), 194, Kindle.

4. Curtis Yee, "The Death of George Winne Jr. and the Fight for a More Peaceful World," *The Triton*, May 10, 2017, https://triton.news/2017/05/death-george-winne-jr-fight-peaceful-world/.

5. *Herbert's Hippopotamus: Marcuse and Revolution in Paradise*, documentary, Paul Alexander Juutilainen, 1997, video, shantiq, YouTube, March 4, 2011, 08:18, https://www.youtube.com/watch?v=gbzhmMDFcFQ.

6. James F. Clarity, "Rap Brown Wounded Here in Shootout After Holdup," *New York Times*, October 17, 1971, https://www.nytimes.com/1971/10/17/archives/rap-brown-wounded-here-in-shootout-after-hold-up-he-and-3-other.html.

7. Marcuse, *The New Left and the 1960s: Collected Papers of Herbert Marcuse*, vol. 3, 27.

8. Marcuse, 129.

9. "Rap Brown Calls Nation on 'Eve' of a Negro Revolt," *New York Times*, September 11, 1967, http://timesmachine.nytimes.comhttp://timesmachine.nytimes.com/timesmachine/1967/09/11/93872422.html?pageNumber=76.

10. Malcolm McLaughlin, *The Long, Hot Summer of 1967: Urban Rebellion in America*, 2014th ed. (New York: Palgrave Macmillan, 2014), 122.

11. Max Elbaum, *Revolution in the Air: Sixties Radicals Turn to Lenin, Mao and Che* (London: Verso, 2002), 69–70.

12. Bernardine Dohrn, "Communiqué #1 from the Weatherman Underground," transcript of audio, 1970, https://socialhistoryportal.org/sites/default/files/raf/0419700521.pdf.

13. Becky W. Thompson, *A Promise and a Way of Life: White Antiracist Activism* (Minneapolis: University of Minnesota Press, 2001).

14. Chaplin and Mooney, *The Global 1960s*.

15. Michael Horowitz, "Portrait of the Marxist as an Old Trouper," *Playboy*, September 1970.

16. Herbert Marcuse, *An Essay on Liberation* (Boston: Beacon Press, 1971), 61–62, Kindle.

17. Horowitz, "Portrait of the Marxist as an Old Trouper."

18. Theodor Adorno and Herbert Marcuse, "Correspondence on the German Student Movement," *New Left Review*, no. 233 (February 1, 1999): 128.

19. Adorno and Marcuse, 128.

20. Stuart Jeffries, *Grand Hotel Abyss: The Lives of the Frankfurt School* (London: Verso, 2017), 345, 2.

21. Adorno and Marcuse, "Correspondence on the German Student Movement," 125.

22. Adorno and Marcuse, 130.

23. John L. McClellan et al., *The Weather Underground: Report of the Subcommittee to Investigate the Administration of the Internal Security Act and Other Internal Security Laws*, US Senate Committee, 94th Congress (US Senate Committee on the Judiciary, January 1975), 75; Herbert Marcuse, Bernardine Dohrn, and Jamil Al-Amin, "Radical Perspectives," speeches, December 5, 1968, New York, NY, Radio Free People audio recording, Carl Oglesby Papers (MS 514), Special Collections and University Archives, University of Massachusetts Amherst Libraries, https://credo.library.umass.edu/view/full/mums514-b080-i006.

24. Judith Moore, "Marxist Professor Herbert Marcuse's Years at UCSD: Angel of the Apocalypse," *San Diego Reader*, September 11, 1986, https://www.sandiegoreader.com/news/1986/sep/11/angel-apocalypse/; "Regents Ruling Evokes Varied UC Reactions," *Triton Times*, October 4, 1968, https://library.ucsd.edu/dc/object/bb4164952s/_1.pdf.

25. Melvin J. Lasky, "Ulrike & Andreas," *New York Times*, May 11, 1975, https://timesmachine.nytimes.com/timesmachine/1975/05/11/92192714.html?pageNumber=286; Christina

L.Stefanik, "West German Terror: The Lasting Legacy of the Red Army Faction" (master's thesis, Bowling Green State University, 2009), https://etd.ohiolink.edu/apexprod/rws_etd /send_file/send?accession=bgsu1245696702&disposition=inline; Michael A. Schmidtke, "Cultural Revolution or Cultural Shock? Student Radicalism and 1968 in Germany," *South Central Review* 16/17 (1999): 77–89, https://doi.org/10.2307/3190078.

26. Stephen Gennaro and Douglas Kellner, "Under Surveillance: Herbert Marcuse and the FBI," in *Current Perspectives in Social Theory*, ed. Harry F. Dahms (Bingley, UK: Emerald, 2009), 306, https://doi.org/10.1108/S0278-1204(2009)0000026014.

27. Federal Bureau of Investigation, "FBI File, Subject: Herbert Marcuse, File Number: 9-48255," 1968–76, PDF document in author's files, Black Panther support, 517, 557; Communist Party officials, 490; Davis connections, 470, 493, 595; Germany meeting, 595; Brown support, 362.

28. McClellan et al., *The Weather Underground*, 31.

29. McClellan et al., 32.

30. Anna Robinson-Sweet, "Audio Interview with Naomi Jaffe," Activism at The New School Oral History Program, January 9, 2019, accessed November 28, 2022, https://digital .archives.newschool.edu/index.php/Detail/objects/NS070104_Jaffe_20190109.

31. Karin Ashley et al., "You Don't Need a Weatherman to Know Which Way the Wind Blows," originally from *New Left Notes*, July 18, 1969, Students for a Democratic Society archival website, accessed November 2, 2022, https://www.sds-1960s.org/sds_wuo/weather /weatherman_document.txt.

32. Ron Jacobs, *The Way the Wind Blew: A History of the Weather Underground* (London: Verso Books, 1997).

33. Ashley et al., "You Don't Need a Weatherman to Know Which Way the Wind Blows."

34. Jacobs, *The Way the Wind Blew*, 23–31.

35. Bryan Burrough, *Days of Rage: America's Radical Underground, the FBI, and the Forgotten Age of Revolutionary Violence* (New York: Penguin, 2015), 84–86, Kindle. In an appearance on C-Span in 2009, Dohrn argued that her comment about Manson was meant as an ironic joke, but contemporaneous accounts from left-wing sources suggest otherwise. See *In Depth*, "In Depth with Bill Ayers," aired June 7, 2009, C-SPAN, https://www.c-span.org /video/?c4460430/user-clip-professor-bernardine-dohrn-remarks-manson-family-remarks; *Guardian*, "Weatherman Conducts a 'War Council,'" January 10, 1970, reprinted at Marxists.org, https://www.marxists.org/history/erol/ncm-1/war-council.htm.

36. Jacobs, *The Way the Wind Blew*, 24.

37. Burrough, *Days of Rage*, 76.

38. Doug McAdam in "Picking Up the Pieces," *Making Sense of the Sixties*, Part 5, documentary (PBS, 1990).

39. Harold Jacobs, ed., *Weatherman* (Berkeley, CA: Ramparts Press, 1970), 202, https://www .sds-1960s.org/books/weatherman.pdf.

40. Larry Grathwohl in *No Place to Hide: The Strategy and Tactics of Terrorism*, documentary (Western Goals Foundation, 1982), video, thetruthisoutthere32, YouTube, November 1, 2013, 48:20, https://www.youtube.com/watch?v=9bQEI2RAznY.

41. Marcuse, *An Essay on Liberation*, 69.

42. Jacobs, *Weatherman*, 214.

43. Dohrn, "Communiqué #1 from the Weatherman Underground."

44. Burrough, *Days of Rage*, 56, 121, 127, 134, 163, 230, 315.

45. Weather Underground, *Prairie Fire: The Politics of Revolutionary Anti-Imperialism* (San Francisco: Communications Co., 1974), 2, 95.

46. Wade Greene, "The Militants Who Play with Dynamite," *New York Times*, October 25, 1970, https://www.nytimes.com/1970/10/25/archives/the-militants-who-play-with -dynamite-bombing-the-police-report-is.html.

47. Marcuse, *An Essay on Liberation*, 85.

48. Marcuse, 86.

49. Herbert Marcuse in "Interview with Pierre Viansson-Ponte," *Le Monde*, June 1969, trans. Anne Fremantle, Marxists.org, accessed November 4, 2022, https://www.marxists.org /reference/archive/marcuse/works/1969/interview.htm.

50. Marcuse, *The New Left and the 1960s: Collected Papers of Herbert Marcuse*, vol. 3, 133.

51. Arthur M. Eckstein, *Bad Moon Rising: How the Weather Underground Beat the FBI and Lost the Revolution* (New Haven, CT: Yale University Press, 2016), chap. 3, e-pub.

52. McClellan et al., *The Weather Underground*.

53. "314. Bernardine Rae Dohrn," Federal Bureau of Investigation Most Wanted posters, accessed November 4, 2022, https://www.fbi.gov/wanted/topten/topten-history/hires _images/FBI-314-BernardineRaeDohrn.jpg/view.

54. Burrough, *Days of Rage*, 78.

55. Burrough, 92, 220.

56. *Documents of the Black Liberation Army* (A Radical Reprint, 2021), 147–48, Google Books.

57. Burrough, *Days of Rage*, 74.

58. Herbert Marcuse, *Counterrevolution and Revolt* (Boston: Beacon Press, 2010), 5–6, Kindle.

59. Marcuse, *The New Left and the 1960s: Collected Papers of Herbert Marcuse*, vol. 3, 185.

60. Marcuse, 183.

61. Herbert Marcuse, *Marxism, Revolution and Utopia: Collected Papers of Herbert Marcuse*, vol. 6, ed. Douglas Kellner and Clayton Pierce (New York: Routledge, 2017), 427, Kindle.

62. "Communism: 125 Years Later," *New York Times*, August 15, 1972, https://www.nytimes .com/1972/08/15/archives/marx-and-paramarx-on-capitalist-contradictions.html.

Chapter 3: The Long March Through the Institutions

1. For the correspondence between Marcuse and Dutschke, see Herbert Marcuse, *Marxism, Revolution and Utopia: Collected Papers of Herbert Marcuse*, vol. 6, ed. Douglas Kellner and Clayton Pierce (New York: Routledge, 2017), 334–36, Kindle.

2. Herbert Marcuse, *Towards a Critical Theory of Society: Collected Papers of Herbert Marcuse*, vol. 2, ed. Douglas Kellner (New York: Routledge, 2013), chap. IX, Kindle.

3. Herbert Marcuse, *Counterrevolution and Revolt* (Boston: Beacon Press, 2010), 55, Kindle.

4. Marcuse, 28.

5. Herbert Marcuse, "The Movement in a New Era of Repression: An Assessment," speech transcript, University of California, Berkeley, February 3, 1971, Marcuse Family Website, accessed November 2, 2022, https://www.marcuse.org/herbert/publications/1970s/1971 -movement-in-new-era-of-repression.pdf.

6. Marcuse, *Towards a Critical Theory of Society*, chap. IX.

7. Marcuse, *Counterrevolution and Revolt*, 42.

8. Marcuse, 133.

9. Max Elbaum, "Mark Rudd's Self-Criticism," *Frontline* 6, no. 15 (February 13, 1989), republished at Marxists.org, accessed November 13, 2022, https://www.marxists.org/history/erol /ncm-7/lom-mark-rudd.htm.

10. Weather Underground, *Prairie Fire: The Politics of Revolutionary Anti-Imperialism* (San Francisco: Communications Co., 1974), introduction.

11. Weather Underground, 1.

12. Weather Underground, 48.

13. Weather Underground, 119.

14. Weather Underground, 9.

15. Weather Underground, 13.

16. Weather Underground, 148.

17. Weather Underground, 144.

18. Weather Underground, 3–4.

19. Ron Jacobs, "A Second Wind for Weather Underground? The Prairie Fire Statement," *Verso Books* (blog), November 3, 2017, https://www.versobooks.com/blogs/3469-a-second-wind -for-weather-underground-the-prairie-fire-statement.

20. Bryan Burrough, *Days of Rage: America's Radical Underground, the FBI, and the Forgotten Age of Revolutionary Violence* (New York: Penguin, 2015), 369–70, Kindle.

21. See Franks, "The Seeds of Terror"; Burrough, "Days of Rage," 370–72.

22. Marcuse, *Counterrevolution and Revolt*, 51.

23. Paul Buhle, *Marxism in the United States: A History of the American Left* (London: Verso, 2013), 263.

24. Lucinda Franks, "The Seeds of Terror," *New York Times*, November 22, 1981, https://www.nytimes.com/1981/11/22/magazine/the-seeds-of-terror.html.

25. "Marcuse Scholars and Activists," Marcuse Family Website, accessed November 5, 2022, https://www.marcuse.org/herbert/scholars-activists/index-full.html.

26. Bernardine Dohrn, "Communiqué #1 from the Weatherman Underground," transcript of audio, 1970, https://socialhistoryportal.org/sites/default/files/raf/0419700521.pdf.

27. Author's database of Weathermen biographies, assembled from public sources.

28. Bruce Bawer, *The Victims' Revolution: The Rise of Identity Studies and the Closing of the Liberal Mind* (New York: Broadside Books, 2012), 12, Kindle.

29. Neil Gross and Solon Simmons, "The Social and Political Views of American Professors," January 1, 2007, 42.

30. Mitchell Langbert, "Homogenous: The Political Affiliations of Elite Liberal Arts College Faculty," *Academic Questions* 31 (Summer 2018): 186–97, https://doi.org/10.1007/s12129-018-9700-x.

31. Mitchell Langbert, Anthony J. Quain, and Daniel B. Klein, "Faculty Voter Registration in Economics, History, Journalism, Law, and Psychology," *Character Issues* 13, no. 3 (September 2016): 428–29.

32. Marcuse, *The Essential Marcuse*, 50.

33. Marcuse, *Marxism, Revolution and Utopia: Collected Papers of Herbert Marcuse*, vol. 6, 381.

34. Eric Kaufmann, "Academic Freedom in Crisis: Punishment, Political Discrimination, and Self-Censorship" (Center for the Study of Partisanship and Ideology, March 1, 2021), https://cspicenter.org/wp-content/uploads/2021/03/AcademicFreedom.pdf.

35. Burrough, *Days of Rage*, 361.

36. Jacob Bennett, "White Privilege: A History of the Concept" (master's thesis, Georgia State University, 2012), 15, https://scholarworks.gsu.edu/history_theses/54.

37. "Deconstructing Whiteness Working Group," Division of Equity and Inclusion, University of Oregon, accessed November 5, 2022, https://inclusion.uoregon.edu/deconstructing-whiteness-working-group.

38. Cristina Combs, "Recovery from White Conditioning: Building Anti-Racist Practice and Community" (webinar, University of Minnesota, School of Social Work), accessed November 5, 2022, https://practicetransformation.umn.edu/continuing-education/part-i-recovery-from-white-conditioning-building-anti-racist-practice-and-community/.

39. Author analysis of Google Scholar and Semantic Scholar academic databases.

40. Herbert Marcuse, *An Essay on Liberation* (Boston: Beacon Press, 1971), 8, Kindle.

41. Bennett M. Berger, "Just What the Movement Needed, an Elder Who Isn't an Adult," *New York Times*, July 9, 1972, https://www.nytimes.com/1972/07/09/archives/counterrevolution-and-revolt-by-herbert-marcuse-138-pp-boston.html.

42. Arnold Beichman, "Six 'Big Lies' About America," *New York Times*, June 6, 1971, sec. Archives, https://www.nytimes.com/1971/06/06/archives/six-big-lies-about-america-six-big-lies-about-america.html.

43. Herbert Marcuse, Bernardine Dohrn, and Jamil Al-Amin, "Radical Perspectives," speeches, December 5, 1968, New York, NY, Radio Free People audio recording, Carl Oglesby Papers (MS 514), Special Collections and University Archives, University of Massachusetts Amherst Libraries, https://credo.library.umass.edu/view/full/mums514-b080-i006.

44. Zach Goldberg, "How the Media Led the Great Racial Awakening," *Tablet Magazine*, August 4, 2020, https://www.tabletmag.com/sections/news/articles/media-great-racial-awakening.

45. Marcuse, *An Essay on Liberation*, 34.

46. Erica Sherover-Marcuse, *Emancipation and Consciousness: Dogmatic and Dialectical Perspectives in the Early Marx* (Oxford: Blackwell, 1986).

47. Marcuse, *Marxism, Revolution and Utopia: Collected Papers of Herbert Marcuse*, vol. 6, 391.

48. "Erica Sherover-Marcuse; Created Workshops on Racism," *Los Angeles Times*, Obituaries, December 25, 1988, https://www.latimes.com/archives/la-xpm-1988-12-25-mn-1350-story.html.

49. Marcuse, *Marxism, Revolution and Utopia: Collected Papers of Herbert Marcuse*, vol. 6, 391.

50. Christian Parenti, "The First Privilege Walk," *Nonsite.org* (blog), November 18, 2021, https://nonsite.org/the-first-privilege-walk/; Ricky Sherover-Marcuse, "Compilation of Working Assumptions on Racism, Alliance-Building, Diverse Working Groups, Liberation Theory, Recruiting Whites as Allies," document, July 1988, https://communityfoodfunders.org/wp-content/uploads/2015/01/Ricky-Sherover-Marcuse.pdf.

51. Ricky Sherover-Marcuse, "Liberation Theory: A Working Framework," Films for Action, undated, republished June 16, 2017, https://www.filmsforaction.org/articles/liberation-theory-a-working-framework/.

52. Parenti, "The First Privilege Walk."

53. Sherover-Marcuse, "Compilation of Working Assumptions on Racism, Alliance-Building, Diverse Working Groups, Liberation Theory, Recruiting Whites as Allies."

54. Ricky Sherover-Marcuse, "Ten Things Everyone Should Know About Race," Unlearning Racism, undated, accessed November 5, 2022, http://www.lovingjustwise.com/unlearning_racism.htm.

55. Herbert Marcuse and Douglas Kellner, *One-Dimensional Man: Studies in the Ideology of Advanced Industrial Society*, 2nd ed. (Boston: Beacon Press, 2012), 88, Kindle.

56. New England Center for Investigative Reporting, "New Analysis Shows Problematic Boom in Higher Ed Administrators," February 6, 2014, https://web.archive.org/web/20180616113604/https://www.necir.org/2014/02/06/new-analysis-shows-problematic-boom-in-higher-ed-administrators/.

57. Richard Vedder, "900,000 Costly Bureaucrats Work on Campus—How Many Do We Really Need?," Minding the Campus, June 12, 2017, https://www.mindingthecampus.org/2017/06/12/900000-costly-bureaucrats-work-on-campus-how-many-do-we-really-need/.

58. "The Rise of Universities' Diversity Bureaucrats," *The Economist*, May 18, 2018, https://www.economist.com/the-economist-explains/2018/05/08/the-rise-of-universities-diversity-bureaucrats.

59. Samuel J. Abrams, "Think Professors Are Liberal? Try School Administrators," *New York Times*, October 16, 2018, https://web.archive.org/web/20210816155242/https:/www.nytimes.com/2018/10/16/opinion/liberal-college-administrators.html.

60. University of California, Berkeley, "Vice Chancellor for Equity and Inclusion," informational memorandum, 2021, 2, PDF in author's files.

61. Jay P. Greene and James D. Paul, "Diversity University: DEI Bloat in the Academy," Backgrounder, Heritage Foundation, July 27, 2021, 2, https://www.heritage.org/education/report/diversity-university-dei-bloat-the-academy.

62. Richard Vedder, "Diversity and Other Administrative Monstrosities: The Case of the University of Michigan," *Forbes*, July 23, 2018, accessed November 5, 2022, https://www.forbes.com/sites/richardvedder/2018/07/23/diversity-and-other-administrative-monstrousities-the-case-of-the-university-of-michigan/.

63. Jay P. Greene, "Growth of Virginia Universities' Diversity-Industrial Complex," Heritage Foundation, September 17, 2021, https://www.heritage.org/education/commentary/growth-virginia-universities-diversity-industrial-complex.

64. University of Pittsburgh, "Pitt's Commitment to Social Justice," Office of the Provost, November 4, 2022, https://www.provost.pitt.edu/pitts-commitment-social-justice.

65. Dean Bonner, "Response to Black Senate Leaders Letter," August 17, 2020, University of Pittsburgh, https://www.studentaffairs.pitt.edu/wp-content/uploads/2020/08/ResponseBlackSenate-20200817-final2.pdf.

66. Natalie Frank, "'A Good Stepping Stone': Students, Professors Review New Anti-Racism Course," *Pitt News*, September 16, 2020, https://pittnews.com/article/160071/top-stories /a-good-stepping-stone-students-professors-review-new-anti-racism-course/; University of Pittsburgh, "Anti-Black Racism: History, Ideology, and Resistance (PITT 0210)—Final Course Syllabus," Office of the Provost, 2020, https://www.provost.pitt.edu/anti-black -racism-history-ideology-and-resistance-final-course-syllabus.

67. Angela Morabito, "UPitt to Hire Professor of 'Oppression,'" Campus Reform, September 3, 2021, https://campusreform.org/article?id=18089.

68. University of Pittsburgh, "Diversity Statement for Leadership Candidates," School of Medicine, June 10, 2020, https://www.pediatrics.pitt.edu/about-us/diversity-inclusion-and -equity/our-goals/faculty-level/diversity-statement-leadership; Bonner, "Response to Black Senate Leaders Letter."

69. "Waverly Duck Publishes New Book, 'Tacit Racism,'" University of Pittsburgh, accessed November 28, 2022, https://www.pitt.edu/pittwire/accolades-honors/waverly-duck -publishes-new-book-tacit-racism.

70. Lending Equity, "Creating Student Activists Through Social Justice Mathematics with Dr. Kari Kokka," Lending Equity Center, accessed November 5, 2022, https://www .leadingequitycenter.com/63.

71. University of Pittsburgh, "GSWS Faculty Fellowships," Gender, Sexuality, & Women's Studies Program, November 4, 2022, https://www.wstudies.pitt.edu/people/ant-236.

72. Michael Vanyukov, "Letter to the Editor: Racial Equity Consciousness Institute Criticized," *University Times*, September 23, 2021, https://www.utimes.pitt.edu/news/letter-editor -racial-0.

73. Abigail Thompson, "A Word From . . . ," *Notices of the American Mathematical Society* 66, no. 11 (December 2019): 1778–79.

74. Mark Perry, interview with the author, September 2021.

75. Herbert Marcuse, *The New Left and the 1960s: Collected Papers of Herbert Marcuse*, vol. 3, ed. Douglas Kellner (New York: Routledge, 2005), 152, Kindle.

76. John M. Ellis et al., *A Crisis of Competence: The Corrupting Effect of Political Activism in the University of California* (National Association of Scholars, April 2012).

77. Langbert, "Homogenous."

78. Michael Levenson, "University Must Reinstate Professor Who Tweeted About 'Black Privilege,'" *New York Times*, May 19, 2022, https://www.nytimes.com/2022/05/19/us/twitter -florida-professor-reinstated.html; Gordon Klein, "Why I Am Suing UCLA," *Common Sense* (blog), September 30, 2021, https://www.commonsense.news/p/why-i-am-suing -ucla.

79. Larry Gordon, "Leftism at UC Leaves Many with Unbalanced Education, Study Says," *Los Angeles Times*, April 1, 2012, https://www.latimes.com/local/la-xpm-2012-apr-01-la-me -0401-uc-critics-20120402-story.html.

80. Marcuse, *The New Left and the 1960s: Collected Papers of Herbert Marcuse*, vol. 3, 60.

81. Marcuse, *An Essay on Liberation*, 87, 89.

82. Marcuse, *The Essential Marcuse*, 45.

83. Sherover-Marcuse, "Compilation of Working Assumptions on Racism, Alliance-Building, Diverse Working Groups, Liberation Theory, Recruiting Whites as Allies."

84. Marcuse, *The New Left and the 1960s: Collected Papers of Herbert Marcuse*, vol. 3, 125.

85. Marcuse, *An Essay on Liberation*, 74.

86. Marcuse, *The Essential Marcuse*, 52.

87. Marcuse, *The New Left and the 1960s: Collected Papers of Herbert Marcuse*, vol. 3, 84.

88. Marcuse, 85.

89. Marcuse, 85.

Chapter 4: The New Ideological Regime

1. Herbert Marcuse, *Counterrevolution and Revolt* (Boston: Beacon Press, 2010), 56, Kindle.

2. Herbert Marcuse, *Soviet Marxism: A Critical Analysis* (New York: Columbia University Press, 1958).

3. For the political theory of the integrated managerial state that serves as the "vital center," see John Marini, *Unmasking the Administrative State: The Crisis of American Politics in the Twenty-First Century*, ed. Ken Masugi (New York: Encounter Books, 2019).

4. Herbert Marcuse, *An Essay on Liberation* (Boston: Beacon Press, 1971), 89, Kindle.

5. Herbert Marcuse, *The Essential Marcuse: Selected Writings of Philosopher and Social Critic Herbert Marcuse*, ed. Andrew Feenberg and William Leiss (Boston: Beacon Press, 2007), 42, Kindle.

6. Marcuse, *Counterrevolution and Revolt*, 55.

7. Sidney Hook, "An Essay on Liberation," *New York Times*, April 20, 1969, https://www.nytimes.com/1969/04/20/archives/an-essay-on-liberation-by-herbert-marcuse-91-pp-boston-the-beacon.html.

8. Bennett M. Berger, "Just What the Movement Needed, an Elder Who Isn't an Adult," *New York Times*, July 9, 1972, https://www.nytimes.com/1972/07/09/archives/counterrevolution-and-revolt-by-herbert-marcuse-138-pp-boston.html.

9. Kenneth A. Briggs, "Marcuse, Radical Philosopher, Dies," *New York Times*, July 31, 1979, https://www.nytimes.com/1979/07/31/archives/marcuse-radical-philosopher-dies-largely-unnoticed-before-60s.html.

10. Writer interview with author, September 2021.

11. Zach Goldberg, "How the Media Led the Great Racial Awakening," *Tablet Magazine*, August 4, 2020, https://www.tabletmag.com/sections/news/articles/media-great-racial-awakening.

12. Writer interview with author, September 2021.

13. Kerry Flynn, "As Subscriber Growth Slows, the New York Times Reveals 100 Million Registered Users," CNN Business, May 5, 2021, accessed November 10, 2022, https://www.cnn.com/2021/05/05/media/new-york-times-earnings-q1-2021/index.html.

14. Goldberg, "How the Media Led the Great Racial Awakening."

15. For an in-depth case study in the ideological capture of Reuters, see Christopher F. Rufo, "The Price of Dissent," *City Journal*, January 5, 2022, https://www.city-journal.org/black-lives-matter-thomson-reuters-and-the-price-of-dissent.

16. Marcuse, *An Essay on Liberation*, 8.

17. To understand the origins and rise of the managerial state, see James Burnham, *The Managerial Revolution: What Is Happening in the World* (New York: John Day, 1941).

18. Fiona Hill, "Public Service and the Federal Government," *Brookings* (blog), May 27, 2020, https://www.brookings.edu/policy2020/votervital/public-service-and-the-federal-government/.

19. Robert Rector and Vijay Menon, *Understanding the Hidden $1.1 Trillion Welfare System and How to Reform It*, Backgrounder, Heritage Foundation, April 5, 2018, http://report.heritage.org/bg3294.

20. Veronique de Rugy, "A Nation of Government Dependents?," George Mason University, Mercatus Center, 2010, https://www.mercatus.org/research/data-visualizations/nation-government-dependents.

21. Contribution information in this section is based on analysis of the OpenSecrets political contribution database during the 2020 election cycle.

22. Jackie Gu, "The Employees Who Gave Most to Trump and Biden," Bloomberg, November 2, 2020, https://www.bloomberg.com/graphics/2020-election-trump-biden-donors/.

23. Joseph R. Biden Jr., "Executive Order 14035: Diversity, Equity, Inclusion, and Accessibility in the Federal Workforce," The White House, June 25, 2021, https://www.whitehouse.gov/briefing-room/presidential-actions/2021/06/25/executive-order-on-diversity-equity-inclusion-and-accessibility-in-the-federal-workforce/.

24. See investigative reports on Treasury Department, Department of Education, National Credit Union Association, Department of Homeland Security, Centers for Disease Control and Prevention, Department of State, Environmental Protection Agency, and Department of

Veterans Affairs in Christopher F. Rufo, "Critical Race Theory Briefing Book," May 4, 2022, https://rufo.substack.com/p/crt-briefing-book/.

25. Christopher F. Rufo, "Nuclear Consequences," August 12, 2020, https://rufo.substack .com/p/nuclear-consequences/.

26. Funding information in this section is based on author analysis of the US Government System for Award Management database during the years 2009 through 2020.

27. US Government System for Award Management database.

28. Ibid. See also Heather Mac Donald, *The Diversity Delusion: How Race and Gender Pandering Corrupt the University and Undermine Our Culture* (New York: St. Martin's Press, 2018), chap. 11, Kindle.

29. In-depth ongoing investigative coverage of "diversity, equity, and inclusion" ideology in American business is found in my *City Journal* series at https://www.city-journal.org /christopher-rufo-on-woke-capital.

30. Gu, "The Employees Who Gave Most to Trump and Biden."

31. Tracy Jan, Jena McGregor, and Meghan Hoyer, "Corporate America's $50 Billion Promise," *Washington Post*, August 23, 2021, https://www.washingtonpost.com/business/interactive /2021/george-floyd-corporate-america-racial-justice/.

32. Cisco [@cisco], "At Cisco, we stand in solidarity with those taking action to eradicate systemic racism and inequality. Cisco CEO @chuckrobbins announced a $5M donation to @ eji_org, @NAACP_LDF, @ColorofChange, @Blklivesmatter and our Fighting Racism and Discrimination Fund. #BlackLivesMatter," tweet, Twitter, June 1, 2020, 2:02 p.m., https:// twitter.com/cisco/status/1267547077892026375; Ramon Laguarta, "PepsiCo CEO: 'Black Lives Matter, to Our Company and to Me.' What the Food and Beverage Giant Will Do Next," *Fortune*, June 16, 2020, https://fortune.com/2020/06/16/pepsi-ceo-ramon-laguarta -black-lives-matter-diversity-and-inclusion-systemic-racism-in-business/; Lauren Thomas, "Read Nike CEO John Donahoe's Note to Employees on Racism: We Must 'Get Our Own House in Order,'" CNBC, June 5, 2020, https://www.cnbc.com/2020/06/05/nike-ceo-note -to-workers-on-racism-must-get-our-own-house-in-order.html.

33. Thornton McEnery, "Mending JPM Chief Drops into Mt. Kisco Chase Branch," *New York Post*, June 5, 2021, https://nypost.com/2020/06/05/mending-jpm-chief-drops-into-mt -kisco-chase-branch/.

34. McDonald's, "One of Us," video, McDonald's, YouTube, 2020, 01:00, https://www .youtube.com/watch?v=3HaC5D_TaEo.

35. For detailed investigations into "diversity, equity, and inclusion" programs at the Fortune 100 companies, see "Christopher Rufo on Woke Capital," *City Journal*, 2022, https://www .city-journal.org/christopher-rufo-on-woke-capital.

36. Christopher F. Rufo, "The Woke-Industrial Complex," *City Journal*, May 20, 2021, https:// www.city-journal.org/lockheed-martins-woke-industrial-complex.

37. Christopher F. Rufo, "The Woke Defense Contractor," *City Journal*, July 6, 2021, https:// www.city-journal.org/raytheon-adopts-critical-race-theory.

38. Walmart, "The Walmart.org Center for Racial Equity Awards over $14 Million in First Round of Grants," press release, February 1, 2021, https://corporate.walmart.com /newsroom/2021/02/01/the-walmart-org-center-for-racial-equity-awards-over-14-million -in-first-round-of-grants; Walmart, "Center for Racial Equity," Walmart.org, 2022, https:// walmart.org/diversity-equity-and-inclusion/center-for-racial-equity.

39. Christopher F. Rufo, "Walmart vs. Whiteness," *City Journal*, October 14, 2021, https://www .city-journal.org/walmart-critical-race-theory-training-program.

40. Kim Souza, "Top Six Walmart Execs Compensation a Combined $112.39 Million in 2019," *Talk Business & Politics* (blog), April 24, 2020, https://talkbusiness.net/2020/04/top-six -walmart-execs-compensation-a-combined-112-39-million-in-2019/.

41. All of the best available evidence suggests that diversity trainings do not achieve their stated intentions. According to Professors Frank Dobbin and Alexandra Kalev, who reviewed thirty years of data from more than eight hundred American corporations, diversity training does

not "reduce bias, alter behavior, or change the workplace." At best, the potential benefits fade within a few days; at worst, diversity training programs can "awaken biases," "make [stereotypes] more salient in trainees' minds," and "provoke resistance in white men who feel unjustly accused of discrimination." Frank Dobbin and Alexandra Kalev, "Why Doesn't Diversity Training Work? The Challenge for Industry and Academia," *Anthropology Now* 10, no. 2 (May 4, 2018): 48–55, https://doi.org/10.1080/19428200.2018.1493182; "Frank Dobbin and Alexandra Kalev Explain Why Diversity Training Does Not Work," *The Economist*, May 21, 2021, accessed December 5, 2022, https://www.economist.com/by-invitation/2021/05/21/frank-dobbin-and-alexandra-kalev-explain-why-diversity-training-does-not-work.

42. Tamara Chaplin and Jadwiga E. Pieper Mooney, eds., *The Global 1960s: Convention, Contest, and Counterculture* (New York: Routledge, 2017), 288.

43. Federal Bureau of Investigation, "FBI File, Subject: Herbert Marcuse, File Number: 9-48255," 1968–76, PDF document in author's files, 601.

44. Judith Moore, "Marxist Professor Herbert Marcuse's Years at UCSD: Angel of the Apocalypse," *San Diego Reader*, September 11, 1986, https://www.sandiegoreader.com/news/1986/sep/11/angel-apocalypse/.

45. Marcuse moderated somewhat toward the end of his life, perhaps in the interest of reshaping his image in posterity. The year before his death, a journalist named Myriam Malinovich visited Marcuse in La Jolla and interviewed him for a profile for the *New York Times Magazine*. Marcuse had fallen out of favor and the three remaining leaders of the Red Army Faction had recently committed suicide in Germany's Stammheim Prison, marking the end of their guerrilla uprising. Malinovich interrogated the professor about his desire to suspend civil rights for political opponents, his work's connection to violent political factions, and his idea of the dictatorship of the intellectuals. Marcuse admitted that he would apply "repressive tolerance" to anyone who would oppose the liberal welfare state, including conservatives in academia. But he denied serving as the inspiration for left-wing militant organizations such as the Red Army Faction and the Weather Underground. "I have never advocated terror," he said, arguing that although he had previously voiced support for political violence, "there is a difference between violence and terror," and that he renounced the Red Army Faction's bombing campaigns. Myriam Miedzian Malinovich, "Herbert Marcuse in 1978: An Interview by Myriam Miedzian Malinovich," in Herbert Marcuse, *Marxism, Revolution and Utopia: Collected Papers of Herbert Marcuse*, vol. 6.

46. Herbert Marcuse, *The New Left and the 1960s: Collected Papers of Herbert Marcuse*, vol. 3, ed. Douglas Kellner (New York: Routledge, 2005), 114, Kindle.

47. Herbert Marcuse, *An Essay on Liberation* (Boston: Beacon Press, 1971), 17, Kindle.

48. See Derald Wing Sue et al., "Racial Microaggressions in Everyday Life: Implications for Clinical Practice," *American Psychologist* 62, no. 4 (2007): 271–86, https://doi.org/10.1037/0003-066X.62.4.271.

49. Harold Marcuse, "Death, Burial, and Grave of Herbert Marcuse in Berlin," Marcuse Family Website, 2004, accessed November 13, 2022, https://www.marcuse.org/herbert/newsevents/2003berlinburial/gravestone.htm.

50. Peter Marcuse, "Burying Herbert's Ashes in Berlin: A Personal Reflection on the Interconnections between the Personal and the Political, the Private and the Symbolic," Marcuse Family Website, July 22, 2003, accessed November 13, 2022, https://www.marcuse.org/herbert/newsevents/2003berlinburial/AshesPeter037hm038pm.htm.

51. Marcuse, *The New Left and the 1960s: Collected Papers of Herbert Marcuse*, vol. 3, 199.

Chapter 5: Angela Davis

1. Later published in the February 1971 issue of *Ramparts* magazine as "Angela Davis in Prison: A Letter."

2. Herbert Marcuse, *An Essay on Liberation* (Boston: Beacon Press, 1971), 52, Kindle.

3. Herbert Marcuse, "Angela Davis in Prison: A Letter."

4. Angela Y. Davis, *Angela Davis: An Autobiography* (New York: International, 2013), 144, Kindle.

5.   Cecil Williams and Angela Davis, "A Conversation with Angela," *Black Scholar* 3, no. 7/8 (April 1972): 36.

6.   Williams and Davis, 36–37.

7.   Williams and Davis, 40.

8.   Marcuse, "Angela Davis in Prison: A Letter," 22.

9.   Sol Stern, "The Campaign to Free Angela Davis . . . and Mitchell Magee," *New York Times*, June 27, 1971, https://www.nytimes.com/1971/06/27/archives/the-campaign-to-free -angela-davis-and-ruchell-magee-the-campaign-to.html.

10.   Yana Skorobogatov, "Our Friend Angela: Soviet Schoolchildren, a Letter-Writing Campaign, and the Legend of Angela Davis," *The Drift*, October 21, 2020, https://www .thedriftmag.com/our-friend-angela/.

11.   Skorobogatov, "Our Friend Angela." Extensive international Free Angela records and documents are housed at Stanford University's Manuscript Division, "National United Committee to Free Angela Davis," collection number M0262, Stanford, California.

12.   Angela Y. Davis, ed., *If They Come in the Morning . . . : Voices of Resistance* (1971; reprint, New York: Verso, 2016), 48, Kindle.

13.   Angela Y. Davis, *Angela Davis: An Autobiography*, Part Two, Kindle.

14.   Angela Y. Davis, "Reflections on Race, Class, and Gender in the USA," in *The Angela Y. Davis Reader* (Malden, MA: Blackwell, 1998), 315.

15.   Jennifer L. Greer, "Invisible Line down Birmingham Street Was Potentially Deadly," *ComebackTown* (blog), January 20, 2021, https://comebacktown.com/2021/01/20/invisible-line -down-birmingham-street-was-potentially-deadly/.

16.   For the detail history of this period in Birmingham, see Glenn T. Eskew, *But for Birmingham: The Local and National Movements in the Civil Rights Struggle* (Chapel Hill: University of North Carolina Press, 1997).

17.   Cynthia A. Young, *Soul Power: Culture, Radicalism, and the Making of a U.S. Third World Left* (Durham, NC: Duke University Press, 2006), 187–89, Kindle.

18.   Davis, *Angela Davis: An Autobiography*, 78.

19.   Davis, 79.

20.   Davis, 92, 89–90.

21.   Barbara Epstein, "Free Speech Movement Oral History Project: Barbara Epstein," Regional Oral History Office, Bancroft Library, University of California, Berkeley, 2014, https://digitalassets .lib.berkeley.edu/roho/ucb/text/epstein_barbara_2014.pdf.

22.   Davis, *Angela Davis: An Autobiography*, 19.

23.   Davis, 111.

24.   Davis, 112.

25.   Davis, 135.

26.   Davis, 145.

27.   Rick Heimlich, "Third College: Hope for the Third World," *Triton Times*, October 16, 1970, https://library.ucsd.edu/dc/object/bb0205870h/_1.pdf.

28.   Davis, "Reflections on Race, Class, and Gender in the USA," 317.

29.   Davis, *Angela Davis: An Autobiography*, 159.

30.   Davis, 187–89.

31.   Davis, 191–92.

32.   For an academic perspective on Davis's appointment, see "Academic Freedom and Tenure: The University of California at Los Angeles," *AAUP Bulletin* 57, no. 3 (Autumn 1971): 382–420.

33.   Charles L. Sanders, "The Radicalization of Angela Davis," *Ebony*, July 1971.

34.   Davis, ed., *If They Come in the Morning . . .* , 206.

35.   "Angela Davis Speaking at UCLA 10/8/1969," audio, University of California, Los Angeles, UCLA Comm Studies, YouTube, 2013, 11:30, 06:35, 25:50, https://www.youtube.com /watch?v=AxCqTEMgZUc.

36.   "Herbert Marcuse and Angela Davis at Berkeley," recording of speeches, University of Cali-

fornia, Berkeley, Pacifica Radio Archives, 1969, 38:00, https://www.pacificaradioarchives.org/recording/az1025.

37. Bettina Aptheker, *The Morning Breaks: The Trial of Angela Davis*, 2nd ed. (Ithaca, NY: Cornell University Press, 2014), 213, Kindle.

38. Aptheker, 210, 211, 234.

39. Aptheker, 213–14.

40. Lawrence V. Cotj, "The Facts Behind the Angela Davis Case," *Human Events*, June 17, 1972.

41. "Justice: A Bad Week for the Good Guys," *Time*, August 17, 1970, https://web.archive.org/web/20080913023405/http://www.time.com/time/magazine/article/0,9171,909547-1,00.html.

42. "Another Vital and Necessary Level Has Been Reached in the Revolutionary Struggle in America," *Black Panther*, August 21, 1970, housed at Kennesaw State University Archives, https://soar.kennesaw.edu/bitstream/handle/11360/3547/black-panther-newspaper-FINAL.pdf.

43. Aptheker, *The Morning Breaks*, 209.

44. "Justice: A Bad Week for the Good Guys."

45. Aptheker, *The Morning Breaks*, 189–90.

46. Cotj, "The Facts Behind the Angela Davis Case."

47. Davis, *Angela Davis: An Autobiography*, 5–6.

48. "The Angela Davis Case," *Newsweek*, October 26, 1970.

49. Linda Charlton, "F.B.I. Seizes Angela Davis in Motel Here," *New York Times*, October 14, 1970, https://archive.nytimes.com/www.nytimes.com/books/98/03/08/home/davis-fbi.html.

50. Aptheker, *The Morning Breaks*, 23.

51. Carole Alston and Leo Branton, "In Defense of Angela: Profile of the Davis Defense Team," *Black Law Journal* 2, no. 1 (1972): 51.

52. Davis, *Angela Davis: An Autobiography*, 44–45, 64–66.

53. Davis, ed., *If They Come in the Morning . . .* , 36, 34, 37.

54. Cotj, "The Facts Behind the Angela Davis Case."

55. Angela Y. Davis, "Statement to the Court," January 5, 1971, in Davis, ed., *If They Come in the Morning . . .* , 224–25.

56. See attorney Howard J. Moore Jr.'s chapter in Davis, ed., *If They Come in the Morning . . .* , 206.

57. "People v. Angela Y. Davis, Trial Transcript, June 4, 1972, Angela Davis," Papers of Angela Y. Davis, 1937–2017, Legal Files, 1965–97, MC940 52.5, Schlesinger Library, Radcliffe Institute, Harvard University, Cambridge, MA, accessed November 8, 2022, https://iiif.lib.harvard.edu/manifests/view/drs:491929913$5i.

58. Cotj, "The Facts Behind the Angela Davis Case."

Chapter 6: "Kill the Pigs"

1. Angela Y. Davis, *Angela Davis: An Autobiography* (New York: International, 2013), 398, Kindle.

2. The newspaper *Neues Deutschland* wrote on September 11, 1972, that she "was welcomed enthusiastically by 50,000 people."

3. Davis, *Angela Davis: An Autobiography*, Epilogue.

4. "Miss Davis Hails Soviet's Policies," *New York Times*, September 10, 1972, https://www.nytimes.com/1972/09/10/archives/miss-davis-hails-soviets-policies-but-the-comments-on-tour-arouse.html.

5. For a discussion of the "neo-slave narrative," see Mechthild Nagel, "Women Outlaws: Politics of Gender and Resistance in the US Criminal Justice System," State University of New York at Cortland, 2006, accessed November 10, 2022, https://web.cortland.edu/nagelm/papers_for_web/davis_assata06.htm.

6. Angela Davis, "Angela Davis Speaks on the Topic of Oppression and Repression in the U.S.

at California State University Fullerton," speech, video recording, California State University Fullerton, University Archives and Special Collections, California Revealed, November 17, 1972, https://calisphere.org/item/8cef4824d3eb83e821b886c4c3f9e15b/.

7. "San Quentin Six to Open Defense," *New York Times*, June 28, 1976, https://www.nytimes.com/1976/06/28/archives/san-quentin-six-to-open-defense-prosecutor-rests-case-with-review.html.

8. Lacey Fosburgh, "Ruchell Magee, Once Angela Davis' Co-Defendant, Gets Life for Kidnapping," *New York Times*, January 24, 1975, https://www.nytimes.com/1975/01/24/archives/ruchell-magee-once-angela-davis-codefendant-gets-life-for.html.

9. "Hijacker Convicted in California Case; Gets Life Sentence," *New York Times*, July 25, 1972, https://www.nytimes.com/1972/07/25/archives/hijacker-convicted-in-california-case-gets-life-sentence.html.

10. Gregory Jaynes, "'I Hate You . . . I Hope I Killed You,'" *Atlanta Constitution*, November 1, 1972.

11. Davis, "Angela Davis Speaks on the Topic of Oppression and Repression in the U.S. at California State University Fullerton."

12. Black Liberation Army, "Message to the Black Movement: A Political Statement from the Black Underground," undated booklet, Michigan State University Archives, American Radicalism Collection, 1, https://archive.lib.msu.edu/DMC/AmRad/messageblackmovement.pdf.

13. Eldridge Cleaver, *Soul on Ice* (1968; reprint, New York: Delta, 1999), 32–33.

14. Cleaver, 33.

15. Angela Davis, "Angela Davis Speaking at UCLA 10/8/1969," audio, University of California Los Angeles Department of Communication, special collection, 25:40, https://comm.ucla.edu/angela-davis-10-8-1969/.

16. Eldridge Cleaver, "On the Case of Angela Davis," *Black Panther*, January 23, 1971, Utah State University Libraries, Digital Exhibits, http://exhibits.lib.usu.edu/files/original/1a27cd0588d0593b76d1b880af54d46a.jpg.

17. Eldridge Cleaver, "On the Ideology of the Black Panther Party, Part 1," Black Panther Party, 1970, 1–2, Freedom Archives, http://www.freedomarchives.org/Documents/Finder/Black%20Liberation%20Disk/Black%20Power%21/SugahData/Books/Cleaver.S.pdf.

18. Karl Marx and Frederick Engels, *Manifesto of the Communist Party*, authorized English translation, edited and annotated by Frederick Engels (Chicago: Charles H. Kerr, 1888, 1910), 29.

19. Cleaver, "On the Ideology of the Black Panther Party, Part 1," 4.

20. Eldridge Cleaver, "On Lumpen Ideology," *Black Scholar* 4, no. 3 (1972): 4.

21. Cleaver, "On the Ideology of the Black Panther Party, Part 1," 10.

22. Cleaver, "On Lumpen Ideology," 10.

23. Curtis J. Austin, *Up Against the Wall: Violence in the Making and Unmaking of the Black Panther Party* (Fayetteville: University of Arkansas Press, 2008), 169–70, Kindle.

24. Huey P. Newton, *Revolutionary Suicide* (London: Penguin, 2009), 121, Google Books.

25. Jama Lazerow and Yohuru Williams, eds., *In Search of the Black Panther Party: New Perspectives on a Revolutionary Movement* (Durham, NC: Duke University Press, 2006), 374.

26. Black Panther Party, "The Black Panther Party Ten-Point Program," October 15, 1966, https://www.marxists.org/history/usa/workers/black-panthers/1966/10/15.htm.

27. Huey P. Newton, "In Defense of Self Defense: The Correct Handling of a Revolution," *Black Panther*, July 20, 1967, 3, https://www.marxists.org/history/usa/pubs/black-panther/01n05-Jul%2020%201967.pdf.

28. Eldridge Cleaver, "Education and Revolution," *Black Scholar* 1, no. 1 (November 1969): 52, https://doi.org/10.1080/00064246.1969.11414451.

29. Austin, *Up Against the Wall*, 186, 95.

30. Hugh Pearson, *Shadow of the Panther: Huey Newton and the Price of Black Power in America* (Reading, MA: Addison-Wesley, 1994), 3. Years later, in a haze of smoke at a gin and crack cocaine party, Newton reportedly admitted to the killing (*Shadow of the Panther*, 7).

31. Austin, *Up Against the Wall*, 165–68.

32. Austin, 89–90. Referring to testimony before the United States Senate, Hearings Before the Subcommittee to Investigate the Administration of the Internal Security Act and other Internal Security Laws of the Committee on the Judiciary, Assaults on Law Enforcement Officers, 91st Cong., 2nd sess. (Washington, DC: US Government Printing Office, 1970).

33. Elaine Brown, *A Taste of Power: A Black Woman's Story* (New York: Anchor Books, 1994), 13.

34. "Hoover Calls Panthers Top Threat to Security," *Washington Post, Times Herald*, July 16, 1969, https://www.proquest.com/docview/147638465/abstract/81DAF4E98E63453EPQ/1.

35. Frank J. Donner, *Protectors of Privilege: Red Squads and Police Repression in Urban America* (Berkeley: University of California Press, 1990), 180.

36. Austin, *Up Against the Wall*, 105.

37. Bryan Burrough, *Days of Rage: America's Radical Underground, the FBI, and the Forgotten Age of Revolutionary Violence* (New York: Penguin, 2015), 192, Kindle.

38. Austin, *Up Against the Wall*, 297–98.

39. Austin, 305–6.

40. Burrough, *Days of Rage*, 200.

41. Black Liberation Army, "Message to the Black Movement: A Political Statement from the Black Underground," ii.

42. Field Marshall D.C., *On Organizing Urban Guerilla Units*, pamphlet, self-published, October 8, 1970.

43. "Machine-Gun Fire Hits 2 Policemen," *New York Times*, May 20, 1971, https://www.nytimes.com/1971/05/20/archives/machinegun-fire-hits-2-policemen-machinegun-fire-hits-2-policemen.html.

44. Burrough, *Days of Rage*, 176.

45. Robert Daley, *Target Blue: An Insider's View of the NYPD* (1973; reprint, Riviera Productions, 2011), Book 2, Part 1, Kindle.

46. The Officer Down Memorial Page website provides information on American fallen law enforcement officers. The site provides details on the deaths of John Victor Young, James Richard Greene, Gregory Philip Foster, Rocco W. Laurie, and Werner Foerster, all of whom were killed by members of the BLA.

47. "Policeman Is Hurt in $90,000 Holdup of Bank in Bronx," March 17; "2 Attempt to Rob a Bank with 11 F.B.I. Men Inside," September 30; "Teller on Her First Day Pays Out to Gunman," April 11; all from the *New York Times*, 1972.

48. "Suspect in Kidnapping Sought in the Killing of Two Policemen," *New York Times*, December 29, 1972, sec. Archives, https://www.nytimes.com/1972/12/29/archives/suspect-in-kidnapping-sought-in-the-killing-of-two-policemen.html.

49. Robert Hanley, "Miss Chesimard Flees Jersey Prison, Helped by 3 Armed 'Visitors,'" *New York Times*, November 3, 1979, https://www.nytimes.com/1979/11/03/archives/miss-chesimard-flees-jersey-prison-helped-by-3-armed-visitors-miss.html.

50. Kim Hjelmgaard, "In 1972, Melvin McNair Helped Hijack a Plane to Join Black Panthers in Algeria. 'I Am at Peace with What I Did,'" *USA Today*, August 20, 2021, https://www.usatoday.com/in-depth/news/nation/2021/07/29/melvin-mcnair-black-panthers-hijackers-algeria-1972/7042889002/; Raphael Minder and James Barron, "Telling the Story of 41 Years on the Run," *New York Times*, October 29, 2011, https://www.nytimes.com/2011/10/29/nyregion/george-wright-tells-story-of-hijacking-from-portugal.html.

51. Daley, *Target Blue*, Book 5, Part 4; Black Liberation Army, "Black Liberation Army Communiques," 1971–72, Freedom Archives, accessed November 10, 2022, http://freedomarchives.org/Documents/Finder/DOC513_scans/BLA/513.BLA.communiques.pdf.

52. Maryland State Police, Criminal Intelligence Division, *The Black Liberation Army: Understanding, Monitoring, Controlling*, October 1991, 12, https://www.ojp.gov/pdffiles1/Digitization/136568NCJRS.pdf.

53. Black Liberation Army, "Message from the Black Liberation Army: Spring Came Early This Year," newsletter, 1972, pt. III, obtained by author from Harvard University Archives.

54. Black Liberation Army, pt. III.

55. Bill Weinberg, "Interview with Dhoruba Bin Wahad," transcript, n.d., The Shadow, accessed November 8, 2022, http://www.spunk.org/texts/colon/sp001068.txt.

56. Akinyele Omowale Umoja, "Repression Breeds Resistance: The Black Liberation Army and the Radical Legacy of the Black Panther Party," *New Political Science* 21, no. 2 (June 1999): 143–45, https://doi.org/10.1080/07393149908429859.

57. Maryland State Police, *The Black Liberation Army*.

58. Umoja, "Repression Breeds Resistance," 146.

59. Henry Giniger, "Black Panthers in Algiers Halt Operations in Rift with Regime," *New York Times*, September 9, 1972, https://www.nytimes.com/1972/09/09/archives/black-panthers-in-algiers-halt-operations-in-rift-with-regime.html.

60. Morris Kaplan, "9 Allegedly in Black Army Indicted Here," *New York Times*, August 24, 1973, https://www.nytimes.com/1973/08/24/archives/9-allegedly-in-black-army-indicted-here-9-allegedly-in-black.html.

61. Michael T. Kaufman, "Slaying of One of the Last Black Liberation Army Leaders Still at Large Ended a 7-Month Manhunt," *New York Times*, November 16, 1973, https://www.nytimes.com/1973/11/16/archives/slaying-of-one-of-the-last-black-liberation-army-leaders-still-at.html; Paul L. Montgomery, "3D Suspect Linked to Police Slayings," *New York Times*, February 20, 1972, https://www.nytimes.com/1972/02/20/archives/3d-suspect-linked-to-police-slayings-hes-believed-to-have-fled-at.html.

62. Maryland State Police, *The Black Liberation Army*, 19–20.

63. Austin, *Up Against the Wall*, 325.

64. Karl Marx, *The Class Struggles in France: 1848–1850* (London: Wellred Books, 1968), pt. I, Google Books.

65. Austin, *Up Against the Wall*, 156–57. Some contemporary left-wing commentators understood that the Black Panther Party was driven more by nihilism than by utopianism. "Adventurous black youth joining the Panthers did not see themselves as building a successful social revolution, but anticipated 'leaving the Party in a pine box' with a dead cop to their credit, having done their share to avenge the centuries-old oppression of their people," the editorialists of the *Worker Vanguard* warned in a damning 1972 critique. "The ghetto uprisings did not give the black masses a sense of their own power. They did just the opposite. During the rioting, it was blacks' own homes that were burned down and the cops who went on a killing rampage." *Workers Vanguard*, no. 4, January 1972, republished at https://www.marxists.org/history/etol/newspape/workersvanguard/1972/0004_00_01_1972.pdf.

66. Cleaver, "On the Ideology of the Black Panther Party, Part 1," 3.

67. Global Terrorism Database, "197303270003" (College Park: University of Maryland, 2022), https://www.start.umd.edu/gtd/search/IncidentSummary.aspx?gtdid=197303270003. For contemporaneous news reporting, see "Brooklyn Grocery Owner Is Slain During Robbery," *New York Times*, March 28, 1973, https://www.nytimes.com/1973/03/28/archives/brooklyn-grocery-owner-is-slain-during-robbery.html.

68. Wallace Turner, "Ex–Black Panther Chief Arrested on Fraud Charges," *New York Times*, April 17, 1985, https://www.nytimes.com/1985/04/17/us/ex-black-panther-chief-arrested-on-fraud-charges.html.

69. Cynthia Gorney, "Mistrial Declared in Newton Murder Case," *Washington Post*, March 25, 1979, https://www.washingtonpost.com/archive/politics/1979/03/25/mistrial-declared-in-newton-murder-case/b6408217-1cf0-4c67-a425-9d25b6ac600f/.

70. Associated Press, "Huey Newton Killed; Was a Co-Founder of Black Panthers," *New York Times*, August 23, 1989, https://www.nytimes.com/1989/08/23/us/huey-newton-killed-was-a-co-founder-of-black-panthers.html; "Huey P. Newton (February 17, 1942–August 22, 1989)," National Archives, African American Heritage, 2016, accessed November 9, 2022, https://www.archives.gov/research/african-americans/individuals/huey-newton.

71. Newell G. Bringhurst, "Eldridge Cleaver's Passage through Mormonism," *Journal of Mormon History* 28, no. 1 (2002): 88.

72. David Hilliard, *Huey: Spirit of the Panther* (New York: Basic Books, 2009), chap. 3, Google Books.

73. Daley, *Target Blue*, Book 5, Part 4.

74. Judith Cummings, "Angela Davis Asks Support for 'Political Prisoners,'" *New York Times*, October 8, 1973, https://www.nytimes.com/1973/10/08/archives/angela-davis-asks-support-for-political-prisoners.html.

Chapter 7: From Black Liberation to Black Studies

1. "Lumumba-Zapata College: B.S.C.-M.A.Y.A. Demands for the Third College, U.C.S.D.," University of California, San Diego, March 14, 1969, PDF, https://library.ucsd.edu/dc/object/bb2392060k.

2. Angela Davis, *Lectures on Liberation* (New York Committee to Free Angela Davis, 1971), 4, PDF, https://archive.org/stream/AngelaDavis-LecturesOnLiberation/AngelaDavis-LecturesOnLiberation_djvu.txt.

3. Davis, 4, 5, 10.

4. Angela Y. Davis, "Women and Capitalism: Dialectics of Oppression and Liberation," in *The Angela Davis Reader* (Malden, MA: Blackwell, 1998), 174, 171, 170, 160, 175.

5. Angela Davis, "Reflections on the Black Woman's Role in the Community of Slaves," *Black Scholar* 3, no. 4 (December 1, 1971): 9, https://doi.org/10.1080/00064246.1971.11431201.

6. Davis, "Reflections on the Black Woman's Role in the Community of Slaves," 15.

7. Combahee River Collective, *The Combahee River Collective Statement*, pamphlet, April 1977, retrieved from the Library of Congress, https://www.loc.gov/item/lcwaN0028151/#:~:text=Summary,Original%20Statement%20Dated%20April%201977.

8. The authors readily acknowledge that they have cut out the majority from their coalition and that there are "problems in organizing Black feminists," but they plow forward into solipsism, misandry, and incoherence all the same. They suggest, quoting another feminist author, that they "haven't the faintest notion what possible revolutionary role white heterosexual men could fulfill, since they are the very embodiment of reactionary-vested-interest-power"—in the same breath that they appeal to Karl Marx. They expect the entire society to yield to their personal preoccupations, because their subjective freedom "necessitate[s] the destruction of all systems of oppression," including capitalism, private property, the nuclear family, and the constitutional system of government. Combahee River Collective, *The Combahee River Collective Statement*.

9. Combahee River Collective, *The Combahee River Collective Statement*.

10. Eldridge Cleaver, *Soul on Ice* (1968; reprint, New York: Delta, 1999), 90–91.

11. Cleaver, 92.

12. Cleaver, 95.

13. Cleaver, 104–5.

14. Davis, *Lectures on Liberation*, 3.

15. Angela Y. Davis, *Freedom Is a Constant Struggle: Ferguson, Palestine, and the Foundations of a Movement* (Chicago: Haymarket Books, 2006), 69, Kindle.

16. Davis, 35.

17. Angela Davis, "From the Prison of Slavery to the Slavery of Prison: Frederick Douglas and the Convict Lease System," in *The Angela Y. Davis Reader*, ed. Joy James (Malden, MA: Blackwell, 1998), 80.

18. Davis, *Freedom Is a Constant Struggle*, 69.

19. Eldridge Cleaver, "An Address Given by Eldridge Cleaver at a Rally in His Honor a Few Days Before He Was Scheduled to Return to Jail," *Ramparts*, December 14, 1968, 194.

20. Cleaver, 193–94.

21. David Bird, "Police Investigate Apparent Escape Effort by Black Liberationists," *New York Times*, February 18, 1975, https://www.nytimes.com/1975/02/18/archives/police-investigate-apparent-escape-effort-by-black-liberationists.html.

22. Robert Hanley, "No Checking Was Done on Chesimard 'Visitors,'" *New York Times*, No-

vember 6, 1979, https://www.nytimes.com/1979/11/06/archives/no-checking-was-done-on-chesimard-visitors-identification-required.html.

23. Davis, *Freedom Is a Constant Struggle*, 6.
24. Davis, 48.
25. "Social Analysis 139X," Subseries 2.6, Speeches and Lectures 1967–1981, carton 2, folders 76–81, Eldridge Cleaver Papers, Bancroft Library, University of California, Berkeley.
26. "Cleaver Omits Obscenities in 'Scholarly' First UC Lecture," *Los Angeles Times*, October 9, 1968.
27. Roz Payne, "Eldridge Cleaver Controversy at UC-Berkeley (196 Images)," photography, 1968–69, Roz Payne Sixties Archive, Center for Digital Research in the Humanities, University of Nebraska–Lincoln, https://rozsixties.unl.edu/items/show/789.
28. "Cleaver: No More Neutrality," *Indicator*, October 9, 1968, https://library.ucsd.edu/dc/object/bb39947572/_1.pdf; Eldridge Cleaver, "Eldridge Cleaver Speaking at UCLA 10/4/1968," video, October 4, 1968, University of California, Los Angeles, Department of Communication, special collection, https://www.youtube.com/watch?v=mfRxv_Nz4MY.
29. "Cleaver: No More Neutrality."
30. Fabio Rojas, *From Black Power to Black Studies: How a Radical Social Movement Became an Academic Discipline* (2007; reprint, Baltimore: Johns Hopkins University Press, 2010), 73, Kindle; Helene Whitson, "STRIKE! . . . Concerning the 1968–69 Strike at San Francisco State College," Foundsf.org, accessed November 12, 2022, https://www.foundsf.org/index.php?title=STRIKE%21..._Concerning_the_1968-69_Strike_at_San_Francisco_State_College.
31. Eldridge Cleaver, "Eldridge Cleaver, Speaker's Platform: October 9, 1968," audio, San Francisco State University, 1968, 07:16, Poetry Center Digital Archive, https://diva.sfsu.edu/collections/poetrycenter/bundles/222902.
32. Cleaver, "Eldridge Cleaver, Speaker's Platform: October 9, 1968," 15:56.
33. Martha Biondi, *The Black Revolution on Campus* (Berkeley: University of California Press, 2014), 48.
34. Jason Ferreira, "1968: The Strike at San Francisco State," SocialistWorker.org, December 13, 2018, http://socialistworker.org/2018/12/13/1968-the-strike-at-san-francisco-state.
35. See Bruce Bawer, *The Victims' Revolution: The Rise of Identity Studies and the Closing of the Liberal Mind* (New York: Broadside Books, 2012), 125–26.
36. Rojas, *From Black Power to Black Studies*, 27, 284.
37. Even veteran civil rights activists questioned the value of the new black studies programs. Bayard Rustin issued a critique in 1969 that captures the spirit. "Is Black Studies an educational program or a forum for ideological indoctrination?" Rustin asked. "Is it designed to train qualified scholars in a significant field of intellectual inquiry, or is it hoped that its graduates will form political cadres prepared to organize the impoverished residents of the black ghetto? Is it a means to achieve psychological identity and strength, or is it intended to provide a false and sheltered sense of security, the fragility of which would be revealed by even the slightest exposure to reality? And finally, does it offer the possibility for better racial understanding, or is it a regression to racial separatism?" Martin Kilson and Bayard Rustin, *Black Studies: Myths and Realities*, Current Educational Fund Publications (New York: A. Philip Randolph Educational Fund, 1969).
38. Bawer, *The Victims' Revolution*, 123–25.
39. Abdul Alkalimat et al., *African American Studies 2013: A National Web-Based Survey* (University of Illinois at Urbana-Champaign, Department of African American Studies, 2013).
40. Combahee River Collective, *The Combahee River Collective Statement*.
41. Kwame Ture and Charles V. Hamilton, *Black Power: The Politics of Liberation* (New York: Random House, 1967).
42. Huey P. Newton, "Huey Newton Talks to The Movement," *The Movement*, August 1968, https://archive.lib.msu.edu/DMC/AmRad/hueynewtontalks.pdf; John Brown Society, *An Introduction to the Black Panther Party* (Berkeley, CA: Radical Education Project, 1969),

https://freedomarchives.org/Documents/Finder/DOC513_scans/BPP_General/513.BPP
.intro.bpp.5.1969.pdf.

43. By 1971, Davis had established the essential statistical and political logic of the black liberationist argument that continues to this day. "Within the contained, coercive universe of the
prison, the captive is confronted with the realities of racism, not simply as individual acts
dictated by attitudinal bias; rather he is compelled to come to grips with racism as an institutional phenomenon collectively experienced by the victims," Davis wrote. "The disproportionate representation of the Black and Brown communities, the manifest racism of parole
boards, the intense brutality inherent in the relationship between prison guards and Black
and Brown inmates—all this and more cause the prisoner to be confronted daily, hourly, with
the concentrated, systematic existence of racism." Angela Y. Davis, ed., *If They Come in the
Morning . . . : Voices of Resistance* (1971; reprinted, New York: Verso, 2016), 38, Kindle.

44. Herbert Aptheker, *Anti-Racism in U.S. History: The First Two Hundred Years* (Westport, CT:
Greenwood, 1992).

45. Citation counts derived from an analysis of Google Scholar academic database.

46. Tanzina Vega and John Eligon, "Deep Tensions Rise to Surface After Ferguson Shooting,"
New York Times, August 16, 2014, https://www.nytimes.com/2014/08/17/us/ferguson-mo
-complex-racial-history-runs-deep-most-tensions-have-to-do-police-force.html; Joe Davidson, "Democrats Seek to Undo Institutional Racism Embedded in Pivotal New Deal Law,"
Washington Post, June 12, 2021, https://www.washingtonpost.com/politics/new-deal-law
-racism/2021/06/11/bd3a2612-ca2c-11eb-93fa-9053a95eb9f2_story.html; Caleb Ecarma,
"'We Tried Band-Aiding the Problem': Black Lives Matter Activists Split on How Radical
Change Should Be," *Vanity Fair*, June 18, 2020, https://www.vanityfair.com/news/2020/06
/black-lives-matter-protests-split-police-brutality-solutions.

47. I. Imari Abubakari Obadele, *Foundations of the Black Nation: A Textbook of Ideas Behind
the New Black Nationalism and the Struggle for Land in America* (Detroit: House of Songhay
/Julian Richardson Associates, 1975).

48. Davis, *Freedom Is a Constant Struggle*, 2.

49. For primary-source documentation on the ideological capture of K–12 education, see the
investigative series "Christopher Rufo on Woke Education" in *City Journal*, https://www
.city-journal.org/christopher-rufo-on-woke-education.

50. For an example of the campaign to "decarcerate, decriminalize, and depolice" in a major
American city, see Christopher F. Rufo, "Chaos by the Bay," *City Journal*, April 14, 2020,
https://www.city-journal.org/san-francisco-experiment-in-lawlessness.

51. Angela Davis describes this deeper ambition in her jailhouse interview, Cecil Williams and
Angela Davis, "A Conversation with Angela," *Black Scholar* 3, no. 7/8 (April 1972): 36–48.

52. Davis, *Freedom Is a Constant Struggle*, 72–73.

53. J. M. Brown, "Angela Davis, Iconic Activist, Officially Retires from UC–Santa Cruz," *Mercury News*, October 27, 2008, https://www.mercurynews.com/2008/10/27/angela-davis
-iconic-activist-officially-retires-from-uc-santa-cruz/.

Chapter 8: BLM

1. Mike Gonzalez, *BLM: The Making of a New Marxist Revolution* (New York: Encounter
Books, 2021), chap. 3, Kindle.

2. Patrisse Cullors, "Abolition and Reparations: Histories of Resistance, Transformative Justice, and Accountability," *Harvard Law Review*, vol. 132, no. 6 (April 2019): 1685–86.

3. "TimesTalks: Patrisse Cullors and Angela Davis," recorded live stream, February 20, 2018, New York Times Events, YouTube, 2018, https://www.youtube.com
/watch?v=BiAUYJXv2Yo, 01:18:21; "Angela Davis & BLM Co-Founder Alicia Garza in
Conversation across Generations," Democracy Now!, YouTube, 2017, 07:14. https://
www.youtube.com/watch?v=_gqGVni8Oec; Nelson George, "The Greats: Angela Davis," *New York Times Style Magazine*, October 19, 2020, https://www.nytimes.com
/interactive/2020/10/19/t-magazine/angela-davis.html.

4. During his Weather Underground years, Mann was convicted of assault and battery during a protest at a Boston high school, spent eighteen months in prison for his role in ransacking the Harvard Center for International Affairs, and was charged and then cleared of conspiracy to attempt murder after his group of Weathermen allegedly fired shots through a police station window. Jeff Magalif, "Judge Convicts Mann on Charge of Assault," *Harvard Crimson*, November 8, 1969, https://www.thecrimson.com/article/1969/11/8/judge-convicts-mann-on-charge-of/; Eric Mann and Lian Hurst Mann Papers, 1967–2007, Call no.: MS 657, Robert S. Cox Special Collections & University Archives Research Center, University of Massachusetts Amherst, http://scua.library.umass.edu/mann-eric/; *The Weather Underground: Report of the Subcommittee to Investigate the Administration of the Internal Security Act and Other Internal Security Laws of the Committee on the Judiciary*, United States Senate, Ninety-Fourth Congress, First Session (Washington, DC: US Government Printing Office, 1975), 19.

5. Mike Gonzalez, "To Destroy America," *Heritage Foundation* (blog), September 3, 2020, https://www.heritage.org/civil-society/commentary/destroy-america.

6. Cullors, "Abolition and Reparations," 1688.

7. George, "The Greats: Angela Davis."

8. Angela Y. Davis, *Freedom Is a Constant Struggle: Ferguson, Palestine, and the Foundations of a Movement* (Chicago: Haymarket Books, 2006), 87, Kindle.

9. Black Liberation Army, "Message to the Black Movement: A Political Statement from the Black Underground," undated, ii, Michigan State University Archives, https://archive.lib .msu.edu/DMC/AmRad/messageblackmovement.pdf.

10. Alicia Garza, "Left Forum 2015—Saturday Evening Event," panel session, video recording, May 30, 2015, John Jay College of Criminal Justice, New York, NY, Other Voices, Other Choices, YouTube, 2016, 26:17, https://www.youtube.com/watch?v=ETdStVAXwgk.

11. Foreword by Angela Davis, in Patrisse Khan-Cullors and Asha Bandele, *When They Call You a Terrorist: A Black Lives Matter Memoir* (New York: St. Martin's Griffin, 2018), xi, xiv, Kindle.

12. Alicia Garza, "A Herstory of the #BlackLivesMatter Movement," *Feminist Wire* (blog), October 7, 2014, https://thefeministwire.com/2014/10/blacklivesmatter-2/.

13. The chant is derived from the poem "To My People," originally written and recorded by Assata Shakur while incarcerated at Middlesex County Jail in 1973. Reprinted in Assata Shakur, *Assata: An Autobiography* (Brooklyn, NY: Lawrence Hill Books, 2020), 49–52, Kindle.

14. Khan-Cullors and Bandele, *When They Call You a Terrorist*, 257.

15. Black Liberation Army, "Message from the Black Liberation Army: Spring Came Early This Year," newsletter, 1972, PDF acquired by author from Harvard University archives.

16. The evidence on police shootings does not comport with the BLM narrative. See the reports on Michael Brown and Jacob Blake later in this chapter. For more context on race and police shootings, see Heather Mac Donald's testimony before the House Judiciary Committee, reprinted as Heather Mac Donald, "Repudiate the Anti-Police Narrative," *City Journal*, June 10, 2020.

17. Angela Davis, "The Soledad Brothers," *Black Scholar* 2, no. 8/9 (May 1971): 2.

18. Davis, 2.

19. Angela Y. Davis, ed., *If They Come in the Morning . . . : Voices of Resistance* (New York: Verso, 2016), 188, Kindle.

20. Department of Justice, *Department of Justice Report Regarding the Criminal Investigation into the Shooting Death of Michael Brown by Ferguson, Missouri Police Officer Darren Wilson*, March 4, 2015, https://www.justice.gov/sites/default/files/opa/press-releases /attachments/2015/03/04/doj_report_on_shooting_of_michael_brown_1.pdf.

21. Michael D. Graveley, *Report on the Officer Involved Shooting of Jacob Blake*, Kenosha County District Attorney, January 2021, https://www.kenoshacounty.org/DocumentCenter /View/11827/Report-on-the-Officer-Involved-Shooting-of-Jacob-Blake.

22. See Heather Mac Donald's testimony before the Senate Judiciary Committee, reprinted as Heather Mac Donald, "The Myth of Criminal-Justice Racism," *City Journal*, October 22, 2015.

23. Alicia Garza, "Black People Deserve a Revolution," video, BBC Select Takes, YouTube, 2021, 01:00, https://www.youtube.com/watch?v=9JUQoMem8mU.

24. Alicia Garza, "I Am Very Optimistic About the Future," video, BBC Select Takes, YouTube, 2022, https://www.youtube.com/watch?v=uZD_7FSzaRw.

25. George, "The Greats: Angela Davis."

26. Zach Goldberg, "How the Media Led the Great Racial Awakening," *Tablet Magazine*, August 4, 2020, https://www.tabletmag.com/sections/news/articles/media-great-racial-awakening.

27. Samantha Neal, "Views of Racism as a Major Problem Increase Sharply, Especially Among Democrats," Pew Research Center, August 29, 2017, accessed November 12, 2022, https://www.pewresearch.org/fact-tank/2017/08/29/views-of-racism-as-a-major-problem-increase-sharply-especially-among-democrats/.

28. Lawrence D. Bobo et al., "The Real Record on Racial Attitudes," in *Social Trends in American Life: Findings from the General Social Survey since 1972*, ed. Peter V. Marsden (Princeton, NJ: Princeton University Press, 2012), 49.

29. Nancy Krieger et al., "Trends in US Deaths Due to Legal Intervention Among Black and White Men, Age 15–34 Years, by County Income Level: 1960–2010," *Harvard Public Health Review* 3 (January 2015), https://doi.org/10.54111/0001c/1.

30. See, for example, Wilfred Reilly, "America Run Riot," *Commentary*, June 16, 2020, https://www.commentary.org/articles/wilfred-reilly/george-floyd-destructive-narrative-riots/. As Reilly notes: "The *total* number of unarmed black persons killed by police during 2019 was *15*. There are 42 million Black people in the United States. The overall number of unarmed individuals killed by police during that year was 56. Even adding in all those armed with a weapon or attacking officers, police in 2019 took exactly 229 black lives, out of a total of 1,004 among the 330 million people living in America. Nor was 2019 an outlier year. While preparing my book *Taboo: Ten Facts You Can't Talk About*, I reviewed the fairly typical year of 2015 in depth. That year, not even 365 days into the Black Lives Matter movement and resultant attempts at police reform, police killed at most 1,200 people, 258 of whom were African American and just 17 of whom were unarmed black men killed by white officers—numbers virtually identical to 2019's."

31. Megan Brenan, "Ratings of Black-White Relations at New Low," Gallup.com, July 21, 2021, accessed November 13, 2022, https://news.gallup.com/poll/352457/ratings-black-white-relations-new-low.aspx.

32. Kevin McCaffree and Anondah Saide, *How Informed Are Americans about Race and Policing?*, Skeptic Research Center, February 2021, https://www.skeptic.com/research-center/reports/Research-Report-CUPES-007.pdf.

33. *Washington Post*, "Police Shootings Database 2015–2022," Fatal Force, accessed November 11, 2022, https://www.washingtonpost.com/graphics/investigations/police-shootings-database/?itid=lk_inline_manual_5.

34. Alicia Garza, "A Herstory of the #BlackLivesMatter Movement," *The Feminist Wire* (blog), October 7, 2014, https://thefeministwire.com/2014/10/blacklivesmatter-2/; "Black Lives Matter," Auschwitz Institute for the Prevention of Genocide and Mass Atrocities, accessed November 13, 2022, http://www.auschwitzinstitute.org/black-lives-matter/.

35. Hannah Gilberstadt and Andrew Daniller, "Liberals Make Up the Largest Share of Democratic Voters, but Their Growth Has Slowed in Recent Years," Pew Research Center, accessed November 13, 2022, https://www.pewresearch.org/fact-tank/2020/01/17/liberals-make-up-largest-share-of-democratic-voters/.

36. Pew Research Center, *Beyond Red vs. Blue: The Political Typology*, November 2021, 94–100, https://www.pewresearch.org/politics/wp-content/uploads/sites/4/2021/11/PP_2021.11.09_political-typology_REPORT.pdf.

37. Arelis R. Hernández, "George Floyd's America: A Knee on His Neck," *Washington Post*, October 26, 2022, https://www.washingtonpost.com/graphics/2020/national/george-floyd-america/policing/.

38. "George Floyd Arrest Transcript," District Court, State of Minnesota, June 15, 2020, PDF,

https://int.nyt.com/data/documenthelper/7070-exhibit-final07072020/4b81216735f2203a0
8cb/optimized/full.pdf#page=1.

39. CBS News Minnesota, "'It's Real Ugly': Protesters Clash with Minneapolis Police After George Floyd's Death," CBS News, May 25, 2020, https://www.cbsnews.com/minnesota/news/hundreds-of-protesters-march-in-minneapolis-after-george-floyds-deadly-encounter-with-police/.

40. Farah Stockman, "'They Have Lost Control': Why Minneapolis Burned," *New York Times*, July 3, 2020, https://www.nytimes.com/2020/07/03/us/minneapolis-government-george-floyd.html.

41. FBI Counterterrorism Division, "Black Identity Extremists Likely Motivated to Target Law Enforcement Officers," intelligence assessment, Federal Bureau of Investigation, August 3, 2017, 5, https://s3.documentcloud.org/documents/4067711/BIE-Redacted.pdf.

42. FBI Counterterrorism Division, 4.

43. Joel Finkelstein et al., *Network-Enabled Anarchy: How Militant Anarcho-Socialist Networks Use Social Media to Instigate Widespread Violence Against Political Opponents and Law Enforcement*, Network Contagion Research Institute, Miller Center for Community Protection and Resilience, Rutgers University, New Brunswick, NJ, September 14, 2020, 2–7.

44. Finkelstein et al., *Network-Enabled Anarchy*, 8–12; Willem Van Spronsen, "Written Manifesto of Willem Van Spronsen," KIRO News, Tacoma, WA, 2019, PDF, https://mediaweb.kirotv.com/document_dev/2019/07/15/Manifesto_15897725_ver1.0.pdf.

45. Finkelstein et al., *Network-Enabled Anarchy*, 13.

46. Gillian Flaccus, "Portland's Grim Reality: 100 Days of Protests, Many Violent," Associated Press, September 4, 2020, https://apnews.com/article/virus-outbreak-ap-top-news-race-and-ethnicity-id-state-wire-or-state-wire-b57315d97dd2146c4a89b4636faa7b70.

47. Finkelstein et al., *Network-Enabled Anarchy*, 13.

48. Finkelstein et al., 16.

49. US Crisis Monitor, "US Crisis Monitor Releases Full Data for 2020," Armed Conflict Location & Event Data Project (ACLED), February 5, 2021, accessed November 13, 2022, https://acleddata.com/2021/02/05/us-crisis-monitor-releases-full-data-for-2020/.

50. Anita Snow, "AP Tally: Arrests at Widespread US Protests Hit 10,000," Associated Press, June 4, 2020, https://apnews.com/article/american-protests-us-news-arrests-minnesota-burglary-bb2404f9b13c8b53b94c73f818f6a0b7; Lois Beckett, "At Least 25 Americans Were Killed During Protests and Political Unrest In 2020," *Guardian*, October 31, 2020, https://archive.ph/D2Tdx.

51. Thomas Johansmeyer, "How 2020 Protests Changed Insurance Forever," World Economic Forum, February 22, 2021, accessed November 13, 2022, https://www.weforum.org/agenda/2021/02/2020-protests-changed-insurance-forever/.

52. Local news outlets in Portland, Oregon, documented the destruction of statues in detail during the riots. Sergio Olmos, Ryan Haas, and Rebecca Ellis, "Portland Protesters Tear Down Roosevelt, Lincoln Statues During 'Day of Rage,'" Oregon Public Broadcasting, October 12, 2020, https://www.opb.org/article/2020/10/12/portland-protesters-tear-down-roosevelt-lincoln-statues-during-day-of-rage/; Latisha Jensen, "Portland Man Describes Tearing Down Thomas Jefferson Statue: 'It's Not Vandalism,'" *Willamette Week*, June 20, 2020, https://www.wweek.com/news/2020/06/20/portland-man-describes-tearing-down-thomas-jefferson-statue-its-not-vandalism/; Kristian Foden-Vencil, "Some of Portland's Most Prominent Public Art Tumbled This Year. Which Ones Should Come Back?," Oregon Public Broadcasting, December 28, 2020, https://www.opb.org/article/2020/12/28/portland-oregon-statues-protest-black-lives-matter-elk/; Rob Manning, "Thomas Jefferson Statue Pulled Down at Portland's Jefferson High," Oregon Public Broadcasting, June 14, 2020, https://www.opb.org/news/article/thomas-jefferson-statue-pulled-down-portland-jefferson-high/; Bryant Clerkley, "George Washington Statue Toppled in Portland," KGW8 News, June 20, 2020, https://www.kgw.com/article/news/local/statue-of-george-washington-toppled-and-spray-pained-in-hollywood-neighborhood/283-6f3d5c28-74c6-43 07-88d7-493c5dfcd59b; Shane Dixon Kavanaugh, "Will They Return? Toppled Portland

Statues of Lincoln, Roosevelt Mired in Delays, Uncertainty and Suspicion," *Oregonian/ OregonLive*, October 21, 2021, https://www.oregonlive.com/news/2021/10/will-they-return -toppled-portland-statues-of-lincoln-roosevelt-mired-in-delays-uncertainty-and-suspicion .html.

53.   Ava DuVernay, "Ava DuVernay Talks to Angela Davis About Black Lives Matter," *Vanity Fair*, September 2020, https://www.vanityfair.com/culture/2020/08/angela-davis-and-ava -duvernay-in-conversation.

54.   Eldridge Cleaver, *Soul on Ice* (1968; reprinted, New York: Delta, 1999), 90–92.

55.   DuVernay, "Ava DuVernay Talks to Angela Davis About Black Lives Matter."

56.   Andrew Court, "Aggressive Crowd of BLM Protesters Accost White Diners Outside DC Restaurants," *Daily Mail*, updated November 2, 2020, https://www.dailymail.co.uk/news /article-8664345/Aggressive-crowd-BLM-protesters-accost-white-diners-outside-DC -restaurants.html.

57.   Basic Schwab Leader President Dr RollerGator PhD [@drrollergator], "PITTSBURGH PA," tweet, Twitter, September 6, 2020, https://twitter.com/drrollergator/status /1302741208570236935.

58.   Andy Ngô [@MrAndyNgo], "New York: #BLM Protesters Tell White People Dining Out- side to 'Get the f—out of New York' & That Their White-Owned Taquerias Aren't Wel- come. The Crowd Chant along. Https://T.Co/E8D7B2rkQ8," tweet, Twitter, April 21, 2021, https://twitter.com/MrAndyNgo/status/1384670611348365313.

59.   During communist times, the Czech dissident Václav Havel wrote a famous parable about the greengrocers who are silently compelled to hang "workers of the world, unite" signs in their store windows as an expression of obedience to the dominant regime. "I think it can safely be assumed that the overwhelming majority of shopkeepers never think about the slogans they put in their windows, nor do they use them to express their real opinions," Havel wrote. "He put them all into the window simply because it has been done that way for years, because everyone does it, and because that is the way it has to be. If he were to refuse, there could be trouble. He could be reproached for not having the proper decoration in his window; someone might even accuse him of disloyalty. He does it because these things must be done if one is to get along in life. It is one of the thousands of details that guarantee him a relatively tranquil life 'in harmony with society.'" Václav Havel, "The Power of the Powerless," October 1978, Florida International University, Václav Havel Program from Human Rights & Diplomacy, accessed November 12, 2022, https://havel.fiu.edu/about-us /publications-and-resources/the-power-of-the-powerless.pdf.

60.   For a full analysis of the Reuters coverage, see Christopher F. Rufo, "The Price of Dissent," *City Journal*, January 5, 2022, https://www.city-journal.org/black-lives-matter-thomson -reuters-and-the-price-of-dissent.

61.   David Schuman [@david_schuman], "BREAKING: Mayor Jacob Frey Is Here and Making His Way to the Front to Speak Https://T.Co/IjyIwXv9Rh," tweet, Twitter, June 6, 2020, https://twitter.com/david_schuman/status/1269394658926514176; "Video: Minneapolis Mayor Booed Out of Rally," *New York Times*, 2020, https://www.nytimes.com/video/us/politics /100000007178355/minneapolis-mayor-booed-out-of-rally.html.

62.   David Schuman [@david_schuman], "Paused for a Seated, Fists-up Call and Repeat. This Is Peaceful Protesting, and Has Been for 3+ Hours @WCCO," tweet, Twitter, June 6, 2020, https://twitter.com/david_schuman/status/1269391464859144194.

63.   "Video: Minneapolis Mayor Booed Out of Rally."

64.   David Schuman [@david_schuman], "'We're Not Here for Police Reform Bulls**t. Abolish the Police, Then the Prisons.' Roar from the Crowd," tweet, Twitter, June 6, 2020, https:// twitter.com/david_schuman/status/1269352694306820097.

65.   Common, "Angela Davis Is on the 2020 TIME 100 List," *Time*, September 22, 2020, https:// time.com/collection/100-most-influential-people-2020/5888290/angela-davis/.

66.   Ibram X. Kendi, "100 Women of the Year: 1971: Angela Davis," *Time*, March 5, 2020, https://time.com/5793638/angela-davis-100-women-of-the-year/.

67. Shakur, *Assata: An Autobiography*, 169.
68. DuVernay, "Ava DuVernay Talks to Angela Davis About Black Lives Matter."

Chapter 9: Mob Rule in Seattle
1. Livestream video during Capitol Hill Autonomous Zone protests obtained by author. First reported in Christopher F. Rufo, "Burn It Down," *City Journal*, Autumn 2020, https://www.city-journal.org/seattle-movement-to-deconstruct-justice-and-social-order.
2. 8toAbolition, "8 to Abolition: Abolitionist Policy Changes to Demand from Your City Officials," 8toAbolition.com, 2020, newsletter, PDF, https://static1.squarespace.com/static/5edbf321b6026b073fef97d4/t/5ee0817c955eaa484011b8fe/1591771519433/8toAbolition_V2.pdf.
3. Decriminalize Seattle Coalition, "Individual Sign On: Support the Call to Defund the Seattle Police Department," online petition, Defund Seattle Police, Summer 2020, accessed November 14, 2022, https://docs.google.com/forms/d/e/1FAIpQLSeLx0UBq_-FmE6YQPgG2aGSmNOI7_LCjpGiNGH4HSq2nWpGSA/viewform?usp=embed_facebook.
4. Ketil Freman et al., "City of Seattle Draft Resolution," Pub. L. No. Draft Public Safety Dept Reorg (2020), http://seattle.legistar.com/View.ashx?M=F&ID=8699266&GUID=CF75D7B1-35AC-421F-A691-D2000894E7E2&fbclid=IwAR2xqZ44izad2BtyyuNhyJX9nqBMcls3Cmo3eiN7GikEbEGjyyap6QU-Lew.
5. Every Day March social media feeds monitored by author; Louis Casiano, "Seattle Mayor, Councilmembers See Offensive Messages Written Outside Homes: 'Resign Bi---,'" Fox News, July 27, 2020, https://www.foxnews.com/us/seattle-mayor-councilmembers-offensive-messages-outside-homes-resign-bi.
6. Livestream video obtained by author. First reported in Rufo, "Burn It Down."
7. Kshama Sawant, "An Ordinance Relating to the Seattle Police Department; Banning the Ownership, Purchase, Rent, Storage, or Use of Crowd Control Weapons; and Adding a New Section 3.28.146 to the Seattle Municipal Code.," Pub. L. No. CB 119805 (2020), https://seattle.legistar.com/LegislationDetail.aspx?ID=4564636&GUID=90EDF5B4-7607-43BB-A99C-514C0B51CB56&FullText=1.
8. Letter obtained by author and reported in Christopher F. Rufo [@realchrisrufo], "The Seattle Police Chief Is Sending Out Letters Telling Residents: 'We Cannot Enforce the Law. You Are on Your Own,'" tweet, Twitter, July 25, 2020, https://twitter.com/realchrisrufo/status/1286902138996572160.
9. EMC Research, "Survey of Likely November 2021 Voters, City of Seattle, WA" telephone survey report, July 2020.
10. Law enforcement interview with author, first reported in Rufo, "Burn It Down."
11. Internal documents obtained by author, including: King County Department of Adult and Juvenile Detention, "NYZ EHM Community Supports Meeting," King County, WA, July 21, 2020.
12. Internal email obtained by author and released to the public. John Diaz, "A New Vision for Adult and Youth Detention," King County Department of Adult and Juvenile Detention, July 21, 2020. Subsequently confirmed by King County Executive Dow Constantine in his State of the County speech three days later. Dow Constantine, "2020 State of the County," transcript of speech delivered in Seattle, WA, July 24, 2020, https://kingcounty.gov/elected/executive/constantine/news/speeches/2020-state-of-the-county.aspx.
13. Corrections department official interview with author, first reported in Rufo, "Burn It Down."
14. King County Department of Adult and Juvenile Detention, "NYZ EHM Community Supports Meeting."
15. Budget for Justice, "Budget for Justice Divestment and Reinvestment Strategies," proposal, 2019, PDF, 3, 20, https://roominate.com/blogg/mckenna/Budget-For-Justice-Council-Ask_10-8-18.pdf.

16. Budget for Justice, 20, 12, 1.

17. Claudia Rowe, "King County Sticks with Peace Circles for Juvenile Crime, Even After a Murder Charge," *Seattle Times*, June 4, 2018, https://www.seattletimes.com/education-lab /king-county-sticks-with-peace-circles-for-juvenile-crime-even-after-a-murder-charge/.

18. Interview with author, first reported in Rufo, "Burn It Down."

19. Jamie Tompkins and David Rose, "Police: Teen Killed in West Seattle Park Was Set up, Lured There by a Girl," FOX 13 News, October 20, 2017, https://www.q13fox.com/news /police-teen-killed-in-west-seattle-park-was-set-up-lured-there-by-a-girl.

20. Social media feed monitored by author, including seattleeverydayresistence, "Dow Constantine Speaks with Us," video, Instagram, July 31, 2020, https://www.instagram.com/tv /CDS7UsNpZAL/.

21. Criminal justice reform organizations have proposed variations on these policies over the years. See King County Public Defense Advisory Board, "2018 Annual Report," 21–22; Budget for Justice proposal to Seattle City Council, October 8, 2018; Anita Khandelwal, "DPD Presentation to Law, Justice, Health and Human Services Committee regarding COVID's Impact on Our Work and Our Clients," King County Department of Public Defense, February 1, 2022; Letter from Budget for Justice to the City of Seattle, reprinted in *South Seattle Emerald*, "Budget for Justice Calls for 'Ongoing, Real and Progressive Policy and System Change,'" November 9, 2018, https://southseattleemerald.com/2018/11/09/budget-for -justice-calls-for-ongoing-real-and-progressive-policy-and-system-change/.

22. King County, "Law Enforcement Assisted Diversion (LEAD)," accessed November 30, 2022, https://kingcounty.gov/depts/community-human-services/mental-health-substance -abuse/diversion-reentry-services/lead.aspx.

23. See Christopher F. Rufo, "Seattle Under Siege," *City Journal*, August 2018, https://www .city-journal.org/seattle-homelessness.

24. Matt Markovich, "Controversial Sentence of 75-Time Offender Results in Months-Long Effort to Block Judge," KOMO News, February 26, 2020, https://komonews.com/news /operation-crime-justice/controversial-sentence-of-75-time-offender-results-in-months -long-effort-to-block-judge?fbclid=IwAR29J4jezUYlNTId2lE5C9M22dHI19V2dhfjsqjrX M6r1Oq7-qfPja1zEms.

25. For a detailed analysis of "prolific offenders," see Scott P. Lindsay, *System Failure: Report on Prolific Offenders in Seattle's Criminal Justice System*, Downtown Seattle Association, February 2019, https://downtownseattle.org/files/advocacy/system-failure-prolific-offender -report-feb-2019.pdf.

26. Author interview and correspondence with Judge Edward McKenna, 2020.

27. King County DPAA Equity & Justice Workgroup, letter to Criminal Division Leadership, King County Prosecuting Attorney's Office, July 17, 2020.

28. David Kroman, "Seattle's Arrest Alternative, LEAD, Moves Beyond Police," Crosscut, July 17, 2020, https://crosscut.com/2020/07/seattles-arrest-alternative-lead-moves-beyond-police.

29. Kroman.

30. Kshama Sawant, "CB 119810 An Ordinance Related to Taxation," Seattle City Council meeting, Seattle, Washington, July 6, 2020.

31. This on-the-ground reporting on the Capitol Hill Autonomous Zone was first published in a series of stories for *City Journal*. See Christopher F. Rufo, "Anarchy in Seattle," *City Journal*, June 10, 2020; Christopher F. Rufo, "The State of CHAZ," *City Journal*, June 15, 2020; Christopher F. Rufo, "The End of CHAZ," *City Journal*, July 1, 2020.

32. Livestream video obtained by author. First reported in Rufo, "The State of CHAZ."

33. blackstarfarmers, "All My BIPOC Folks Come on Out. We Got a Bed Just for You. #blacklandmatters," photo, Instagram, June 13, 2020, https://www.instagram.com/p /CBYd0SBjhTO/.

34. Matt Baume, "Meet the Farmer Behind CHAZ's Vegetable Gardens," The Stranger, June 12, 2020, https://www.thestranger.com/slog/2020/06/12/43897621/meet-the-farmer-behind -chazs-vegetable-gardens.

35. Hannah Weinberger, "In Seattle's CHAZ, a Community Garden Takes Root," Crosscut, June 15, 2020, https://crosscut.com/environment/2020/06/seattles-chaz-community -garden-takes-root.

36. Joshua McNichols, "CHAZ Community Chews on What to Do Next," KUOW/NPR, June 12, 2020, https://www.kuow.org/stories/chaz-community-chews-on-what-to-do-next.

37. Livstream video obtained by author. First reported in Rufo, "The State of CHAZ."

38. Livestream video obtained by author. First reported in Rufo, "Anarchy in Seattle."

39. Livestream video and police radio monitored by author. First reported in Rufo, "The State of CHAZ."

40. Rufo, "The End of CHAZ."

41. Rufo, "The End of CHAZ."

42. Sam Smith, "Special Meeting of City Council," transcript of city council meeting, Seattle Municipal Archives, July 27, 1977, accessed November 30, 2022, https://www.seattle.gov /cityarchives/exhibits-and-education/seattle-voices/central-area-police-precinct.

43. FBI crime data cited in Jeff Asher, "Murder Rose by Almost 30% in 2020. It's Rising at a Slower Rate in 2021," *New York Times*, September 22, 2021, sec. The Upshot, https://www .nytimes.com/2021/09/22/upshot/murder-rise-2020.html.

44. Paul G. Cassell, "Explaining the Recent Homicide Spikes in U.S. Cities: The 'Minneapolis Effect' and the Decline in Proactive Policing," *Federal Sentencing Reporter* 33, no. 83, University of Utah Law Research Paper no. 377 (December 2020), https://papers.ssrn.com /abstract=3690473; Tanaya Devi and Roland G. Fryer Jr., *Policing the Police: The Impact of "Pattern-or-Practice" Investigations on Crime* (Cambridge, MA: National Bureau of Economic Research, June 2020), https://doi.org/10.3386/w27324.

45. Chief Adrian Diaz, "Chief Diaz's Remarks on Investigation of Officers in DC and Year-End Crime Data," SPD Blotter, Seattle Police Department, January 11, 2021, accessed November 14, 2022, https://spdblotter.seattle.gov/2021/01/11/chief-diazs-remarks/.

46. Tammy Mutasa, "Dad of Slain CHOP Victim Now a Shooting Victim Himself: 'I'm Glad to Be Alive,'" KOMO News, June 12, 2021, https://komonews.com/news/local/dad-of-slain -chop-victim-now-a-shooting-victim-himself-im-glad-to-be-alive.

47. Observational reporting in downtown Seattle, summer 2020.

48. Angela Davis, *Lectures on Liberation* (New York Committee to Free Angela Davis, 1971), 11, PDF, https://archive.org/stream/AngelaDavis-LecturesOnLiberation/AngelaDavis -LecturesOnLiberation_djvu.txt.

Chapter 10: Paulo Freire

1. Catherine Halley, "Paulo Freire's Pedagogy of the Oppressed at Fifty," JSTOR Daily, September 30, 2020, https://daily.jstor.org/paulo-freires-pedagogy-of-the-oppressed-at-fifty/.

2. Elliott Green, "What Are the Most-Cited Publications in the Social Sciences (According to Google Scholar)?," *LSE Impact* (blog), London School of Economics and Political Science, May 12, 2016, accessed November 15, 2022, https://blogs.lse.ac.uk/impactofsocialsciences /2016/05/12/what-are-the-most-cited-publications-in-the-social-sciences-according-to -google-scholar/.

3. Paulo Freire, *Pedagogy of the Oppressed*, trans. Myra Bergman Ramos (1970; reprint, New York: Bloomsbury Academic, 2018), 139–40, Kindle.

4. Freire, 149.

5. Freire, 158–59.

6. Paulo Freire, *Letters to Cristina* (1996; reprint, London: Routledge, 2016), 53, Kindle.

7. Freire, 49.

8. Andrew J. Kirkendall, *Paulo Freire and the Cold War Politics of Literacy* (Chapel Hill: University of North Carolina Press, 2010), 25–26, Kindle; for Freire's social analysis of Northeast Brazil, see Paulo Freire, *The Politics of Education: Culture, Power, and Liberation*, trans. Donaldo Macedo (Westport, CT: Bergin & Garvey, 1985), chap. 7, Kindle.

9. Kirkendall, *Paulo Freire and the Cold War Politics of Literacy*, 14–15.

10. Freire, *Letters to Cristina*, 14.

11. Freire, 17–18.

12. E. Teofilo and D. Prado Garcia, "Brazil: Land Politics, Poverty and Rural Development," in *Land Reform: Land Settlement and Cooperatives*, ed. P. Groppo, vol. 3 (Rome: FAO Information Division, 2003), https://www.fao.org/3/y5026e/y5026e04.htm.

13. Kirkendall, *Paulo Freire and the Cold War Politics of Literacy*, 21.

14. Paulo Freire, *Education for Critical Consciousness* (1974; reprint, London: Bloomsbury Academic, 2013), 128, Kindle.

15. Freire, *Letters to Cristina*, 81–82.

16. Freire, 82–83.

17. Freire, 86–87.

18. Freire, *The Politics of Education*, chap. 7.

19. Freire, *Pedagogy of the Oppressed*, 54–55.

20. Ana Maria Araujo-Freire and Donaldo Macedo, introduction to Paulo Freire, *The Paulo Freire Reader*, ed. Ana Maria Araujo-Freire and Donaldo Macedo (New York: Continuum, 1998), 21.

21. Paulo Freire, "Conscientisation," *CrossCurrents* 24, no. 1 (Spring 1974): 28.

22. For documentation on the crimes of twentieth-century communist regimes, see Karel Bartosek et al., *The Black Book of Communism: Crimes, Terror, Repression* (Cambridge, MA: Harvard University Press, 1999).

23. Freire, *Pedagogy of the Oppressed*, 54–55.

24. Freire, "Conscientisation," 28.

25. Freire, *The Politics of Education*, chap. 7.

26. Freire, *Pedagogy of the Oppressed*, 124.

27. Kirkendall, *Paulo Freire and the Cold War Politics of Literacy*, 40.

28. Kirkendall, 42–44.

29. Andrew J. Kirkendall, "Entering History: Paulo Freire and the Politics of the Brazilian Northeast, 1958–1964," *Luso-Brazilian Review* 41, no. 1 (2004): 169, https://doi.org/10.1353/lbr.2004.0014.

30. Jorge Ferreira, "The Brazilian Communist Party and Joao Goulart's Administration," *Revista Brasileira de História* 33 (December 2013): 117, https://doi.org/10.1590/S0102-01882013000200007.

31. Kirkendall, *Paulo Freire and the Cold War Politics of Literacy*, 47–48.

32. Kirkendall, 53–56.

33. Freire, *Letters to Cristina*, 18.

34. Kirkendall, *Paulo Freire and the Cold War Politics of Literacy*, 57.

35. Freire, *Letters to Cristina*, 116.

36. Kirkendall, 57.

37. Freire, *Pedagogy of the Oppressed*, 136–37.

38. Paulo Freire, *Pedagogy in Process: The Letters to Guinea-Bissau*, trans. Carman St. John Hunter (1978; reprint, London: Bloomsbury, 2016), Introduction: Part 1, loc. 202, Kindle.

39. Freire, Letter 11, loc. 1819.

40. Freire, Introduction: Part 2, loc. 1086.

41. Freire, Letter 3, loc. 1372.

42. Freire, Letter 3, loc. 1420.

43. Timothy W. Luke, "Cabral's Marxism: An African Strategy for Socialist Development," *Studies in Comparative Communism* 14, no. 4 (1981): 329, https://www.jstor.org/stable/45367474.

44. Freire, *Pedagogy in Process*, letter 11, Introduction: Part 1, loc. 202.

45. Shirley Washington, "New Institutions for Development in Guinea-Bissau," *Black Scholar* 11, no. 5 (May 1980): 20, https://doi.org/10.1080/00064246.1980.11414116.

46. Luke, "Cabral's Marxism," 315.

47. Kirkendall, *Paulo Freire and the Cold War Politics of Literacy*, 111.

48. Luke, "Cabral's Marxism," 325.

49. Freire, *Pedagogy in Process*, Letter 15, loc. 2362-2415.

50. Frank Dikötter, *The Cultural Revolution: A People's History, 1962–1976* (New York: Bloomsbury, 2016), 230–31, 229, Kindle.

51. Judith Shapiro, *Mao's War Against Nature: Politics and the Environment in Revolutionary China*, illustrated ed. (Cambridge: Cambridge University Press, 2001), 137.

52. "Chen Yonggui; Disgraced in China Over 'Model' Commune," *Los Angeles Times*, April 5, 1986, https://www.latimes.com/archives/la-xpm-1986-04-05-fi-21793-story.html.

53. Pao-yu Ching, *Revolution and Counterrevolution: China's Continuing Class Struggle Since Liberation* (Manila: Institute of Political Economy, 2012), 52.

54. Paulo Freire, *The Politics of Education: Culture, Power, and Liberation*, trans. Donaldo Macedo (Westport, CT: Bergin & Garvey, 1985), chap. 8, loc. 1430, Kindle.

55. Paulo Freire, "Reading the World and Reading the Word: An Interview with Paulo Freire," *Language Arts* 62, no. 1 (1985): 16.

56. Rosemary E. Galli, "The Food Crisis and the Socialist State in Lusophone Africa," *African Studies Review* 30, no. 1 (1987): 23, https://doi.org/10.2307/524502.

57. Freire, *Pedagogy in Process*, letter 17, letter 3.

58. Kirkendall, *Paulo Freire and the Cold War Politics of Literacy*, 109, Kindle.

59. Linda M. Harasim, "Literacy and National Reconstruction in Guinea Bissau: A Critique of the Freirean Literacy Campaign" (PhD diss., University of Toronto, 1983).

60. See footnotes 9–11 in Bianca Facundo, "The Lessons of Guinea-Bissau, Section 7 of Freire-Inspired Programs in the United States and Puerto Rico: A Critical Evaluation," essay, Suppression of Dissent, 1984, accessed November 16, 2022, https://www.bmartin.cc/dissent/documents/Facundo/section7.html.

61. Harasim is quoted in Facundo's "The Lessons of Guinea-Bissau."

62. "Guinea-Bissau Inflation Rate 1988–2022," Macrotrends, 2021, accessed November 16, 2022, https://www.macrotrends.net/countries/GNB/guinea-bissau/inflation-rate-cpi.

63. William D. Montalbano, "Leave Marxist Roots, Pope Urges Guinea-Bissau, Africa: John Paul II Advises the Revolutionary Government to Avoid Corruption and Abuse of Power as It Moves Toward a More Open Society," *Los Angeles Times*, January 28, 1990, https://www.latimes.com/archives/la-xpm-1990-01-28-mn-1246-story.html.

64. Loro Horta, "Guinea Bissau: Africa's First Narcostate," essay, African Studies Center, University of Pennsylvania, October 2007, accessed November 16, 2022, https://www.africa.upenn.edu/Articles_Gen/guinbisauhorta.html.

65. World Bank International Comparison Program, "GDP per Capita, PPP (Current International $)," World Bank, 2021, accessed November 16, 2022, https://data.worldbank.org/indicator/NY.GDP.PCAP.PP.CD?end=2020&most_recent_value_desc=false&start=1990&view=chart&year_high_desc=true; United Nations World Food Programme, "Guinea-Bissau," World Food Program USA, accessed November 16, 2022, https://www.wfpusa.org/countries/guinea-bissau/.

66. US Department of State, Bureau of Democracy, Human Rights, and Labor, "2020 Country Reports on Human Rights Practices: Guinea-Bissau," March 30, 2021, https://www.state.gov/reports/2020-country-reports-on-human-rights-practices/guinea-bissau/.

67. UNESCO Institute for Statistics, Guinea-Bissau, "Literacy Rate, Adult Total (% of People Ages 15 and Above)," "Literacy Rate, Adult Female (% of Females Age 15 and Above)," 2014, https://data.worldbank.org/indicator/SE.ADT.LITR.FE.ZS?locations=GW.

68. Freire, *Pedagogy in Process*, Letter 15, loc. 2378.

Chapter 11: "We Must Punish Them"

1. Andrew J. Kirkendall, *Paulo Freire and the Cold War Politics of Literacy* (Chapel Hill: University of North Carolina Press, 2010), 90, Kindle.

2. Isaac Gottesman, "Sitting in the Waiting Room: Paulo Freire and the Critical Turn in the Field of Education," *Educational Studies* 46, no. 4 (July 28, 2010): 376–99, https://doi.org/10.1080/00131941003782429.

3. Jonathan Kozol, "Coming Up for Freire," *New York Review of Books*, October 22, 1970, https://www.nybooks.com/articles/1970/10/22/coming-up-for-freire/.

4. Isaac Gottesman, *The Critical Turn in Education: From Marxist Critique to Poststructuralist Feminism to Critical Theories of Race* (New York: Routledge, 2016), 24, Kindle.

5. Mark Hudson, "Education for Change: Henry Giroux and Transformative Critical Pedagogy," Against the Current, December 1983, https://againstthecurrent.org/atc083/p1734/.

6. Gottesman, "Sitting in the Waiting Room," 390.

7. Kozol, "Coming Up for Freire."

8. Henry A. Giroux, "Paulo Freire's Approach to Radical Educational Reform," ed. Paulo Freire, *Curriculum Inquiry* 9, no. 3 (1979): 267, https://doi.org/10.2307/3202124.

9. Paulo Freire, *Education for Critical Consciousness* (London: Bloomsbury Academic, 2013), 30–31, Kindle.

10. Freire, 5.

11. Kirkendall, *Paulo Freire and the Cold War Politics of Literacy*, 96, Kindle.

12. Paulo Freire, *The Politics of Education: Culture, Power, and Liberation*, trans. Donaldo Macedo (Westport, CT: Bergin & Garvey, 1985), sec. Rethinking Critical Pedagogy, loc. 2374, Kindle.

13. Federal Bureau of Investigation, "Freire FBI File," declassified document, US Department of Justice, 1971, PDF in author's files.

14. Freire in correspondence with Adrian Resnick, February 19, 1973, World of Council of Churches, Archives, Geneva, Switzerland, quoted in Kirkendall, *Paulo Freire and the Cold War Politics of Literacy*, 96.

15. Kirkendall, 99.

16. Freire quotes this Simone de Beauvoir phrase (from *La Pensée de Droite, Aujord'hui*, 1963) in Paulo Freire, *Pedagogy of the Oppressed*, trans. Myra Bergman Ramos (New York: Bloomsbury Academic, 2018), 74, Kindle.

17. Freire, 74.

18. Freire, *The Politics of Education*, sec. Rethinking Critical Pedagogy, loc. 2374.

19. Freire, chap. Ten, loc. 1826.

20. Henry A. Giroux, *Teachers as Intellectuals: Toward a Critical Pedagogy of Learning* (Westport, CT: Bergin & Garvey, 1988), 24, 27, Google Books.

21. Henry Giroux, "Henry Giroux: Where Is the Outrage? Critical Pedagogy in Dark Times," video, September 14, 2015, Distinguished Scholar Speaker Series in Critical Pedagogy, McMaster University, MacPherson Institute, Hamilton, ON, YouTube, October 22, 2015, 1:16, https://www.youtube.com/watch?v=CAxj87RRtsc.

22. Sol Stern, "Pedagogy of the Oppressor," *City Journal*, Spring 2009, https://www.city-journal.org/html/pedagogy-oppressor-13168.html.

23. Gottesman, *The Critical Turn in Education*, 24–25, Kindle.

24. Author analysis of Google Scholar and Semantic Scholar academic databases.

25. "Paulo Freire Organizations," Freire Institute, accessed November 18, 2022, https://www.freire.org/paulo-freire-organizations; "Paulo Freire Democratic Project Awards," Chapman University, accessed November 18, 2022, https://www.chapman.edu/education/centers-and-partnerships/paulo-freire/pfdp-awards.aspx.

26. Gottesman, *The Critical Turn in Education*, 1.

27. Gottesman, 10.

28. California Department of Education, "Ethnic Studies Model Curriculum," collection of Microsoft Word documents, adopted by the state legislature on March 18, 2021, https://www.cde.ca.gov/ci/cr/cf/esmc.asp.

29. From R. Tolteka Cuauhtin, *Rethinking Ethnic Studies* (Milwaukee: Rethinking Schools, 2019). The material on Tolteka Cuauhtin and the model ethnic studies curriculum was first reported in Christopher F. Rufo, "Revenge of the Gods," *City Journal*, March 10, 2021, https://www.city-journal.org/calif-ethnic-studies-curriculum-accuses-christianity-of-theocide.

30. Draft version of California Department of Education, "Ethnic Studies Model Curriculum."

Following the "Revenge of the Gods" report in *City Journal* and an ensuing public backlash, the Department of Education removed the chant to the Aztec gods from the model curriculum before final adoption.

31. California Department of Education, "Ethnic Studies Model Curriculum." In Chapter 3, "Instructional Guidance for K–12 Education," the authors outline the theory of "ethnic studies pedagogy" (4) and cite Freire's *Pedagogy of the Oppressed* (4, 14).

32. R. Tolteka Cuauhtin, "The Matrix of Social Identity and Intersectional Power: A Classroom Resource," in *Rethinking Ethnic Studies*, ed. Miguel Zavala et al. (Milwaukee: Rethinking Schools, 2019), 38–47.

33. Internal documents, video, and presentation slides obtained by author, first reported in Christopher F. Rufo, "Merchants of Revolution," published in *City Journal*, April 13, 2021, https://www.city-journal.org/california-ethnic-studies-programs-merchants-of-revolution.

34. California State Assembly Bill 101, "Pupil Instruction: High School Graduation Requirements: Ethnic Studies," signed into law October 8, 2021, https://leginfo.legislature.ca.gov/faces/billTextClient.xhtml?bill_id=202120220AB101.

35. Internal document obtained by author, first reported in Rufo, "Merchants of Revolution."

36. Matthew Richmond, *The Hidden Half: School Employees Who Don't Teach*, Thomas B. Fordham Institute, August 2014, https://fordhaminstitute.org/sites/default/files/publication/pdfs/hidden-half-school-employees-who-dont-teach-final0.pdf.

37. US Bureau of Labor Statistics, "Education Administrators, Kindergarten through Secondary," Occupational Employment and Wage Statistics, accessed November 18, 2022, https://www.bls.gov/oes/current/oes119032.htm.

38. *The Condition of Education 2016* (Washington, DC: National Center for Education Statistics, US Department of Education, May 2016), chap. 3.

39. Jay P. Greene and James Paul, *Equity Elementary: "Diversity, Equity, and Inclusion" Staff in Public Schools*, Backgrounder, Heritage Foundation, October 2021, 2, https://www.heritage.org/education/report/equity-elementary-diversity-equity-and-inclusion-staff-public-schools.

40. Seattle Public Schools, "2020–21 Fast Facts & Figures," PDF, 2021, https://www.seattleschools.org/wp-content/uploads/sps/district/File/District/Departments/Communications/seattle-public-schools-quick_facts.pdf; Seattle Public Schools, "Black Studies," PDF, October 2021, https://www.seattleschools.org/wp-content/uploads/2021/10/black_studies23.pdf; Seattle Public Schools, *Seattle Public Schools 2021–2022 Adopted Budget* (Seattle: Seattle Public Schools, 2021).

41. "Department of Racial Equity Advancement Staff," Contact Us, Seattle Public Schools, accessed November 18, 2022, https://archive.ph/ef6tL.

42. Internal Seattle Public Schools training documents obtained by author, first reported in Christopher F. Rufo, "Teaching Hate," *City Journal*, December 18, 2020, https://www.city-journal.org/racial-equity-programs-seattle-schools.

43. Seattle Public Schools, "Black Studies."

44. Paulo Freire, Ubiratan D'Ambrosio, and Maria Do Carmo Mendonça, "A Conversation with Paulo Freire," *For the Learning of Mathematics* 17, no. 3 (1997): 7–10.

45. Seattle Public Schools, "K–12 Math Ethnic Studies Framework," 2019, PDF, https://www.k12.wa.us/sites/default/files/public/socialstudies/pubdocs/Math%20SDS%20ES%20Framework.pdf.

46. Department of Equity & Race Relations, "Racial Equity Team," Seattle Public Schools, n.d., PDF, https://www.seattleschools.org/wp-content/uploads/sps/district/File/District/Departments/DREA/racial-equity-teams-conflict-copy.pdf.

47. Department of Equity & Race Relations, "Racial Equity Team"; James Bush, *2020–2021 Annual Report for Policy 0030—Ensuring Educational and Racial Equity* (Seattle: Seattle Public Schools, June 2021), PDF.

48. Seattle Public Schools, "Building and Program Racial Equity Teams," 2018, PDF, https://www.seattlewea.org/file_viewer.php?id=14901.

49. Internal training documents obtained by author, first reported in Rufo, "Teaching Hate."

50. Paulo Freire, *Letters to Cristina* (London: Routledge, 2016), 159–60, Kindle.

51. Freire, 174–76.

52. Freire, *Pedagogy of the Oppressed*, 152–53.

53. Freire, *Letters to Cristina*, 52–54.

54. Eric Pace, "Paulo Freire, 75, Is Dead; Educator of the Poor in Brazil," *New York Times*, May 6, 1997, https://www.nytimes.com/1997/05/06/world/paulo-freire-75-is-dead-educator-of -the-poor-in-brazil.html.

55. Susan L. Cooke, "Paulo Freire Personal Vita," accessed November 18, 2022, https:// roghiemstra.com/pvitapf.html.

56. Freire, *Letters to Cristina*, 136–37.

57. Freire, 188.

58. Paulo Freire, *Pedagogy in Process: The Letters to Guinea-Bissau*, trans. Carman St. John Hunter (London: Bloomsbury, 2016), Introduction, Part 1, loc. 311, Kindle.

59. For an account of Freire's funeral, see Dada Maheshvarananda, "A Personal Remembrance and Conversation with Paulo Freire, Educator of the Oppressed," *Neohumanist Educational Futures: Liberating the Pedagogical Intellect*, ed. Sohail Inayatullah, Marcus Bussey, and Iva-na Milojević (New Taipei City: Tamkang University Press, 2006), 297–304.

Chapter 12: Engineers of the Human Soul

1. Orlando Figes, *Revolutionary Russia, 1891–1991: A History* (New York: Henry Holt, 2014), 186.

2. Mao Zedong, laying the foundation for his first purge, told the artists and teachers at the Yan'an Forum on Literature and Art: "[Our purpose is] to ensure that literature and art fit well into the whole revolutionary machine as a component part, that they operate as powerful weapons for uniting and educating the people and for attacking and destroying the enemy, and that they help the people fight the enemy with one heart and one mind." His propagandists coined the term *xinao*—literally, "washing the brain"—and Mao saw artists as a means of achieving it. "Proletarian literature and art are part of the whole proletar-ian revolutionary cause," he said. "They are, as Lenin said, cogs and wheels in the whole revolutionary machine." Mao Zedong, "Talks at the Yenan Forum on Literature and Art," May 1942, *Selected Works*, vol. 3, 70, 86, https://www.marxists.org/reference/archive/mao /selected-works/volume-3/mswv3_08.htm.

3. Lilia I. Bartolomé, "Insurgent Multiculturalism," in *Dancing with Bigotry: Beyond the Poli-tics of Tolerance*, ed. Donaldo Macedo and Lilia I. Bartolomé (New York: Palgrave Macmil-lan, 1999), 95.

4. Peter McLaren, *Che Guevara, Paulo Freire, and the Pedagogy of Revolution* (Lanham, MD: Rowman & Littlefield, 2000), 184–85, Kindle.

5. Peter McLaren et al., *Rethinking Media Literacy: A Critical Pedagogy of Representation* (New York: Peter Lang, 1995), 87–124.

6. McLaren, *Che Guevara, Paulo Freire, and the Pedagogy of Revolution*, 183, 161.

7. McLaren et al., *Rethinking Media Literacy*, 121.

8. Internal documents obtained by author, first reported in Christopher F. Rufo, "Failure Fac-tory," *City Journal*, February 23, 2021, https://www.city-journal.org/buffalo-public-schools -critical-race-theory-curriculum.

9. McLaren, *Che Guevara, Paulo Freire, and the Pedagogy of Revolution*, 192.

10. The merging of ideology and technology has already begun. The new movement combines technical methods with revolutionary ambitions, using the neutral language of social science in pursuit of political soulcraft. Private research firms administer surveys in public schools to gather detailed information on students, categorizing them into identity groups, then probing them with questions about race, sexuality, and political opinion. The firm Panorama, for example, has surveyed 13 million students in 23,000 schools, allowing the company and its partners to employ a range of new psychological and pedagogical techniques, such as

"social-emotional learning," "culturally responsive practices," and "restorative justice," to manipulate student behavior. The company has pledged to use social-emotional learning, in particular, as "a vehicle to dismantle systemic oppression" and eliminate "white supremacy within systems and self." The last phrase, "within systems and self," is crucial. The new pedagogists, whose ranks now includes teams of data scientists and social psychologists, believe that reforming individual psyches can transform the collective society. The schoolhouse is the institutional base and delivery mechanism for this process. "Education represents one of the most important levers for change in America," says Panorama's chief executive, Aaron Feuer. "A reimagined education system is our antiracist protest," he continues, quoting the words of a colleague. See District of Columbia Public Schools, "Parents and Guardians: Complete Guide to the Panorama Survey," undated, https://dcps.dc.gov/sites/default /files/dc/sites/dcps/page_content/attachments/Family-Panorama-Survey-Guide.pdf; Nick Woolf, "How Panorama Aligns with CASEL's SEL Roadmap for a Successful Second Se- mester," Panorama Education, accessed December 8, 2022, https://www.panoramaed.com /blog/how-panorama-aligns-with-casel-sel-roadmap-second-semester-2021; Nick Woolf, "How to Implement Restorative Practices in Your School," Panorama Education, accessed December 8, 2022, https://www.panoramaed.com/blog/restorative-practices-to-implement; Aaron Feuer, "Letter from Panorama Education's CEO: Our Stand Against Systemic Rac- ism," Panorama Education, accessed December 8, 2022, https://www.panoramaed.com /blog/panoramas-stand-against-systemic-racism; Panorama Education, "SEL as Social Jus- tice: Dismantling White Supremacy Within Systems and Self," presentation, 2021.

11. McLaren, *Che Guevara, Paulo Freire, and the Pedagogy of Revolution*, 182–83.
12. Barbara Applebaum, *Being White, Being Good: White Complicity, White Moral Responsibil- ity, and Social Justice Pedagogy* (Lanham, MD: Lexington, 2010), 8–9, Kindle.
13. Applebaum, 10.
14. Applebaum, 179, 140.
15. Stephanie M. Wildman with Adrienne D. Davis, "Language and Silence: Making Systems of Privilege Visible," in *Readings for Diversity and Social Justice*, ed. Maurianne Adams, Warren J. Blumenfeld, Rosie Castaneda, Heather W. Hackman, Madeline L. Peters, and Ximena Zuniga (New York: Routledge, 2000), 56.
16. Internal documents obtained by author, including Henry Maxfield and Daina Weber, "White Privilege: Understanding Power and Privilege in Education," San Diego Unified School District, undated, PDF. First reported in Christopher F. Rufo, "The Whitest Privilege," December 3, 2020, https://rufo.substack.com/p/the-whitest-privilege/.
17. Internal documents obtained by author regarding Bettina Love, "Abolitionist Teaching, Co-Conspirators & Educational Justice," presentation, September 29, 2020, slides, photo- graphs, and contemporaneous notes. First reported in Christopher F. Rufo, "Radicalism in San Diego Schools," *City Journal*, January 5, 2021, https://www.city-journal.org/radicalism -in-san-diego-schools.
18. DeMicia Inman, "San Diego Teachers Invited to Attend 'White Privilege' Training," *The Grio* (blog), December 7, 2020, accessed November 19, 2022, https://thegrio.com/2020/12/07 /san-diego-teachers-white-privilege-training/.
19. Noel Ignatin, "The White Blindspot Documents," in *Revolutionary Youth & the New Work- ing Class*, ed. Carl Davidson (Pittsburgh: Changemaker, 2011), 145–81. Ignatiev was born and published early work under the name Ignatin. For consistency, this book will use Igna- tiev throughout the main text.
20. Ignatin, 149–50.
21. Ignatin, 157.
22. Noel Ignatiev, "Abolish the White Race," *Harvard Magazine*, September/October 2002, 30.
23. Ignatin, "The White Blindspot Documents," 163.
24. Internal emails obtained by author, first reported in Christopher F. Rufo, "Gone Crazy," *City Journal*, February 18, 2021, https://www.city-journal.org/east-side-community-school-tells -parents-to-become-white-traitors.

25. Barnor Hesse, "The 8 White Identities," infographic, Slow Factory Foundation, January 8, 2021, https://www.instagram.com/p/CJyvriYFHMb.

26. Barnor Hesse, "Racialized Modernity: An Analytics of White Mythologies," *Ethnic and Racial Studies* 30, no. 4 (July 2007): 644–45, https://doi.org/10.1080/01419870701356064.

27. Mike Sargent and Jack Rico, hosts, "Dr. Barnor Hesse Discusses His '8 White Identities' (Part 1)," *The Brown & Black Podcast*, 47 mins., March 28, 2021.

28. Rufo, "Gone Crazy."

29. Paulo Freire, *The Politics of Education: Culture, Power, and Liberation*, trans. Donaldo Macedo (Westport, CT: Bergin & Garvey, 1985), sec. Rethinking Critical Pedagogy, loc. 2374, Kindle.

30. Freire, chap. 7, loc. 1009.

31. Paulo Freire, "Reading the World and Reading the Word: An Interview with Paulo Freire," *Language Arts* 62, no. 1 (1985): 15–21, http://www.jstor.org/stable/41405241.

32. Paulo Freire, *Education, the Practice of Freedom* (London: Writers and Readers Publishing Cooperative, 1967), 35.

33. Peter McLaren, "Unthinking Whiteness, Rethinking Democracy: Or Farewell to the Blonde Beast; Towards a Revolutionary Multiculturalism," *Educational Foundations* 11, no. 2 (1997): 13, 30–34.

34. "Buffalo Public Schools, New York," Demographics, Ballotpedia, accessed November 19, 2022, https://ballotpedia.org/Buffalo_Public_Schools,_New_York.

35. Fatima Morrell and Kriner Cash, *Culturally & Linguistically Responsive Initiatives Strategic Plan 2019–2021* (Buffalo, NY: Buffalo Public Schools, 2019).

36. Internal presentation video obtained by author, first reported in Rufo, "Failure Factory."

37. Internal presentation video obtained by author, first reported in Rufo, "Failure Factory."

38. Internal curriculum materials obtained by author, first reported in Rufo, "Failure Factory."

39. Black Lives Matter at School, "BLM at School 14 Principles," PDF, accessed November 19, 2022, https://www.buffaloschools.org/cms/lib/NY01913551/Centricity/Domain/9000/BLM%20at%20School%2014%20Principles.pdf; Black Lives Matter at School, "National Black Lives Matter in School Week of Action Starter Kit," Google Doc, accessed November 19, 2022, https://docs.google.com/document/d/1kjnmt8y-7d0_8y6eVxRG_OeGv5Sy4yHudDIpmiaoLFg/.

40. Internal curriculum materials obtained by author, first reported in Rufo, "Failure Factory."

41. Chancellor Williams, *Destruction of Black Civilization: Great Issues of a Race From: 4500 B.C to 2000 A.D* (1971; reprint, Lulu Press, 2019), 160, 303–4, Google Books.

42. William R. Hite Jr., "The School District of Philadelphia's Anti-Racism Declaration," School District of Philadelphia, accessed November 19, 2022, https://www.philasd.org/antiracism/.

43. Hanako Franz, "Why Do Educators Need Anti-Racist Training?," video recording, Black Lives Matter Week of Action 2020, Racial Justice, YouTube, February 5, 2020, 0:08, https://www.youtube.com/watch?v=7GMTpAZb4Hw.

44. This initiative was created by the Racial Justice Organizing Committee of the Caucus of Working Educators, which is part of the Philadelphia Federation of Teachers. Philadelphia Racial Justice Organizing Committee, "Mission & Vision," accessed November 19, 2022, https://www.phillyrj.org/about/mission-vision.

45. Philadelphia School District, "School Information," District Performance Office, accessed November 19, 2022, https://www.philasd.org/performance/programsservices/open-data/school-information/.

46. Internal curriculum materials, video, and photographs obtained by author, including "Black Communist Case Study: Angela Davis," School District of Philadelphia, PDF, accessed November 19, 2022, https://www.documentcloud.org/documents/20477743-philadelphia-public-schools. First reported in Christopher F. Rufo, "Bad Education," *City Journal*, September 10, 2020, https://www.city-journal.org/philadelphia-fifth-graders-forced-to-celebrate-black-communism.

47. Crystal M. Edwards, "Welcome to William D. Kelley School!," William D. Kelley School, accessed November 19, 2022, https://archive.ph/l1lXZ.

48. Educator interview with author, first published in Rufo, "Bad Education."

49. "Buffalo City SD Financial Transparency Report," New York State Education Department, accessed November 19, 2022, https://data.nysed.gov/expenditures.php?year=2020&inst id=800000052968; School District of Philadelphia, "Philadelphia Public School Enrollment, 2019–20 and 2020–21," Office of Research and Evaluation, June 2021, PDF, https://www .philasd.org/research/wp-content/uploads/sites/90/2021/06/Enrollment-Rates-in-2019-20 -and-2020-21-Research-Brief-June-2021.pdf; School District of Philadelphia, "Quick Budget Facts," Office of Management & Budget, accessed November 19, 2022, https://www .philasd.org/budget/budget-facts/quick-budget-facts/.

50. Organisation for Economic Co-operation and Development, Online Education Database, retrieved October 7, 2021, from https://stats.oecd.org/Index.aspx. See *Digest of Education Statistics 2021*, table 605.10.

51. New York State Education Department, "Buffalo City School District Grades 3–8 ELA Assessment Data, 2019," Buffalo City School District, accessed November 19, 2022, https://data.nysed.gov/assessment38.php?subject=ELA&year=2019&instid=80000005 2968; New York State Education Department, "Buffalo City School District Grades 3–8 Mathematics Assessment Data, 2019," Buffalo City School District, accessed November 19, 2022, https://data.nysed.gov/assessment38.php?subject=Mathematics&year=2019&ins tid=800000052968.

52. Philadelphia School District, "School Performance," District Performance Office, accessed November 19, 2022, https://www.philasd.org/performance/programsservices/open-data /school-performance/.

53. Franz, *Why Do Educators Need Anti-Racist Training?*

54. Paulo Freire, *Pedagogy in Process: The Letters to Guinea-Bissau*, trans. Carman St. John Hunter (London: Bloomsbury, 2016), Letter 3, Kindle.

55. Educator interview with author, first published in Rufo, "Failure Factory."

56. Racial Justice Organizing Committee, "Mission & Vision," accessed November 19, 2022, https://www.phillyrj.org/about/mission-vision; Melanated Educators Collective and the Racial Justice Organizing Committee, "10 Demands for Radical Education Transformation," accessed November 19, 2022, https://archive.ph/jkW6v.

57. Bettina L. Love, *We Want to Do More Than Survive: Abolitionist Teaching and the Pursuit of Educational Freedom* (Boston: Beacon Press, 2019), 25–26; spirit-murder, 34, Kindle.

58. Love, 145.

59. Love, 101.

60. Love, 22.

61. Love, 50, 143, 74, 72, 64.

62. Love, 55.

63. Love, 159–60.

64. Love, 114.

65. Ira Shor and Paulo Freire, *Pedagogy for Liberation: Dialogues on Transforming Education* (Westport, CT: Bergin & Garvey, 1986), 47.

66. Presentation slides and contemporaneous notes obtained by author. Bettina Love, "Hip Hop, Creativity, Social Justice, & Civics," presentation, CAST UDL Symposium, August 7, 2020.

Chapter 13: The Child Soldiers of Portland

1. Andy Ngô [@MrAndyNgo], "'Death to America' Portland Antifa Group Youth Liberation Front Has Announced Their Plans for Wednesday," tweet, Twitter, November 4, 2020, https://twitter.com/mrandyngo/status/1323896207643602946; Luke Mogelson, "In the Streets with Antifa," *New Yorker*, October 25, 2020, https://www.newyorker.com /magazine/2020/11/02/trump-antifa-movement-portland.

2. Nur Ibrahim, "Does Video Show Toddlers Holding Profane Signs at Protest?," Snopes, accessed November 19, 2022, https://www.snopes.com/fact-check/toddlers-signs-profanities -protest/.
3. Maxine Bernstein, "'What Are We Marching For?' Protesters and Observers Wonder Alike in Portland," *Oregonian*, January 23, 2021, https://www.oregonlive.com/portland/2021/01 /what-are-we-marching-for-protesters-and-observers-wonder-alike-in-portland.html.
4. "A Resolution of the Tigard-Tualatin School Board of Directors," Tigard-Tualatin School District, June 2020, accessed November 19, 2022, https://www.ttsdschools.org/Page /http%3A%2F%2Fwww.ttsdschools.org%2Fsite%2Fdefault.aspx%3FPageID%3D9770.
5. "Tigard-Tualatin School District Names First Equity and Inclusion Director," *Times*/Pamplin Media Group, July 26, 2020, accessed November 19, 2022, https://pamplinmedia .com/ttt/89-news/474892-383876-tigard-tualatin-school-district-names-first-equity-and -inclusion-director.
6. Internal document obtained by author. Zinnia Un, "What Will It *Really* Take to Make the Change Towards an Anti-Racist School District?," Tigard-Tualatin School District, June 2020. First reported in Christopher F. Rufo, "The Child Soldiers of Portland," *City Journal*, Spring 2021, https://www.city-journal.org/critical-race-theory-portland-public-schools.
7. Internal document obtained by author. Anna Stamborski, Nikki Zimmermann, and Bailie Gregory, "Scaffolded Anti-Racist Resources," PDF, June 23, 2020, first reported in Rufo, "The Child Soldiers of Portland."
8. Educator interview with author, first reported in Rufo, "The Child Soldiers of Portland."
9. Internal document obtained by author. Nick Sidlin and Alfonso Ramirez, "Political Strife in the Classroom: A Restorative Response?," Tigard-Tualatin School District, 2020, first reported in Rufo, "The Child Soldiers of Portland."
10. Educator interview with author, first reported in Rufo, "The Child Soldiers of Portland."
11. US Census Bureau, "QuickFacts: Beaverton City, Oregon," accessed December 1, 2022, https://www.census.gov/quickfacts/beavertoncityoregon.
12. Internal curriculum materials obtained by author, first reported in Rufo, "The Child Soldiers of Portland."
13. Family interview with author, first reported in Rufo, "The Child Soldiers of Portland."
14. House Bill 2845, 79th Oregon Legislative Assembly, enrolled June 19, 2017, https://olis .oregonlegislature.gov/liz/2017R1/Downloads/MeasureDocument/HB2845/Enrolled.
15. "Critical Ethnic Studies Association," accessed November 19, 2022, https://www .criticalethnicstudies.org/.
16. Oregon Department of Education, "Ethnic Studies Grade Level Standards Recommendation July 2019," PDF, draft version, updated February 2020; Oregon Department of Education, "2021 Social Science Standards Integrated w/ES," PDF, 2021.
17. Oregon Department of Education, "Ethnic Studies Update, August 19, 2020," PowerPoint, accessed November 19, 2022, https://drive.google.com/file/d /14fwjOksAp0QzPyna7dXZIOkHW_Dla9zf/view?usp=embed_facebook.
18. Author review of news reports, law enforcement announcements, livestream video, and social media feeds during the riots. See footnote later in this chapter detailing Portland Police Bureau announcements for details on crimes and weapons.
19. Jamie Goldberg, "Insurers Balk at Covering Portland Businesses; Brokers Say Downtown Upheaval Has Made Carriers Wary," *Oregonian*/OregonLive, updated May 14, 2021, https:// www.oregonlive.com/business/2020/12/insurers-balk-at-covering-portland-businesses -brokers-say-downtown-upheaval-has-made-carriers-wary.html.
20. Portland Public Schools, "Leading with Racial Equity & A Bold Commitment to Social Justice: Our Collective Plan and Framework," PDF, 2019, https://www.pps.net/cms/lib /OR01913224/Centricity/Domain/4/RESJ_FrameworkandPlan_V3.GGJG.pdf.
21. Educator interview with author, first reported in Rufo, "The Child Soldiers of Portland."
22. Internal document obtained by author. Luis Versalles, "SPELLing Out Institutional Barriers to Just Schooling: Moving from Compliance to Equity and Excellence," Pacific Education

Group, presentation and training document for Portland Public Schools, January 11, 2013. First reported in Rufo, "The Child Soldiers of Portland."

23. Internal materials obtained by author, including: "Staff Meeting, September, 15, 2020"; "Staff Meeting, December 2, 2020"; "Staff Meeting, December 8, 2020"; "Anti-Racism Through Technology, August 2020." First reported in Rufo, "The Child Soldiers of Portland."

24. Educator interview with author, first reported in "The Child Soldiers of Portland."

25. Internal materials obtained by author, including: "Anti-Racism Through Technology August 2020"; video messages to students, 2020; collection of various social media images. First reported in Rufo, "The Child Soldiers of Portland."

26. Internal documents obtained by author. Jessica Mallare-Best, "Critical Race Studies" and "Critical Race Studies 3/4," Portland Public Schools, Google Docs, 2020.

27. *BLM Parade*, photograph, n.d., JPEG, accessed November 19, 2022, https://www.pps.net /cms/lib/OR01913224/Centricity/ModuleInstance/9817/BLM%20Parade%20copy.jpg.

28. Kelly Kenoyer, "Why Did Portland Public Schools Put an Activist Teacher on Indefinite Leave?," *Portland Mercury*, April 4, 2018, accessed December 8, 2022, https://www .portlandmercury.com/news/2018/04/04/19790749/why-did-portland-public-schools-put -an-activist-teacher-on-indefinite-leave; Bethany Barnes, "Portland Public Schools Listens to Families, Won't Fire Teacher for Black Lives Matter Walkout," *Oregonian*, August 3, 2018, https://www.oregonlive.com/education/2018/04/portland_public_schools_listen.html.

29. "Kids Organize March for George Floyd, March Through NE Portland in Day 15 of Protests," KPTV, June 11, 2020, https://www.kptv.com/news/kids-organize-march-for-george -floyd-march-through-ne-portland-in-day-15-of-protests.

30. Courtney Vaughn, "Protesters Overtake Multnomah Village," *SouthwestConnection*/Pamplin Media Group, November 7, 2020, https://pamplinmedia.com/scc/103-news/487224 -392206-protesters-overtake-multnomah-village.

31. Hal Bernton, "Meet the Youth Liberation Front Behind a Militant Marathon of Portland Protests," *Seattle Times*, July 12, 2020, https://www.seattletimes.com/seattle-news/meet -the-youth-liberation-front-the-militant-group-promoting-a-marathon-of-angry-portland -protests/.

32. Portland Police Bureau, "Update: Three Arrested During Riot, Scope of Property Damage Becoming Clear," January 1, 2021, https://web.archive.org/web/20220129111509/https:// www.portlandoregon.gov/police/news/read.cfm?id=271441; Portland Police Bureau, "Suspect Charged with Several Offenses After Committing Crimes During Civil Unrest in Portland," January 14, 2021, https://web.archive.org/web/20221126154059/https://www .portlandoregon.gov/police/news/read.cfm?id=281464&ec=1; Portland Police Bureau, "Rocks and Other Items Thrown at Officers, Unlawful Assembly Declared at Kelly Building," August 31, 2020, https://web.archive.org/web/20220421002347/https://www .portlandoregon.gov/police/news/read.cfm?id=261156; Portland Police Bureau, "Update: 12 Adults Arrested, 1 Juvenile Detained—New Criminal Tactic Used on Police Vehicles, Spike Devices Seized," August 7, 2020, https://web.archive.org/web/20210329024133 /https://www.portlandoregon.gov/police/news/read.cfm?id=261076; Portland Police Bureau, "Update: Juvenile Threatening with Gun," August 4, 2020, https://web .archive.org/web/20210302050610/https://www.portlandoregon.gov/police/news/read .cfm?id=251066&ec=2&ch=twitter; Portland Police Bureau, "Update: Arrests After Fire Set to Union Building, Riot Declared," August 29, 2020, https://web.archive.org /web/20210302043753/https://www.portlandoregon.gov/police/news/read.cfm?id=261151; Portland Police Bureau, "Update: Adult Suspect Arrested for Assault During May 30, 2020 Demonstrations," June 8, 2020, https://web.archive.org/web/20210612233938/https:// www.portlandoregon.gov/police/news/read.cfm?id=250842&ec=2.

33. The independent journalist Andy Ngo carefully documented arrests and court proceedings in Portland during the George Floyd riots.

34. Author review of publicly accessible Portland Public Schools employee directories.

Chapter 14: Derrick Bell

1. "Derrick Bell in 2010 on Racism in the Era of Obama," video segment of unknown origin, republished by BuzzFeed, March 7, 2012, YouTube, 02:03, 03:13, 04:09, https://www.youtube.com/watch?v=9Fig-2dStzU.

2. Derrick Bell, *Race, Racism, and American Law*, Law School Casebook Series (Boston: Little, Brown, 1973).

3. Derrick Bell and Martha A. Field, "The Supreme Court, 1984 Term," *Harvard Law Review* 99, no. 1 (1985): 83, https://doi.org/10.2307/1341120.

4. Derrick Bell, *Faces at the Bottom of the Well: The Permanence of Racism* (New York: Basic Books, 2018), xxi, Kindle.

5. Bell, 7.

6. Bell, 120.

7. Bell, 115–17.

8. Bell, 15.

9. See Chapter 17.

10. Daniel Solórzano, "Critical Race Theory's Intellectual Roots: My Email Epistolary with Derrick Bell," in *Handbook of Critical Race Theory in Education* (New York: Routledge, 2013), 52.

11. This description of critical race theory is made by the critical race theorists themselves, who cite the influence of critical theory, postmodernism, black nationalism, and Marxism. See: Mari J. Matsuda et al., eds., *Words That Wound: Critical Race Theory, Assaultive Speech, and the First Amendment* (1993; reprint, New York: Routledge, 2018), 5, Kindle; Gary Peller, "History, Identity, and Alienation Commentary: Critical Race Theory: A Commemoration: Response," *Connecticut Law Review* 43, no. 5 (2011): 1494, https://opencommons.uconn.edu/cgi/viewcontent.cgi?article=1122&context=law_review.

12. National Visionary Leadership Project, "Derrick Bell: My Family," video, Visionary Project, YouTube, 2010, https://www.youtube.com/watch?v=uQJdtbpvl30.

13. Derrick Bell, *Confronting Authority: Reflections of an Ardent Protester* (Boston: Beacon Press, 1994), 10–14.

14. Bell, 15.

15. Bell, 10–15.

16. Bell, 14.

17. Derrick Bell, *Silent Covenants: Brown v. Board of Education and the Unfulfilled Hopes for Racial Reform* (Oxford: Oxford University Press, 2004), 3, Kindle.

18. Derrick Bell, *The Derrick Bell Reader* (New York: New York University Press, 2005), e-pub.

19. Bell, *Silent Covenants*, 98.

20. Stuart Crainer, "Ethics and Ambition: An Interview with Derrick Bell," *Business Strategy Review* 14, no. 1 (Spring 2003): 3.

21. John Herbers, "Rural School in Mississippi Enrolls One Negro Girl Under Heavy Guard," *New York Times*, September 2, 1964, https://www.nytimes.com/1964/09/02/archives/rural-school-in-mississippi-enrolls-one-negro-girl-under-heavy.html?searchResultPosition=5.

22. Herbers.

23. John Herbers, "Grade Schools in Mississippi Are Integrated," *New York Times*, September 1, 1964, https://www.nytimes.com/1964/09/01/archives/grade-schools-in-mississippi-are-integrated.html.

24. "Mississippi Loses in Three School Cases; Integration Ordered by U.S. Judge Who Deplores It," *New York Times*, July 8, 1964, https://www.nytimes.com/1964/07/08/archives/mississippi-loses-in-3-school-cases-integration-ordered-by-us-judge.html.

25. Derrick Bell, *Ethical Ambition: Living a Life of Meaning and Worth* (New York: Bloomsbury, 2008), 158, Kindle.

26. Winson Hudson and Constance Curry, *Mississippi Harmony: Memoirs of a Freedom Fighter* (New York: Palgrave Macmillan, 2002), xviii.

27. Bell, *Confronting Authority*, 29.

28. Bell, 156.
29. For a summary and key quotations from Bell, *Race, Racism, and American Law*, see "Scholarship," Derrick Bell Official Site, https://professorderrickbell.com/scholarship/.
30. Bell, *Silent Covenants*, 187.
31. Solórzano, "Critical Race Theory's Intellectual Roots," 58.
32. National Visionary Leadership Project, "Derrick Bell: Civil Rights Cases," video, Visionary Project, YouTube, 2010, 05:50, https://www.youtube.com/watch?v=LJ54Goo6u4M.
33. "City Talk: Derrick Bell," *City Talk*, CUNY TV, March 20, 2007, 04:36, https://www.youtube.com/watch?v=E7zYD1q8B30. This quote is edited for clarity; some spoken filler words are omitted.
34. Derrick Bell, "The Dialectics of School Desegregation Symposium: Judicially Managed Institutional Reform," *Alabama Law Review* 32, no. 2 (1980–81): 285.
35. Derrick A. Bell, "*Brown v. Board of Education* and the Interest-Convergence Dilemma," *Harvard Law Review* 93, no. 3 (1980): 524, https://doi.org/10.2307/1340546.
36. Bell.
37. Bell, "The Dialectics of School Desegregation Symposium."
38. Bell, *Silent Covenants*, 196.
39. Derrick Bell, "Racism: A Major Source of Property and Wealth Inequality in America," *Indiana Law Review* 34 (2001): 1270–71.
40. "City Talk: Derrick Bell," 25:20. This quote is edited for clarity; some spoken filler words are omitted.
41. Derrick A. Bell, *And We Are Not Saved: The Elusive Quest for Racial Justice* (New York: Basic Books, 2008), 12–13, Kindle.
42. Bell, 18.
43. Bell, 172.
44. Derrick Bell and Martha A. Field, "The Supreme Court, 1984 Term," *Harvard Law Review* 99, no. 1 (1985): 7, 9, 10, https://doi.org/10.2307/1341120.
45. Solórzano, "Critical Race Theory's Intellectual Roots," 52.
46. Bell, *And We Are Not Saved*, 70–71.
47. Bell, *Faces at the Bottom of the Well*, 3.
48. Bell, 14.

Chapter 15: "I Live to Harass White Folks"

1. Dorothy Gilliam, "An Insult to a Law Professor," *Washington Post*, August 4, 1986, https://www.washingtonpost.com/archive/local/1986/08/04/an-insult-to-a-law-professor/d503c162-b8bd-434a-99e6-37ee6c8348a5/.
2. Charles R. Lawrence III, "Doing 'the James Brown' at Harvard: Professor Derrick Bell as Liberationist Teacher," *Harvard BlackLetter Law Journal* 8 (1991): 263, https://scholarspace.manoa.hawaii.edu/server/api/core/bitstreams/c449967c-a4a9-46a4-970d-fc06cecfda36/content.
3. Lawrence, 264.
4. Lawrence, 272.
5. Lawrence, 265.
6. Lawrence, 265.
7. Heather Mac Donald, "Law School Humbug," *City Journal*, Autumn 1995, https://www.city-journal.org/html/law-school-humbug-11925.html.
8. Jennifer A. Kingson, "Harvard Tenure Battle Puts 'Critical Legal Studies' on Trial," *New York Times*, August 30, 1987.
9. Reclaim Harvard Law School, "Timeline of Student Activism for Diversity and Inclusion," https://reclaimharvardlaw.wordpress.com/timeline-of-student-inclusion-requests/.
10. Bell, *The Derrick Bell Reader*, Introduction, 28–29.
11. Regina Austin, "Sapphire Bound!," in *Critical Race Theory: The Key Writings That Formed the Movement*, ed. Kimberlé Crenshaw et al. (New York: New Press, 1995), 426.

12. Fox Butterfield, "Harvard Law School Torn by Race Issue," *New York Times*, April 26, 1990, https://www.nytimes.com/1990/04/26/us/harvard-law-school-torn-by-race-issue.html.

13. Derrick Bell, *Faces at the Bottom of the Well: The Permanence of Racism* (New York: Basic Books, 2018), chap. 7, 159, Kindle.

14. Bell, 160.

15. Bell, 160.

16. Bell, 163.

17. Bell, 168.

18. Derrick Bell, "The Final Report: Harvard's Affirmative Action Allegory," *Michigan Law Review* 87, no. 8 (August 1989): 2389.

19. HLS News Staff, "Roger Fisher (1922–2012)," Harvard Law School, accessed October 25, 2022, https://hls.harvard.edu/today/roger-fisher-1922-2012/.

20. Derrick Bell, *Confronting Authority: Reflections of an Ardent Protester* (Boston: Beacon Press, 1994), 86.

21. Josh Getlin, "Raising Hell for a Cause," *Los Angeles Times*, November 5, 1992, https://www.latimes.com/archives/la-xpm-1992-11-05-vw-1558-story.html.

22. Derrick Bell, *Confronting Authority: Reflections of an Ardent Protester* (Boston: Beacon Press, 1994), 96–97.

23. Susan Chira, "Derrick Bell: The Charms of a Devoutly Angry Man," *New York Times*, October 28, 1992, https://www.nytimes.com/1992/10/28/garden/at-lunch-with-derrick-bell-the-charms-of-a-devoutly-angry-man.html.

24. Bell, *Confronting Authority*, 96.

25. Derrick A. Bell, *And We Are Not Saved: The Elusive Quest for Racial Justice* (1987; reprint, New York: Basic Books, 2008), chap. 1, Kindle.

26. Derrick Bell, "Constitutional Conflicts: The Perils and Rewards of Pioneering in the Law School Classroom," *Seattle University Law Review* 21 (1998): 1040.

27. Bell, 1042.

28. Vinay Harpalani, "From Roach Powder to Radical Humanism: Professor Derrick Bell's 'Critical' Constitutional Pedagogy," *Seattle University Law Review* 36, no. i (2013): xxv.

29. Derrick Bell, "Racism: A Prophecy for the Year 2000," *Rutgers Law Review* 42, no. 1 (1989–90): 94. Bell originally delivered this material as a speech on March 28, 1989, as the first C. Willard Heckel Lecture.

30. Bell, *And We Are Not Saved*, 62–63.

31. Derrick Bell, *Silent Covenants: Brown v. Board of Education and the Unfulfilled Hopes for Racial Reform* (Oxford: Oxford University Press, 2004), 53–54, Kindle.

32. Bell, *And We Are Not Saved*, 76–77. Bell is quoting Professor Boris Bittker here.

33. Bell, 84–85.

34. Bell, 84–85.

35. Bell, *Faces at the Bottom of the Well*, chap. 3, "The Racial Preference Licensing Act."

36. Bell, *And We Are Not Saved*, chap. 10, "The Chronicle of the Black Crime Cure," 259.

37. Bell, *Faces at the Bottom of the Well*, 148.

38. Bell, chap. 9.

39. Bell, 203.

40. Bell, 225.

41. Bell, 233.

42. Bell, 241.

43. Bell, *Confronting Authority*, ix–x.

44. Angela Onwuachi-Willig, "On Derrick Bell as Pioneer and Teacher: Teaching Us How to Have the Nerve," *Seattle University Law Review* 36, no. i (2013): xlv.

45. Bell, *Confronting Authority*, 29.

46. Chira, "Derrick Bell: The Charms of a Devoutly Angry Man."

47. Bell, *Faces at the Bottom of the Well*, 193.

48. Bell, 144.

49. Thomas Sowell, "Racial-Quota Fallout," *National Review Online*, March 15, 2012, https://www.nationalreview.com/2012/03/racial-quota-fallout-thomas-sowell/.

50. "Derrick Bell on the 'Permanence of Racism,'" interview with Terry Gross, *Fresh Air*, NPR (WHYY, October 7, 1992), audio, 13:33, https://freshairarchive.org/segments/derrick-bell-permanence-racism. Bell used a similar line, "Maybe I'm paranoid," in his interview "City Talk: Derrick Bell," *City Talk*, CUNY TV, March 20, 2007, 06:31, https://www.youtube.com/watch?v=E7zYD1q8B30.

51. Bell, *Faces at the Bottom of the Well*, 131–32.

52. Bell, 116.

53. Derrick Bell, "The Racism Is Permanent Thesis: Courageous Revelation or Unconscious Denial of Racial Genocide," *Capital University Law Review* 22 (Summer 1993): 571, 578.

54. "Derrick Bell on the 'Permanence of Racism,'" *Fresh Air*, 03:06.

55. Bell, "The Racism Is Permanent Thesis," 571.

56. Bell, 572.

57. Bell, 583.

58. Derrick Bell, "Racial Realism," *Connecticut Law Review* 24, no. 2 (Winter 1992): 378, https://www.law.nyu.edu/sites/default/files/Racial%20Realism.pdf.

59. Bell, "Racial Realism," 379.

60. Bell, *Faces at the Bottom of the Well*, iv.

61. "The College Years," *Hannity Show*, Fox News, March 13, 2012, video, 05:23, https://www.youtube.com/watch?v=wxYu90mxvh0.

Chapter 16: The Rise of Critical Race Theory

1. Richard Delgado and Jean Stefancic, eds., *Critical Race Theory: An Introduction*, 3rd ed. (New York: New York University Press, 2017), xv, Kindle.

2. Kimberlé Crenshaw, "The First Decade: Critical Reflections, or 'A Foot in the Closing Door,'" *UCLA Law Review* 49 (2002): 1360–61.

3. "2019 ASA Presidential Session: Intersectionality and Critical Race Theory," panel discussion, Honolulu, American Studies Association, video, YouTube, 2020, 45:27, https://www.youtube.com/watch?v=elaIUgX-zZE.

4. Crenshaw, "The First Decade," 1363.

5. Richard Delgado and Jean Stefancic, "Living History Interview with Richard Delgado & Jean Stefancic," *Transnational Law & Contemporary Problems* 19, no. 221 (2011): 225.

6. "2019 ASA Presidential Session: Intersectionality and Critical Race Theory."

7. Delgado and Stefancic, "Living History Interview with Richard Delgado & Jean Stefancic," 225.

8. Crenshaw, "The First Decade," 1360.

9. Kimberlé Crenshaw et al., eds., *Critical Race Theory: The Key Writings That Formed the Movement* (New York: New Press, 1995), 338.

10. Mari J. Matsuda et al., eds., *Words That Wound: Critical Race Theory, Assaultive Speech, and the First Amendment* (New York: Routledge, 2018), 5–7, Kindle.

11. Richard Delgado and Jean Stefancic, eds., *Critical Race Theory: An Introduction* (1995; reprint, New York: New York University Press, 2001), 104. This quote is from the book's second edition and, after criticism, was removed in subsequent editions.

12. Crenshaw et al., eds., *Critical Race Theory: The Key Writings That Formed the Movement*, xiv.

13. Kimberlé Crenshaw, "Race, Reform, and Retrenchment: Transformation and Legitimation in Antidiscrimination Law," *Harvard Law Review* 101, no. 7 (May 1988): 1336, https://doi.org/10.2307/1341398.

14. Crenshaw et al., eds., *Critical Race Theory: The Key Writings That Formed the Movement*, xxv.

15. Crenshaw et al., eds., xxix.

16. "Creator of Term 'Critical Race Theory' Kimberlé Crenshaw Explains What It Really Is,"

The Reidout, MSNBC, June 21, 2021, video, 08:35, https://www.msnbc.com/the-reidout /watch/critical-race-theory-explained-as-not-marxist-or-racist-by-its-leading-scholar -kimberle-crenshaw-115226693996.

17. Delgado and Stefancic, *Critical Race Theory: An Introduction,* 3rd ed., 3.

18. Crenshaw et al., eds., *Critical Race Theory: The Key Writings That Formed the Movement*, 342.

19. Charles R. Lawrence III, "Doing the James Brown" at Harvard: Professor Derrick Bell as Liberationist Teacher," *Harvard BlackLetter Law Journal*, 8 (1991), 266, https://scholarspace .manoa.hawaii.edu/server/api/core/bitstreams/c449967c-a4a9-46a4-970d-fc06cecfda36 /content.

20. Delgado and Stefancic, *Critical Race Theory: An Introduction*, 2001, 104. This quote is from the book's second edition and, after criticism, was removed in subsequent editions.

21. Gary Peller, "Race-Consciousness," in *Critical Race Theory: The Key Writings That Formed the Movement*, ed. Kimberlé Crenshaw et al. (New York: New Press, 1995), 142.

22. Peller, 142–43.

23. Charles R. Lawrence III, "The Word and the River: Pedagogy as Scholarship as Struggle," in *Critical Race Theory: The Key Writings That Formed the Movement*, ed. Kimberlé Crenshaw et al. (New York: New Press, 1995), 343.

24. Lawrence, 336.

25. Lawrence., 343.

26. Lawrence, 338–40.

27. Lawrence, 339.

28. Lawrence, 340.

29. Kimberlé Crenshaw, "Demarginalizing the Intersection of Race and Sex: A Black Feminist Critique of Antidiscrimination Doctrine, Feminist Theory and Antiracist Politics," *University of Chicago Legal Forum*, no. 1, article 8 (1989): 151–52, https://chicagounbound.uchicago .edu/cgi/viewcontent.cgi?article=1052&context=uclf.

30. Kimberlé Crenshaw, "Mapping the Margins: Intersectionality, Identity Politics, and Violence Against Women of Color," in *Critical Race Theory: The Key Writings That Formed the Movement*, 375.

31. Karl Marx, appendix to Friedrich Engels, *Ludwig Feuerbach and the End of Classical German Philosophy*, 1886, republished at https://www.marxists.org/archive/marx/works/1845 /theses/theses.htm. This epigram was deeply important to Marx and was engraved on his tomb.

32. Delgado and Stefancic, *Critical Race Theory*, 3rd ed., 8.

33. Delgado and Stefancic, 105–6.

34. Kimberlé Crenshaw, "Race, Reform, and Retrenchment: Transformation and Legitimation in Anti-discrimination Law," in *Critical Race Theory: The Key Writings That Formed the Movement*, 108.

35. Crenshaw, 115.

36. Crenshaw, 114.

37. Crenshaw, 119.

38. Mari Matsuda, "Critical Race Theory and Critical Legal Studies: Contestation and Coalition," in Crenshaw et al., eds., *Critical Race Theory: The Key Writings That Formed the Movement*, 63.

39. Matsuda, 74.

40. Matsuda, 64.

41. John O. Calmore, "Critical Race Theory, Archie Shepp, and Fire Music: Securing an Authentic Intellectual Life in a Multicultural World," in Crenshaw et al., eds., *Critical Race Theory: The Key Writings That Formed the Movement*, 317.

42. Derrick A. Bell, "Who's Afraid of Critical Race Theory," *University of Illinois Law Review* 1995, no. 4 (1995): 893.

43. Bell, 900.

44. Randall L. Kennedy, "Racial Critiques of Legal Academia," *Harvard Law Review* 102, no. 8 (June 1989): 1745–1819, https://doi.org/10.2307/1341357.
45. Kennedy, 1778.
46. Kennedy, 1779.
47. Kennedy, 1782.
48. Kennedy, 1796.
49. Kennedy, 1809.
50. Kennedy, 1801.
51. Randall L. Kennedy, "Derrick Bell and Me," Harvard Public Law Working Paper No. 19-13, July 11, 2019, 48, http://dx.doi.org/10.2139/ssrn.3350497.
52. Kennedy, 19.
53. "LDF Mourns the Loss of Leroy D. Clark, Former LDF Counsel and Venerated Law Professor," *NAACP Legal Defense Fund* (blog), December 6, 2019, https://www.naacpldf.org /press-release/ldf-mourns-the-loss-of-leroy-d-clark-former-ldf-counsel-and-venerated-law -professor/.
54. Leroy D. Clark, "A Critique of Professor Derrick A. Bell's Thesis of the Permanence of Racism and His Strategy of Confrontation," *Denver Law Review* 73, no. 1 (January 1995): 24.
55. Clark, 27–29.
56. Clark, 33.
57. Clark, 36–37.
58. Clark, 27.
59. Clark, 49.
60. Clark, 50.
61. James Traub, "For Whom the Bell Tolls: Derrick Bell, Civil Rights Emblem," *New Republic*, February 28, 1993, https://newrepublic.com/article/63271/whom-the-bell-tolls.
62. Henry Louis Gates Jr., "Black Demagogues and Pseudo-Scholars," *New York Times*, July 20, 1992, https://www.nytimes.com/1992/07/20/opinion/black-demagogues-and-pseudo -scholars.html.
63. Susan Chira, "Derrick Bell: The Charms of a Devoutly Angry Man," *New York Times*, October 28, 1992, https://www.nytimes.com/1992/10/28/garden/at-lunch-with-derrick-bell-the -charms-of-a-devoutly-angry-man.html.
64. Traub, "For Whom the Bell Tolls."
65. Henry Louis Gates Jr., "Let Them Talk: Why Civil Liberties Pose No Threat to Civil Rights," *New Republic*, September 20, 1993, https://newrepublic.com/article/149558/let-talk.
66. Gates.
67. Gates.
68. Gates.
69. Derrick Bell, "Racial Realism," in Crenshaw et al., eds., *Critical Race Theory: The Key Writings That Formed the Movement*, 304.

Chapter 17: DEI and the End of the Constitutional Order

1. Delgado and Stefancic, *Critical Race Theory: An Introduction,* 3rd ed., 158.
2. "Preferential Policies," *Booknotes*, C-SPAN, May 24, 1990, video, 38:30, https://www.c -span.org/video/?12648-1/preferential-policies.
3. "Preferential Policies," *Booknotes*, 34:57.
4. Author analysis of Google Scholar and Semantic Scholar citation databases.
5. For a comprehensive and updated listing of critical race theory in the universities, see Legal Insurrection, *Critical Race Training in Education*, database, https://criticalrace.org/schools/.
6. Kimberlé Crenshaw, "The First Decade: Critical Reflections, or 'A Foot in the Closing Door,'" *UCLA Law Review* 49 (2002): 1361.
7. Richard Delgado and Jean Stefancic, "Living History Interview with Richard Delgado & Jean Stefancic," *Transnational Law & Contemporary Problems* 19, no. 221 (2011): 226.
8. Max Eden, "Ethnic Studies: Evidence-Based Curriculum, or CRT Trojan Horse?," Real-

ClearPolicy, April 19, 2022, https://www.realclearpolicy.com/articles/2022/04/19/ethnic _studies_evidence-based_curriculum_or_crt_trojan_horse_827733.html.

9. See "Christopher Rufo on Woke Education," *City Journal*, accessed October 27, 2022, https://www.city-journal.org/christopher-rufo-on-woke-education

10. "Detroit School District Pushes Back against Anti-CRT Legislation," Chalkbeat Detroit, November 15, 2021, https://detroit.chalkbeat.org/2021/11/15/22784151/detroit-school -district-pushes-back-against-anti-crt-bills-black-history.

11. Biography of Dr. Conrad Webster, Project Manager for Seattle Public Schools, Department of Racial Equity, https://www.seattleschools.org/departments/drea/connect.

12. Christopher F. Rufo, "Going All In," *City Journal*, July 15, 2021, https://www.city-journal .org/nea-to-promote-critical-race-theory-in-schools.

13. Derrick Bell, *Confronting Authority: Reflections of an Ardent Protester* (Boston: Beacon Press, 1994), 110.

14. Cheryl I. Harris, "Whiteness as Property," *Harvard Law Review* 106, no. 8 (1993): 1788, https://doi.org/10.2307/1341787.

15. See Mari J. Matsuda et al., eds., *Words That Wound: Critical Race Theory, Assaultive Speech, and the First Amendment* (New York: Routledge, 2018), Kindle.

16. See investigative stories on critical race theory in the federal government, listed in Christopher F. Rufo, "Critical Race Theory Briefing Book," June 29, 2022, https://rufo.substack.com/p /crt-briefing-book/.

17. Christopher F. Rufo, "Pushing the Narrative," July 20, 2020, https://rufo.substack.com/p /pushing-the-narrative/.

18. Christopher F. Rufo, "The Smallest Injustice," August 3, 2021, https://rufo.substack.com/p /the-smallest-injustice/.

19. Christopher F. Rufo, "Mind Virus," September 14, 2020, https://rufo.substack.com/p /mind-virus/.

20. Christopher F. Rufo, "Federal Agencies Violate Presidential Order on Critical Race Theory," September 21, 2021, https://rufo.substack.com/p/federal-agencies-violate-presidential -order-on-critical-race-theory/.

21. Patrick Witt, "Here's How I Found Out Just How Deep Critical Race Theory Goes in U.S. Government," *The Federalist*, September 13, 2021, https://thefederalist.com/2021/09/13 /heres-how-i-found-out-how-deep-critical-race-theory-goes-in-the-u-s-government/.

22. Christopher F. Rufo, "Lockheed Martin's Woke-Industrial Complex," *City Journal*, May 26, 2021, https://www.city-journal.org/lockheed-martins-woke-industrial-complex.

23. Christopher F. Rufo, "The Woke Defense Contractor," *City Journal*, July 6, 2021, https:// www.city-journal.org/raytheon-adopts-critical-race-theory.

24. Treasury Department employee interview with author, June 2020.

25. Original source documents and audio transcript obtained by author. First published in Christopher F. Rufo, "Pushing the Narrative," July 20, 2020, https://rufo.substack.com/p /pushing-the-narrative/.

26. Christopher F. Rufo, "'White Fragility' Comes to Washington," *City Journal*, July 18, 2020, https://www.city-journal.org/white-fragility-comes-to-washington.

27. David Twersky, "A New Kind of Democrat?," *Commentary*, February 1993, https://www .commentary.org/articles/david-twersky/a-new-kind-of-democrat/.

28. Notes and agenda from the Angola Support Conference, May 28–30, 1976, Chicago, African Activist Archive, Michigan State University, https://web.archive.org/web/20111106060723 /http://www.historicalvoices.org/pbuilder/pbfiles/Project39/Scheme361/african_activist _archive-a0a7j3-b_12419.pdf.

29. Michael Kelly, "Ideology Seems to Doom Cabinet Contender," *New York Times*, December 17, 1992, https://www.nytimes.com/1992/12/17/us/ideology-seems-to-doom-cabinet -contender.html.

30. Testimony submitted by Hon. Larry McDonald, "Threats to Orderly Observances of the Bicentennial, Part I—The July 4 Coalition—Sponsors and Endorsers," US House of Repre-

sentatives, June 28, 1976, https://www.govinfo.gov/content/pkg/GPO-CRECB-1976-pt17 /pdf/GPO-CRECB-1976-pt17-3-3.pdf.

31. Twersky, "A New Kind of Democrat?"
32. Original source documents and audio transcript obtained by author. First published in Rufo, "Pushing the Narrative."
33. Mari Matsuda, "Looking to the Bottom: Critical Legal Studies and Reparations," in Crenshaw et al., eds., *Critical Race Theory: The Key Writings That Formed the Movement*, 66.
34. Matsuda, 66.
35. Neil Gotanda, "A Critique of 'Our Constitution Is Color-Blind,'" in Crenshaw et al., eds., *Critical Race Theory: The Key Writings That Formed the Movement*, 257.
36. Gotanda, 272.
37. Gotanda, 272.
38. Derrick Bell, "Racism: A Prophecy for the Year 2000," *Rutgers Law Review* 42, no. 1 (1989–90): 106.
39. Mari J. Matsuda et al., eds., *Words That Wound: Critical Race Theory, Assaultive Speech, and the First Amendment* (1993; reprint, New York: Routledge, 2018), 15, Kindle.
40. Cheryl I. Harris, "Whiteness as Property," *Harvard Law Review* 106, no. 8 (1993): 1776, https://doi.org/10.2307/1341787.
41. Harris, 1709.
42. Harris, 1778.
43. Harris, 1778.
44. Harris, 1778.
45. Harris, 1790.
46. Harris, 1716.
47. Harris, 1780, 1788.
48. Harris, 1779.
49. See, in addition to Matsuda, Richard Delgado, and Jean Stefancic, *Must We Defend Nazis? Why the First Amendment Should Not Protect Hate Speech and White Supremacy* (New York: New York University Press, 2018), https://doi.org/10.2307/j.ctvf3w49r.
50. Matsuda et al., *Words That Wound: Critical Race Theory, Assaultive Speech, and the First Amendment*, 62.
51. Matsuda et al., 1.
52. Matsuda et al., 80.
53. Matsuda et al., 38.
54. Matsuda et al., 24.
55. Matsuda et al., 38–39.
56. Matsuda et al., 37.
57. Matsuda et al., 24.
58. Matsuda et al., 72.
59. Charles R. Lawrence III, "The Id, the Ego, and Equal Protection: Reckoning with Unconscious Racism," *Stanford Law Review* 39, no. 2 (January 1987): 317, https://doi.org/10.2307/1228797.
60. Matsuda et al., *Words That Wound*, 69.
61. Phil Galewitz, "Vermont to Give Minority Residents Priority for COVID Vaccines," *Scientific American*, April 6, 2021, https://www.scientificamerican.com/article/vermont-to-give-minority-residents-priority-for-covid-vaccines/; "EPPC and Boyden Gray & Associates Demand HHS Hold New Hampshire Accountable for Unlawful Racial Set-Asides in COVID-19 Vaccine Distribution," Ethics & Public Policy Center, September 28, 2021, https://eppc.org/news/eppc-and-boyden-gray-associates-demand-hhs-hold-new-hampshire -accountable-for-unlawful-racial-set-asides-in-covid-19-vaccine-distribution/.
62. Erika D. Smith, "Guaranteed Income or Reparations? A Test Case in Oakland," *Los Angeles Times*, March 27, 2021, https://www.latimes.com/california/story/2021-03-27/oakland -guaranteed-income-reparations-slavery-black-california; Houston Keene, "California City

to Give Universal Income to Transgender, Nonbinary Residents," Fox News, April 5, 2022, https://www.foxnews.com/politics/california-city-universal-income-transgender-residents.

63. Christopher F. Rufo, "Woke Segregation and the Ghost of Jim Crow," *City Journal*, January 19, 2022, https://www.city-journal.org/woke-segregation-and-the-ghost-of-jim-crow.

64. Rufo.

65. S.162—117th Congress (2021–22): Anti-Racism in Public Health Act of 2021.

66. Christopher Rufo, "The DEI Regime," *City Journal*, July 13, 2022, https://www.city-journal .org/the-diversity-equity-and-inclusion-regime.

67. See also: Ibram X. Kendi, "Is Critical Race Theory Getting Canceled?," *A Word . . . with Jason Johnson*, transcript of Slate podcast, https://slate.com/transcripts/ekpZWlM0Z0hkVn QyaXlPVllGelBkWVNvRXk3cExkV0JYM2s5Zmw3bWVyZz0=; Jason Johnson, "Critical Race Theory Is a Convenient Target for Conservatives," Slate, June 12, 2021, https://slate .com/news-and-politics/2021/06/critical-race-theory-ibram-kendi-racism-racists.html.

68. Ibram X. Kendi, "Pass an Anti-Racist Constitutional Amendment," *Politico*, 2019, https:// politico.com/interactives/2019/how-to-fix-politics-in-america/inequality/pass-an-anti -racist-constitutional-amendment/.

69. For a more detailed analysis of how critical race theory as public policy might work, see Christopher Rufo, "Critical Race Theory Would Not Solve Racial Inequality: It Would Deepen It," Domestic Policy Studies report, Heritage Foundation, March 23, 2021, 5, https://www.heritage.org/progressivism/report/critical-race-theory-would-not-solve-racial -inequality-it-would-deepen-it.

Conclusion: The Counter-Revolution to Come

1. Herbert Marcuse, *Marxism, Revolution and Utopia: Collected Papers of Herbert Marcuse*, vol. 6, ed. Douglas Kellner and Clayton Pierce (New York: Routledge, 2017), 388, Kindle.

2. Verso Books, "Angela Davis on International Solidarity and the Future of Black Radicalism," *Literary Hub* (blog), August 31, 2020, https://lithub.com/angela-davis-on-international -solidarity-and-the-future-of-black-radicalism/.

3. Eldridge Cleaver, *Soul on Ice* (1968; reprint, New York: Delta, 1999), 90.

4. In Brazil, Freire's influence has been profound, but has also generated a significant backlash. During his successful campaign for president in 2018, populist right-wing leader Jair Bolsonaro vowed to "combat the Marxist rubbish that has spread in educational institutions." He told his followers that he wanted to "enter the Education Ministry with a flamethrower to remove Paulo Freire," blaming the critical pedagogist for Brazil's dismal educational outcomes. During his first inaugural address, Bolsonaro declared: "This is the beginning of Brazil's liberation from socialism, inverted values, the bloated state, and political correctness. . . . We are going to unite the people, rescue the family, [respect] our Judeo-Christian tradition, combat gender ideology, [and conserve] our values." Within months, Bolsonaro's Education Ministry had dismantled its "diversity department," announced a plan to overhaul national textbooks, proposed defunding university departments captured by "cultural Marxism," and pledged to stop schools from turning students into "political militants." Meanwhile, the president's allies advocated for stripping the "Patron of Brazilian Education" title from Freire and reassigning it to Saint Joseph de Anchieta, a Jesuit missionary who helped found modern Brazil and educated the country's native tribes. See: "Brazil Plans Overhaul of Education to Oust 'Marxist Ideology,'" *Christian Science Monitor*, accessed December 12, 2022, https://www.csmonitor.com/World/Americas/2019/0206/Brazil-plans -overhaul-of-education-to-oust-Marxist-ideology; Dom Phillips, "Bolsonaro Declares Bra-zil's 'Liberation from Socialism' as He Is Sworn In," *Guardian*, January 1, 2019, sec. World news, https://www.theguardian.com/world/2019/jan/01/jair-bolsonaro-inauguration-brazil -president; Elizabeth Redden, "In Brazil, a Hostility to Academe," Inside Higher Ed, May 6, 2019, https://www.insidehighered.com/news/2019/05/06/far-right-government-brazil -slashes-university-funding-threatens-cuts-philosophy-and; "Who Gets to Be Brazil's Patron of Education under Bolsonaro? Paulo Freire or a Jesuit Saint?," America Magazine, July 1,

2019, https://www.americamagazine.org/politics-society/2019/07/01/who-gets-be-brazils-patron-education-under-bolsonaro-paulo-freire-or.

5. A translation of the Jena Lectures on the Philosophy of Spirit (1805–1806) with commentary, found in Leo Rauch, *Hegel and the Human Spirit* (Detroit: Wayne State University Press, 1983), accessed November 20, 2022, https://www.marxists.org/reference/archive/hegel/works/jl/ch03a.htm.

6. Herbert Marcuse, *The Essential Marcuse: Selected Writings of Philosopher and Social Critic Herbert Marcuse*, ed. Andrew Feenberg and William Leiss (Boston: Beacon Press, 2007), 34–35, Kindle.

7. Political theorist John Marini traces this process all the way back to the German idealist philosopher Georg Wilhelm Friedrich Hegel, who pioneered the theory of the modern rational state and inspired a long line of political thought from the "scientific socialism" of Karl Marx to the critical theory of Herbert Marcuse. Marini argues that the modern political Left has abandoned the principles of natural right and limited government in favor of the principles of the "rational state" and the "universal class" of bureaucratic experts, which have the power to administer society, and, following the imperatives of the social sciences, establish social justice. "In the rational state," Marini writes, "the authority of science—and the new disciplines of the social sciences—would provide the theoretical and practical knowledge necessary to transform society and administer progress. The Hegelian idea of the state was meant to reestablish a political whole that would reunite the social and economic, the public and private, and make citizenship the ground of freedom and public virtue. John Marini, *Unmasking the Administrative State: The Crisis of American Politics in the Twenty-First Century*, ed. Ken Masugi (New York: Encounter Books, 2019): 8, 88.

8. Alasdair MacIntyre, "On Marcuse," *New York Review of Books*, October 23, 1969, https://www.nybooks.com/articles/1969/10/23/on-marcuse/.

9. Martin Jay, *The Dialectical Imagination: A History of the Frankfurt School and the Institute of Social Research, 1923–1950* (Berkeley: University of California Press, 1996), 279, Kindle.

10. Martin Jay, a second-generation critical theorist who had studied at the feet of Theodor Adorno and Leo Löwenthal, elucidates the substance of this paradox in his book. "[Critical Theory] was superb at attacking other systems' pretensions to truth, but when it came to articulating the ground of its own assumptions and values, it fared less well," he writes. "Critical Theory had a basically insubstantial concept of reason and truth, rooted in social conditions and yet outside them, connected with praxis yet keeping its distance from it. If Critical Theory can be said to have had a theory of truth, it appeared in its immanent critique of bourgeois society, which compared the pretensions of bourgeois ideology with the reality of its social conditions." Jay, *The Dialectical Imagination*, 63.

11. Herbert Marcuse, *An Essay on Liberation* (Boston: Beacon Press, 1971), 88, Kindle.

12. Herbert Marcuse, *Soviet Marxism* (1958; reprint, New York: Columbia University Press, 1985).

13. Rudi Dutschke, *The Student Rebellion* (Milan: Feltrinelli, 1968), 47–134.

14. Rudi Dutschke, "On Anti-Authoritarianism," in *The New Left Reader*, ed. Carl Oglesby (New York: Grove Press, 1969), 249, 250, 246.

15. For statistics on family, crime, marriage, and the half-century-long decline of America's working class, see Charles Murray, *Coming Apart: The State of White America, 1960–2010* (New York: Crown Forum, 2013).

16. Frantz Fanon, *The Wretched of the Earth*, trans. Richard Philcox (New York: Grove, 2004), 51.

17. Eldridge Cleaver, "On Lumpen Ideology," *Black Scholar* 4, no. 3 (1972): 8.

18. Isabel Vincent, "Inside BLM Co-Founder Patrisse Khan-Cullors' Real-Estate Buying Binge," *New York Post*, April 10, 2021, https://nypost.com/2021/04/10/inside-blm-co-founder-patrisse-khan-cullors-real-estate-buying-binge/.

19. Alexandra Del Rosario, "Black Lives Matter Co-Founder Alicia Garza Signs with ICM Partners," Deadline, August 20, 2020, https://deadline.com/2020/08/black-lives-matter-co-founder-alicia-garza-inks-deal-with-icm-partners-1203019086/.

20. Joshua Rhett Miller, "Black Lives Matter Used Donations to Buy $6 Million Southern California Home: Report," *New York Post*, April 8, 2022, https://nypost.com/2022/04/04/black-lives-matter-used-donations-to-buy-6-million-southern-california-home-report/.

21. Noah Goldberg, "Black Lives Matter Leader Accused of Stealing $10 Million from Organization," *Los Angeles Times*, September 2, 2022, https://www.latimes.com/california/story/2022-09-02/black-lives-matter-leader-accused-of-stealing-10-million-from-organization. The leader, Shalomyah Bowers, denied the allegations of financial misconduct.

22. Harriet Alexander, "BLM 'Transferred Millions to Canadian Charity Run by Wife of Co-Founder for Toronto Mansion,'" *Daily Mail*, January 30, 2022, https://www.dailymail.co.uk/news/article-10457275/BLM-transferred-millions-Canadian-charity-run-wife-founder-Toronto-mansion.html; Joe Schoffstall, "Black Lives Matter Paid Nearly $4M to Board Secretary, Co-Founder's Brother, and Father of Her Child," Fox News, May 17, 2022, https://www.foxnews.com/politics/black-lives-matter-paid-4m-board-secretary-co-founders-brother-father-child.

23. Marcuse, *Marxism, Revolution and Utopia: Collected Papers of Herbert Marcuse*, vol. 6, 377.

24. Derrick Bell, *Confronting Authority: Reflections of an Ardent Protester* (Boston: Beacon Press, 1994), 7.

25. Derrick Bell, *Faces at the Bottom of the Well: The Permanence of Racism* (New York: Basic Books, 2018), 245–46, Kindle.

26. For more background on the social pathologies of poor American communities, see the documentary film *America Lost*, directed by Christopher F. Rufo (PBS, 2019), americalostfilm.com.

27. For a deeper argument on critical race theory and inequality, see Christopher F. Rufo, "Critical Race Theory Would Not Solve Racial Inequality: It Would Deepen It," Backgrounder, no. 3597, Heritage Foundation, March 23, 2021.

28. Karl Marx, *The Class Struggles in France: 1848–1850* (London: Wellred Books, 1968). Google Books.

29. The reaction against the left-wing cultural revolution, characterized as a force of Thermidor—that is, the reaction against the French Revolution—was a constant preoccupation of Marcuse's during the Nixon years. Herbert Marcuse, *The New Left and the 1960s: Collected Papers of Herbert Marcuse*, vol. 3, ed. Douglas Kellner (New York: Routledge, 2005), 200, Kindle.

30. Karl Marx, "The Victory of the Counter-Revolution in Vienna," trans. Marx-Engels Institute, originally published in *Neue Rheinische Zeitung* no. 136, November 1848, republished at Marxists.org, accessed November 20, 2022, https://www.marxists.org/archive/marx/works/1848/11/06.htm.

31. Karl Korsch, "State and Counterrevolution," *Modern Quarterly* 11, no. 2 (1939): 60–67.

32. Marcuse, *An Essay on Liberation*, 19.

33. Richard Nixon, "Letter to the Citizens of New Hampshire," January 31, 1968, Richard Nixon Foundation, https://www.nixonfoundation.org/2018/01/rn-announces-68-campaign/. Nixon is, in many ways, the original architect of the counter-revolution. A dedicated study to Nixon's policies and politics would illuminate many of the opportunities for counter-mobilization against the critical theory–based movements and bureaucracies.

INDEX